MASTERING

GERMAN

HEAR IT · SPEAK IT · WRITE IT · READ IT

Developed for the
**FOREIGN SERVICE INSTITUTE,
DEPARTMENT OF STATE**

D0596251

Cover design by Milton Glaser, Inc.

This edition published in 1985 by Barron's Educational Series, Inc.

The title of the original course is German Basic Course

This course was developed for the Foreign Service Institute, Department of State under the supervision of Dr. Samuel A. Brown by Ilse Christoph with the assistance of Maria-Luise Bissonnette, Freidrich Lehmann, Gerhard Matzel, Margarete Plischke, and Erika Quaid.

All inquiries should be addressed to:
Barron's Educational Series, Inc.
250 Wireless Boulevard
Hauppauge, New York 11788

Paper Edition
International Standard Book No. 0-8120-2210-6

A large part of the text of this book is recorded on the accompanying tapes, as follows:

Unit 1	Tape 1A and Tape 1B
Unit 2	Tape 1B (part), Tape 2A, and Tape 2B (part)
Unit 3	Tape 2B (part), Tape 3A, and Tape 3B
Unit 4	Tape 4A and Tape 4B
Unit 5	Tape 5A, Tape 5B, and Tape 6A (part)
Unit 6	Tape 6A (part), Tape 6B, and Tape 7A (part)
Unit 7	Tape 7A (part) and Tape 7B
Unit 8	Tape 8A, Tape 8B, and Tape 9A (part)
Unit 9	Tape 9A (part), Tape 9B, and Tape 10A (part)
Unit 10	Tape 10A (part) and Tape 10B
Unit 11	Tape 11A and Tape 11B
Unit 12	Tape 12A and Tape 12B

On the tapes selected statements about Germany and its culture adapted from:

German at a Glance by Henry Strutz

Learn German the Fast and Fun Way by Paul Graves

1001 Pitfalls in German by Henry Strutz

PRINTED IN THE UNITED STATES OF AMERICA
   12   800   9 8

Preface

This course in <u>Mastering German</u> is part of a new series being offered by Barron's Educational Series. If you are a serious language student, this course will provide you with the opportunity to become truly fluent in German.

This is one of the famous courses developed by the Foreign Service Institute of the United States. These courses were designed to train United States Government representatives who need to be able to communicate clearly and accurately in a foreign language.

<u>Mastering German</u> provides an excellent opportunity for you to learn German on your own, studying at your own pace. In addition, these tapes are ideal for students who are studying German in school and who would like to supplement their classroom work with additional practice in the spoken language.

INTRODUCTION

AIM

This course will provide the student with a grasp of the structure of spoken German and with the basic vocabulary likely to be of most immediate use. This solid foundation will enable the student to continue developing still greater fluency in German in the future.

MATERIALS

The materials in this first volume of the text are organized into twelve lessons or units. Each unit contains a set of basic sentences for memorization. These are in the form of a dialog based on one or sometimes two specific situations in which a person might find himself in Germany. Notes to the basic sentences are provided as necessary to clarify occasional difficulties in vocabulary and idiom and to provide additional background on some cultural features unfamiliar to Americans. Notes on pronunciation are included in each of the first eight units. Phonological features which have been found to be particularly difficult for American students are here presented with explanations and pronunciation practice drills. The notes on grammar in each unit single out those structural features illustrated in the basic sentences which are appropriate for systematic consideration at that stage in the course. Substitution drills provide for the manipulation of forms by substituting specific items in fixed sentence frames. They are intended to build habits of association, so that in a given syntactic environment the appropriate grammatical form automatically comes to mind. As the German vocabulary is all familiar, no English equivalents are given in these drills. Variation drills provide for the manipulation of larger syntactic patterns. In each group a model sentence, underscored, serves as a guide. Associated with it are additional sentences incorporating the same syntactic pattern but in which most of the individual word items have been replaced. English equivalents are given to serve as cues for recall of the German variant sentences. Vocabulary drills provide both practice in the use of new vocabulary items and also allow for manipulation of sentence elements whose particular form and arrangement depends upon their association with that vocabulary item. The manipulation of both variation and vocabulary drills depends on the use of English equivalents. Specific translation drills are also provided, however. In most cases they present the material of the basic dialog in the form of a narrative. They thus provide content review of the basic sentences and practice in the transformation from active dialog to descriptive narration. The response drills are question and answer drills on the situations of the basic dialogs. Conversation practice and additional situations in outline bridge the gap to free conversation with small pieces of supplementary dialog for acting out and situations providing for a freer play of the student's imagination. The finder list in each unit notes all new vocabulary which has been presented.

METHOD AND PROCEDURE

This is a course that emphasizes spoken German. The forms and patterns of the language presented here are intentionally colloquial. An indispensable component of the learning process in a course like this is the voice of a native German speaker. This is provided on the tapes, in the voices of the instructors and tutors. The method of instruction uses <u>guided imitation</u>, <u>repetition</u>, <u>memorization</u>, and <u>pattern practice</u>.

The voices on the tapes provide models for speech and guide the student to accurate imitation by constant repetition. Students who are not sure how accurately they are repeating the sounds may want to use a second tape recorded to record their speech. They can then listen to themselves and compare their pronunciation with the instructor's.

When beginning a new section, students should listen to the tape before looking at the book. It is not a good idea to read from the text before hearing the word or utterance as the instructor speaks it. Only by constant repetition after an authentic model can fluent and accurate reproduction of the sounds and forms of a foreign language be achieved.

The <u>basic sentences</u> are preceded by "build-ups" giving the component parts of the utterance separately. Each new item which is introduced appears first as a build-up. The tutor will ask the students to repeat the build-ups separately first, then combined into larger units and finally the complete new sentence or utterance. The basic sentences are sub-divided into numbered sections, each to be treated as a unit, repeated individually, with and without build-ups, until the students' imitation is satisfactory. Then a new section may be begun. After acceptable imitation and accurate pronunciation has been achieved in one or more sections they are assigned for <u>memorization</u> outside of class or repeated in class until memorized. The student should be able to give either the German sentence or its English equivalent on request or switch from one to the other and back again. The tutor will drill by repeating each sentence for each student in the class, then by giving each student a different sentence, repeating it for him first, and finally asking the students to recite the sentences in order, the first student the first sentence, the second student the second sentence, etc., without receiving a cue from the instructor. Repetition outside of class, preferably using recorded materials as a guide, should be continued to the point of <u>overlearning</u>. The student should not only be able to give the correct German sentence immediately upon hearing an English equivalent, at random selection, he should also be able to give the correct German sentence with equal ease and speed of response upon hearing its German cue. As a final step the students are expected to act out the basic dialog in entirety from memory, with the tutor or with other students. Only when the basic sentences have been mastered to this extent can they be considered to provide an adequate basis for control of the spoken language. It should be noted at this point that the English text accompanying the basic sentences is <u>not</u> primarily a <u>translation</u> but rather a set of conversational equivalents. Many apparent discrepancies will be found if the student, or the tutor, looks for word-for-word correspondence between the English and German text. It does not exist. Rather, in such and such a situation <u>this</u> is what is said in German and <u>this</u> is what is said in English.

The <u>pronunciation practice drills</u> are to be taken up after the presentation of the basic sentences has been completed and memorization has been started. Items are arranged in groups according to the particular phonological feature concerned. Words in vertical columns present the same phonological feature in different environments. Several columns in a practice group contain related phonological features or related phonological environments in which the same feature recurs. Words are to be repeated, first following the vertical columns and later, for variation and comparison, horizontally across the page. Particular attention should be paid to items in <u>contrast</u>. These are minimum meaningfully distinctive sound patterns, accurate control of which is important for communication and comprehension. Contrasting word pairs are linked by a dash, and after separate practice for accuracy the items should be repeated by pairs to bring out the exact distinctions between them.

The <u>notes on grammar</u> are earmarked for home study. In each unit one or more grammatical features are presented, and the basic sentences have been designed, as far as is possible consistent with natural expression, to incorporate and illustrate those features. Each point of grammar discussed is illustrated by sentences which are natural utterances in the language. They are taken in nearly every case from the basic sentences of the current or preceding units. Thus the examples are already familiar to the student, and the <u>patterns</u> they contain, which will be drilled and practiced in the sections to follow, are patterns which the student has already begun to assimilate by memorizing the sentences of the dialog.

After the basic sentences of a unit have all been repeated several times and memorization has been well begun, work can be started on the <u>drills</u>. The material is designed to provide a maximum of additional experience in using the forms and patterns of the language learned in the basic sentences. It is <u>not</u> assumed, however, that the learner is automatically able to transfer the experience gained in the basic sentences to error-free manipulation of these forms and patterns. The drills are by no means a test of what the student can do with the elements given him. It is a matter of no great importance whether he can or cannot "figure them out" by himself. The goal is to learn to speak the language <u>accurately</u> and <u>fluently</u>, and this aim can only be achieved by <u>correct</u> repetition of the forms and patterns involved. Therefore all the sentences in each drill group are first to be repeated after the tutor in their correct form.

In the <u>substitution drills</u>, repeat the model sentence and its variants after the tutor. Sometimes the cue will fit exactly into the sentences. Sometimes changes in the basic sentence will have to be made. Regardless of which type of cue is given, or how simple or complex the exercise may appear to be, the student's task is to make the substitution without hesitation and to repeat the sentence accurately at normal conversation speed. Although no English equivalents are given in the substitution drills and the first goal is rapid, fluent and accurate manipulation of the material in <u>German</u>, the student should be able to give English equivalents for all the sentences.

In most of the variation drills and in all of the vocabulary drills the cues take the form of equivalent English sentences. Basic procedure remains the same as in the substitution drills. The student may work with the book, covering the right side of the page on which the German sentences are printed and taking the cues from the English sentences on the left side of the page.

<u>Conversion drills</u> require the conversion of one or more elements in a sentence from one form to another--singular to plural, present tense to past tense, etc. As a rule, no English is provided for these sentences, but the student should be able to translate them.

All drill material is provided with both a cue and a correct response, so it may be repeated and practiced as often as necessary to achieve complete accuracy and fluency.

Translation and response drills, as noted above, are in most cases directly related to the basic sentences. These are not recorded. In the translation drills, students can test themselves by working with the German covered. In the response drills, students should again practice with the answers covered.

The other sections that are not recorded--the conversation practice and situations--provide additional opportunities for students to create their own conversations.

The narratives, which begin in the fifth unit, are reading material. In the early units they introduce a minimum of additional vocabulary and unfamiliar forms, and students may want to try retelling the story in other words. In later units, some features or expository prose--matters of both form and style-- that differ from normal spoken usage are introduced through the narratives to bridge the gap between conversational German and those reading skills that require particular attention.

TABLE OF CONTENTS

UNITS 1 - 12

Tape 1A   WIR SIND IN DEUTSCHLAND

Basic Sentences

I	I
good	guten
morning	Morgen
Good morning.	Guten Morgen.
Mr.	Herr
Becker	Becker
Mr. Becker	Herr Becker
Good morning, Mr. Becker.	Guten Morgen, Herr Becker.
day	Tag
Hello (Good day).	Guten Tag.
Mrs.	Frau
Kunze	Kunze
Mrs. Kunze	Frau Kunze
Hello, Mrs. Kunze.	Guten Tag, Frau Kunze.
evening	Abend
Good evening.	Guten Abend.
Miss	Fräulein
Schneider	Schneider
Miss Schneider	Fräulein Schneider
Good evening, Miss Schneider.	Guten Abend, Fräulein Schneider.

II	II
Hello, Miss Schneider.	Guten Tag, Fräulein Schneider.
Hello, Mr. Becker.	Guten Tag, Herr Becker.
how	wie
goes	geht
it	es
to you, with you	Ihnen
How are you? (How goes it with you?)	Wie geht es Ihnen?
thanks	danke
very	sehr
good, well	gut
Fine, Thanks.	Danke, sehr gut.
and	und
And how are you, **Mr. Becker?**	Und wie geht es Ihnen, Herr Becker?
also, too	auch
Thank you, I'm fine too.	Danke, auch gut.

III	III
understand	verstehen
you	Sie
Do you understand Mrs. Kunze?	Verstehen Sie Frau Kunze?
no	nein
I	ich
I understand	ich verstehe
not	nicht
No, I don't understand Mrs. Kunze.	Nein, ich verstehe Frau Kunze nicht.
me	mich
Do you understand me?	Verstehen Sie mich?
yes	ja
Yes, I understand you well.	Ja, ich verstehe Sie gut.

IV	IV
where	wo
is	ist
the airport	der Flughafen
Where's the airport?	Wo ist der Flughafen?
there	dort
over there	drüben
The airport is over there.	Der Flughafen ist dort drüben.
please	bitte
I beg your pardon. What did you say?	Wie bitte?
speak	sprechen
slow, slowly	langsam
Please speak slowly.	Sprechen Sie bitte langsam.
The airport is over there.	Der Flughafen ist dort drüben.
Do you understand?	Verstehen Sie?
thank you	danke schön
Yes, I understand. Thank you.	Ja, ich verstehe. Danke schön.
you're welcome	bitte schön
You're welcome.	Bitte schön.

V	V
that	das
the railroad station	der Bahnhof
Is that the railroad station?	Ist das der Bahnhof?

No, that' not the station.

> he, it
> to the left

It's there to the left.

> the restaurant

Is the restaurant there too?

> it

Yes, it's there too.

VI

> what
> there

What's that there?

> the hotel

That's the hotel.

> here
> to the right
> the embassy

Is the embassy here to the right?

> she, it

Yes, it's here to the right.

VII

> excuse me
> the café

Excuse me, where is the café?

> straight ahead

There, straight ahead.

> the bank
> isn't it? (not true?)

The bank is there too, isn't it?

Yes, it's there too.

> thanks

Thanks.

> you're welcome

You're welcome.

Nein, das ist nicht der Bahnhof.

> er
> links

Er ist dort links.

> das Restaurant

Ist das Restaurant auch dort.

> es

Ja, es ist auch dort.

VI

> was
> da

Was ist das da?

> das Hotel

Das ist das Hotel.

> hier
> rechts
> die Botschaft

Ist die Botschaft hier rechts?

> sie

Ja, sie ist hier rechts.

VII

> Verzeihung
> das Café

Verzeihung, wo ist das Café?

> geradeaus

Dort, geradeaus.

> die Bank
> nicht wahr

Die Bank ist auch da, nicht wahr?

Ja, sie ist auch da.

> danke

Danke.

> bitte

Bitte.

VIII

Good morning.

     I would like
     with pleasure
     I'd like very much
     some cigars
     to have

I'd like to have some cigars.

     how many

All right. How many?

     five
     and
     some matches

Five, and some matches too, please.

Here you are.

     how much
     costs

How much does that cost?

     the cigars
     cost
     two
     Mark

The cigars cost two Marks.

     the matches
     ten
     penny, pennies

The matches cost ten pennies.

     would like
     would you like
     some cigarettes

Would you like to have some cigarettes too?

     they
     they cost

Yes, how much do they cost?

     one

One Mark.

Here you are.

Thank you.

VIII

Guten Morgen.

     ich möchte
     gern
     ich möchte gern
     Zigarren
     haben

Ich möchte gern Zigarren haben.

     wieviele

Gern. Wieviele?

     fünf
     und
     Streichhölzer

Fünf, und bitte auch Streichhölzer.

Hier, bitte.

     wieviel
     kostet

Wieviel kostet das?

     die Zigarren
     kosten
     zwei
     Mark

Die Zigarren kosten zwei Mark.

     die Streichhölzer
     zehn
     Pfennig

Die Streichhölzer kosten zehn Pfennig.

     möchten
     möchten Sie
     Zigaretten

Möchten Sie auch Zigaretten haben?

     sie
     sie kosten

Ja, wieviel kosten sie?

     eine

Eine Mark.

Bitte schön.

Danke schön.

IX

Good evening.

 to eat

Would you like to eat?

 sausage and sauerkraut

Yes, sausage and sauerkraut please.

 some, a little
 bread

And a little bread.

X

 the wine

How's the wine, and how's the beer?

 are

The wine and the beer are good.

 but
 the coffee

But the coffee's not good.

 the tea
 not ... either

And the tea isn't good either.

 the milk

Is the milk good?

Yes, the milk is very good.

 the water

How's the water here?

The water is good.

XI

zero - one - two - three - four

five - six - seven - eight

nine - ten - eleven - twelve

IX

Guten Abend.

 essen

Möchten Sie essen?

 Bratwurst mit Sauerkraut

Ja, Bratwurst mit Sauerkraut, bitte.

 etwas
 Brot

Und etwas Brot.

X

 der Wein

Wie ist der Wein und wie ist das Bier?

 sind

Der Wein und das Bier sind gut.

 aber
 der Kaffee

Aber der Kaffee ist nicht gut.

 der Tee
 auch nicht

Und der Tee ist auch nicht gut.

 die Milch

Ist die Milch gut?

Ja, die Milch ist sehr gut.

 das Wasser

Wie ist hier das Wasser?

Das Wasser ist gut.

XI

null - eins - zwei - drei - vier

fünf - sechs - sieben - acht

neun - zehn - elf - zwölf

FÜNF

How much is three and five?	Wieviel ist drei und fünf?
Three and five is eight.	Drei und fünf ist acht.
How much is seven and four?	Wieviel ist sieben und vier?
Seven and four is eleven.	Sieben und vier ist elf.
How much is two and ten?	Wieviel ist zwei und zehn?
Two and ten is twelve.	Zwei und zehn ist zwölf.
again	nochmal
Say it again, please.	Nochmal, bitte.
Two and ten is twelve.	Zwei und zehn ist zwölf.

XII

XII

one, you	man
says	sagt
does one say	sagt man
in German	auf deutsch

How do you say 'good bye' in German?	Wie sagt man 'good bye' auf deutsch?
good bye	Auf Wiedersehen
You say 'Auf Wiedersehen'.	Man sagt 'Auf Wiedersehen'.

Notes on Pronunciation

The spelling of a language only symbolizes to the native speaker the sounds which he already knows. You will learn these sounds directly from your instructor; the spelling will serve as an aid to listening. No spelling system adequately represents the sounds of the spoken language, and no attempt will be made at this point to outline exactly what sounds are represented by what symbols of the German spelling system. We will however present for particular drill and attention in each unit certain sounds which have shown themselves to be difficult for speakers of American English. In the meantime we ask you to remember two cardinal points:

1. The German of your text is printed in the standard German written style.

2. The letter-symbols used, although in most cases the same symbols we use in written English, in most cases do not represent exactly the same sounds we use in English. Therefore, DO NOT EXPECT GERMAN WRITTEN SYMBOLS TO REPRESENT SOUND VALUES YOU KNOW IN ENGLISH.

Pronunciation Practices. To be drilled in class.

A. Short Vowels

The German short vowels i,e,a and u are not dissimilar from English sounds. The o, however, is probably different from any sound that you have in English. Do not try to replace it by a sound from English, but rather reproduce the pronunciation. The German front rounded vowels ö and ü do not occur in English. To produce the ö, put your tongue in the position for the German e and round your lips; for ü, put your tongue in the position for the German i and round your lips. You will then produce a sound similar to the German sound. Do not worry about the meaning of the words in these practices. Concentrate instead on the sounds.

Practice 1(a)

Short   i --------- e --------- a --------- o --------- u

bitte	denn	das	kostet	muss
ist	essen	Mann	Sonne	Mutter
in	etwas	an	Doktor	und

Short   ö -------- ü ------------------------------- e(unstressed)

können	Mütter	bitte	genug
möchte	fünf	danke	gesehen
öfter	Hütte	Sonne	bekommen

Practice 1(b)

mit	— Mütter	kennen	— können
missen	— müssen	stecke	— Stöcke

B.   Long Vowels

    There are no sounds in English exactly like the German long vowels. If you will pronounce English gate and then listen to the German geht, you will notice that the English vowel sound seems to change during its pronunciation, but the German sound seems tense and stable throughout its duration. Your tongue actually moves during the production of the English vowel sound, but during the production of the German sound the tongue remains in the same position. The long ö and ü are formed approximately like short ö and ü. Pronounce German long e and round your lips to form ö, and pronounce German long i and round your lips to form ü

Practice 2(a)

Long   i -------- e ------- a --------- o ------- u ------- ö ------- ü

wie	geht	Tag	Sohn	gut	König	für
ihnen	Tee	Abend	oder	du	schön	Tür
viel	den	Bahn	wo	Flug	öde	über

Practice 2(b)

vier	— für	lesen	— lösen
Tier	— Tür	Sehne	— Söhne

C. Distinguishing Long and Short Vowels

It is NOT ALWAYS POSSIBLE to distinguish long and short vowels in written
German, as the German spelling system does not consistently mark them as such.
Your best guide to the pronunciation of any given word is the way your native
instructor pronounces it. However, a few hints can be given which will help
you to recognize them most of the time. If you look back at the practice lists
above you will see that the short vowels in most cases are followed by two or
more consonants and they are always written with a single letter symbol. Then
note that the long vowels are not always written with a single letter symbol and
usually are followed by only one consonant. The following combinations of
letters always designate long vowels: ie, ih - eh, ee - ah, aa - oh, oo - uh -
öh - üh

D. DIPHTHONGS

These combinations of two vowel sounds in German are very similar, though
not identical to certain vowel combinations in English.

Practice 3

ei	au	eu (äu)
nein	auch	deutsch
eins	Tau	neun
Wein	Laut	läute

Notes on Grammar (not recorded)
(For Home Study)

A. The German Noun-Classification ('Gender') System

I. The three classes of nouns.

Der Wein ist nicht gut.	The wine isn't good.
Das Bier ist gut.	The beer is good.
Die Milch ist auch gut.	The milk is good too.

1. German has three words for 'the': der, das and die; and German nouns
    can be divided into three classes according to which of the three words
    for 'the' they go with. Wein goes only with der, never with das, never
    with die. Bier goes only with das, and so on.

2. We will refer to these three classes of nouns, for obvious reasons, as
    der-nouns, das-nouns and die-nouns. ('Wein is der-noun.' 'Hotel is a
    das-noun.')

3. The traditional statement about this phenomenon is: 'German nouns have
    three genders--masculine, feminine, and neuter.' We will not use this
    terminology because it tends to mislead English-speaking students by
    suggesting that the German noun classification has something to do with
    sex differentiation. It doesn't. See paragraph III.

4. Insofar as the basic stock of German nouns is concerned (nouns like
    house, grass, sky, wine, beer, milk), there is absolutely no sense or
    rationale to the classification system; there is no way at all of
    anticipating which class any given noun belongs to. You must simply
    learn the word for 'the' as a part of the noun: the German word for
    'wine' is der Wein. And you must practice saying der Wein often enough
    so that das Wein or die Wein sounds as wrong to you as 'The father of
    his country -- Henry Washington.'

5. Now, Henry Washington is a perfectly good name; but it's wrong, and every American knows it's wrong. By the same token, <u>das Wein</u> is a perfectly good form; but it's wrong, and every German knows it's wrong. In time, you will too.

6. With <u>derivative</u> nouns (that is, nouns made from other words, like our happi-ness, brother-hood) your problem is easier. The classification of German derivative nouns is fairly orderly and consistent. Nouns ending in -ung, for example, are always <u>die</u>-nouns: <u>die Verzeihung</u> 'the forgive-ness, the pardon.' And nouns ending with the diminutive suffixes -lein and -chen are always <u>das</u>-nouns: <u>das Fräulein</u> 'the miss, waitress,' <u>das Mädchen</u> 'the little girl.' We will deal with the formation of the various kinds of derivative nouns as we go along through the units.

7. But if the classification of derivative nouns is orderly and consistent, the classification of the basic stock of German nouns remains virtually chaotic. There really is no system at all for guessing which class a noun belongs to; it's not something you can reason out or get the knack of. It is not the same as our <u>he-she-it</u> system, as we'll see in a minute. There is absolutely nothing in English like it. Your only solution is to use the nouns until you know them as well as you know 'George Washington.'

II. Pronouns Corresponding to the Three Classes of Nouns.

Wo ist <u>der</u> Bahnhof?	<u>Er</u> ist dort.	Where is <u>the</u> station?	<u>It</u>'s there.
Wo ist <u>das</u> Hotel?	<u>Es</u> ist dort.	Where is <u>the</u> hotel?	<u>It</u>'s there.
Wo ist <u>die</u> Botschaft?	<u>Sie</u> ist dort.	Where is <u>the</u> embassy?	<u>It</u>'s there.

1. As these examples show, there is a special <u>pronoun</u> for each of the three classes of nouns. Notice the correspondence in the final sounds of the pairs <u>der-er</u>, <u>das-es</u>, and <u>die-sie</u>. This is no coincidence.

III. Contrast between German and English Pronoun Usage.

Wo ist <u>der</u> Bahnhof?	<u>Er</u> ist dort.	Where's <u>the</u> station?	<u>It</u>'s there.
Wo ist <u>der</u> Mann?	<u>Er</u> ist dort.	Where's <u>the</u> man?	<u>He</u>'s there.
Wo ist <u>das</u> Hotel?	<u>Es</u> ist dort.	Where's <u>the</u> hotel?	<u>It</u>'s there.
Wo ist <u>das</u> Kind ?	<u>Es</u> ist dort.	Where's <u>the</u> child?	<u>He</u>'s there.
			or <u>She</u>'s there.
Wo ist <u>die</u> Botschaft?	<u>Sie</u> ist dort.	Where's <u>the</u> embassy?	<u>It</u>'s there.
Wo ist <u>die</u> Frau?	<u>Sie</u> ist dort.	Where's <u>the</u> woman?	<u>She</u>'s there.

1. These examples show that the German pronouns <u>er</u>, <u>sie</u>, and <u>es</u> do not match up with the English pronouns 'he', 'she', and 'it'. The English <u>he-she-it</u> system has an entirely different foundation from the German noun-classification ('gender') system. In the English system, the choice of pronoun depends upon the sex (male, female, or sexless) of some non-linguistic entity--a man ('he'), a woman ('she'), or a table ('it'). In the German system, on the other hand, the choice of pronoun depends upon the linguistic classification of the noun you are replacing, except in reference to human beings.

IV. Pronouns Referring to People.

Wo ist <u>das</u> Fräulein?	Where's <u>the</u> waitress?
<u>Sie</u> ist dort.	<u>She</u>'s there.

1. Since all German nouns referring to men are <u>der</u>-nouns and virtually all German nouns referring to women are <u>die</u>-nouns, <u>er</u> and <u>sie</u> correspond to 'he' and 'she' -- when they refer to <u>human beings</u>. Consequently, one says <u>sie</u> when referring to <u>das Fräulein</u>, who is, after all, <u>die junge Dame</u> 'the young lady', <u>die Tochter</u> 'the daughter', <u>die Schwester</u> 'the sister', and so on, as well as <u>das Fräulein</u>.

V. No classification in the Plural.

Wo sind <u>die</u> Bahnhöfe?	<u>Sie</u> sind hier.	Where are <u>the</u> stations?	<u>They</u>'re here.
Wo sind <u>die</u> Hotels?	<u>Sie</u> sind hier.	Where are <u>the</u> hotels?	<u>They</u>'re here.
Wo sind <u>die</u> Frauen?	<u>Sie</u> sind hier.	Where are <u>the</u> women?	<u>They</u>'re here.

1. As these examples show, the three-fold classification we've been discussing applies only to nouns in the singular. In the plural, there is only one word for 'the', and only one pronoun.

B. The Pointing-Word <u>das</u>.

<u>Das</u> ist der Bahnhof, nicht wahr?	<u>This</u> is the station, isn't it?
Ja, <u>das</u> ist er.	Yes, <u>that</u>'s it.
Ist <u>das</u> die Milch?	Is <u>that</u> the milk?
<u>Das</u> ist Wasser.	<u>This</u> is water.
Sind <u>das</u> die Streichhölzer?	Are <u>these</u> the matches?
<u>Das</u> sind die Zigarren.	<u>Those</u> are the cigars.

1. The pointing-word <u>das</u> (often accompanied by a pointing gesture) is used to call any <u>object</u> or <u>group of objects</u> to the hearer's attention, without any reference to noun classification or to the number of objects.

2. The pointing-word <u>das</u> is an entirely different entity from the <u>das</u> of <u>das Hotel</u>. The English equivalents of the pointing-word <u>das</u> are 'this', 'that', 'these', and 'those'.

SUBSTITUTION DRILL.

This section is made up of a number of model sentences. One or two words in each sentence are underscored. Below each group will be found a series of isolated words. The drill consists in substituting these words, one by one, for the one that is underscored in the model sentence, and making necessary changes in the rest of the sentence.

1. Der Flughafen ist dort.

  a. Bahnhof - Kaffee - Tee - Wein

    der Bahnhof - der Kaffee - der Tee - der Wein

  b. Restaurant - Bier - Wasser - Hotel - Café

    das Restaurant - das Bier - das Wasser - das Hotel - das Café

  c. Bank - Milch - Botschaft

    die Bank - die Milch - die Botschaft

  d. Streichhölzer - Zigarren

    die Streichhölzer - die Zigarren

  e. Bahnhof - Hotel - Tee - Milch - Kaffee - Restaurant - Streichhölzer - Botschaft - Flughafen - Bier - Wein - Wasser - Zigarren - Café

    der Bahnhof - das Hotel - der Tee - die Milch - der Kaffee - das Restaurant - die Streichhölzer - die Botschaft - der Flughafen - das Bier - der Wein - das Wasser - die Zigarren - das Café

2. Wo ist der Bahnhof?

  a. Flughafen - Kaffee - Tee - Wein

    der Flughafen - der Kaffe - der Tee - der Wein

  b. Restaurant - Bier - Wasser - Café - Hotel

    das Restaurant - das Bier - das Wasser - das Café - das Hotel

  c. Bank - Milch - Botschaft

    die Bank - die Milch - die Botschaft

  d. Streichhölzer - Zigarren

    die Streichhölzer - die Zigarren

  e. Restaurant - Flughafen - Bank - Kaffee - Wasser - Milch - Streichhölzer - Bahnhof - Tee - Hotel - Wein - Bier - Botschaft - Zigarren - Café

    das Restaurant - der Flughafen - die Bank - der Kaffee - das Wasser - die Milch - die Streichhölzer - der Bahnhof - der Tee - das Hotel - der Wein - das Bier - die Botschaft - die Zigarren - das Café

3. Wieviel kostet der Kaffee?

  a. Wein - Tee

    der Wein - der Tee

  b. Bier

    das Bier

  c. Zigarren - Streichhölzer

    die Zigarren - die Streichhölzer

  d. Wein - Zigarren - Tee - Streichhölzer - Bier

    der Wein - die Zigarren - der Tee - die Streichhölzer - das Bier

4. Wie ist das Bier?

  a. Wasser - Hotel - Restaurant - Café

    das Wasser - das Hotel - das Restaurant - das Café

  b. Kaffee - Tee - Wein -

    der Kaffee - der Tee - der Wein

  c. Bank - Milch

    die Bank - die Milch

  d. Zigarren - Streichhölzer

    die Zigarren - die Streichhölzer

  e. Bier - Tee - Hotel - Wein - Wasser - Kaffee - Milch - Zigarren - Café - Bank - Streichhölzer

    das Bier - der Tee - das Hotel - der Wein - das Wasser - der Kaffee - die Milch - die Zigarren - das Café - die Bank - die Streichhölzer

5. <u>Das Hotel</u> ist gut.

   a. Bier - Restaurant - Wasser -   das Bier - das Restaurant - das
       Café   Wasser - das Café

   b. Wein - Kaffee - Tee   der Wein - der Kaffee - der Tee

   c. Milch - Bank   die Milch - die Bank

   d. Zigarren - Streichhölzer   die Zigarren - die Streichhölzer

   e. Bier - Wein - Restaurant -   das Bier - der Wein - das Restaurant -
       Kaffee - Bank - Tee - Hotel -   der Kaffee - die Bank - der Tee -
       Streichhölzer - Wasser -   das Hotel - die Streichhölzer - das
       Zigarren - Café - Milch   Wasser - die Zigarren - das Café -
                                          die Milch

6. <u>Das Hotel</u> ist da drüben.

   a. Restaurant - Bier - Wasser -   das Restaurant - das Bier - das
       Café   Wasser - das Café

   b. Flughafen - Bahnhof - Kaffee -   der Flughafen - der Bahnhof - der
       Tee - Wein   Kaffee - der Tee - der Wein

   c. Botschaft - Milch - Bank   die Botschaft - die Milch - die Bank

   d. Streichhölzer - Zigarren   die Streichhölzer - die Zigarren

   e. Hotel - Restaurant - Tee -   das Hotel - das Restaurant - der Tee -
       Milch - Bier - Kaffee -   die Milch - das Bier - der Kaffee -
       Botschaft - Wein - Zigarren -   die Botschaft - der Wein - die
       Streichhölzer - Café - Bank   Zigarren - die Streichhölzer - das
                                          Café - die Bank

7. Das ist <u>der Flughafen</u>.

   a. Bahnhof - Wein - Tee - Kaffee   der Bahnhof - der Wein - der Tee -
                                          der Kaffee

   b. Hotel - Restaurant - Bier -   das Hotel - das Restaurant - das Bier -
       Café   das Café

   c. Bank - Botschaft - Milch   die Bank - die Botschaft - die Milch

   d. Streichhölzer - Zigarren   die Streichhölzer - die Zigarren

   e. Botschaft - Flughafen - Hotel -   die Botschaft - der Flughafen - das
       Milch - Restaurant - Bahnhof -   Hotel - die Milch - das Restaurant -
       Bier - Wein - Tee - Zigarren -   der Bahnhof - das Bier - der Wein -
       Café - Bank   der Tee - die Zigarren - das Café -
                                          die Bank   (End of Tape 1A)

Tape 1B

8. Hier ist <u>Herr Becker</u>. Hier ist <u>er</u>.

   a. Flughafen - Bahnhof - Wein -   der Flughafen.er - der Bahnhof.er -
       Tee - Kaffee - Herr Keller   der Wein.er - der Tee.er - der Kaffee.
                                          er - Herr Keller.er

   b. Frau Kunze - Milch - Botschaft -   Frau Kunze.sie - die Milch.sie -
       Bank - Frau Schneider   die Botschaft.sie - die Bank.sie -
                                          Frau Schneider.sie

   c. Restaurant - Bier - Wasser -   das Restaurant.es - das Bier.es -
       Café - Hotel   das Wasser.es - das Café.es - das
                                          Hotel.es

d. Streichhölzer - Zigarren - Herr und Frau Becker	die Streichhölzer.sie - die Zigarren. sie - Herr und Frau Becker.sie
e. Bier - Milch - Wasser - Wein - Streichhölzer - Bahnhof - Restaurant - Zigarren - Hotel - Herr und Frau Becker - Botschaft - Tee - Café - Frau Schneider - Flughafen - Herr Keller - Bank - Kaffee	das Bier.es - die Milch.sie - das Wasser.es - der Wein.er - die Streichhölzer.sie - der Bahnhof.er - das Restaurant.es - die Zigarren.sie - das Hotel.es - Herr und Frau Becker. sie - die Botschaft.sie - der Tee.er - das Café.es - Frau Schneider.sie - der Flughafen.er - Herr Keller.er - die Bank.sie - der Kaffee.er

VARIATION DRILL

This section is made up of several groups of sentences. Each group is headed by a model sentence which is underscored.

While doing this drill, STUDENTS MUST COVER THE RIGHT-HAND SIDE OF THE PAGE.

English versions must be read silently, and the German version must be given without stopping, with the proper pronunciation, including intonation. If you have to 'translate' word by word you need more practice with the basic sentences.

1. Ich verstehe Sie.   I understand you.

    a. I understand you well.   Ich verstehe Sie gut.
    b. I understand you very well.   Ich verstehe Sie sehr gut.
    c. I understand you well, too.   Ich verstehe Sie auch gut.
    d. I don't understand you.   Ich verstehe Sie nicht.
    e. I don't understand you either.   Ich verstehe Sie auch nicht.

2. Verstehen Sie mich?   Do you understand me?

    a. Do you understand me well?   Verstehen Sie mich gut?
    b. Do you understand me well to?   Verstehen Sie mich auch gut?
    c. Don't you understand me?   Verstehen Sie mich nicht?
    d. Don't you understand me either?   Verstehen Sie mich auch nicht?
    e. Don't you understand me well   Verstehen Sie mich auch nicht gut?
       either?

3. Wo ist der Flughafen?   Where is the airport?

    a. There is the airport.   Da ist der Flughafen.
    b. Is that the airport?   Ist das der Flughafen?
    c. Yes, that's the airport.   Ja, das ist der Flughafen.
    d. No, that's not the airport.   Nein, das ist nicht der Flughafen.
    e. Is the airport over there?   Ist der Flughafen da drüben?
    f. Yes, it's over there.   Ja, er ist da drüben.
    g. No, it's not over there.   Nein, er ist nicht da drüben.

Repeat the same drill and for airport substitute: hotel - embassy - restaurant - station.

4. <u>Wo sind die Streichhölzer</u>?   <u>Where are the matches</u>?

  a. Where are they?   Wo sind sie?
  b. There are the matches.   Da sind die Streichhölzer.
  c. There they are.   Da sind sie.
  d. Are the matches over there?   Sind die Streichhölzer da drüben?
  e. Yes, the matches are over   Ja, die Streichhölzer sind da drüben.
     there.
  f. They're over there.   Sie sind da drüben.

Repeat the same drill and for potatoes substitute: cigars - Mr. and Mrs. Kunze.

5. <u>Wie ist die Milch</u>?   <u>How's the milk</u>?

  a. It's good.   Sie ist gut.
  b. It's very good.   Sie ist sehr gut.
  c. The water is good too.   Das Wasser ist auch gut.
  d. It's very good too.   Es ist auch sehr gut.

6. <u>Wie ist das Bier</u>?   <u>How's the beer</u>?

  a. It's good.   Es ist gut.
  b. It's very good.   Es ist sehr gut.
  c. The cigars are good too.   Die Zigarren sind auch gut.
  d. They're very good too.   Sie sind auch sehr gut.

7. <u>Wie ist der Tee</u>?   <u>How's the tea</u>?

  a. It's not good.   Er ist nicht gut.
  b. It's very good.   Er ist sehr gut.
  c. The milk isn't good either.   Die Milch ist auch nicht gut.
  d. It's not very good either.   Sie ist auch nicht sehr gut.

8. <u>Wie sind die Streichhölzer</u>?   <u>How are the matches</u>?

  a. They're not good.   Sie sind nicht gut.
  b. They're not very good.   Sie sind nicht sehr gut.
  c. The wine is not good either.   Der Wein ist auch nicht gut.
  d. It's not very good either.   Er ist auch nicht sehr gut.

9. <u>Das kostet viel</u>.   <u>That costs a lot</u>.

  a. How much does that cost?   Wieviel kostet das?
  b. Does that cost much?   Kostet das viel?
  c. That doesn't cost much.   Das kostet nicht viel.
  d. That doesn't cost much either.   Das kostet auch nicht viel.
  e. That costs three marks.   Das kostet drei Mark.
  f. That costs three marks, too.   Das kostet auch drei Mark.

10. <u>Das Bier ist gut</u>.   <u>The beer is good</u>.

  a. The wine is not good.   Der Wein ist nicht gut.
  b. The coffee is good, too.   Der Kaffee ist auch gut.
  c. The restaurant is very good.   Das Restaurant ist sehr gut.
  d. Is the tea good?   Ist der Tee gut?
  e. No, the tea isn't very good.   Nein, der Tee ist nicht sehr gut.
  f. Is the café good?   Ist das Café gut?

11. <u>Die Streichhölzer sind nicht</u>   <u>The matches are not very good</u>.
    <u>sehr gut</u>.

  a. The beer and the wine are good.   Das Bier und der Wein sind gut.
  b. The cigars are good, too.   Die Zigarren sind auch gut.
  c. Are the coffee and the tea good?   Sind der Kaffee und der Tee gut?
  d. Yes, they are very good.   Ja, sie sind sehr gut.

12. **Wo ist der Flughafen?** **Er ist dort rechts.**

   Where is the airport? **It's there to the right.**

   a. Where is the café? It's there to the left.

   Wo ist das Café? Es ist dort links.

   b. Where is the restaurant? It's there, too.

   Wo ist das Restaurant? Es ist auch dort.

   c. Where is the bank? It's there straight ahead.

   Wo ist die Bank? Sie ist dort geradeaus.

   d. Where is Mr. Schneider? He is here.

   Wo ist Herr Schneider? Er ist hier.

   e. Where is Mrs. Schneider? She's here, too.

   Wo ist Frau Schneider? Sie ist auch hier.

   f. Where is the station? It's over there, to the right.

   Wo ist der Bahnhof? Er ist da drüben, rechts.

13. **Wie ist der Kaffee?** **Er ist gut.**

   How is the coffee? **It is good.**

   a. How is the milk? It's very good.

   Wie ist die Milch? Sie ist sehr gut.

   b. How is the water? It's good, too.

   Wie ist das Wasser? Es ist auch gut.

   c. How is the hotel? It's not very good.

   Wie ist das Hotel? Es ist nicht sehr gut.

   d. How is the beer? It's very good here.

   Wie ist das Bier? Es ist hier sehr gut.

   e. How is the tea? It's not good.

   Wie ist der Tee? Er ist nicht gut.

   f. How is the wine? It's very good, too.

   Wie ist der Wein? Er ist auch sehr gut.

14. **Ich möchte gern Zigaretten haben.**

   I'd like to have some cigarettes, please.

   a. Would you like to have some cigars, too?

   Möchten Sie auch Zigarren haben?

   b. I'd like to have some matches.

   Ich möchte gern Streichhölzer haben.

   c. Would you like to have some bread?

   Möchten Sie etwas Brot haben?

   d. I'd like to have some milk.

   Ich möchte gern Milch haben.

   e. I'd like to have some sausage and sauerkraut.

   Ich möchte gern Bratwurst mit Sauerkraut haben.

15. **Ich möchte gerne essen.**

   I'd like to eat.

   a. What would you like to eat?

   Was möchten Sie essen?

   b. I'd like to eat some sausage and sauerkraut.

   Ich möchte Bratwurst mit Sauerkraut essen.

   c. Would you also like to eat some bread?

   Möchten Sie auch Brot essen?

   d. Yes, I'd like to eat some bread.

   Ja, ich möchte gern etwas Brot essen.

16. **Das ist der Bahnhof.**

   That's the railroad station.

   a. Is that the embassy?

   Ist das die Botschaft?

   b. No, that's not the embassy.

   Nein, das ist nicht die Botschaft.

   c. That's the hotel.

   Das ist das Hotel.

   d. Is that Mr. Kunze?

   Ist das Herr Kunze?

   e. No, that's not Mr. Kunze.

   Nein, das ist nicht Herr Kunze.

   f. That's Mr. Schneider.

   Das ist Herr Schneider.

17. <u>Hier ist das Hotel.</u>   <u>Here is the hotel.</u>

    a. There's the restaurant.   Dort ist das Restaurant.
    b. Over there is the airport.   Da drüben ist der Flughafen.
    c. There to the right is the   Dort rechts ist die Botschaft.
       embassy.
    d. Here on the left is the station. Hier links ist der Bahnhof.
    e. Over there, to the right is the Da drüben, rechts, ist das Café.
       café.

18. <u>Die Zigarren kosten fünf Mark.</u>   <u>The cigars cost five marks.</u>

    a. The beer costs one mark.   Das Bier kostet eine Mark.
    b. The wine costs two marks ten.   Der Wein kostet zwei Mark zehn.
    c. The matches cost ten pennies.   Die Streichhölzer kosten zehn Pfennig.
    d. The coffee costs three marks   Der Kaffee kostet drei Mark acht.
       eight.
    e. The tea costs two marks four.   Der Tee kostet zwei Mark vier.
    f. The milk costs twelve pennies.   Die Milch kostet zwölf Pfennig.
    g. Bratwurst and sauerkraut costs Bratwurst mit Sauerkraut kostet
       two marks five.   zwei Mark fünf.

19. <u>Drei und vier ist sieben.</u>   <u>Three and four is seven.</u>

    a. Five and three is eight.   Fünf und drei ist acht.
    b. How much is two and six?   Wieviel ist zwei und sechs?
    c. Seven and five is twelve.   Sieben und fünf ist zwölf.
    d. Three and three is six.   Drei und drei ist sechs.
    e. How much is seven and four?   Wieviel ist sieben und vier?
    f. Is nine and one eleven?   Ist neun und eins elf?
    g. No, nine and one is ten.   Nein, neun und eins ist zehn.

TRANSLATION DRILL (Not recorded)

Unless students can do this drill confidently, they need more preparation.

1. Is that the embassy?   Ist das die Botschaft?
2. No, that's not the embassy, that's Nein, das ist nicht die Botschaft, das
   the hotel.   ist das Hotel.
3. The embassy is over there, to the Die Botschaft ist da drüben, links.
   left.
4. How is the beer, is it good?   Wie ist das Bier, ist es gut?
5. No, it's not very good.   Nein, es ist nicht sehr gut.
6. What is that there, the airport?   Was ist das dort, der Flughafen?
7. Yes, that's the airport.   Ja, das ist der Flughafen.
8. Is Mr. Becker here?   Ist Herr Becker hier?
9. No, he isn't (here).   Nein, er ist nicht hier.
10. Is the wine good here?   Ist hier der Wein gut?
11. Yes, it is (good here).   Ja, er ist gut hier.
12. Where is Miss Schneider?   Wo ist Fräulein Schneider?
13. Isn't she here?   Ist sie nicht hier?
14. No, she isn't (here).   Nein, sie ist nicht hier.
15. How much does sausage and sauerkraut Wieviel kostet Bratwurst mit
   cost?   Sauerkraut?
16. It doesn't cost much.   Es kostet nicht viel.
17. Where are the cigars?   Wo sind die Zigarren?
18. Aren't they here?   Sind sie nicht hier?

19. No, they aren't (here).	Nein, sie sind nicht hier.
20. They cost four marks.	Sie kosten vier Mark.
21. Do you understand me?	Verstehen Sie mich?
22. What did you say?	Wie bitte?
23. Yes, I understand you very well.	Ja, ich verstehe Sie sehr gut.
24. Would you like to eat?	Möchten Sie gern essen?
25. Yes, I would.	Ja, gerne.

RESPONSE DRILL (Not recorded)

Students are to prepare this drill at home. The questions are generally directed toward the situation or situations presented in the Basic Sentences. The answers suggested are obviously not the only possible answers to these questions, and the student should feel free to vary them or to replace them by his own formulations ad libitum, within the limitations of structure and vocabulary covered.

1. Wo ist Herr Becker?	Er ist dort drüben.
2. Ist das Frau Kunze?	Nein, das ist nicht Frau Kunze.
3. Wo sind Herr und Frau Schneider?	Herr und Frau Schneider sind hier.
4. Wie geht es Ihnen?	Danke gut. Und Ihnen?
5. Verstehen Sie mich?	Ja, ich verstehe Sie gut.
6. Verstehen Sie mich auch gut?	Nein, ich verstehe Sie nicht.
7. Wo ist der Bahnhof?	Der Bahnhof ist dort rechts.
8. Ist das der Bahnhof?	Nein, das ist nicht der Bahnhof. Er ist dort, geradeaus.
9. Wo ist der Flughafen?	Er ist dort drüben.
10. Ist das Hotel dort links?	Nein, es ist dort rechts.
11. Das Restaurant ist dort drüben, nicht wahr?	Ja, es ist dort drüben, geradeaus.
12. Was ist das dort?	Das ist die Botschaft.
13. Wo ist hier die Bank?	Die Bank ist hier links.
14. Ist das die Botschaft da drüben?	Ja, das ist die Botschaft.
15. Wie ist das Café?	Das Café ist sehr gut.
16. Ist das Restaurant auch gut?	Nein, das Restaurant ist nicht sehr gut.
17. Wie sagt man "good bye" auf deutsch?	Man sagt "Auf Wiedersehen".
18. Wie sagt man "thank you" auf deutsch?	Man sagt "Danke schön".
19. Was möchten Sie haben?	Ich möchte zehn Zigaretten haben.
20. Möchten Sie auch Zigarren haben?	Ja, ich möchte auch Zigarren haben.
21. Wieviele möchten Sie haben?	Vier, bitte.
22. Möchten Sie auch Streichhölzer haben?	Ja, ich möchte auch Streichhölzer haben.
23. Wieviel kosten die Zigarren?	Die Zigarren kosten eine Mark.
24. Kostet das Bier eine Mark?	Nein, es kostet eine Mark zehn.
25. Wieviel kostet der Wein?	Er kostet sechs Mark fünf.
26. Wieviel kosten der Kaffee und der Tee?	Der Kaffee und der Tee kosten fünf Mark zwölf.
27. Möchten Sie gern etwas essen?	Ja, ich möchte gern etwas essen.
28. Was möchten Sie essen?	Ich möchte Bratwurst mit Sauerkraut essen.
29. Möchten Sie auch Brot essen?	Ja, ich möchte auch etwas Brot essen.
30. Wie ist hier das Bier?	Das Bier ist hier sehr gut.
31. Ist der Wein auch gut?	Ja, der Wein ist auch sehr gut.
32. Wie ist der Kaffee?	Der Kaffee ist nicht gut.
33. Ist der Tee auch nicht gut?	Nein, er ist auch nicht gut.
34. Ist die Milch gut?	Ja, die Milch ist sehr gut.
35. Wieviel ist zwei und zwei?	Zwei und zwei ist vier.
36. Ist drei und vier acht?	Nein, drei und vier ist sieben.
37. Wieviel ist fünf und vier?	Fünf und vier ist neun.
38. Ist sechs und fünf zwölf?	Nein, sechs und fünf ist nicht zwölf. Sechs und fünf ist elf.

CONVERSATION PRACTICE (not recorded)

1

A: Wo ist die Botschaft hier in Bonn?
B: Die Botschaft ist dort, geradeaus.
A: Wie bitte?
B: Sie ist dort, geradeaus. Verstehen Sie mich?
A: Ja, danke. Und wo ist der Flughafen?
B: Der Flughafen ist da links.
A: Danke schön.

2

S: Guten Tag, Herr Becker.
K: Guten Tag, Herr Kunze. Wie geht es Ihnen?
S: Danke, gut. Und Ihnen?
K: Auch gut, danke.
S: Wie ist das Bier hier?
K: Es ist sehr gut und der Wein ist auch gut.
S: Wieviel kostet das Bier?
K: Es kostet eine Mark zehn.
S: Möchten Sie auch etwas essen?
K: Nein, danke.

3

C: Guten Morgen.
   Ich möchte gern zehn Zigarren haben.
D: Bitte. Möchten Sie auch Zigaretten haben?
C: Nein, danke. Aber ich möchte Streichhölzer haben.
D: Hier bitte.
C: Wieviel kosten die Zigarren?
D: Sie kosten fünf Mark sieben.

4

E: Verzeihung, wo ist das Restaurant?
F: Das Restaurant ist dort, rechts.
E: Ist das der Flughafen dort drüben?
F: Nein, das ist nicht der Flughafen, das ist der Bahnhof.
   Der Flughafen ist dort, links.
E: Wie bitte? Ich verstehe Sie nicht. Sprechen Sie bitte langsam.
F: Das ist nicht der Flughafen, das ist der Bahnhof.
   Der Flughafen ist dort, links. Verstehen Sie mich?
E: Ja, ich verstehe Sie. Auf Wiedersehen.

SITUATIONS (not recorded)

You are now ready for free conversation. Act out the following situations, which are slight variations on the basic sentences, as freely and fluently as you can, making use of all the patterns you have learned.

Finding the Way

An American has just arrived in Germany and doesn't understand too well yet. He asks a German on the street where the hotel is. The German tells him it's over there to the left. The American doesn't understand him and asks him to say it again please. He still does not understand and asks the German to speak slowly. The latter repeats much slower and asks the American if he understands. The American says he does, thanks him and says good-bye.

Go through this conversation again with the American asking for the embassy, café, airport, etc., and the German giving different directions: straight ahead, over there, to the right, etc.

At the Cigar Store

Mr. Becker is the proprietor of a cigar store. Mr. Schneider stops in for some cigarettes. They exchange greetings, and Mr. Becker asks what Mr. Schneider would like. After getting him the cigarettes he asks if Mr. Schneider would like some cigars, too. He says no thanks, but he would like some matches. Figuring up his own bill he says that costs one mark ten, doesn't it, but Mr. Becker says no, it costs two marks. Mr. Schneider gives him the money, and they say good-bye to each other.

At the Restaurant

Miss Schneider is the waitress in a restaurant. Mr. Kunze greets her as he comes in and asks how she is. She returns his greeting and asks if he is well, too. He says yes, thanks, and asks if they have sausage and sauerkraut, and how the beer and the wine are, etc. Finally he says he'd like to have sausage and sauerkraut, beer and some bread. After the meal he pays her - it costs three marks - and says good-bye.

FINDER LIST

	Abend	evening
	aber	but
	acht	eight
	auch	also, too
	auch nicht	not ... either
	auf deutsch	in German
	Auf Wiedersehen!	good-bye
der	Bahnhof	station
die	Bank	bank
das	Bier	beer
	bitte	please
	bitte schön	here you are
die	Botschaft	embassy
	Bratwurst mit Sauerkraut	sausage and sauerkraut
	Brot	bread
das	Café	café
	da	there
	danke	thanks
	danke schön	many thanks
	das	that
	dort	there
	drei	three
	drüben	over there
	eins	one

	elf	eleven
	er	he, it
	es	it
	essen	eat
	etwas Brot	some bread
der	Flughafen	airport
	Frau	Mrs.
	Frau Kunze	Mrs. Kunze
	Fräulein	Miss
	Fräulein Schneider	Miss Schneider
	fünf	five
	geht	goes
	geradeaus	straight ahead
	gern(e)	with pleasure
	gut	good, well
	guten Abend	good evening
	guten Morgen	good morning
	guten Tag	hello (good ɪy)
	haben	have
	Herr	Mr.
	Herr Becker	Mr. Becker
	hier	here
das	Hotel	hotel
	ich	I
	Ihnen	to you, with you
	ist	is
	ja	yes
der	Kaffee	coffee
	kosten	cost
	kostet	costs
	langsam	slow, slowly
	links	left, to the left
	man	one, you
	Mark	Mark, Marks
	eine Mark	one Mark
	zwei Mark	two Marks
	mich	me (acc)
die	Milch	milk
	möchten	would like
	möchten Sie	would you like
	ich möchte	I would like
	ich möchte gern	I'd like very much
	Morgen	morning
	nein	no
	neun	nine
	nicht	not
	nicht wahr?	isn't it (not true)?
	nochmal	again
	null	zero
	Pfennig	penny, pennies
	rechts	to the right
das	Restaurant	restaurant
	sagt	says
	sagt man	does one say
	sechs	six
	sehr	very
	sie	she, it
	Sie	you
	sieben	seven
	sind	are
	sprechen	speak
die	Streichhölzer	matches
	Tag	day
der	Tee	tea

	und	and
	verstehen	understand
	verstehen Sie	do you understand
	ich verstehe	I understand
	Verzeihung	excuse me
	vier	four
	was	what
das	Wasser	water
der	Wein	wine
	wie	how
	wie bitte?	I beg your pardon. What did you say?
	wieviel	now much
	wieviele	how many
	wo	where
	zehn	ten
	Zigaretten	cigarettes
die	Zigarren	cigars
	zwei	two
	zwölf	twelve

IN MÜNCHEN

Basic Sentences

I

to meet, encounter	treffen
he meets	er trifft
Mr. (object)	Herrn (accusative form)
in	in
Munich	München

Mr. Becker meets Mr.and Mrs.Allen
in Munich.

Herr Becker trifft Herrn und Frau Allen
in München.

the Allens	Allens
the American	der Amerikaner
Americans	Amerikaner
the diplomat (used loosely to designate any Foreign Service Officer abroad)	der Diplomat
a diplomat, a Foreign Service Officer	Diplomat

The Allens are Americans. Mr. Allen
is a Foreign Service Officer.

Allens sind Amerikaner. Herr Allen
ist Diplomat.

II

(No English equivalent. Unstressed particle express- ing polite interest or con- cern.)	denn

MR. ALLEN

Hello, Mr. Becker. How are you?

HERR ALLEN

Guten Tag, Herr Becker. Wie geht es
Ihnen denn?

MR. BECKER

Fine, thanks.

HERR BECKER

Danke, gut.

to know, be acquainted with	kennen
you know (speaking to family or intimate friends)	du kennst
(no exact equivalent. Here: unstressed particle stressing an obvious fact.)	doch

MR. ALLEN

Mary, you know Mr. Becker, don't you?

HERR ALLEN

Maria, du kennst doch Herrn Becker,
nicht wahr?

of course	natürlich
we	wir
we have	wir haben
for a long time	lange
seen	gesehen

MRS. ALLEN	FRAU ALLEN
Yes, of course. We haven't seen you for a long time, Mr. Becker.	Ja, natürlich. Wir haben Sie lange nicht gesehen, Herr Becker.

I was	ich war
the month	der Monat
for two months	zwei Monate
Bonn	Bonn

MR. BECKER	HERR BECKER
I was in Bonn for two months.	Ich war zwei Monate in Bonn.

how long	wie lange
to stay, remain	bleiben

MR. ALLEN	HERR ALLEN
How long are you staying here in Munich?	Wie lange bleiben Sie hier in München?

probably	wahrscheinlich
the year	das Jahr
one year	ein Jahr

MR. BECKER	HERR BECKER
Probably for one year.	Wahrscheinlich ein Jahr.

III

to please	gefallen
it pleases	es gefällt
you like it	es gefällt Ihnen
(polite way of addressing a married woman. Here: 'Mrs.Allen')	gnädige Frau

MR. BECKER	HERR BECKER
How do you like it in Munich, Mrs. Allen?	Wie gefällt es Ihnen in München, gnädige Frau?

to us	uns (dative)
we like it	es gefällt uns
beautiful	schön
the city	die Stadt
a beautiful city	eine schöne Stadt

MRS. ALLEN	FRAU ALLEN
We like it here very much. Munich is a beautiful city.	Es gefällt uns hier sehr gut. München ist eine schöne Stadt.

to live, dwell	wohnen
the vicinity, 'nearness'	die Nähe
in the vicinity, near	in der Nähe
the consulate	das Konsulat
of the consulate	vom Konsulat

MR. BECKER	HERR BECKER
Do you live in the vicinity of the consulate?	Wohnen Sie in der Nähe vom Konsulat?
in the Bayrischen Hof (Hotel)	im Bayrischen Hof
MRS. ALLEN	FRAU ALLEN
Yes, in the Bayrischen Hof.	Ja, im Bayrischen Hof.
nice	nett
It's very nice there.	Es ist dort sehr nett.

IV	IV
to plan to do you plan to do now	vorhaben Sie haben ... vor jetzt
MR. BECKER	HERR BECKER
What do you plan to do now?	Was haben Sie denn jetzt vor?
to want or intend (to) we want, we intend (to) to go and eat	wollen wir wollen essen gehen
MR. ALLEN	HERR ALLEN
We're planning to go and eat.	Wir wollen essen gehen.
to come along	mitkommen
Don't you want to come along?	Wollen Sie nicht mitkommen?
MR. BECKER	HERR BECKER
I'd be very glad to. Where are you going to eat?	Sehr gern. Wo essen Sie denn?
on Ludwigstrasse	in der Ludwigstrasse
MR. ALLEN	HERR ALLEN
Do you know the restaurant on Ludwigstrasse?	Kennen Sie das Restaurant in der Ludwigstrasse?
the food	das Essen
The food is very good there.	Das Essen ist dort sehr gut.

V

who	wer
actually, really	eigentlich
the lady	die Dame

MRS. ALLEN

FRAU ALLEN

I wonder who the lady over there is?

Wer ist eigentlich die Dame dort?

she is speaking, talking	sie spricht
just	gerade
with	mit
the waiter	der Ober
with the waiter	mit dem Ober

She's just talking to the waiter.

Sie spricht gerade mit dem Ober.

MR. BECKER

HERR BECKER

That's Miss Adams.

Das ist Fräulein Adams.

her (object)	sie (accusative)

Don't you know her?

Kennen Sie sie nicht?

to believe	glauben
I believe	ich glaube

MRS. ALLEN

FRAU ALLEN

No, I don't believe so.

Nein, ich glaube nicht.

to go	gehen
I go	ich gehe
often	oft
to the movies	ins Kino

MR. BECKER

HERR BECKER

I often go to the movies with her.

Ich gehe oft mit ihr ins Kino.

or	oder
the American (lady)	die Amerikanerin
an American (lady)	Amerikanerin
the German (lady)	die Deutsche
a German (lady)	Deutsche

MRS. ALLEN

FRAU ALLEN

Is she an American or a German?

Ist sie Amerikanerin oder Deutsche?

MR. BECKER

HERR BECKER

She's an American.

Sie ist Amerikanerin.

German	deutsch
English	englisch

MRS. ALLEN

FRAU ALLEN

Do you speak English or German
with her?

Sprechen Sie deutsch oder englisch
mit ihr?

26

to be able
she can

	könnten
	sie kann

MR. BECKER

She can speak German very well.

HERR BECKER

Sie kann sehr gut deutsch sprechen.

VI

to go, ride (in a vehicle)
to that place
today

fahren
hin
heute

MR. ALLEN

Where are you going today?

HERR ALLEN

Wo fahren Sie heute hin?

I intend, I plan
then
to, toward

ich will
dann
nach

MR. BECKER

I'm planning to go to Schwabing
and then to Tölz.

HERR BECKER

Ich will nach Schwabing fahren,
und dann nach Tölz.

whom (object)
to visit

wen (accusative)
besuchen

MR. ALLEN

Who are you going to visit there?

HERR ALLEN

Wen wollen Sie denn dort besuchen?

the parents
of
Mr. (object)

die Eltern
von
Herrn (dative)

MR. BECKER

Mr. Keller's parents.

You know Mr. Keller, don't you?

HERR BECKER

Die Eltern von Herrn Keller.

Sie kennen doch Herrn Keller, nicht
wahr?

to work
he works

arbeiten
er arbeitet

I believe he works at the consulate
too.

Ich glaube, er arbeitet auch im
Konsulat.

even, as a matter of fact

sogar

MR. ALLEN

Yes, as a matter of fact I know him
very well.

HERR ALLEN

Ja, ich kenne ihn sogar sehr gut.

to live
he lives
now
quite
in my vicinity, near me

wohnen
er wohnt
jetzt
ganz
in meiner Nähe

He lives quite near me now.

Er wohnt jetzt ganz in meiner Nähe

I go, I ride	ich fahre
him (object)	ihm (dative)
with	mit
with him	mit ihm
home	nach Hause

I often ride home with him.   Ich fahre oft mit ihm nach Hause.

can you	können Sie
me, to me	mir (dative)
the address	die Adresse
new	neu
his new address	seine neue Adresse
to give	geben

MR. BECKER   **HERR BECKER**

Can you give me his new address?   Können Sie mir seine neue Adresse
                                      geben?

MR. ALLEN   **HERR ALLEN**

Gladly   Gerne.

BEI DER PASSKONTROLLE UND BEIM ZOLL

VII   ### VII

to be allowed (to)	dürfen
may I	darf ich
the passport	der Pass
your passport (object)	Ihren Pass (accusative)
to see	sehen

THE OFFICIAL   **DER BEAMTE**

May I see your passport?   Darf ich Ihren Pass sehen?

MR. BRAUER   **HERR BRAUER**

Here you are.   Hier, bitte.

| to be called, named | heissen |
| you are called, your name is | Sie heissen |

THE OFFICIAL   **DER BEAMTE**

What is your name, Bauer or Brauer?   Wie heissen Sie, Bauer oder Brauer?

| I am called, my name is | ich heisse |

MR. BRAUER   **HERR BRAUER**

My name is Brauer.   Ich heisse Brauer.

were you, have you been	waren Sie
already, before	schon
once (Here: 'ever')	einmal
Germany	Deutschland

THE OFFICIAL   **DER BEAMTE**

Have you ever been in Germany before? Waren Sie schon einmal in Deutschland?

| still, yet | noch |
| not yet | noch nicht |

MR. BRAUER	HERR BRAUER
No, not yet.	Nein, noch nicht.

THE OFFICIAL	DER BEAMTE
Where are you going (to)?	Wo fahren Sie hin?
Frankfort	Frankfurt

MR. BRAUER	HERR BRAUER
To Frankfurt.	Nach Frankfurt.

well	also
to have to	müssen
now	jetzt
the customs office	der Zoll
to	zu
to the customs office	zum Zoll

THE OFFICIAL	DER BEAMTE
Well, then you still have to /go/ to the customs office.	Also, dann müssen Sie jetzt noch zum Zoll.

MR. BRAUER	HERR BRAUER
Where is the customs office?	Wo ist denn der Zoll?
to see	sehen

THE OFFICIAL	DER BEAMTE
Over there, do you see (it)?	Da drüben, sehen Sie?

MR. BRAUER	HERR BRAUER
Yes, thanks.	Ja, danke.

VIII

to come	kommen
from that place	her

THE OFFICIAL	DER BEAMTE
Where do you come from?	Wo kommen Sie her?
out of, from	aus
America	Amerika

MR. BRAUER	HERR BRAUER
I come from America.	Ich komme aus Amerika.
to declare	verzollen
to declare, to be declared	zu verzollen

THE OFFICIAL	DER BEAMTE
Do you have anything to declare?	Haben Sie etwas zu verzollen?

MR. BRAUER	HERR BRAUER
I don't believe so.	Ich glaube nicht.

the baggage, luggage	das Gepäck
your baggage, luggage	Ihr Gepäck
to show	zeigen
THE OFFICIAL	DER BEAMTE

Show me your luggage, please.	Zeigen Sie mir bitte Ihr Gepäck.

MR. BRAUER	HERR BRAUER
Here.	Bitte.

(to) whom	wem (dative)
to belong	gehören
he, it belongs	er gehört
the suitcase	der Koffer
this suitcase	dieser Koffer
THE OFFICIAL	DER BEAMTE

Who does this suitcase here belong to?	Wem gehört dieser Koffer hier?

that one	der
MR. BRAUER	HERR BRAUER

That one doesn't belong to me.	Der gehört mir nicht.

only	nur
these two suitcases	diese zwei Koffer

I only have these two suitcases.	Ich habe nur diese zwei Koffer.

THE OFFICIAL	DER BEAMTE
Thanks very much.	Danke sehr.

everything	alles
the order	die Ordnung
in order	in Ordnung

Everything's in order.	Alles in Ordnung.

the trip	die Reise
a good trip	gute Reise

/Have/ a good trip!	Gute Reise!

(End of Tape 1B)

Tape 2A Basic Sentences

Notes on Pronunciation

A. **Long and short vowels.**

   Practice 1:

ihn	– in	Beet	– Bett	Staat	– Stadt	bog	– Bock
bieten	– bitten	beten	– Betten	wate	– Watte	wohne	– Wonne
Lied	– litt	den	– denn	Wahn	– wann	lohte	– Lotte
mieten	– mitten	Sehne	– Senne	bahne	– banne	Ofen	– offen

Mus - muss	König - können	Hüte - Hütte
Pute - Putte	Höhle - Hölle	fühle - fülle
bucht - Bucht	böge - Böcke	müder - Mütter
Muhme - Mumme	Goethe - Götter	Lüge - Lücke

B. Diphthongs.

Listen to the German Wein, then say English 'wine.' Notice that the duration of the German vowel combination is considerably shorter than the English.

Practice 2:

mein	Haus	neu
Wein	Maus	neun
nein	auch	deutsch
leider	glaube	Leute

C. Post-vocalic r

Post-vocalic r in German has a vowel-like sound. It does not sound like the English r. Listen carefully to the following pairs of words and imitate them.

Practice 3:

diese - dieser	Miete - Mieter	älter - Eltern	Gästen - gestern
eine - einer	Alte - Alter	Vetter - Vettern	locken - lockern
Liebe - lieber	bitte - bitter	Kinder - Kindern	fetten - Vettern
Ode - oder	welche - welcher		

Note that the syllable with post-vocalic r is in every case slightly longer than the syllable without it.

Now practice the following groups, first the long vowels and then the pairs of long and short vowels with post-vocalic r, and finally the vowels followed by r and a consonant.

Practice 4:

hier	sehr	Uhr	Ohr	her - Herr
Bier	mehr	fuhr	Tor	wir - wirr
wir	her	nur	Mohr	Star - starr

Mark	dort	Herrn	Furt	Wirt
Park	Dorf	gern	Durst	First
darf	Wort	herb	Wurm	Schirm
hart	Kork	Kerl	Kurve	Birne

D.   Pre-vocalic r (voiceless).

The pre-vocalic r differs from the post-vocalic r. Most speakers of German make the pre-vocalic r with slight friction between the back of the tongue and the soft palate, the region back of the mouth near the uvula. This sound is very similar to the final sound in noch and nach. Practice the following groups:

Practice 5:

noch	lachen	Dachau
doch	pochen	Bochum
nach	tauchen	Bucholz
auch		

Now try making the same sound right after the initial consonants in the following groups:

Practice 6:

Frau	Trost	Prost	Krone
fragen	traute	prall	Kragen
froh	treffen	Preis	krumm

You may find it necessary at first to whisper an extra syllable at the beginning of these words and pronounce Fochau, Tochost, pochall, Kochone, etc. Don't hesitate to try this if necessary.

Notes on Grammar (not recorded)
(For Home Study)

A.   PRONOUNS - FORMS AND FUNCTIONS.

I. Forms.

1. In the following English sentences the pronouns are underlined. Note their forms.

I know him and he knows me. Do you know her? She knows you.

Most English pronouns have two different forms: I-me, he-him, she-her, etc. Some, like the pronouns you and it, have only one form however.

2. Note the forms of the German pronouns in the following sentences.

Verstehen Sie mich?	Do you understand me?
Ja, ich verstehe Sie gut.	Yes, I understand you well.
Wie geht es Ihnen?	How goes it with-regard-to-you?
	(How are you?)
Er spricht englisch mit mir.	He speaks English with me.

Some German pronouns have two different forms, like Sie and Ihnen above. Many German pronouns however have three different forms like ich, mich and mir above.

3. The following table gives the forms of the most common German pronouns:

	'I'	'we'	'he'	'it'	'she'	'they'	'you'	'who?'	'what?'
a. NOMINATIVE forms:	ich	wir	er	es	sie	sie	Sie	wer	was
b. ACCUSATIVE forms:	mich	uns	ihn	es	sie	sie	Sie	wen	was
c. DATIVE forms :	mir	uns	ihm	ihm	ihr	ihnen	Ihnen	wem	---
	'me'	'us'	'him'	'it'	'her'	'them'	'you'	('whom?')	'what'

The English forms at the top of the table correspond to the set of German forms above the line. Those at the bottom of the table correspond to the <u>two</u> sets of German forms below the line. The pronouns <u>wer</u> and <u>was</u> are used only in questions. The pronouns for familiar address, <u>du</u> and <u>ihr</u>, will be taken up later.

II. Functions.

1. The NOMINATIVE form: In German, as in English, the basic sentence structure is an ACTOR-ACTION pattern: somebody doing something. The ACTOR is called the SUBJECT of the sentence, and in German a pronoun designating the ACTOR always has the NOMINATIVE form.

<u>Ich</u> verstehe sehr gut.	<u>I</u> understand very well.
<u>Er</u> wohnt ganz in meiner Nähe.	<u>He</u> lives quite near me.
<u>Wir</u> wollen gerade essen gehen.	<u>We</u>'re just planning to go and eat.

2. The ACCUSATIVE form: In many sentences in both English and German there is another element, the GOAL or OBJECT of the action, the person or thing toward which the action is aimed. In German a pronoun designating the OBJECT of an action is usually in the ACCUSATIVE form.

Ich kenne <u>ihn</u> sehr gut.	I know <u>him</u> very well.
Verstehen Sie <u>mich</u>?	Do you understand <u>me</u>?
Wir treffen <u>sie</u> dort.	We're meeting <u>them</u> (or <u>her</u>) there.

3. The DATIVE form: The third form of the German pronoun is used to designate the INTERESTED BYSTANDER, the person <u>to whom</u> or <u>for whom</u> or <u>with regard to whom</u> the action of the sentence is being performed. In some cases this is referred to as the INDIRECT OBJECT.

Können Sie <u>mir</u> seine Adresse geben?	Can you give <u>me</u> his address?
Sie müssen <u>ihm</u> Ihren Pass zeigen.	You have to show your passport <u>to him.</u>
Wie geht es <u>Ihnen</u>?	How are you? (How goes it <u>with-regard-to-you</u>?)
Gefällt es <u>Ihnen</u> in München?	Do you like it in Munich? (Is it pleasing <u>to you</u> in Munich?)
Der Koffer gehört <u>mir</u> nicht.	The suitcase doesn't belong <u>to me.</u>

4. Another use of the DATIVE form is illustrated by the following sentences you have learned:

Sprechen Sie englisch mit <u>ihr</u>?	Do you speak English with <u>her</u>?
Ich fahre oft mit <u>ihm</u> nach Hause.	I often ride home with <u>him</u>.

The DATIVE forms <u>ihr</u> and <u>ihm</u> are used here because they follow the word <u>mit</u>, and that's all there is to it. Any pronoun that follows <u>mit</u> has the DATIVE form, always and without fail. This has nothing to do with the INTERESTED BYSTANDER usage; it's something entirely different.

B. The Principle of Substitution.

1. Languages, like automobiles, are made up of replaceable parts; but the part you substitute must fit the frame into which it is put. For example, in the frame <u>Er kennt mich</u> 'He knows me', the Accusative form <u>mich</u> may be replaced only by other Accusative forms -- that is, forms from the same horizontal line in the table of pronoun forms as <u>mich</u>, the line labeled 'ACCUSATIVE forms'.

Er kennt mich.	He knows me.
uns	us
ihn	him
es	it
sie	her
sie	them
Sie	you
wen?	who (m)?

2. Similarly, Dative forms must be replaced by other Dative forms, and Nominative forms by other Nominative forms.

Ich gehe oft ins Kino mit ihr.	I often go to the movies with her.
ihm	him
ihnen	them

Kennen Sie Herrn Becker?	Do you know Mr. Becker?
wir	we
sie	they

C. VERB FORMS AND FUNCTIONS - THE PRESENT

I. Forms.

1. In German, and in English, when you substitute one Nominative form for another, that is, change the SUBJECT in a sentence, you sometimes have to change the form of the verb as well. The subject and the verb have to fit together. Note the following English forms:

I, you, we, they	sing	do	(no ending)
he, it, she	sings	does	(ending -s)

2. All but a very few German verbs have the following forms:

ich	komme	gebe	(ending -e)
er, es, sie	kommt	gibt	(ending -t)
wir, sie ('they'), Sie	kommen	geben	(ending -en)

Note that German verbs have a special form with the pronoun <u>ich</u>. Otherwise the pronouns and verbs are grouped as they are in English: <u>er</u>, <u>es</u>, <u>sie</u> occur with one verb form just as 'he, it and she' and <u>wir</u>, <u>sie</u>, <u>Sie</u> with another verb form just as 'we, they, you.' Notice that the vowel in the STEM of <u>geben</u> appears as <u>i</u> in the <u>er</u>-form: <u>er gibt</u>. This is something like the English <u>says</u> or <u>does</u> /sez, duz/ versus <u>say</u> or <u>do</u>, except that in German the vowel-change is shown even more clearly in the writing system. There are several verbs in German that have this kind of irregular <u>er</u>-form, but unfortunately there is no simple way of determining which verbs they are. They are not very numerous however, and we'll point them out to you as we encounter them.

3. Two German verbs you have encountered show a very slight modification in the <u>er</u>-form. They are <u>arbeiten</u> and <u>kosten</u>.

    er, es, sie   arbeitet   (connecting vowel -e- and ending -t)

After a -t- (or a -d-) a connecting vowel -e- occurs before the ending -t so that the ending is heard distinctly.

4. We have four verbs so far that exhibit the following pattern:

	'can' 'be able to'	'may' 'be allowed to'	'must' have to'	'want to'	
ich er es sie	kann	darf	muss	will	(no ending)
wir sie Sie	können	dürfen	müssen	wollen	(ending -en)

There are three more verbs with the same pattern, making a total of seven in all. Notice that the English equivalents of the verbs listed above have no -<u>s</u> ending in the <u>he</u> form: <u>He can</u>, <u>he may</u>, <u>he must</u>, and <u>he will</u> (in the sense of <u>he insists</u>.)

5. The following forms of <u>haben</u> "to have", <u>sein</u> "to be" and <u>möchte(n)</u> "would like to" complete the inventory:

ich	habe	bin	möchte
er, es, sie	hat	ist	möchte
wir, sie, Sie	haben	sind	möchten

The patterns of the first two of these verbs are unique and are found in no other German verbs. The forms <u>möchte</u> and <u>möchten</u> are special forms which we will deal with somewhat later.

6. Here is a table of verb forms:

	A	B	(7)	(1)	(1)		special form
ich	komme	treffe	kann	habe	bin		möchte
er, es, sie	kommt	trifft		hat	ist		
wir, sie, Sie	kommen	treffen	können	haben	sind		möchten

All verbs in German follow pattern A or pattern B except the nine indicated in the table and one more that is still to come.

II. Functions.

1. English uses a verb form with the ending <u>-ing</u> very freely: <u>he's singing</u>, <u>we're waiting</u>, <u>it's raining</u>. German has no corresponding form and uses the simple form of the verb for such expressions.

> he gives
> he's giving   er gibt
> he does give
>
> is he giving?
> does he give?   gibt er?

2. For COMMANDS, German uses the verb form with the ending <u>-en</u>, followed by the pronoun <u>Sie</u>. The German form is like Biblical English: 'Go ye into all the world, and preach the gospel...'

> Bitte <u>sprechen Sie</u> langsam.   Please <u>speak</u> slowly.
>
> <u>Zeigen Sie</u> mir bitte Ihr   <u>Show</u> me your luggage please.
> Gepäck.

3. Two verb forms can be used together in German or in English as a VERB PHRASE. Although German doesn't have verb phrases like <u>is going</u> or <u>does believe</u>, it has others, as follows.

> Ich <u>möchte</u> gern Wasser   <u>I'd like to have</u> water.
> <u>haben</u>.
>
> <u>Können</u> Sie mich gut   <u>Can</u> you <u>understand</u> me well?
> <u>verstehen</u>?
>
> <u>Darf</u> ich Ihren Pass <u>sehen</u>?   <u>May</u> I <u>see</u> your passport?
>
> Sie <u>müssen</u> zum Zoll <u>gehen</u>.   You <u>have to go</u> to the customs office.

The second part of the German verb phrase comes at the end of the sentence, and is called the INFINITIVE. It is the form with the ending <u>-en</u>, but it never has a subject and is unaffected by any change of subject: Ich kann <u>gehen</u>. Wir können <u>gehen</u>. There is only one irregular infinitive in German: <u>sein</u> 'to be'; the infinitive of every other verb is the same as the <u>wir</u>-form.

III. List of verbs in units 1 and 2.

1. Pattern A

arbeite	besuche	bleibe	gehe
arbeitet	besucht	bleibt	geht
arbeiten	besuchen	bleiben	gehen
gehöre	glaube	heisse	kenne
gehört	glaubt	heisst	kennt
gehören	glauben	heissen	kennen

komme	(koste)	sage	verstehe	wohne	zeige
kommt	kostet	sagt	versteht	wohnt	zeigt
kommen	kosten	sagen	verstehen	wohnen	zeigen

Pattern B

esse	gebe	sehe	spreche	treffe	fahre	gefalle
isst	gibt	sieht	spricht	trifft	fährt	gefällt
essen	geben	sehen	sprechen	treffen	fahren	gefallen

D. __Hin__ and __her__

Wo wohnen Sie?	Where do you live?
Wo kommen Sie her?	Where do you come from?
Wo gehen Sie hin?	Where are you going (to)?

1. __Wo__ by itself means 'where?' in the sense of 'in what place?'. To give it the meaning 'where from?' the little word __her__ is added; to give it the meaning 'where to?' the little word __hin__ is added.

2. The position of __hin__ and __her__ is usually at the end of the sentence or question. They may occur alternately however at the beginning after __wo__. The writing system joins __hin__ and __her__ to the preceding question word or adverb. __Woher__? 'Where from?'; __Wohin__? 'Where to?'; __dahin__, __dorthin__ 'to there'

Wo fahren Sie heute hin?	
Wohin fahren Sie heute?	Where are you going today?
Wir fahren dorthin.	We are going (to) there.

SUBSTITUTION DRILL

The basic procedure in this drill is the same as was outlined for Unit 1: Repeat the pattern sentence after your instructor and make the substitutions and any additional changes indicated as he gives you the cue. Remember, you are being drilled on fluency, accuracy and speed of response. This is __not__ a test or an intellectual excercise.

1. __Ich__ verstehe Sie sehr gut.

   er - sie (sg) - wir - sie (pl) - Frau Kunze - Fräulein Schneider und ich

2. Sie trifft __ihn__ in Frankfurt.

   sie (sg) - mich - uns - sie (pl) - Herrn und Frau Becker

3. Können Sie __mir__ seine Adresse geben?

   ihm - ihr - uns - ihnen - Herrn Becker - Frau Allen

4. __Er__ kommt aus Amerika.

   sie (pl) - Herr Becker - wir - sie (sg) - ich

5. __Ich__ habe nur diese zwei Koffer.

   er - Frau Kunze - sie (pl) - wir - sie (sg) - Herr und Frau Becker

6. Kennen <u>Sie</u> sie nicht?

sie (pl) - sie (sg) - er - wir - ich - Herr und Frau Becker - Fräulein Schneider

7. Ich kann <u>ihn</u> nicht gut verstehen.

sie (sg) - Herrn Allen - Sie - Fräulein Schneider - sie (pl)

8. Wie geht es <u>Ihnen</u>?

ihr - ihm - ihnen - Herrn Becker

9. Wie lange bleiben <u>Sie</u> hier in München?

er - sie (sg) - wir - sie (pl) - Herr Becker - Frau Kunze

10. Wohnt <u>Frau Becker</u> in der Nähe vom Konsulat?

Herr und Frau Allen - ich - er - sie (pl) - wir - sie (sg)

11. <u>Herr und Frau Allen</u> treffen ihn im Konsulat.

sie (sg) - sie (pl) - Herr Becker und ich - Sie - er - ich - wir

12. Kennen Sie <u>Herrn Keller</u>?

ihn - Frau Kunze - sie (sg) - mich - Fräulein Schneider - Herrn und Frau Allen - sie (pl) - uns

13. Was möchten <u>Sie</u> essen?

er - sie (pl) - sie (sg) - Herr und Frau Allen

14. Ich fahre oft mit <u>ihm</u> nach Hause.

ihr - ihnen - Herrn Becker - Fräulein Schneider - Herrn und Frau Becker

15. Wo essen <u>Sie</u> heute?

er - Herr und Frau Allen - sie (sg) - wir - Fräulein Schneider - sie (pl)

16. Es gefällt <u>uns</u> hier sehr gut.

ihr - ihm - mir - ihnen - Frau Keller

17. Dann müssen <u>Sie</u> jetzt noch zum Zoll.

er - Frau Becker und ich - sie (sg) - sie (pl) - wir - Fräulein Schneider

18. <u>Sie</u> kann aber auch gut deutsch sprechen.

Herr Keller - sie (pl) - er - wir - ich - Fräulein Keller

19. Darf <u>ich</u> mitkommen?

wir - Herr Becker - sie (sg) - sie (pl) - er

20. <u>Er</u> arbeitet auch im Konsulat.

wir - sie (pl) - sie (sg) - Fräulein Schneider und ich

21. Wo fahren <u>Sie</u> hin?

er - Herr Allen und Herr Becker - Sie - sie (sg) - sie (pl) - Frau Allen

22. <u>Wir</u> wollen gerade essen gehen.

Herr Becker und ich - er - sie (pl) - Frau Keller - sie (sg) - ich

23. Wo ist der <u>Flughafen</u>?

  a. Bahnhof - Wein - Kaffee - Tee - Amerikaner - Diplomat - Ober - Pass - Beamte - Koffer - Zoll

der Bahnhof - der Wein - der Kaffee - der Tee - der Amerikaner - der Diplomat - der Ober - der Pass - der Beamte - der Koffer - der Zoll

  b. Restaurant - Café - Konsulat - Kino - Gepäck - Bier - Essen - Hotel

das Restaurant - das Café - das Konsulat - das Kino - das Gepäck - das Bier - das Essen - das Hotel

c. Stadt - Bank - Adresse -
Dame - Amerikanerin - Deutsche -
Milch - Botschaft

die Stadt - die Bank - die Adresse -
die Dame - die Amerikanerin - die
Deutsche - die Milch - die Botschaft

d. Streichhölzer - Zigarren
Kartoffeln - Eltern

die Streichhölzer - die Zigarren -
die Kartoffeln - die Eltern

e. Beamte - Dame - Konsulat - Tee -
Kino - Eltern - Milch - Pass -
Restaurant - Bier - Amerikanerin -
Café - Koffer - Streichhölzer -
Bank - Diplomat - Ober - Gepäck -
Adresse - Kartoffeln - Bahnhof

der Beamte - die Dame - das Konsulat -
der Tee - das Kino - die Eltern - die
Milch - der Pass - das Restaurant -
das Bier - die Amerikanerin - das Café -
der Koffer - die Streichhölzer - die
Bank - der Diplomat - der Ober - das
Gepäck - die Adresse - die Kartoffeln -
der Bahnhof

VARIATION DRILL

1. Ich komme.

I'm coming.

   a. I'm coming too.
   b. I'm not coming.
   c. I'm not coming either.

   Ich komme auch.
   Ich komme nicht.
   Ich komme auch nicht.

2. Bleibt sie?

Is she staying?

   a. Is she staying too?
   b. Isn't she staying?
   c. Isn't she staying either?

   Bleibt sie auch?
   Bleibt sie nicht?
   Bleibt sie auch nicht?

3. Wir arbeiten dort.

We work there.

   a. We work there too.
   b. We don't work there.
   c. We don't work there either.

   Wir arbeiten auch dort.
   Wir arbeiten nicht dort.
   Wir arbeiten auch nicht dort.

4. Können sie kommen?

Can they come?

   a. Can they come too?
   b. Can't they come?
   c. Can't they come either?
   d. Can they come now?
   e. Can't they come now?
   f. Can't they come now either?

   Können sie auch kommen?
   Können sie nicht kommen?
   Können sie auch nicht kommen?
   Können sie jetzt kommen?
   Können sie jetzt nicht kommen?
   Können sie jetzt auch nicht kommen?

5. Er will sie treffen.

He intends to meet her.

   a. He intends to meet her too.
   b. He doesn't intend to meet her.
   c. He doesn't intend to meet her
      either.
   d. He doesn't intend to meet her
      there.
   e. He doesn't intend to meet her
      there either.

   Er will sie auch treffen.
   Er will sie nicht treffen.
   Er will sie auch nicht treffen.

   Er will sie dort nicht treffen.

   Er will sie dort auch nicht treffen.

6. Allens sind Amerikaner.

Allens are Americans.

   a. We're Americans too.
   b. Is Mrs. Kunze German?
   c. No, she is an American.
   d. I'm an American (man).

   Wir sind auch Amerikaner.
   Ist Frau Kunze Deutsche?
   Nein, sie ist Amerikanerin.
   Ich bin Amerikaner.

7. <u>Wo fahren Sie heute hin?</u> <u>Ich fahre</u>
<u>nach München.</u>

<u>Where are you going today?</u> <u>I'm going</u>
<u>to Munich.</u>

   a. Where is he going now?
      He's going to Bonn.
   b. Where are you going?
      I'm going to the movies.
   c. Where is she going?
      She's just going /out/ to eat.
   d. Where are they going?
      They're going to Schwabing.

Wo fährt er jetzt hin?
Er fährt nach Bonn.
Wo gehen Sie hin?
Ich gehe ins Kino.
Wo geht sie hin?
Sie geht gerade essen.
Wo fahren sie hin?
Sie fahren nach Schwabing.

8. <u>Ich glaube, er kennt Sie.</u>

<u>I think he knows you.</u>

   a. He says he comes from Germany.
   b. I think they work at the
      consulate.
   c. She says she speaks German too.
   d. He thinks I know him.
   e. You say I know him too?
   f. He says she lives in the
      Bayrischen Hof.

Er sagt, er kommt aus Deutschland.
Ich glaube, sie arbeiten im Konsulat.

Sie sagt, sie spricht auch deutsch.
Er glaubt, ich kenne ihn.
Sie sagen, ich kenne ihn auch?
Er sagt, sie wohnt im Bayrischen Hof.

9. <u>Wir möchten hier bleiben.</u>

<u>We'd like to stay here.</u>

   a. They want to drive to Tölz.
   b. May we speak German?
   c. I can visit you in Bonn.
   d. He has to work right now.

Sie wollen nach Tölz fahren.
Dürfen wir deutsch sprechen?
Ich kann Sie in Bonn besuchen.
Er muss gerade arbeiten.

10. <u>Wo kommen Sie her?</u> <u>Ich komme aus</u>
<u>Amerika.</u>

<u>Where do you come from?</u> <u>I come from</u>
<u>America.</u>

   a. Where does he come from? He
      comes from Germany.
   b. Where does she come from? Does
      she come from Bonn too?
   c. Does he come from America, or
      where does he come from?
   d. Where do they come from? They
      come from Frankfort.

Wo kommt er her? Er kommt aus
Deutschland.
Wo kommt sie her? Kommt sie auch aus
Bonn?
Kommt er aus Amerika, oder wo kommt
er her?
Wo kommen sie her? Sie kommen aus
Frankfurt.

                                (End of Tape 2A)

Tape 2B   **VOCABULARY DRILL**

1. <u>treffen</u> – "to meet"

   a. Er trifft Herrn Allen in Bonn.
   b. Ich treffe sie in München.
   c. Wir treffen Herrn und Frau
      Keller in Amerika.
   d. Treffen Sie Fräulein Schneider
      heute?
   e. Sie trifft Frau Bauer in
      Frankfurt.

He's meeting Mr. Allen in Bonn.
I'm meeting her in Munich.
We meet Mr. and Mrs. Keller in America.

Are you meeting Miss Schneider today?

She meets Mrs. Bauer in Frankfurt.

2. <u>es gefällt mir</u> – "I like it"

   a. Wie gefällt es Ihnen in
      München?
   b. Gefällt es Ihnen in Deutschland?
   c. Es gefällt uns hier sehr gut.
   d. Mir gefällt es sehr gut in Bonn.
   e. Es gefällt ihr hier auch sehr
      gut.

How do you like it in Munich?

Do you like it in Germany?
We like it very much here.
I like it in Bonn very much.
She likes it very much here too.

3. kennen - "to know"

    a. Kennen Sie Herrn Becker?   Do you know Mr. Becker?
    b. Wir kennen ihn gut.   We know him well.
    c. Kennen Sie auch Frau Bauer?   Do you know Mrs. Bauer, too?
    d. Nein, ich kenne sie nicht.   No, I don't know her.
    e. Sie kennen ihn auch, nicht wahr? You know him too, don't you?

4. wohnen - "to live"

    a. Wohnen Sie in der Nähe vom   Do you live in the vicinity of the
       Konsulat?   consulate?
    b. Wohnt er auch in München?   Does he live in Munich too?
    c. Er wohnt hier in der Nähe.   He lives here in the vicinity.
    d. Wo wohnen Sie?   Where do you live?
    e. Ich wohne im Bayrischen Hof.   I live in the Bayrischen Hof.

5. ins Kino gehen - "to go to the
                   movies"

    a. Ich gehe ins Kino.   I'm going to the movies.
    b. Gehen Sie auch ins Kino?   Are you going to the movies too?
    c. Nein, ich gehe heute nicht ins No, I'm not going to the movies today.
       Kino.
    d. Mit wem geht sie ins Kino?   Who's she going to the movies with?
    e. Sie geht heute mit uns ins Kino. She's going to the movies with us
                               today.

6. wer - "who"

    a. Wer ist die Dame dort?   Who is the lady there?
    b. Wer wohnt im Bayrischen Hof?   Who lives in the Bayrischen Hof?
    c. Wer kennt Herrn und Frau Allen? Who knows Mr. and Mrs. Allen?
    d. Wer kann hier deutsch sprechen? Who can speak German here?
    e. Wer will heute ins Kino gehen?   Who wants to go to the movies today?

7. sprechen - "to speak"

    a. Ich spreche oft englisch mit   I often speak English with her.
       ihr.
    b. Wir sprechen oft deutsch mit   We often speak German with him.
       ihm.
    c. Er spricht oft englisch mit uns. He often speaks English with us.
    d. Sprechen Sie bitte oft deutsch Please speak German with me often.
       mit mir.
    e. Spricht sie auch oft englisch   Does she often speak English with
       mit Ihnen?   you too?

8. heissen - " my, your, his, her,
                etc.) name is"

    a. Wie heissen Sie?   What is your name?
    b. Er heisst Fritz Keller.   His name is Fritz Keller.
    c. Sie heisst Elisabeth, nicht   Her name is Elizabeth, isn't it?
       wahr?
    d. Ich heisse Heinz Becker.   My name is Heinz Becker.
    e. Heissen Sie Bauer oder Brauer? Is your name Bauer or Brauer?

9. besuchen - "to visit"

    a. Wen wollen Sie dort besuchen?   Who are you planning to visit there?
    b. Wen besuchen Sie in Bonn?   Who are you visiting in Bonn?
    c. Er will uns heute besuchen.   He's planning to visit us today.
    d. Wir wollen Herrn und Frau Allen We're planning to visit Mr. and Mrs.
       besuchen.   Allen.
    e. Wen besucht sie in Deutschland? Who's she visiting in Germany?

10. gehören - "to belong"

    a. Der Pass gehört mir.   The passport belongs to me.
    b. Gehört Ihnen dieser Koffer hier? Does this suitcase here belong to
                                 you?
    c. Wem gehören die Streichhölzer? Who do the matches belong to?
    d. Ich glaube, das Gepäck gehört   I believe the luggage belongs to her.
       ihr.
    e. Er sagt, die Zigarren gehören   He says the cigars don't belong to
       ihm nicht.   him.

11. vorhaben - "to plan to do, to have
             planned"

    a. Was haben Sie heute vor?   What do you plan to do today?
    b. Wir haben heute viel vor.   We have a lot planned for today.
    c. Haben Sie heute schon etwas   Do you already have something planned
       vor?   for today?
    d. Was hat Fräulein Kunze vor?   What does Miss Kunze plan to do?
    e. Was haben Herr und Frau Allen vor? What are Mr. and Mrs. Allen planning to do?

12. nicht wahr? "isn't it? don't you?
            doesn't he? she, etc,"

    a. Sie wohnen in der Ludwigstrasse, You live on 'Ludwigstrasse', don't
       nicht wahr?   you?
    b. Sie fährt heute nach Tölz.   She's driving to Tölz today.
       nicht wahr?   isn't she?
    c. Er ist Diplomat, nicht wahr?   He's a Foreign Service Officer,
                                  isn't he?
    d. Sie geben ihm die Adresse, nicht You'll give him the address, won't
       wahr?   you?
    e. Das Konsulat ist hier in der   The consulate is here in the vicinity,
       Nähe, nicht wahr?   isn't it?

TRANSLATION DRILL (not recorded)

1. Mr. Becker was in Bonn for two   Herr Becker war zwei Monate in Bonn.
   months.
2. Now he is in Munich.   Jetzt ist er in München.
3. He's probably going to stay there   Er bleibt dort wahrscheinlich ein
   for a year.   Jahr.
4. He meets Mr. and Mrs. Allen in   Er trifft Herrn und Frau Allen in
   Munich.   München.
5. He knows them very well.   Er kennt sie sehr gut.
6. They are Americans.   Sie sind Amerikaner.
7. Mr. Allen works at the consulate. Herr Allen arbeitet im Konsulat.
8. He is a Foreign Service Officer.   Er ist Diplomat.
9. The Allens live at the Bayrischen Allens wohnen im Bayrischen Hof.
   Hof.
10. The hotel is very nice.   Das Hotel ist sehr nett.
11. It is in the vicinity of the   Es ist in der Nähe vom Konsulat.
    consulate.
12. The Allens like it in Munich very Allens gefällt es sehr gut in
    much.   München.
13. It's very nice at the Bayrischen   Im Bayrischen Hof ist es auch sehr
    Hof too.   nett.
14. Mr. Becker and the Allens go and   Herr Becker und Allens gehen essen.
    eat.
15. The restaurant is on Ludwigstrasse. Das Restaurant ist in der Ludwig-
                                  strasse.
16. There is Miss Adams, says Mr.   Dort ist Fräulein Adams, sagt Herr
    Becker.   Becker.
17. Who is Miss Adams?   Wer ist Fräulein Adams?

18. Mrs. Allen doesn't know her.	Frau Allen kennt sie nicht.
19. However, Mr. Becker knows her well.	Aber Herr Becker kennt sie gut.
20. She is an American.	Sie ist Amerikanerin.
21. Can she speak German too?	Kann sie auch deutsch sprechen?
22. Yes, she speaks German very well in fact.	Ja, sie spricht sogar sehr gut deutsch.
23. The Allens want to go and eat.	Allens wollen essen gehen.
24. Mr. Becker wants to come along.	Herr Becker will mitkommen.
25. Then he likes to go to Schwabing.	Dann möchte er nach Schwabing fahren.
26. Mr. Keller's parents live there.	Dort wohnen die Eltern von Herrn Keller.
27. He wants to visit them.	Er will sie besuchen.
28. Mr. Keller works at the consulate too.	Herr Keller arbeitet auch im Konsulat.
29. Mr. Allen knows him.	Herr Allen kennt ihn.
30. He often rides home with him.	Er fährt oft mit ihm nach Hause.
31. Mr. Becker would like to have Mr. Keller's new address.	Herr Becker möchte die neue Adresse von Herrn Keller haben.
32. Mr. Allen gives it to him.	Herr Allen gibt sie ihm.
33. He lives in the vicinity.	Er wohnt in der Nähe.
34. Mr. Brauer comes from America.	Herr Brauer kommt aus Amerika.
35. He's not familiar with Germany yet.	Er kennt Deutschland noch nicht.
36. Where does he intend to go?	Wo will er hinfahren?
37. He intends to go to Frankfort.	Er will nach Frankfurt fahren.
38. He has to show his passport.	Er muss seinen Pass zeigen.
39. The official says: "Everything's in order."	Der Beamte sagt: "Alles in Ordnung!"
40. Then Mr. Brauer has to go to the customs office.	Dann muss Herr Brauer zum Zoll gehen.
41. He shows the baggage there.	Er zeigt dort das Gepäck.
42. How many suitcases belong to him?	Wieviele Koffer gehören ihm?
43. He only has two suitcases.	Er hat nur zwei Koffer.
44. The official says: "Have a good trip!"	Der Beamte sagt: "Gute Reise!"

RESPONSE DRILL (not recorded)

1. Wen trifft Herr Becker?	Herr Becker trifft Herrn und Frau Allen.
2. Wo trifft Herr Becker Herrn und Frau Allen?	Er trifft sie in München.
3. Sind Allens Amerikaner oder Deutsche?	Allens sind Amerikaner.
4. Was ist Herr Allen?	Herr Allen ist Diplomat.
5. Kennt Frau Allen Herrn Becker?	Ja, Frau Allen kennt Herrn Becker.
6. Wie lange war Herr Becker in Bonn?	Er war zwei Monate in Bonn.
7. Wie lange bleibt Herr Becker in München?	Er bleibt wahrscheinlich ein Jahr in München.
8. Wie gefällt es Frau Allen in München?	Es gefällt ihr dort sehr gut.
9. Wo wohnen Herr und Frau Allen?	Sie wohnen im Bayrischen Hof.
10. Was haben Allens vor?	Sie wollen essen gehen und dann ins Kino.
11. Wo ist das Restaurant?	Das Restaurant ist in der Ludwig-strasse.
12. Wie ist das Essen dort?	Das Essen ist dort sehr gut.
13. Wer ist die Dame dort?	Das ist Fräulein Adams.
14. Mit wem spricht sie gerade?	Sie spricht gerade mit dem Ober.
15. Kennt Frau Allen Fräulein Adams?	Nein, Frau Allen kennt Fräulein Adams nicht.
16. Ist Fräulein Adams Deutsche?	Nein, sie ist Amerikanerin.
17. Kann sie auch deutsch sprechen?	Ja, sie kann auch gut deutsch sprechen.

18. Wo fährt Herr Becker heute hin?	Er will nach Schwabing fahren.
19. Wer will nach Schwabing fahren?	Herr Becker will dorthin fahren.
20. Wen will Herr Becker in Schwabing besuchen?	Er will die Eltern von Herrn Keller besuchen.
21. Kennt Herr Allen Herrn Keller?	Ja, er kennt ihn sogar sehr gut.
22. Wo arbeitet Herr Keller?	Er arbeitet im Konsulat.
23. Wer fährt oft mit ihm nach Hause?	Herr Allen fährt oft mit ihm nach Hause.
24. Was sagt der Beamte bei der Passkontrolle?	Der Beamte sagt:" Darf ich Ihren Pass sehen?"
25. Heisst der Herr Bauer oder Brauer?	Er heisst Brauer.
26. War er schon einmal in Deutschland?	Nein, er war noch nicht in Deutschland.
27. Wo will Herr Brauer hinfahren?	Er will nach Frankfurt fahren.
28. Wo muss Herr Brauer jetzt noch hingehen?	Er muss jetzt noch zum Zoll gehen.
29. Wo ist der Zoll?	Der Zoll ist dort drüben.
30. Wo kommt Herr Brauer her?	Herr Brauer kommt aus Amerika.
31. Hat Herr Brauer etwas zu verzollen?	Nein, ich glaube nicht.
32. Was sagt der Beamte beim Zoll?	Der Beamte sagt:" Zeigen Sie mir bitte Ihr Gepäck.
33. Wieviele Koffer hat Herr Brauer?	Er hat zwei Koffer.

34. Sind Sie Amerikaner?
35. Wo kommen Sie her?
36. Wo wohnen Sie hier?
37. Kennen Sie München?
38. Können Sie deutsch sprechen?
39. Können Sie mich gut verstehen?
40. Wo gehen Sie jetzt hin?
41. Wo wollen Sie essen?
42. Ist das Essen dort gut?
43. Was möchten Sie denn essen?
44. Ist das Bier dort gut?
45. Und wie ist der Wein?
46. Wer ist das dort?
47. Kennen Sie ihn?
48. Sind Sie Herr Maler?
49. Kennen Sie ihn nicht?
50. Mit wem gehen Sie heute ins Kino?
51. Kommen Sie mit?
52. Wo arbeiten Sie denn?
53. Kommen Sie aus Amerika?

CONVERSATION PRACTICE (not recorded)

1

B: Kennen Sie Herrn Allen?
C: Wo arbeitet er denn?
B: Er arbeitet im Konsulat.
   Er ist Diplomat.
C: Nein, ich glaube, ich kenne ihn nicht.

2

D: Was haben Sie heute vor?
F: Wir wollen nach München fahren und Kellers besuchen.
D: Ist Frau Keller nicht Amerikanerin?
F: Ja, sie kommt aus Washington.

3

A: Wir haben Sie lange nicht gesehen, Herr Becker.
   Wie geht es Ihnen denn?
B: Danke, gut.
   Ich war vier Monate in Amerika.
A: Wie lange bleiben Sie jetzt hier in Bonn?
B: Wahrscheinlich nur ein Jahr.
A: Wo wohnen Sie hier?
B: Ich wohne im Bayrischen Hof.
A: Gefällt es Ihnen dort gut?
B: Ja, es ist dort sehr nett.

4

E: Ich möchte jetzt gern essen gehen.
   Wollen Sie mitkommen?
H: Wo essen Sie denn?
E: In der Ludwigstrasse.
   Kennen Sie das Restaurant dort?
H: Nein, das kenne ich nicht.
   Wie ist dort das Essen?
E: Es ist sehr gut.
H: Gut, ich komme gern mit und dann
   können wir ins Kino gehen.

5

G: Kennen Sie die Dame dort?
F: Wo ist sie denn?
G: Da drüben.
   Sie spricht gerade mit dem Ober.
F: Ja, das ist Fräulein Adams.
   Sie ist Amerikanerin.
G: Kann sie deutsch sprechen?
F: Sie spricht sogar sehr gut deutsch.

6

B: Haben Sie etwas zu verzollen?
S: Nein, ich glaube nicht.
B: Zeigen Sie mir bitte Ihr Gepäck.
S: Gerne.
   Diese Koffer hier gehören mir.
B: Gehört das Gepäck dort drüben auch
   Ihnen?
S: Nein, ich habe nur diese drei
   Koffer.
B: Gut, - alles in Ordnung.
   Auf Wiedersehen!

7

K: Wo wohnen eigentlich die Eltern
   von Herrn Keller?
L: Sie wohnen in München.
K: Können Sie mir ihre Adresse geben?
L: Gern; wollen Sie sie besuchen?
K: Ja. Ich muss heute nach Schwabing
   fahren und da will ich sie auch
   besuchen.

SITUATIONS (not recorded)

In a café

Mr. Becker meets Miss Adams in a
café. He says he hasn't seen her for
a long time and asks her how she is,
and if she's going to stay in Munich
now. She says yes, she's probably
staying for four months. She likes it
very much in Munich. Mr. Becker asks
her if she has something planned now
and Miss Adams tells him that she'd
like to go to the movies. Mr. Becker
asks if he may come along and Miss
Adams says she'd be glad to have him.

At the movies

Miss Adams points to Mr. and Mrs.
Jones at the movies and asks Mr.
Becker if he knows them. He says he
doesn't know them and asks who they
are. They are Americans. Mr. Becker
wonders where they live and Miss
Adams tells him they live near her.
Mr. Jones is a Foreign Service Officer
and works at the consulate. Mr. Becker
asks if the Jones' can speak German.
Mr. Jones doesn't speak German very
well but Mrs. Jones does. She is
German

FINDER LIST

die	Adresse	address
	seine neue Adresse	his new address
	alles	everything
	alles in Ordnung	everything's in order
	also	well
	Amerika	America
der	Amerikaner	American
die	Amerikanerin	American (lady)
	arbeiten	work
	er arbeitet	he works
	aus	out of, from
der	Beamte	official
	bei der Passkontrolle	getting the passport checked
	beim Zoll	at the customs office
	besuchen	visit
	bleiben	stay, remain
die	Dame	lady
	danke sehr	thanks very much

	dann	then
	denn	(no English equivalent. Unstressed particle expressing polite interest or concern.)
	der	that one
	deutsch	German
die	Deutsche	German (lady)
	Deutschland	Germany
der	Diplomat	diplomat
	doch	(no exact equivalent. Unstressed particle expressing an obvious fact.)
	dürfen	to be allowed
	darf ich	may I
	eigentlich	actually, really
	einmal	once, ever
die	Eltern	parents
	englisch	English
das	Essen	food
	essen gehen	to go and eat
	fahren	go, ride (in a vehicle)
	er fährt	he goes, rides
	ganz	quite
	geben	give
	gefallen	to please
	es gefällt Ihnen	you like it
	es gefällt uns	we like it
	gehen	go
	gehören	belong
	er gehört	he, it belongs
das	Gepäck	baggage, luggage
	gerade	just
	gesehen	seen
	glauben	believe
	gnädige Frau	polite way of addressing a married woman (Mrs. Allen)
	haben	have
	wir haben .	we have
	heissen	to be called, named
	Sie heissen	your name is
	ich heisse	my name is
	her	from that place
	wo kommen Sie her?	where do you come from?
	Herrn (dat/acc form)	Mr.
	heute	today
	hin	to that place
	wo fahren Sie hin?	where are you going (to)?
	ihm (dat)	him
	ihr (dat)	her
	in	in
	in der Ludwigstrasse	on Ludwigstrasse
das	Jahr	year
	ein Jahr	one year
	jetzt	now
	kennen	to know, be acquainted with
	du kennst	you know (fam sing)
das	Kino	movie theater
	ins Kino	to the movies
der	Koffer	suitcase
	diese zwei Koffer	these two suitcases
	kommen	come
	kommen Sie mit	come along
	können	to be able to
	sie kann	she can
das	Konsulat	consulate
	vom Konsulat	of the consulate

die	Kontrolle	inspection
	lange	for a long time, long
	wie lange	how long
	mit	with
	mit dem Ober	with the waiter
	mit ihr	with her
	mit ihm	with him
	mir (dat)	me, to me
	mitkommen	come along
der	Monat	month
	zwei Monate	two months
	München	Munich
	müssen	to have to
	nach	to, toward
	nach Hause	home
die	Nähe	vicinity, nearness
	in der Nähe	in the vicinity
	natürlich	of course, naturally
	nett	nice
	noch	still, yet
	noch nicht	not yet
	nur	only
der	Ober	waiter
	oder	or
	oft	often
die	Ordnung	order
	in Ordnung	in order
der	Pass	passport
die	Passkontrolle	passport inspection
die	Reise	trip
	gute Reise!	have a good trip
	schön	beautiful
	schon	already, before
	sehen	see
	sie (acc)	her
	sogar	even, as a matter of fact
die	Stadt	city
	eine schöne Stadt	a beautiful city
	treffen	meet
	er trifft	he meets
	uns (dat)	to us
	verzollen	to declare
	zu verzollen	to be declared
	von	of
	vorhaben	to plan to do
	Sie haben vor	you plan to do
	wahrscheinlich	probably
	war	was
	ich war	I was
	waren Sie	were you
	wem (dat)	to whom
	wen (acc)	whom
	wer	who
	wir	we
	wir haben	we have
	wohnen	live
	er wohnt	he lives
	wollen	to want to, to intend to
	ich will	I intend, I plan
	zeigen	show
der	Zoll	customs office
	zu	to
	zum Zoll	to the customs office

STADTPLAN

STADTBESICHTIGUNG

Basic Sentences

I

	I
together	zusammen
down town	in die Stadt

MR. KÖHLER

HERR KÖHLER

Shall we go down town ('together')
today?

Wollen wir heute zusammen in die
Stadt fahren?

MR. BECKER

HERR BECKER

Glad to.

Gerne.

but	aber
before, first	vorher
to	zu
to the	zur (with die-words)
to the bank	zur Bank

But first I'd like to go to the bank.

Aber vorher möchte ich noch zur Bank
gehen.

I have to	ich muss
the money	das Geld
to withdraw	abheben
he withdraws	er hebt ... ab
to change	wechseln

I have to get some money.

Ich muss Geld abheben.

which (object)	welcher (dative form with die-words)
to which bank	zu welcher Bank

MR. KÖHLER

HERR KÖHLER

Which bank are you going to?

Zu welcher Bank gehen Sie?

the street	die Strasse
'Bahnhofstrasse'	die Bahnhofstrasse
on 'Bahnhofstrasse'	in der Bahnhofstrasse
right, just	gleich
next to	neben
next to the hotel	neben dem Hotel
Europa	Europa

MR. BECKER

HERR BECKER

To the bank on 'Bahnhofstrasse' right
next to the Europa Hotel.

Zu der Bank in der Bahnhofstrasse,
gleich neben dem Hotel Europa.

II

II

the museum	das Museum

<u>MR. KÖHLER</u>

Where is the museum actually?

> I know
> unfortunately

<u>MR. BECKER</u>

I'm sorry, I don't know either.

> the doorman (and clerk in
> smaller hotels)

But there's the doorman.

> just
> to ask
> he asks me

We can just ask him.

III

> to say
> he tells me

<u>MR. KÖHLER</u>

Can you tell us where the museum is,
by any chance?

> at, on
> at the, on the
> the market place
> at the market place
> far
> from
> from the
> the town hall
> from the town hall

<u>THE DOORMAN</u>

The museum is at the market place,
not far from the town hall.

> on
> on the map of the city
> he shows it to me

I can show (it to) you here on the
map of the city.

> excellent

<u>MR. KÖHLER</u>

Oh, that's fine!

> the car
> in you car
>   the car
>   in your car

<u>HERR KÖHLER</u>

Wo ist eigentlich das Museum?

> ich weiss
> leider

<u>HERR BECKER</u>

Das weiss ich leider auch nicht.

> der Portier

Aber dort ist der Portier.

> mal
> fragen
> er fragt mich

Wir können ihn mal fragen.

III

> sagen
> er sagt mir

<u>HERR KÖHLER</u>

Können Sie uns vielleicht sagen, wo
das Museum ist?

> an
> am (with <u>der</u>-and-<u>das</u> words)
> der Markt
> am Markt
> weit
> von
> vom (with <u>der</u>-and-<u>das</u> words)
> das Rathaus
> vom Rathaus

<u>DER PORTIER</u>

Das Museum ist am Markt, nicht weit
vom Rathaus.

> auf
> auf dem Stadtplan
> er zeigt es mir

Ich kann es Ihnen hier auf dem
Stadtplan zeigen.

> ausgezeichnet

<u>HERR KÖHLER</u>

Ausgezeichnet!

> der Wagen
> mit Ihrem Wagen
>   das Auto
>   mit Ihrem Auto

the taxi	die Taxe
a taxi (object)	eine Taxe (accusative form)
to take	nehmen
he takes	er nimmt

THE DOORMAN   DER PORTIER

Do you want to go in your car or do   Wollen Sie mit Ihrem Wagen fahren,
you want to take a taxi?   oder wollen Sie eine Taxe nehmen?

the bus	der Omnibus
no, not a	kein
no bus	kein Omnibus
the bus	der Autobus
no bus	kein Autobus

MR. BECKER   HERR BECKER

Isn't there a bus that goes there?   Fährt denn kein Omnibus dahin?

yes (in response to a	doch
negative statement or	
question)	
best	am besten
by bus	mit dem Omnibus
by bus	mit dem Autobus
the streetcar	die Strassenbahn
by streetcar	mit der Strassenbahn

THE DOORMAN   DER PORTIER

Yes, but the best way to go is by   Doch, aber Sie fahren am besten mit
streecar.   der Strassenbahn.

| to stop | halten |
| he stops | er hält |

The bus doesn't stop here.   Der Omnibus hält hier nicht.

| the stop | die Haltestelle |
| the streetcar stop | die Strassenbahnhaltestelle |

MR. BECKER   HERR BECKER

Where's the streetcar stop?   Wo ist die Strassenbahnhaltestelle?

| opposite, across from | gegenüber (von) |
| across from the hotel | gegenüber vom Hotel |

THE DOORMAN   DER PORTIER

Across from the hotel.   Gegenüber vom Hotel.

to know	wissen
the region	die Gegend
in what region	in welcher Gegend
American	amerikanisch
the American Consulate	das amerikanische Konsulat

MR. KÖHLER   HERR KÖHLER

Do you know what part of town the   Wissen Sie, in welcher Gegend das
American Consulate is in?   amerikanische Konsulat ist?

THE DOORMAN	DER PORTIER
It's right near here. On the corner of Kaiser and Schubert street.	Das ist hier ganz in der Nähe. An der Ecke Kaiser- und Schubert-strasse.

(to) there on foot	dorthin zu Fuss

You can walk there, too.	Dorthin können Sie auch zu Fuss gehen.

MR. KÖHLER	HERR KÖHLER
Thanks a lot!	Vielen Dank!

this map of the city to keep he keeps	diesen Stadtplan (acc form) behalten er behält

Can we keep this map of the city?	Können wir diesen Stadtplan behalten?

THE DOORMAN	DER PORTIER
Yes, indeed.	Aber gerne.

IN DER STADT

IV	IV
really the weather nice weather	wirklich das Wetter schönes Wetter

MR. BECKER	HERR BECKER
It's really nice weather today.	Heute ist wirklich schönes Wetter.

to make, to do he makes, he does the walk a walk (object) he takes a walk the university to the to the university	machen er macht der Spaziergang einen Spaziergang (acc form) er macht einen Spaziergang die Universität zur (with die-words) zur Universität

Are you going to take a walk to the university with me?	Machen Sie mit mir noch einen Spaziergang zur Universität?

the idea a good idea	die Idee eine gute Idee

MR. KÖHLER	HERR KÖHLER
That's a good idea.	Das ist eine gute Idee.

to be supposed to, to be said to she, it is supposed to, she, it is said to famous to be	sollen sie soll berühmt sein

It's supposed to be very famous.   Sie soll sehr berühmt sein.

Is it far from here?   Ist sie weit von hier?

        the cathedral   der Dom
        of the   vom (with <u>der</u>-and-<u>das</u> words)
        of the cathedral   vom Dom

        MR. BECKER   HERR BECKER

I think it's in the vicinity of the   Ich glaube, sie ist in der Nähe vom
cathedral.   Dom

        to find   finden

But I can't find it on the map of the   Aber ich kann sie auf dem Stadtplan
city.   nicht finden.

        the policeman   der Polizist
        the policeman (object)   den Polizisten (acc form)
        (unstressed particle   ja
        calling attention to an
        obvious fact)

        MR. KÖHLER   HERR KÖHLER

We can just ask the policeman there.   Wir können ja mal den Polizisten dort
                                               fragen.

                    V   V

        the police sergeant   der Wachtmeister
        officer   Herr Wachtmeister
        to look for   suchen

        MR. KÖHLER   HERR KÖHLER

Officer, we're looking for the   Herr Wachtmeister, wir suchen die
university.   Universität.

        to there   dahin

What's the best way to get there?   Wie kommt man am besten dahin?

        the park   der Park
        the park (object)   den Park (acc form)
        through   durch
        through the park   durch den Park

        THE POLICEMAN   DER POLIZIST

Go through the park here.   Gehen Sie hier durch den Park.

        the minute   die Minute
        in ten minutes   in zehn Minuten

You'll be there in ten minutes.   In zehn Minuten sind Sie da.

        the palace.   das Schloss

        MR. BECKER   HERR BECKER

The palace is there in the vicinity   Das Schloss ist doch auch dort in der
too, isn't it?   Nähe, nicht wahr?

that's right
opposite the cathedral

das stimmt
dem Dom gegenüber

THE POLICEMAN

DER POLIZIST

Yes, that's right, it's opposite
the cathedral.

Ja, das stimmt, es steht dem Dom
gegenüber.

the theater
the municipal theater
the square
the 'Königsplatz'
on 'Königsplatz'

das Theater
das Stadttheater
der Platz
der Königsplatz
am Königsplatz

MR. KÖHLER

HERR KÖHLER

Is the municipal theater on
'Königsplatz'?

Ist das Stadttheater am Königsplatz?

of it, from it

davon

THE POLICEMAN

DER POLIZIST

No, it's on the market place.

Nein, es ist am Markt.

And to the left of it is the
town hall.

Und links davon ist das Rathaus.

the side
on the other side

die Seite
auf der anderen Seite

The museum is on the other side.

Auf der anderen Seite ist das Museum.

MR. KÖHLER

HERR KÖHLER

Thanks a lot.

Vielen Dank.

THE POLICEMAN

DER POLIZIST

You're welcome.

Bitte schön.

VI

VI

I hope
a restaurant

hoffentlich
ein Restaurant

MR. KÖHLER

HERR KÖHLER

I hope there's a restaurant
near here.

Hoffentlich ist hier in der Nähe ein
Restaurant.

why
the thirst
I'm thirsty

warum
der Durst
ich habe Durst

MR. BECKER

HERR BECKER

Why, are you thirsty?

Warum? Haben Sie Durst?

the glass
a glass of beer
to drink

das Glas
ein Glas Bier
trinken

MR. KÖHLER	HERR KÖHLER

Yes, I'd like (to drink) a glass of beer.

Ja, ich möchte gern ein Glas Bier trinken.

the hunger	der Hunger
I'm hungry	ich habe Hunger

And I'm hungry too.

Und ich habe auch Hunger.

which (object)	welches (nom/acc form with das-words)

MR. BECKER	HERR BECKER

So am I, as a matter of fact.

Ich eigentlich auch.

Which restaurant shall we go to?

In welches Restaurant wollen wir gehen?

to the	ins (with das-words)
to the 'Hofbräuhaus'	ins Hofbräuhaus

MR. KÖHLER	HERR KÖHLER

We can go to the 'Hofbräuhaus'.

Wir können ins Hofbräuhaus gehen.

the 'Ratskeller'	der Ratskeller

Or shall we drive to the 'Ratskeller'?

Oder wollen wir zum Ratskeller fahren?

to park	parken

MR. BECKER	HERR BECKER

Can you park there too?

Kann man dort auch parken?

the parking lot	der Parkplatz
big	gross
a big parking lot	ein grosser Parkplatz
next to it	daneben

MR. KÖHLER	HERR KÖHLER

Yes, there's a big parking lot next to it.

Ja, daneben ist ein grosser Parkplatz.

VII	VII

the number	die Zahl
the numbers	die Zahlen
thirteen	dreizehn
twenty	zwanzig

Here are the numbers from thirteen to twenty.

Hier sind die Zahlen von dreizehn bis zwanzig.

thirteen	dreizehn
fourteen	vierzehn
fifteen	fünfzehn
sixteen	sechzehn
seventeen	siebzehn
eighteen	achtzehn
nineteen	neunzehn
twenty	zwanzig

How much is seven and eight?	Wieviel ist sieben und acht?
How much is eleven and five?	Wieviel ist elf und fünf?
How much is nine and nine?	Wieviel ist neun und neun?
How much is six and eight?	Wieviel ist sechs und acht?

Nine and five is fourteen, isn't it? — Neun und fünf ist vierzehn, nicht wahr?

Say in German: 18, 9, 12, 19, 13, 20, 14, 8, 15. — Sagen Sie auf deutsch: 18, 9, 12, 19, 13, 20, 14, 8, 15.

How much is eight and three and seven?	Wieviel ist acht und drei und sieben?
How much is ten and four and five?	Wieviel ist zehn und vier und fünf?
How much is four and eleven and two?	Wieviel ist vier und elf und zwei?

Notes on Pronunciation

A. German b, d, g and p, t, k

1. In most cases the symbols b, d, g and p, t, k represent the same sounds in German as in English. You probably experience little difficulty therefore in pronouncing the following words:

Bahnhof	aber	Pass	(Mappe)	
danke	oder	Taxe	bitte	ist
gut	sagen	kann	Ecke	Bank

b, d, g usually represent what we call voiced sounds; that is, your vocal cords are vibrating when you make these sounds. p, t, k represent what we call voiceless sounds; that is, your vocal cords are not vibrating, and you are actually whispering when you make these sounds.

2. However, b, d, g also represent the voiceless sounds when they occur at the end of a word or syllable and when they are followed by other voiceless sounds:

abheben	"ap-heben"	bleibt	"bleip-t"
hebt ... ab	"hep-t ... ap"	glaubt	"glaup-t"
siebzehn	"siep-zehn"	gibt	"gip-t"
sind	"sin-t"	und	"unt"
Flughafen	"Fluk-hafen"	zeigt	"zeik-t"
Tag	"Tak"	sagt	"sak-t"

This is especially important to realize when considering verb forms. Since there is an alternation between voiced and voiceless endings (-e, -en, -t) many verbs actually have alternate stems which the writing system does not show.

bleib-	or	"bleip-"	sag-	or	"sak-"
(bleibe)		(bleibt)	(sage)		(sagt)

B. Pre-vocalic r in clusters.

Practice 1.

Frau	treffen	Preis	Kraft
Front	Tropfen	Probe	Kreis
Friede	Traum	prima	Krieg

schreibe	Strasse	sprechen
Schramme	streben	springen
Schritt	Strom	Sprung

As noted in Unit 2 you may find it easier to break up the cluster by inserting a vowel between the initial consonant and the r. This may be more necessary in the following group where the r is voiced. For drei try saying darei for example, and for bringen, baringen, etc.

Practice 2

drei	braun	grau
dringen	bringen	Greis
Adresse	Gebrauch	begraben
bedrohen	verbrennen	ergriffen

C. Pre-vocalic r after vowels and initially.

Practice 3.

Bahre	Maria	Rat
Zigarre	beraten	reich
Ehre	erreichen	Rind
ihre	gerieben	roh

D. The German l.

Practice 4

Lied	Loch	beleben
lesen	lösen	Geleit
leider	lud	gelogen
Lack	lügen	beluden

Practice 5.

viel	hohl	Wahl	viele	Aale
Ziel	wohl	Zahl	fehle	male
fehl	Pfuhl	Maul	hole	kühle
Mehl	Stuhl	Gaul	Suhle	fühle

Practice 6.

Wille	will	wild
balle	Ball	bald
helle	hell	hält
solle	soll	Sold

(End of Tape 2B)

<u>Notes on Grammar</u> (not recorded)
(For Home Study)

A. Introduction to Units 3 - 9

  I. Noun Modifiers

    1. The four words 'good', 'these', 'suitcases', and 'two' can only be put
       together in one way so as to make of them a single phrase: 'these two
       good suitcases'. This is also true of the German equivalents of these
       words: they can only appear as <u>diese zwei guten Koffer</u>.

    2. The phrase <u>diese zwei guten Koffer</u> is composed of a NOUN (<u>Koffer</u>) and
       three different kinds of Noun Modifiers: a SPECIFIER (<u>diese</u>), a NUMERAL
       (<u>zwei</u>), and an ADJECTIVE (<u>guten</u>).

    3. Outline Classification of Noun Modifiers

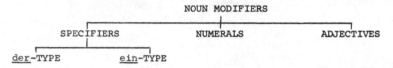

    4. A three-fold treatment of German noun-modifiers is forced upon us by the
       facts of the German language, since these three groups of words exhibit
       different <u>formal patterns</u> - that is, different patterns of endings.

      a. The formal pattern of the NUMERALS is very simple: the numbers from
         zwei 'two' on up never have any endings. (Fractions and numbers
         like 'fourth' and 'seventh' will be dealt with later.)

      b. The formal patterns of the ADJECTIVES will be treated in Units 6 - 9.
         Adjectives are descriptive words (red, white, blue, tall, dark,
         handsome) which have <u>superlative</u> and <u>comparative</u> forms (reddest,
         whitest, taller, darker).

      c. The formal patterns of the SPECIFIERS compel us to divide them into
         two sub-classes: the <u>der</u>-TYPE SPECIFIERS (specifiers which have the
         same pattern of endings as <u>der</u> 'the') and the <u>ein</u>-TYPE SPECIFIERS
         (specifiers which have the same pattern of endings as <u>ein</u> 'a'.)
         The formal patterns of the two subgroups are alike for the most part,
         but there are a couple of differences, so we are forced to deal with
         them separately.

B. <u>der</u>-Type Specifiers: <u>der</u>, <u>dieser</u>, <u>welcher</u>

  I. Forms

        <u>Er</u> kennt <u>ihn</u>.   He knows <u>him</u>.
        <u>Der</u> Ober kennt <u>den</u> Portier.   <u>The</u> waiter knows <u>the</u> doorman.
        <u>Der</u> Portier kennt <u>den</u> Ober.   <u>The</u> doorman knows <u>the</u> waiter.

    1. In German, not only the pronouns, but also the word for 'the' and all
       other Specifiers have Nominative, Accusative, and Dative forms. This is
       entirely different from English, where the word 'the' has no form but
       'the'.

<u>Der</u> Ratskeller soll sehr berühmt sein.	The Ratskeller is supposed to be very famous.
Wir suchen <u>den</u> Dom.	We're looking for <u>the</u> cathedral.
Neben <u>dem</u> Dom ist die Universität.	Next to <u>the</u> cathedral is the university.
<u>Das</u> Museum ist am Markt.	<u>The</u> museum is at the market place.
Wir suchen <u>das</u> Museum.	We're looking for <u>the</u> museum.
Neben <u>dem</u> Museum ist das Stadttheater.	Next to <u>the</u> museum is the municipal theater.
<u>Die</u> Stadt ist nicht weit von hier.	<u>The</u> city's not far from here.
Wir suchen <u>die</u> Stadt.	We're looking for <u>the</u> city.
Das Rathaus ist in <u>der</u> Stadt.	The town hall is in <u>the</u> city.
<u>Die</u> Koffer sind da drüben.	<u>The</u> suitcases are over there.
Wir suchen <u>die</u> Koffer.	We're looking for <u>the</u> suitcases.
Das ist in <u>den</u> Koffern.	That's in <u>the</u> suitcases.

2. By abstracting from these sentences the underscored forms, we can set up the following table of the various forms of the German word for 'the':

	before <u>der</u>-Nouns	before <u>das</u>-Nouns	before <u>die</u>-Nouns	before Plural Nouns
NOMINATIVE forms	der	das	die	die
ACCUSATIVE forms	den	das	die	die
DATIVE forms	dem	dem	der	den (-n)

3. Note: The symbol (-n) signifies that the noun itself, in the DATIVE PLURAL form, adds an -n, if the noun's general plural form does not already end in -n: Nominative Plural die Koffer, Dative Plural den Koffern.

4. Here are similar tables of the forms of dieser 'this' and welcher 'which' with der-nouns, das-nouns, die-nouns and plural nouns and with the pronouns which replace them, as noted in Unit 2.

Nominative:	dieser Koffer	dieses Hotel	diese Bank	diese Zigarren
	welcher Koffer	welches Hotel	welche Bank	welche Zigarren
	er	es	sie	sie

Accusative:	diesen Koffer	dieses Hotel	diese Bank	diese Zigarren
	welchen Koffer	welches Hotel	welche Bank	welche Zigarren
	ihn	es	sie	sie

Dative:	diesem Koffer	diesem Hotel	dieser Bank	diesen Zigarren
	welchem Koffer	welchem Hotel	welcher Bank	welchen Zigarren
	ihm	ihm	ihr	ihnen

5. In Unit 1 your attention was directed to the correspondence of the final sounds in the pairs der-er, das-es, die-sie, and die-sie. If we now make more extensive comparisons of the same sort --das-es-dieses-welches and den-ihn-diesen-welchen-- we begin to see that a relatively simple pattern underlies the profusion of forms. It can be summed up in the following PATTERN CHART:

Pattern Chart 1

Nom.	R	S	E	E
Acc.	N	S	E	E
Dat.	M	M	R	N (-n)

6. Important Note: Pattern Charts are not to be used in the classroom. They are presented for two reasons only: to call to your attention the fact that there is a pattern for whatever part of the language may be concerned, and to display that pattern as clearly and simply as possible. Study the chart at home if you find it helpful, but do not try to use it in class. Your purpose is to learn to speak German, not to learn to look it up in a book.

7. Remember also that substitution of nouns and pronouns operates horizontally on the chart. For example, from the Accusative-form line: Ich sehe den Bahnhof und das Rathaus und die Bank und die Koffer.

8. There are half a dozen more der-type specifiers, all of which exhibit the pattern of Chart 1 above. They are of less frequent occurrence than the three here introduced, and will be pointed out to you as they turn up in later units.

II. Uses

1. Der means 'the' when unstressed, but means 'that' when stressed. Without a noun it means 'that one', and is often followed by da 'there'.

Wir können den Polizisten fragen.	We can ask the policeman.
Wir können den Polizisten dort fragen.	We can ask that policeman there.
Wir können den da fragen.	We can ask that one there.

2. <u>Dieser</u> is used primarily for contrastive purposes. It doesn't just mean 'close to me' as the English <u>this</u> does, but rather 'the one I'm indicating now as opposed to that other one'.

<table>
<tr><td>Ich habe <u>dieses</u> Glas, er hat <u>dás</u> da.</td><td>I have <u>this</u> glass; he has <u>that one</u>.</td></tr>
<tr><td>Ich fahre mit <u>diesem</u> Omnibus nicht mit <u>dém</u> da.</td><td>I'm going on <u>this</u> bus, not <u>that</u> (<u>other</u>) <u>one</u>.</td></tr>
</table>

3. When there is no contrast, but only a pointing indication, the pointing-word <u>das</u> is equivalent to both <u>this</u> and <u>that</u>.

<table>
<tr><td><u>Das</u> ist die Strasse.</td><td><u>This</u> is the street.</td></tr>
<tr><td><u>Das</u> ist die Strasse.</td><td><u>That</u>'s the street.</td></tr>
</table>

4. <u>Welcher</u> is used primarily in questions. When used without a noun, it means 'which one?'.

<table>
<tr><td><u>Welchen</u> Polizisten können wir fragen?</td><td><u>Which</u> policeman can we ask?</td></tr>
<tr><td>Mit <u>welchem</u> spricht er?</td><td><u>Which one</u> is he talking to?</td></tr>
</table>

5. Whenever one of the <u>der</u>-type specifiers is used without a noun, the <u>form</u> of the specifier is exactly the same as if the noun were there.

<table>
<tr><td>Ich spreche mit <u>dem</u>.</td><td>I'm talking to <u>that man</u>.</td></tr>
<tr><td>Ich spreche mit <u>dieser</u>.</td><td>I'm talking to <u>this woman</u> (not to that other one).</td></tr>
<tr><td>Mit <u>welchem</u> sprechen Sie?</td><td><u>Which one</u> (man) are you talking to?</td></tr>
</table>

<u>Note</u>: The stressed <u>der</u>-type specifier has a definite pointing implication. The conventions of polite behavior set certain limitations on the pointing gesture, particularly as applied to persons. In general the same limitations are observed in the use of the <u>der</u>-type specifier without a noun. There are certainly situations where both the pointing gesture and the stressed <u>der</u>-type specifier are not only appropriate but necessary, as in giving directions for instance. However, indiscriminate use is avoided.

C. NOUNS

I. We have noted that German distinguishes <u>der</u>-nouns, <u>das</u>-nouns and <u>die</u>-nouns and furthermore Nominative forms, Accusative forms and Dative forms. The distinctions occur in the pronouns and in the specifiers.

II. Some German NOUNS also show distinctions in form.

<table>
<tr><td><u>Herr</u> Becker trifft <u>Herrn</u> und Frau Allen in München.</td><td>Mr. Becker meets Mr. and Mrs. Allen in Munich.</td></tr>
<tr><td>Dort ist <u>der Polizist</u>.</td><td>There's the policeman.</td></tr>
<tr><td>Ich will <u>den Polizisten</u> dort mal fragen.</td><td>I'll just ask the policeman there.</td></tr>
</table>

Four nouns which we have encountered up to this point have distinctive Nominative and non-Nominative forms. They are listed below for reference:

Nominative form:	der Herr	der Diplomat	der Beamte	der Polizist
Accusative form:	den Herrn	den Diplomaten	den Beamten	den Polizisten
Dative form:	dem Herrn	dem Diplomaten	dem Beamten	dem Polizisten

D. PREPOSITIONAL PHRASES

    I. Dative Prepositions

Ich spreche mit <u>ihm</u>.	I'm talking to <u>him</u>.
Ich spreche mit <u>dem</u> Portier.	I'm talking to <u>the</u> doorman.
Ich spreche mit <u>der</u> Frau.	I'm talking to <u>the</u> woman.
Ich spreche mit <u>den</u> Eltern von Herrn Keller.	I'm talking to <u>the</u> parents of Mr. Keller.
Sie können auch mit <u>der</u> Strassenbahn fahren.	You can go on <u>the</u> streetcar too.

      1. Like pronouns, specifiers which follow <u>mit</u> are in the Dative form. We can refer to <u>mit</u> and other prepositions which are always followed by Dative forms as DATIVE PREPOSITIONS.

Bei <u>der</u> Passkontrolle und <u>beim</u> Zoll.	At the passport inspection and at the customs office.
Rechts <u>vom</u> Dom ist das Museum.	To the right of the cathedral is the museum.
Ich gehe <u>zu der</u> Bank in der Bahnhofstrasse.	I'm going to the bank on 'Bahnhofstrasse'.
Wollen wir <u>zum</u> Ratskeller fahren?	Shall we drive to the 'Ratskeller'?

      2. The prepositions <u>bei</u>, <u>von</u> and <u>zu</u> are also Dative Prepositions. Notice the following contractions:

bei dem	often becomes	beim
von dem	often becomes	vom
zu dem	often becomes	zum
zu der	often becomes	zur

      3. The preposition <u>gegenüber</u> is sometimes followed and sometimes preceded by the specifier in the Dative form. It is generally preceded by the pronoun and by the specifier standing alone without a noun. It often occurs together with the preposition <u>von</u>.

<u>Gegenüber vom</u> Hotel.	Across from the hotel.
Es steht <u>dem</u> Dom <u>gegenüber</u>.	It's opposite the cathedral.
<u>Mir</u> gegenüber.	Across from me.
<u>Dem</u> gegenüber.	Across from that.

  II. Accusative Prepositions

Gehen Sie hier durch <u>den</u> Park.	Go through <u>the</u> park here.

      1. A few prepositions are always and invariably followed by Accusative forms. We will refer to these prepositions as ACCUSATIVE PREPOSITIONS. The only one we've come across so far is <u>durch</u>.

      2. Contraction: <u>durch das</u>   often becomes   <u>durchs</u>

  III. Two-way Prepositions

Es ist an <u>der</u> Ecke Kaiser- und Schubertstrasse.	It (the consulate) is on the corner of Kaiser and Schubert Street.
Gehen Sie an <u>die</u> Ecke Kaiser- und Schubert-strasse.	Go to the corner of Kaiser and Schubert Street.
Er ist auf <u>der</u> Strasse.	He's in ('on') the street.
Er geht auf <u>die</u> Strasse.	He's going into ('onto') the street.

                    Er ist im Hotel.   He's in the hotel.
                    Er geht ins Hotel.   He's going into the hotel.

1. The prepositions an, auf, and in are followed by either a Dative form or
   an Accusative form, with the following difference in meaning:. After a
   Two-way Preposition

   (1) a Dative form tells where some one or something is to be found;

            Er ist auf der Strasse.   He is to be found upon the street;
                                          that's where he is located.

   (2) an Accusative form tells where some one or something (now in motion)
       is going to end up.

            Er geht auf die Strasse.   He is walking, and when he has finish-
                                          ed walking he will be upon the street.

IV. We have now encountered nearly half the prepositions which are of common
    occurrence in German. The following summary lists them by categories.

   1. Accusative Prepositions

            durch 'through'   (always followed by Accusative
                                          forms)

   2. Dative Prepositions

            aus   'out of, from'
            bei   'at'
            mit   'with'   (always followed by Dative forms)
            nach   'toward, to'
            von   'from, of'
            zu   'to'

            gegenüber 'opposite, across from' (always preceded or followed by
                                               Dative forms)

   3. Two-way Prepositions

            an   'to'
            auf   'onto'
            in   'into'   (followed by Accusative forms)
            neben 'up next to'

            an   'at, on'
            auf   'on, upon'   (followed by Dative forms)
            in   'in'
            neben 'next to, beside'

V. Special Pronoun Form with Prepositions

            Links davon ist das   To the left of it is the town hall.
            Rathaus.
            Daneben ist ein grosser   Right next to it is.a big parking lot.
            Parkplatz.

            Ich fahre oft mit ihm   I often ride home with him.
            nach Hause.
            Ich spreche oft englisch   I often speak English with her.
            mit ihr.

When a pronoun in a prepositional phrase refers to a human being, the regular pronoun forms are used; but when a pronoun in a prepositional phrase refers to an inanimate object, the form <u>da-</u> is used for all pronouns. It is put in front of the preposition, and in the writing system is made part of a single word with the preposition (<u>daneben</u>, <u>davon</u>). If the preposition begins with vowel, the pronoun form is dar- (<u>darauf</u>, <u>daran</u>, <u>daraus</u>).

E. VERBS

I. Two verbs have occurred in Unit 3 which are similar to the four irregular verbs <u>dürfen</u>, <u>können</u>, <u>müssen</u> and <u>wollen</u>, which have already been encountered. They are <u>sollen</u> 'to be supposed to' and <u>wissen</u> 'to know (a fact)'. These six verbs occur very frequently in German, and together with one other verb (<u>mögen</u>), occurring very infrequently in the Present, make up the complete list of verbs following this particular irregular pattern. For reference purposes all seven verbs are reproduced below:

<u>ich</u>-form <u>er</u>-form	darf	kann	mag	muss	soll	will	weiss
<u>wir</u>-form	dürfen	können	mögen	müssen	sollen	wollen	wissen

II. There are two other new irregular verbs in this Unit:

	'stop'	'keep'
<u>ich</u>-form	halte	behalte
<u>er</u>-form	hält	behält
<u>wir</u>-form	halten	behalten

F. WORD ORDER

I. In unit 2 we observed that the second part of VERB PHRASES, the INFINITIVE form of the verb, occurs at the end of the sentence:

Ich <u>kann</u> es Ihnen hier auf dem Stadtplan <u>zeigen</u>.	I can show it to you here on the map of the city.

The other part of Verb Phrases, the verb form that has the personal ending, is seen to occur at or near the beginning of the sentence. It is called the FINITE verb form.

II. Observe the position of the FINITE verb form in the following sentences:

a) Sie kommt heute nicht.	She's not coming today.
b) Das Museum ist am Markt.	The museum is on the market place.
c) Das weiss ich leider nicht.	I'm sorry I don't know that.
d) Dort ist der Portier.	There's the doorman.
e) In zehn Minuten sind Sie da.	You'll be there in ten minutes.
f) Wo ist die Strassenbahn-haltestelle?	Where is the streetcar stop?

You will note that the FINITE verb form is always the SECOND ELEMENT of the sentence in the above examples. It can be preceded by: a) a pronoun; b) a noun and its specifier; c) a specifier or pointing word; d) an adverb indicating the time, location or manner in which something occurs or exists; e) a preposition and its object; f) a question word.

III. In QUESTIONS without question words and in COMMANDS the FINITE verb form is the FIRST ELEMENT.

Fährt denn kein Omnibus dahin?	Isn't there a bus that goes there?
Gehen Sie hier durch den Park.	Go through the park here.

Tape 3A   SUBSTITUTION DRILL

The first part of this drill presents forms of the <u>der</u>-type specifiers for
practice. In view of the complex patterning of·the specifiers each sentence
frame is presented with four different substitution groups.

1. Hier ist <u>der Portier</u>.

a. Stadtplan - Markt - Wagen -
   Omnibus - Dom - Polizist -
   Wachtmeister - Platz - Park -
   Ratskeller - Parkplatz

der Stadtplan - der Markt - der Wagen -
der Omnibus - der Dom - der Polizist -
der Wachtmeister - der Platz - der
Park - der Ratskeller - der Parkplatz

b. Theater - Glas - Hofbräuhaus -
   Geld - Museum - Rathaus - Auto -
   Schloss

das Theater - das Glas - das Hofbräuhaus - das Geld - das Museum - das
Rathaus - das Auto - das Schloss

c. Strasse - Taxe - Ecke - Strassenbahn - Haltestelle - Gegend -
   Universität - Bank

die Strasse - die Taxe - die Ecke -
die Strassenbahn - die Haltestelle -
die Gegend - die Universität - die
Bank

d. Glas - Parkplatz - Geld - Park -
   Universität - Wagen - Ecke -
   Theater - Polizist - Taxe -
   Auto - Ratskeller - Museum -
   Stadtplan - Dom - Strasse -
   Gegend - Rathaus - Haltestelle -
   Bank - Portier - Schloss - Omni-
   bus - Strassenbahn - Markt

das Glas - der Parkplatz - das Geld -
der Park - die Universität - der
Wagen - die Ecke - das Theater - der
Polizist - die Taxe - das Auto - der
Ratskeller - das Museum - der
Stadtplan - der Dom - die Strasse -
die Gegend - das Rathaus - die Halte-
stelle - die Bank - der Portier - das
Schloss - der Omnibus - die Strassen-
bahn - der Markt

2. Ich suche <u>den Königsplatz</u>.

a. Markt - Dom - Stadtplan -
   Polizisten - Wachtmeister -
   Portier - Wagen - Omnibus -
   Parkplatz - Ratskeller

den Markt - den Dom - den Stadtplan -
den Polizisten - den Wachtmeister -
den Portier - den Wagen - den Omnibus -
den Parkplatz - den Ratskeller

b. Theater - Schloss - Geld -
   Museum - Rathaus - Gepäck -
   Hofbräuhaus - Stadttheater

das Theater - das Schloss - das Geld -
das Museum - das Rathaus - das Gepäck -
das Hofbräuhaus - das Stadttheater

c. Universität - Bank - Strasse -
   Adresse - Strassenbahnhalte-
   stelle - Amerikanerin -
   Botschaft

die Universität - die Bank - die
Strasse - die Adresse - die Strassenbahnhaltestelle - die Amerikanerin -
die Botschaft

d. Dom - Café - Bank - Ober -
   Gepäck - Wagen - Universität -
   Adresse - Glas - Parkplatz -
   Polizisten - Strassenbahnhalte-
   stelle - Geld - Markt - Stadt-
   theater - Strasse - Hofbräuhaus -
   Omnibus - Schloss - Wachtmeister -
   Botschaft - Gepäck - Portier -
   Amerikanerin - Königsplatz

den Dom - das Café - die Bank - den
Ober - das Gepäck - den Wagen - die
Universität - die Adresse - das Glas -
den Polizisten - die
Strassenbahnhaltestelle - das Geld -
den Markt - das Stadttheater - die
Strasse - das Hofbräuhaus - den
Omnibus - das Schloss - den Wacht-
meister - die Botschaft - das Gepäck -
den Portier - die Amerikanerin - den
Königsplatz

3. Ich spreche von <u>dem Amerikaner</u>.

   a. Polizisten - Herrn - Diplomaten - Portier - Wachtmeister - Dom - Parkplatz - Ratskeller

       dem Polizisten - dem Herrn - dem Diplomaten - dem Portier - dem Wachtmeister - dem Dom - dem Parkplatz - dem Ratskeller

   b. Museum - Rathaus - Geld - Auto - Wetter - Schloss - Stadttheater - Hofbräuhaus

       dem Museum - dem Rathaus - dem Geld - dem Auto - dem Wetter - dem Schloss - dem Stadttheater - dem Hofbräuhaus

   c. Dame - Passkontrolle - Reise - Bank - Strassenbahn - Universität - Taxe

       der Dame - der Passkontrolle - der Reise - der Bank - der Strassenbahn - der Universität - der Taxe

   d. Universität - Dom - Reise - Ratskeller - Geld - Hofbräuhaus - Bank - Herrn - Schloss - Polizisten - Museum - Wetter - Diplomaten - Strassenbahn - Taxe - Parkplatz - Wachtmeister - Dame - Rathaus - Passkontrolle - Portier - Stadttheater

       der Universität - dem Dom - der Reise - dem Ratskeller - dem Geld - dem Hofbräuhaus - der Bank - dem Herrn - dem Schloss - dem Polizisten - dem Museum - dem Wetter - dem Diplomaten - der Strassenbahn - der Taxe - dem Parkplatz - dem Wachtmeister - der Dame - dem Rathaus - der Passkontrolle - dem Portier - dem Stadttheater

4. Wissen Sie, wo <u>das Rathaus</u> ist?

       Konsulat - Flughafen - Bahnhof - Universität - Gepäck - Portier - Beamte - Polizist - Ober - Stadtplan - Kino - Bank - Dom - Schloss - Strassenbahnhaltestelle

       das Konsulat - der Flughafen - der Bahnhof - die Universität - das Gepäck - der Portier - der Beamte - der Polizist - der Ober - der Stadtplan - das Kino - die Bank - der Dom - das Schloss - die Strassenbahnhaltestelle

5. Ich kann <u>den Dom</u> nicht finden.

       Konsulat - Park - Hotel - Universität - Bahnhof - Botschaft - Flughafen - Kino - Theater - Portier - Zigaretten - Geld - Streichhölzer - Pass

       das Konsulat - den Park - das Hotel - die Universität - den Bahnhof - die Botschaft - den Flughafen - das Kino - das Theater - den Portier - die Zigaretten - das Geld - die Streichhölzer - den Pass

6. <u>Sie</u> muss Geld abheben.

       wir - er - sie(pl) - ich - Sie - Herr Keller - Herr und Frau Becker

7. <u>Ich</u> habe Durst.

       er - wir - sie(sg) - Herr Keller - Frau Kunze - sie (pl)

8. Ich kann es <u>Ihnen</u> zeigen.

       ihr - ihm - ihnen - den Eltern - dem Ober - Herrn Köhler - dem Wachtmeister

9. Das weiss <u>ich</u> leider nicht.

       wir - sie(pl) - er - sie(sg) - der Portier - der Polizist - der Beamte

10. <u>Er</u> trinkt ein Glas Bier.

       wir - sie(sg) - Herr und Frau Becker sie(pl) - die Eltern - ich

11. Vielleicht kann er <u>uns</u> einen Stadtplan geben.

       mir - Ihnen - ihr - ihm - Herrn Keller - ihnen - Frau Kunze - dem Diplomaten

12. Vorher möchte <u>ich</u> noch zur Bank gehen.

       wir - er - sie(pl) - Herr und Frau Becker - Fräulein Keller

13. **Die Haltestelle** ist da drüben.
    Sie ist da drüben.

      Autobus - Polizist - Hotel -   der Autobus.er - der Polizist.er -
      Bank - Kino - Restaurant -   das Hotel.es - die Bank.sie - das
      Botschaft - Park - Museum -   Kino.es - das Restaurant.es- die
      Strassenbahn - Ober -   Botschaft.sie - der Park.er - das
            Museum.es - die Strassenbahn.sie -
            der Ober.er

14. Ich fahre zu **der Bank** in der
    Bahnhofstrasse.

      Museum - Hotel - Café -   dem Museum - dem Hotel - dem Café -
      Universität - Kino - Parkplatz -   der Universität - dem Kino - dem
      Botschaft - Restaurant   Parkplatz - der Botschaft - dem
            Restaurant

15. Haben Sie **den Stadtplan** da?

      Geld - Pass - Wagen -   das Geld - den Pass - den Wagen -
      Zigaretten - Streichhölzer -   die Zigaretten - die Streichhölzer -
      Gepäck   das Gepäck

16. In **welches Kino** gehen wir?

      Museum - Bank - Hotel - Café -   welches Museum - welche Bank - welches
      Theater - Park   Hotel - welches Café - welches Theater -
            welchen Park

17. **Das Café** soll sehr berühmt sein.

      Museum - Schloss - Hotel -   das Museum - das Schloss - das Hotel -
      Universität - Restaurant -   die Universität - das Restaurant - der
      Dom - Theater - Ratskeller   Dom - das Theater - der Ratskeller

18. Wir können **zum Ratskeller** fahren.

      Café - Hotel - Bank - Museum -   zum Café - zum Hotel - zur Bank -
      Universität - Bahnhof -   zum Museum - zur Universität - zum
      Restaurant - Flughafen -   Bahnhof - zum Restaurant - zum
      Botschaft - Dom   Flughafen - zur Botschaft - zum
            Dom

19. Wir suchen **den Park**.

      Ratskeller - Rathaus - Schloss -   den Ratskeller - das Rathaus - das
      Bahnhof - Kino - Portier -   Schloss - den Bahnhof - das Kino -
      Wachtmeister - Universität -   den Portier - den Wachtmeister -
      Bank - Polizisten - Dom   die Universität - die Bank - den
            Polizisten - den Dom

20. Wo ist **der Bahnhof**? **Der** ist hier
    ganz in der Nähe.

      Museum - Universität - Konsulat -   das Museum.das - die Universität.die -
      Flughafen - Strassenbahnhalte-   das Konsulat.das - der Flughafen.der -
      stelle - Park - Markt - Bank -   die Strassenbahnhaltestelle.die -
      Dom - Kino   der Park.der - der Markt.der - die
            Bank.die - der Dom.der - das Kino.das

21. Sie können mit **dem Omnibus** fahren.

      Strassenbahn - Wagen - Taxe   der Strassenbahn - dem Wagen - der
            Taxe

22. Er ist im Ratskeller.

      Museum - Schloss - Kino - Stadt -   im Museum - im Schloss - im Kino -
      Universität - Restaurant -   in der Stadt - in der Universität -
      Theater - Bank - Park -   im Restaurant - im Theater - in der
      Botschaft - Rathaus   Bank - im Park - in der Botschaft -
                            im Rathaus

23. In welches Restaurant wollen wir
gehen?

      Café - Kino - Hotel - Park -   welches Café - welches Kino - welches
      Theater - Museum - Bank -   Hotel - welchen Park - welches Theater
      Botschaft   welches Museum - welche Bank - welche
                            Botschaft

24. Dort ist der Polizist. Den können
wir fragen.

      Portier - Ober - Frau Kunze -   der Portier.den - der Ober.den -
      Herr Becker - Herr und Frau   Frau Kunze.die - Herr Becker.den -
      Keller - Beamte - Fräulein   Herr und Frau Keller.die - der Beamte.
      Schneider   den - Fräulein Schneider.die

25. Zu welcher Bank gehen Sie?

      Bahnhof - Museum - Botschaft -   welchem Bahnhof - welchem Museum -
      Hotel - Restaurant -   welcher Botschaft - welchem Hotel -
      Strassenbahnhaltestelle   welchem Restaurant - welcher Stassen-
                            bahnhaltestelle

26. Ich gehe durch den Park.

      Stadt - Museum - Universität -   die Stadt - das Museum - die
      Restaurant   Universität - das Restaurant

27. Vorher möchte ich noch zur Bank
gehen.

      Konsulat - Hotel - Universität -   zum Konsulat - zum Hotel - zur
      Bahnhof - Museum - Botschaft -   Universität - zum Bahnhof - zum
      Flughafen   Museum - zur Botschaft - zum Flughafen

28. Wir können den Portier fragen.

      Polizisten - Eltern - Herrn   den Polizisten - die Eltern - Herrn
      Brauer - Ober - Wachtmeister -   Brauer - den Ober - den Wachtmeister -
      Frau Becker   Frau Becker

29. Die Bank ist neben dem Hotel.

      Restaurant - Bahnhof -   dem Restaurant - dem Bahnhof - der
      Universität - Museum - Kino -   Universität - dem Museum - dem Kino -
      Stadttheater - Rathaus - Dom -   dem Stadttheater - dem Rathaus - dem
      Botschaft - Konsulat - Schloss   Dom - der Botschaft - dem Konsulat -
                            dem Schloss

30. Können wir den Stadtplan behalten?

      Geld - Streichhölzer -   das Geld - die Streichhölzer -
      Zigarren - Koffer   die Zigarren - den Koffer

31. Wollen wir einen Spaziergang <u>zum</u>
    <u>Schloss</u> machen?

    Museum - Bahnhof - Universität -   zum Museum - zum Bahnhof - zur
    Café - Flughafen - Dom   Universität - zum Café - zum
                         Flughafen - zum Dom

32. Wie gefällt Ihnen <u>diese Stadt</u>?

    Wetter - Park - Schloss -   dieses Wetter - dieser Park - dieses
    Rathaus - Gegend - Spaziergang   Schloss - dieses Rathaus - diese
                         Gegend - dieser Spaziergang

33. Kennen Sie <u>diese Strasse</u>?

    Platz - Ecke - Theater - Gegend - diesen Platz - diese Ecke - dieses
    Park - Museum   Theater - diese Gegend - diesen Park -
                         dieses Museum

34. <u>Dieser Park</u> ist sehr schön.

    Gegend - Wagen - Glas - Platz -   diese Gegend - dieser Wagen - dieses
    Seite - Schloss   Glas - dieser Platz - diese Seite -
                         dieses Schloss

35. Fährt dieser Autobus <u>zum</u>
    <u>Königsplatz</u>?

    Stadttheater - Ludwigstrasse -   zum Stadttheater - zur Ludwigstrasse -
    Markt - Ratskeller - Rathaus -   zum Markt - zum Ratskeller - zum
    Universität   Rathaus - zur Universität

36. Sie ist doch <u>im Café</u>, sehen Sie
    sie nicht?

    Taxe - Auto - Park - Strassen-   in der Taxe - im Auto - im Park -
    bahn - Wagen - Omnibus   in der Strassenbahn - im Wagen -
                         im Omnibus

37. Der Beamte <u>besucht</u> den Diplomaten.

    treffen - kennen - suchen -   trifft - kennt - sucht - fragt -
    fragen - finden   findet

38. Wir wohnen nicht weit von <u>diesem</u>
    <u>Park</u>.

    Konsulat - Strasse - Platz -   diesem Konsulat - dieser Strasse -
    Schloss - Universität -   diesem Platz - diesem Schloss -
    Bahnhof   dieser Universität - diesem Bahnhof

                            (End of Tape 3A)

Tape 3B   VOCABULARY DRILL

1. <u>in</u> + Dative - "in, on, at "

   a. Ich esse in diesem Restaurant.   I eat in this restaurant.
    b. Er arbeitet im Konsulat.   He works in the consulate.
    c. Wir wohnen in dieser Strasse.   We live on ('in') this street.
    d. Er ist gerade im Dom.   He's in the cathedral just now.
    e. Die Bank ist in der Schubert-   The bank is on ('in the') Schubert-
       strasse.   strasse.
    f. Sind Herr und Frau Allen im   Are Mr. and Mrs. Allen at ('in') the
       Kino?   movies?
    g. Er wohnt im Hotel Europa.   He lives in the Europa Hotel.

2. <u>in</u> + Accusative - "into, to"

    a. Wir gehen ins Kino.   We're going to the movies.
    b. Fahren Sie heute in die Stadt?   Are you driving down town today?
    c. In welches Theater gehen Sie?   What theater are you going to?
    d. Wollen wir in den Park gehen?   Shall we go to the park?
    e. Herr Köhler geht ins Hotel.   Mr. Köhler is going into the hotel.
    f. Ich möchte gern ins Café gehen.   I'd like to go to the café.

3. <u>zu</u> + Dative - "to"

    a. Ich möchte zur Bank gehen.   I'd like to go to the bank.
    b. Zu welcher Bank gehen Sie?   What bank are you going to?
    c. Wollen wir einen Spaziergang   Shall we take a walk to the cathedral?
        zum Dom machen?
    d. Wir können zum Ratskeller fahren.   We can drive to the 'Ratskeller'.
    e. Wie kommt man am besten zum   What's the best way to get to the
        Flughafen?   airport?
    f. Sie fährt gerade zur Botschaft.   She's just driving to the embassy.

4. <u>neben</u> + Dative - "next to, beside"

    a. Ist der Ratskeller neben dem   Is the 'Ratskeller' next to the town
        Rathaus?   hall?
    b. Die Bank ist neben dem Hotel.   The bank is next to the hotel.
    c. Die Haltestelle ist neben dem   The stop is next to the consulate.
        Konsulat.
    d. Ist der Parkplatz neben der Bank?   Is the parking lot next to the bank?
    e. Sie wohnen neben uns.   They live next (door) to us.
    f. Welches Restaurant ist neben der   Which restaurant is next to the
        Universität?   university?

5. <u>an</u> + Dative - "at, on"

    a. Das Rathaus ist am Markt.   The town hall is at the market place.
    b. Die Strassenbahnhaltestelle ist   The streetcar stop is over there at
        da drüben an der Ecke.   the corner.
    c. Dieser Autobus hält am Markt.   This bus stops at the market place.
    d. Ist der Ratskeller auch am   Is the 'Ratskeller' at the market
        Markt?   place too?
    e. Der Polizist ist dort an der   The policeman is there on the corner.
        Ecke.

6. <u>von</u> + Dative - "of, from"

    a. Das Museum ist nicht weit vom   The museum is not far from the town
        Rathaus.   hall.
    b. Das Museum ist in der Nähe von   The museum is in the vicinity of
        der Universität.   the university.
    c. Rechts vom Dom ist die Botschaft.   To the right of the cathedral is the
                                      embassy.
    d. Gegenüber von diesem Hotel ist   Across from this hotel is the parking
        der Parkplatz.   lot.
    e. Links von der Bank ist das   To the left of the bank is the
        Stadttheater.   municipal theater.
    f. Der Omnibus hält gegenüber vom   The bus stops across from the café.
        Café.

7. <u>auf</u> + Dative - "on, in"

    a. Ich kann es Ihnen auf dem   I can show it to you on the map of
        Stadtplan zeigen.   the city.
    b. Die Strassenbahn hält auf der   The streetcar stops on the other side
        anderen Seite der Strasse.   of the street.
    c. Ich kann die Universität auf   I can't find the university on the
        dem Stadtplan nicht finden.   map of the city.

d. Das Auto ist auf dem Parkplatz.   The car is in ('on') the parking lot.
e. Der Polizist ist auf der anderen   The policeman is on the other side
   Seite der Strasse.   of the street.

8. __fahren mit__ + Dative - "to go on, in, by (a conveyance)"

a. Sie können mit dem Autobus   You can go on the bus.
   fahren.
b. Fahren Sie mit der Strassenbahn   Are you going by streetcar or in your
   oder mit dem Auto?   car?
c. Mit welchem Autobus fährt er?   Which bus is he going on?
d. Ich will mit der Taxe fahren.   I want to go by taxi.
e. Er fährt heute mit dem Wagen.   He's going in his car today.

9. __durch__ + Accusative - "through"

a. Der Omnibus fährt durch den   The bus goes through the park.
   Park.
b. Wir gehen jetzt durch den Park.   We're going through the park now.
c. Fahren Sie durch die Ludwig-   Drive through 'Ludwigstrasse'.
   strasse.
d. Sie können durch den Park gehen.   You can walk through the park.
e. Wollen wir durch die Stadt   Shall we drive through town?
   fahren?

10. __sollen__ - "to be supposed to"

a. Das Bier soll hier sehr gut   The beer is supposed to be very good
   sein.   here.
b. Das Schloss soll sehr berühmt   The palace is supposed to be very
   sein.   famous.
c. Die Haltestelle soll nicht weit   The stop is supposed to be not far
   von hier sein.   from here.
d. Soll der Bahnhof nicht hier in   Isn't the station supposed to be here
   der Nähe sein?   in the vicinity?
e. Das Hotel soll sehr gut sein.   The hotel is supposed to be very
                                             good.
f. Sie sollen sehr nett sein.   They're supposed to be very nice.

11. __wir wollen__ + Infinitive - "shall we"

a. Wollen wir jetzt ins Kino   Shall we go to the movies now?
   gehen?
b. Wollen wir einen Spaziergang   Shall we take a walk?
   machen?
c. Wollen wir ein Glas Bier   Shall we have a glass of beer?
   trinken?
d. Wollen wir den Wachtmeister   Shall we ask the officer?
   fragen?
e. Wollen wir eine Taxe nehmen?   Shall we take a taxi?

12. __mit__ + Dative - "with, to"

a. Sie können mit dem Polizisten   You can talk to the policeman.
   sprechen.
b. Er möchte mit uns ins Theater   He'd like to go to the theater with
   gehen.   us.
c. Ich gehe heute mit Herrn   I'm going down town with Mr. Köhler
   Köhler in die Stadt.   today.
d. Er spricht gerade mit dem   He's just talking to the officer.
   Wachtmeister.
e. Ich gehe mit dieser Dame heute   I'm going to the movies with this
   ins Kino.   lady today.
f. Mit welchem Ober spricht er   Which waiter is he (just) talking to?
   gerade?

13. <u>suchen</u> - "to look for"

    a. Sie sucht gerade den Koffer.   She's just looking for the suitcase.
    b. Was suchen Sie?   What are you looking for?
    c. Er sucht den Pass.   He's looking for the passport.
    d. Suchen Sie den Parkplatz?   Are you looking for the parking lot?
    e. Ich suche die Adresse von   I'm looking for Miss Schneider's
       Fräulein Schneider.   address.

14. <u>fragen</u> - "to ask"

    a. Wir wollen den Portier fragen.   Let's ask the doorman. ('Why don't we
                                        ask...?')
    b. Fragen Sie bitte den Polizisten.   Ask the policeman please.
    c. Er fragt den Ober.   He's asking the waiter.
    d. Ich frage den Wachtmeister.   I'm going to ask the (police) officer.
    e. Können Sie nicht Frau Kunze   Can't you ask Mrs. Kunze?
       fragen?

15. <u>trinken</u> - "to drink, to have (to drink)"

    a. Was möchten Sie trinken?   What would you like to drink?
    b. Er trinkt ein Glas Bier.   He's drinking a glass of beer.
    c. Trinken Sie Kaffee oder Tee?   Are you having coffee or tea?
    d. Ich trinke gern Wein.   I like ('to drink') wine.
    e. Möchten Sie etwas Wasser   Would you like some water to drink?
       trinken?

16. <u>parken</u> - "to park"

    a. Sie können dort drüben parken.   You can park over there.
    b. Ich parke auf dem Parkplatz in   I'll park in the parking lot on
       der Schubertstrasse.   'Schubertstrasse'
    c. Er parkt auf der anderen Seite   He parks on the other side of the
       der Strasse.   street.
    d. Ich parke sehr oft auf diesem   I very often park in this parking lot.
       Parkplatz.
    e. Kann man hier auf der Strasse   Can one park here on the street?
       parken?

17. <u>halten</u> - "to stop"

    a. Hält der Omnibus hier?   Is this where the bus stops? ('Does
                                          the bus stop here?')
    b. Wo hält die Strassenbahn?   Where does the streetcar stop?
    c. Ich halte gegenüber vom Hotel.   I'll stop across from the hotel.
    d. Halten Sie bitte bei der   Stop at the embassy please.
       Botschaft.
    e. Der Autobus soll an dieser Ecke   The bus is supposed to stop at this
       halten.   corner.

VARIATION DRILL

1. <u>Welcher Omnibus fährt nach</u>   <u>Which bus goes to Schwabing</u>?
  <u>Schwabing</u>?

    a. Which hotel is next to the   Welches Hotel ist neben dem Konsulat?
       Consulate?
    b. Which streetcar goes through the   Welche Strassenbahn fährt durch den
       park?   Park?
    c. Which car belongs to the American   Welcher Wagen gehört der Amerikanerin?
       lady?
    d. Which lady is supposed to know   Welche Dame soll die Adresse wissen?
       the address?

2. <u>Dieser Autobus fährt nach Schwabing.</u>   <u>This bus goes to Schwabing.</u>

    a. This gentleman works at the   Dieser Herr arbeitet im Konsulat.
      consulate.
    b. This streetcar goes down town.   Diese Strassenbahn fährt in die Stadt.
    c. This passport is mine.   Dieser Pass gehört mir.
    d. This restaurant is excellent.   Dieses Restaurant ist ausgezeichnet.

3. <u>Fragen Sie diesen Polizisten!</u>   <u>Ask this policeman!</u>

    a. Keep this passport!   Behalten Sie diesen Pass!
    b. Drink this wine!   Trinken Sie diesen Wein!
    c. Take this taxi!   Nehmen Sie diese Taxe!
    d. Change this money!   Wechseln Sie dieses Geld!
    e. Park this car!   Parken Sie diesen Wagen!

4. <u>Welchen Park suchen Sie?</u>   <u>Which park are you looking for?</u>

    a. Which automobile are you   Welches Auto behalten Sie?
      keeping?
    b. Which Foreign Service Officer   Welchen Diplomaten kennen Sie?
      do you know?
    c. Which bank are you looking for?   Welche Bank suchen Sie?
    d. Which beer are you drinking?   Welches Bier trinken Sie?
    e. Which waiter are you going to   Welchen Ober fragen Sie?
      ask?
    f. Which taxi are you taking?   Welche Taxe nehmen Sie?

5. <u>Wohnen Sie in dieser Strasse?</u>   <u>Do you live on this street?</u>

    a. Are you going to this   Gehen Sie zu diesem Restaurant?
      restaurant?
    b. Do you stop on this side?   Halten Sie auf dieser Seite?
    c. Do you work at this bank?   Arbeiten Sie in dieser Bank?
    d. Are you taking this bus?   Fahren Sie mit diesem Autobus?
    e. Are you going to meet us at   Treffen Sie uns an dieser Ecke?
      this corner?

6. <u>In welchem Restaurant essen Sie?</u>   ·<u>Which restaurant are you eating at?</u>

    a. Which streetcar are you taking?   Mit welcher Strassenbahn fahren Sie?
    b. Which corner do you stop at?   An welcher Ecke halten Sie?
    c. Which city do you live in?   In welcher Stadt wohnen Sie?
    d. Which museum are you going to?   Zu welchem Museum gehen Sie?
    e. Which parking lot are you going   Auf welchem Parkplatz parken Sie?
      to park at?

7. <u>Fahren Sie durch die Bahnhofstrasse?</u>   <u>Are you driving through 'Bahnhof-</u>
      <u>strasse'?</u>

    a. The policeman is going to the   Der Polizist geht an die Ecke Kaiser-
      corner Kaiser and Schubert   und Schubertstrasse.
      Street.
    b. We're going to take a walk   Wir machen einen Spaziergang durch
      through the park.   den Park.
    c. Shall we go into the 'Ratskeller'   Wollen wir hier in den Ratskeller
      here?   gehen?
    d. Drive onto the parking lot here.   Fahren Sie hier auf den Parkplatz.

8. <u>Wir fahren mit der Taxe.</u>   <u>We're going by taxi.</u>

    a. The streetcar stops there at the   Die Strassenbahn hält dort an der
      corner.   Ecke.
    b. I'm going to the consulate now.   Ich gehe jetzt zum Konsulat.
    c. We're going to eat at this   Wir essen in diesem Restaurant.
      restaurant.
     (Drill No.8 continued on the next page.)

d. The parking lot is across from
this hotel.

Der Parkplatz ist gegenüber von
diesem Hotel.

e. The museum is next to the bank.

Das Museum ist neben der Bank.

f. He's talking to the waiter.

Er spricht mit dem Ober.

9. Er wechselt mir das Geld.

He'll change the money for me.

a. She's going to show us the city.

Sie zeigt uns die Stadt.

b. We'll give her the map of the
city.

Wir geben ihr den Stadtplan.

c. I'll change the money for him.

Ich wechsele ihm das Geld.

d. He's going to give me the
passport.

Er gibt mir den Pass.

e. We'll show you the suitcases.

Wir zeigen Ihnen die Koffer.

10. Wem zeigt er die Stadt?

Who is he showing the city to?

a. Who is he changing the money for?

Wem wechselt er das Geld?

b. Who are you going to give the
passport to?

Wem geben Sie den Pass?

c. Who is she showing the luggage
to?

Wem zeigt sie das Gepäck?

d. Who is he going to give the
address to?

Wem gibt er die Adresse?

11. Zeigen Sie Herrn Becker das Museum!

Show Mr. Becker the museum!

a. Change the money for this lady!

Wechseln Sie dieser Dame das Geld!

b. Give the Foreign Service Officer
the passport!

Geben Sie dem Diplomaten den Pass!

c. Look for the address for her!

Suchen Sie ihr die Adresse!

d. Show the police sergeant the
suitcase!

Zeigen Sie dem Wachtmeister den Koffer!

12. Der Pass gehört dem Diplomaten.

The passport belongs to the Foreign
Service Officer.

a. This automobile belongs to the
policeman.

Dieses Auto gehört dem Polizisten.

b. The Foreign Service Officer
likes this city.

Diese Stadt gefällt dem Diplomaten.

c. The money belongs to the official.

Das Geld gehört dem Beamten.

d. The American lady likes this
park.

Dieser Park gefällt der Amerikanerin.

13. Er gibt mir den Stadtplan.
Er kann mir den Stadtplan geben.

He's giving me the map of the city.
He can give me the map of the city.

a. Are you going to have a glass of
beer?
Would you like to have a glass
of beer?

Trinken Sie ein Glas Bier?

Möchten Sie ein Glas Bier trinken?

b. I'm going to change the money.
I have to change the money.

Ich wechsele das Geld.
Ich muss das Geld wechseln.

c. We're staying down town today.
We plan to stay down town today.

Wir bleiben heute in der Stadt.
Wir wollen heute in der Stadt bleiben.

d. Is he going to visit you today?
May he visit you today?

Besucht er Sie heute?
Darf er Sie heute besuchen?

e. She's going to drive to the
university now.
She's supposed to drive to the
university.

Sie fährt jetzt zur Universität.

Sie soll jetzt zur Universität fahren.

f. He's coming today.
He can come today.

Er kommt heute.
Er kann heute kommen.

14. **Wo fährt diese Strassenbahn hin?**   **Where does this streetcar go to?**
    Wo soll diese Strassenbahn hin-   **Where is this streetcar supposed <u>to</u>**
    fahren?   **be going to?**

    a. He's coming here by taxi.   Er kommt mit der Taxe her.
      He can come here by taxi.   Er kann mit der Taxe herkommen.
    b. She has something planned for   Sie hat heute etwas vor.
      today.
      She's supposed to have something   Sie soll heute etwas vorhaben.
      planned for today.
    c. He's withdrawing /some_/ money.   Er hebt Geld ab.
      He has to withdraw /some_/ money.   Er muss Geld abheben.
    d. Where does Mr. Köhler come from   Wo kommt eigentlich Herr Köhler her?
      actually?
      Where is Mr. Köhler supposed to   Wo soll eigentlich Herr Köhler
      come from actually?   herkommen?
    e. I'll be glad to come along.   Ich komme gern mit.
      I'd like to come along.   Ich möchte gern mitkommen.
    f. How much are you withdrawing   Wieviel heben Sie von der Bank ab?
      from the bank?
      How much do you want to with-   Wieviel wollen Sie von der Bank
      draw from the bank?   abheben?

15. **Ich fahre heute in die Stadt.**   **I'm driving down town today.**
    Heute fahre ich in die Stadt.   **Today I'm driving down town.**

    a. He's probably going to the   Er geht heute wahrscheinlich ins
      theater today.   Theater.
      Probably he's going to the   Wahrscheinlich geht er heute ins
      theater today.   Theater.
    b. They're coming today, I hope.   Sie kommen hoffentlich heute.
      I hope they're coming today.   Hoffentlich kommen sie heute.
    c. He can perhaps give us this   Er kann uns vielleicht diesen Stadt-
      map of the city.   plan geben.
      Perhaps he can give us this map   Vielleicht kann er uns diesen Stadt-
      of the city.   plan geben.
    d. I'd like to speak to the   Ich möchte vorher mit dem Beamten
      official first.   sprechen.
      First I'd like to speak to the   Vorher möchte ich mit dem Beamten
      official.   sprechen.
    e. Let's go to the cathedral now.   Wir wollen jetzt zum Dom gehen.
      Now let's go to the cathedral.   Jetzt wollen wir zum Dom gehen.

                                               (End of Tape 3B)

TRANSLATION DRILL (not recorded)

1. It's nice weather today.   Heute ist schönes Wetter.
2. Mr. Allen and Mr. Jones are   Herr Allen und Herr Jones wollen
    planning to go down town together.   zusammen in die Stadt fahren.
3. First Mr. Allen would like to get   Vorher möchte Herr Allen noch Geld
    some money.   abheben.
4. He goes to the bank by taxi.   Er fährt mit der Taxe zur Bank.
5. The bank is next to the Europa   Die Bank ist neben dem Hotel Europa.
    Hotel.
6. Then he rides back to the hotel.   Dann fährt er wieder zum Hotel.
7. The hotel is on Ludwigstrasse.   Das Hotel ist in der Ludwigstrasse.
8. Later Mr. Allen and Mr. Jones are   Später wollen Herr Allen und Herr
    planning to go to the museum.   Jones ins Museum gehen.
9. Unfortunately they don't know   Sie wissen leider nicht, wo es ist.
    where it is.
10. They ask the doorman.   Sie fragen den Portier.
11. The doorman shows them the museum   Der Portier zeigt ihnen das Museum
    on the map of the city.   auf dem Stadtplan.
12. It's near the town hall, on the   Es ist in der Nähe vom Rathaus, am
    market place.   Markt.
12. They would like to keep the map.   Sie möchten den Stadtplan gern
      behalten.

14. The doorman gives them the map of the city.

Der Portier gibt ihnen den Stadtplan.

15. Do you want to go by bus or by streetcar, asks the doorman.

Wollen Sie mit dem Autobus oder mit der Strassenbahn fahren, fragt der Portier.

16. Mr. Allen and Mr. Jones want to go by streetcar.

Herr Allen und Herr Jones wollen mit der Strassenbahn fahren.

17. The stop is opposite the hotel.

Die Haltestelle ist dem Hotel gegenüber.

18. They also want to go to the consulate.

Sie wollen auch zum Konsulat fahren.

19. The consulate is near the station, says the doorman.

Das Konsulat ist in der Nähe vom Bahnhof, sagt der Portier.

20. They can walk there too.

Dort können sie auch zu Fuss hingehen.

21. Later they plan to take a walk to the university.

Später wollen sie noch einen Spaziergang zur Universität machen.

22. They don't know where the university is.

Sie wissen nicht, wo die Universität ist.

23. Mr. Allen looks for it on the map of the city.

Herr Allen sucht sie auf dem Stadtplan.

24. He can't find it however.

Er kann sie aber nicht finden.

25. It's supposed to be next to the cathedral.

Sie soll neben dem Dom sein.

26. On the corner on the other side of the street there's a policeman.

An der Ecke, auf der anderen Seite der Strasse ist ein Polizist.

27. They ask the policeman.

Sie fragen den Polizisten.

28. He says the cathedral is on 'Königsplatz'.

Er sagt, der Dom ist am Königsplatz.

29. In ten minutes they can be there.

In zehn Minuten können sie da sein.

30. They take a walk through the park.

Sie machen einen Spaziergang durch den Park.

31. Near the cathedral is the palace, too.

In der Nähe vom Dom ist auch das Schloss.

32. To the left of the palace is the university.

Links vom Schloss ist die Universität.

33. Opposite the university is the municipal theater.

Der Universität gegenüber ist das Stadttheater.

34. Where's the 'Ratskeller', asks Mr. Jones.

Wo ist der Ratskeller, fragt Herr Jones.

35. The 'Ratskeller' is next to the town hall on the market place, says the policeman.

Der Ratskeller ist neben dem Rathaus am Markt, sagt der Polizist.

36. The streetcar stop is in front of the university.

Vor der Universität ist die Strassenbahnhaltestelle.

37. They can take the streetcar to the market place.

Sie können mit der Strassenbahn zum Markt fahren.

38. In the evening Mr. Allen would like to go to a restaurant.

Abends möchte Herr Allen gern in ein Restaurant gehen.

39. He's thirsty and would like to drink a glass of wine.

Er hat Durst und möchte gern ein Glas Wein trinken.

40. Mr. Jones will be glad to come along.

Herr Jones kommt gern mit.

41. He's hungry.

Er hat Hunger.

42. Mr. Jones asks: "Where shall we eat, at the 'Ratskeller' or at the 'Hofbräuhaus'?"

Herr Jones fragt: "Wo wollen wir essen, - im Ratskeller oder im Hofbräuhaus?"

43. They drive to the 'Ratskeller' in their car.

Sie fahren mit dem Auto zum Ratskeller.

44. They can park there too.

Dort können sie auch parken.

RESPONSE DRILL (not recorded)

1. Wohin wollen Herr Köhler und Herr Becker fahren?	Sie wollen in die Stadt fahren.
2. Wo will Herr Becker vorher noch hingehen?	Er will noch zur Bank gehen.
3. Zu welcher Bank geht er?	Er geht zu der Bank in der Bahnhofstrasse.
4. Was will er dort machen?	Er muss Geld abheben.
5. Weiss Herr Becker wo das Museum ist?	Nein, er weiss es leider nicht.
6. Haben sie einen Stadtplan?	Nein, sie haben keinen Stadtplan.
7. Wen fragen sie?	Sie fragen den Portier.
8. Was gibt ihnen der Portier?	Der Portier gibt ihnen einen Stadtplan.
9. Hat Herr Köhler ein Auto?	Ja, Herr Köhler hat ein Auto.
10. Fahren sie mit dem Auto in die Stadt?	Nein, sie fahren mit der Strassenbahn in die Stadt.
11. Wo ist die Strassenbahnhaltestelle?	Die Strassenbahnhaltestelle ist gegenüber vom Hotel.
12. Wo hält der Omnibus?	Der Omnibus hält hier nicht.
13. In welcher Gegend ist das Museum?	Das Museum ist am Markt.
14. Wie kommen sie am besten zum Konsulat?	Sie können zu Fuss dorthin gehen.
15. Wie ist das Wetter?	Das Wetter ist schön.
16. Wohin wollen sie noch einen Spaziergang machen?	Sie wollen noch einen Spaziergang zur Universität machen.
17. Wo ist die Universität?	Die Universität ist am Königsplatz.
18. Wo soll der Dom sein?	Der Dom ist in der Nähe von der Universität.
19. Wen fragen sie, wo die Universität ist?	Sie fragen den Polizisten.
20. Fahren sie mit dem Autobus zur Universität?	Nein, sie gehen zu Fuss dorthin.
21. Wo ist das Stadttheater?	Das Stadttheater ist neben dem Rathaus.
22. Wohin wollen Herr Köhler und Herr Becker abends hingehen?	Sie wollen in ein Restaurant gehen.
23. Wollen sie dort etwas essen?	Sie wollen dort etwas essen und trinken.
24. Ist der Ratskeller in der Nähe vom Hotel?	Nein, der Ratskeller ist neben dem Rathaus.
25. Wie fahren sie dorthin?	Sie fahren mit ihrem Auto dorthin.
26. Wo parken sie den Wagen?	Sie parken den Wagen auf dem Parkplatz.

27. Wo wohnen Sie?
28. In welcher Strasse wohnen Sie?
29. Wie komme ich am besten in die Stadt?
30. Wo parken Sie hier?
31. Kennen Sie diese Stadt gut?
32. Wo kann ich hier Geld wechseln?
33. Ist die Bank hier in der Nähe?
34. Ich habe leider kein Auto; wie komme ich dorthin?
35. Wo ist der Stadtplan?
36. Zeigen Sie mir bitte auf dem Stadtplan, wo das Museum ist.
37. In wieviel Minuten kann ich in der Stadt sein?
38. Wo ist das Theater?
39. Ich habe grossen Durst; wo ist hier ein Restaurant?
40. Wo kann ich das Auto parken?

CONVERSATION PRACTICE (not recorded)

1

M: Guten Tag, Herr Köhler, wo gehen
   Sie denn hin?
K: Ich muss zur Bank gehen und Geld
   abheben.
M: Das Wetter ist heute so schön.
   Gehen Sie zu Fuss?
K: Ja, die Bank ist hier ganz in der
   Nähe.
M: Darf ich mitkommen?
K: Aber gerne!

2

S: Verzeihung, Herr Wachtmeister,
   können Sie mir sagen, wo die
   Universität ist?
W: Die Universität ist in der Ludwig-
   strasse.
S: Wie kommt man am besten dahin?
W: Fahren Sie mit dem Autobus. Er hält
   hier an der Ecke. In zehn Minuten
   sind Sie dort.
S: Vielen Dank.

3

M: Kennen Sie München schon?
S: Ja, aber nicht sehr gut.
M: Ich möchte gern zum Museum fahren.
   Es soll sehr berühmt sein.
   Wollen Sie mitkommen?
S: Gern, haben Sie den Wagen hier?
M: Ja, er ist auf dem Parkplatz. Das
   Theater ist auch in der Nähe vom
   Museum.
S: Gut, und können Sie mir auch das
   Hofbräuhaus zeigen?
M: Aber natürlich!

4

B: Was haben Sie jetzt vor, Herr Allen?
A: Ich möchte essen gehen. Ist das
   Hofbräuhaus nicht hier in der Nähe?
B: Nein, aber der Ratskeller ist nicht
   weit von hier.
A: Hoffentlich ist das Essen dort gut.
   Ich habe Hunger.
B: Ja, es ist sogar sehr gut. Ich
   esse oft dort.

SITUATIONS (not recorded)

At the Hotel

Mr. Allen has just arrived in Germany.
At the hotel where he is staying he
asks the clerk where the cathedral,
palace, museum, etc., are and if there
is a restaurant down town near by.
The clerk answers his questions, shows
him the locations on the map of the
city and tells him how to get to the
various buildings.

At the Restaurant

Mr. Schneider meets Mr. Keller, whom
he hasn't seen for a long time. Mr.
Keller often has to go to Frankfurt, but
he's staying in Munich for two months
now. He asks Mr. Schneider if he'd
like to go and eat. Mr. Schneider
knows a restaurant on Bahnhofstrasse
where they go and order Bratwurst and
Sauerkraut and beer to drink.
Mr. Keller buys some cigars too.

Customs

Mr. Allen goes through customs. The
official asks him where he comes from,
where he is going and what he has to
declare. Mr. Allen does not always
understand and has to ask the official
to repeat and speak slowly. He tells
the official then how many cigars,
cigarettes, etc. he has.

Looking around Town

Mr. Köhler meets Mr. Becker at the hotel
to show him the town. Mr. Becker is
not acquainted with the city, but he
would like to see the museum, cathedral,
palace, city hall, Hofbräuhaus,
Ratskeller, park, Königsplatz, etc.
They take a bus through town, and Mr.
Köhler points out the sights.

FINDER LIST

	abheben	withdraw
	er hebt ab	he withdraws
	am besten	best
	amerikanisch	American
	an	at, on
	auf	on
	ausgezeichnet	excellent
das	Auto	car
der	Autobus	bus
	behalten	keep
	er behält	he keeps
	berühmt	famous
das	Brot	bread
	dahin	to there
	daneben	next to it
	davon	of it, from
	doch	yes (in response to a negative statement or question)
der	Dom	cathedral
	durch (preposition with acc)	through
	durch den Park	through the park
der	Durst	thirst
	ich habe Durst	I am thirsty
die	Ecke	corner
	an der Ecke	at the corner
	finden	find
	fragen	ask
	er fragt mich	he asks me
die	Gegend	region
	gegenüber (von)(preposition with dative)	opposite, across from
	gegenüber vom Hotel	across from the hotel
	dem Dom gegenüber	opposite the cathedral
das	Geld	money
das	Glas	glass
	ein Glas Bier	a glass of beer
	gleich	right, just
	gross	big
	halten	stop
	er hält	he stops
die	Haltestelle	stop
der	Herr	gentleman
	hingehen	go (there)
das	Hofbräuhaus	Hofbräuhaus
	hoffentlich	I hope, it is to be hoped
der	Hunger	hunger
	ich habe Hunger	I am hungry
die	Idee	idea
	eine gute Idee	a good idea
	in der Stadt	down town (location)
	in die Stadt	down town (destination)
	ja	unstressed particle calling attention to an obvious fact
	kein	no, not a
	leider	unfortunately
	machen	make, do
der	Markt	market place
	am Markt	at the market place
die	Minute	minute
	in zehn Minuten	in ten minutes
	mit dem Autobus	by bus
	mit der Strassenbahn	by streetcar

	mit Ihrem Wagen, mit Ihrem Auto	in your car
	neben	next to, beside
das	Museum	museum
	nehmen	take
	er nimmt	he takes
der	Omnibus	bus
der	Park	park
	parken	park
der	Parkplatz	parking lot
der	Platz	square
der	Polizist	policeman
der	Portier	doorman (and clerk in smaller hotels)
das	Rathaus	town hall, city hall
der	Ratskeller	Ratskeller
	sagen	say
	sein	be
die	Seite	side, (page)
	auf der anderen Seite	on the other side
das	Schloss	palace
	sollen	be supposed to
	er soll	he is supposed to
der	Spaziergang	walk
	einen Spaziergang	a walk
	er macht einen Spaziergang	he takes a walk
der	Stadtplan	map of the city
das	Stadttheater	municipal theater, city auditorium
das	stimmt	that's right
die	Strasse	street
die	Strassenbahn	streetcar
die	Strassenbahnhaltestelle	streetcar stop
	suchen	look for
die	Taxe	taxi
das	Theater	theater
	trinken	drink
die	Universität	university
	vielleicht	perhaps, maybe
	von (preposition with dative)	from
	vom (von dem)	from the (with der-and das-words)
	vorher	before, first
der	Wachtmeister	police sergeant
der	Wagen	car
	warum	why
	wechseln	change
	weit	far
	welcher (dative form with die-words)	which (object)
	in welcher Gegend	which region
	zu welcher Bank	to which bank
	welches (nom / acc form with das-words)	which
das	Wetter	weather
	wirklich	really
	wissen	know
	ich weiss	I know
die	Zahl	number
die	Zahlen	numbers
die	Zigaretten	cigarettes
	zu	to
	zu Fuss	on foot
	zum (zu dem) (with der-and das-words)	to the
	zur (zu der) (with die-words)	to the
	zur Bank	to the bank
	zusammen	together

Tape 4A   IM KONSULAT

Basic Sentences

I   I

the visit	der Besuch
the visa	das Visum
the visitor's visa	das Besuchsvisum[1]
a visitor's visa (subject or object)	ein Besuchsvisum (nominative or accusative form)
to apply (for something)	beantragen
he applies	er beantragt

Mr. Köhler wants to apply for a visitor's visa for America.

Herr Köhler will ein Besuchsvisum nach Amerika beantragen.

old	alt
the acquaintance	der Bekannte
an old acquaintance (object)	einen alten Bekannten (acc form)

In the consulate he meets an old acquaintance, Mr. Allen.

Im Konsulat trifft er einen alten Bekannten, Herrn Allen.

MR. KÖHLER

Hello, Mr. Allen.

that

I'm glad I ran into you ('Good that I just /happen to/ meet you').

HERR KÖHLER

Guten Tag, Herr Allen.

dass

Gut, dass ich Sie gerade treffe.

MR. ALLEN

Hello, Mr. Köhler.

HERR ALLEN

Guten Tag, Herr Köhler.

there is, there are	es gibt
is there, are there	gibt's (- gibt es)
that which is new	Neues

What's new with you? ('What is there that is new')

Was gibt's Neues?

to hear	hören
he hears	er hört

I hear you're planning to go to America.

Ich höre, Sie wollen nach Amerika fahren.

to say, to tell

sagen

MR. KÖHLER

Yes; can you tell me where I can apply for a visa?

HERR KÖHLER

Ja; können Sie mir sagen, wo ich ein Visum beantragen kann?

right	gleich mal
the colleague	der Kollege
my colleague (object)	meinem Kollegen (dative form)

MR. ALLEN   HERR ALLEN

Of course; we can go right to my   Natürlich; wir können gleich mal zu
colleague Bill Jones.   meinem Kollegen Bill Jones gehen.

the consul	der Konsul
the vice consul	der Vizekonsul
a vice consul	Vizekonsul[3]
the department, section	die Abteilung
the visa section	die Visa-Abteilung[1]

He's a vice consul in the visa section.   Er ist Vizekonsul in der Visa-
                                            Abteilung.

II   ### II

to introduce	vorstellen
he introduces	er stellt ... vor
the gentlemen	die Herren (plural)

Mr. Allen introduces the gentlemen   Herr Allen stellt die Herren vor.
/to each other/.

acquainted	bekannt
to make acquainted, to introduce	bekannt machen
he introduces them (to each other)	er macht sie bekannt

MR. ALLEN   HERR ALLEN

May I introduce you gentlemen?   Darf ich die Herren bekannt machen?
Mr. Köhler - Mr. Jones.   Herr Köhler - Herr Jones.

for	für (preposition with acc)
to do	tun
he does	er tut

MR. JONES   HERR JONES

What can I do for you, Mr. Köhler?   Was kann ich für Sie tun, Herr Köhler?

MR. KÖHLER   HERR KÖHLER

I want to get a visa.   Ich möchte ein Visum haben.

to emigrate	auswandern
he emigrates	er wandert ... aus
on a visit	auf Besuch

MR. JONES   HERR JONES

Are you planning to emigrate or go on   Wollen Sie auswandern oder auf Besuch
a visit?   fahren?

the business	das Geschäft
the business trip	die Geschäftsreise[1]
a business trip (subj or obj)	eine Geschäftsreise (nom or acc form)
he takes a business trip	er macht eine Geschäftsreise

MR. KÖHLER	HERR KÖHLER

I'm going on business.

Ich muss eine Geschäftsreise machen.

MR. JONES	HERR JONES

How long do you intend to stay?

Wie lange wollen Sie bleiben?

approximately, about	ungefähr
to, up to, until	bis
the week	die Woche
weeks	Wochen

MR. KÖHLER	HERR KÖHLER

Approximately four to six weeks.

Ungefähr vier bis sechs Wochen.

the German	der Deutsche
(a) German	Deutscher[3, 4]

MR. JONES	HERR JONES

You are German, aren't you?

Sie sind Deutscher, nicht wahr?

the state, nation	der Staat
the member (of a nation or family)	der Angehörige
the national, the citizen	der Staatsangehörige[1]
a national, a citizen	Staatsangehöriger[3, 4]

MR. KÖHLER	HERR KÖHLER

Yes, I'm a German citizen.

Ja, ich bin deutscher Staatsangehöriger.

the identification card or paper	der Ausweis
an identification card (obj)	einen Ausweis (acc form)

MR. JONES	HERR JONES

Do you have an identification card?

Haben Sie einen Ausweis?

my passport (subject)	mein Pass (nom form)

MR. KÖHLER	HERR KÖHLER

Here's my passport.

Hier ist mein Pass.

to fill out	ausfüllen
he fills out	er füllt ... aus
the form	das Formular
the questionnaire	der Fragebogen

MR. JONES	HERR JONES

Please fill out this form.

Füllen Sie bitte dieses Formular aus.

the application	der Antrag
your application (subject)	Ihr Antrag (nom form)
he, it will be	er wird
right away	gleich
processed	bearbeitet

MR. JONES	**HERR JONES**
Your application will then be processed right away.	Ihr Antrag wird dann gleich bearbeitet.
MR. KÖHLER	**HERR KÖHLER**
Thank you very much.	Vielen Dank.

III

III

MR. KÖHLER	**HERR KÖHLER**
Do you like it in Bremen, Mr. Allen?	Gefällt es Ihnen in Bremen, Herr Allen?
I like being here, I'm glad to be here	ich bin gern hier
MR. ALLEN	**HERR ALLEN**
Yes, I'm very glad to be here.	Ja, ich bin sehr gern hier.

my wife (subj or obj)
    the climate
    to get used, to get accustomed (to something)
    he gets accustomed
	meine Frau (nom or acc form)
	    das Klima
	    sich gewöhnen (an etwas)
	
	    er gewöhnt sich

Only my wife can't get used to the climate.	Meine Frau kann sich nur nicht an das Klima gewöhnen.

rather, more preferable
    Bavaria
    the son
    our son (subject)
	lieber
	    Bayern
	    der Sohn
	    unser Sohn (nom form)

She'd rather live in Bavaria, and our son /would_7 too.	Sie möchte lieber in Bayern wohnen und unser Sohn auch.
MR. KÖHLER	**HERR KÖHLER**
I can understand that.	Das kann ich verstehen.

the man from Bremen
    a man from Bremen
	der Bremer
	    Bremer[3]

MR. ALLEN	**HERR ALLEN**
Aren't you /originally_7 from Bremen, Mr. Köhler?	Sind Sie nicht Bremer, Herr Köhler?

the home
    the home town, town where one grew up
    my home town (subject or object)
	die Heimat
	    die Heimatstadt
	
	    meine Heimatstadt (nom or acc form)

MR. KÖHLER	**HERR KÖHLER**
No, my /original_7 home town is Berlin.	Nein, meine Heimatstadt ist Berlin.

IV

At the restaurant.

MR. KÖHLER

What would you like to drink, beer
or wine?

    I like (to drink)

MR. ALLEN

I don't care for wine.

I'd like a glass of Pilsner and you?

    I like (to drink) better
    than

MR. KÖHLER

I prefer Würzburger to Pilsner.

    I like (to drink) best

MR. ALLEN

I like Löwenbräu best.

But unfortunately they don't have
it here.

V

    the cigar store
    a cigar store (subject or
    object)

MR. KÖHLER

Is there a cigar store near by?

    the tobacco
    no tobacco (object)
    more

I don't have any tobacco left.

    next door
    one (referring to das-noun)

MR. ALLEN

There's one next door here.

    the cigar
    a cigar (subject or object)

IV

Im Restaurant.

HERR KÖHLER

Was möchten Sie trinken, Bie oder
Wein?

    ich trinke gern

HERR ALLEN

Wein trinke ich nicht gern.

Ich möchte ein Glas Pilsner, und Sie?

    ich trinke lieber
    als

HERR KÖHLER

Ich trinke lieber Würzburger als
Pilsner.

    ich trinke am liebsten

HERR ALLEN

Am liebsten trinke ich ja Löwenbräu.

Aber das haben sie hier leider nicht.

V

    das Zigarrengeschäft
    ein Zigarrengeschäft (nom
    or acc form)

HERR KÖHLER

Gibt es in der Nähe ein Zigarrengeschäft?

    der Tabak
    keinen Tabak (acc form)
    mehr

Ich habe keinen Tabak mehr.

    nebenan
    eins

HERR ALLEN

Hier nebenan ist eins.

    die Zigarre
    eine Zigarre (nom or acc
    form)

MR. ALLEN

But I have some cigars.

    to offer
    he offers

May I offer you one?

MR. KÖHLER

No, thank you.

    to smoke
    he smokes
    the pipe
    a pipe

I only smoke a pipe.

VI

    the Sunday
    next
    (on) next Sunday
    just
    to us, to our house

MR. ALLEN

Why don't you come and see us next Sunday, Mr. Köhler? ('Just come to our house next Sunday, Mr. Köhler.')

    the new building
    a new building (object)
    on the outskirts
    of the town

We live in a new building on the outskirts of town now.

    it suits me, it's con-
    venient for me
    on Sunday

MR. KÖHLER

Sunday is not such a good day for me.

    the engagement
    an engagement (subject or
    object)

I already have an engagement.

    too bad
    the Saturday
    the Saturday
        the Monday
        the Tuesday
        the Wednesday
        the Thursday
        the Friday
    better

HERR ALLEN

Aber ich habe Zigarren.

    anbieten
    er bietet ... an

Darf ich Ihnen eine anbieten?

HERR KÖHLER

Nein, vielen Dank.

    rauchen
    er raucht
    die Pfeife
    Pfeife

Ich rauche nur Pfeife.

VI

    der Sonntag
    nächsten
    am nächsten Sonntag
    mal
    zu uns

HERR ALLEN

Kommen Sie doch mal am nächsten Sonntag zu uns, Herr Köhler.

    der Neubau
    einem Neubau (dative form)
    am Rande
    der Stadt

Wir wohnen jetzt in einem Neubau am Rande der Stadt.

    es passt mir

    am Sonntag

HERR KÖHLER

Am Sonntag passt es mir nicht gut.

    die Verabredung
    eine Verabredung (nom or
    acc form)

Ich habe schon eine Verabredung.

    schade
    der Sonnabend
    der Samstag
        der Montag
        der Dienstag
        der Mittwoch
        der Donnerstag
        der Freitag
    besser

MR. ALLEN	HERR ALLEN
That's too bad; is Saturday any better for you? ('Is it any more convenient for you on Saturay?')	Schade. Passt es Ihnen am Sonnabend besser?

then	da

MR. KÖHLER	HERR KÖHLER
Yes, I'd be glad to come then.	Ja, da komme ich gern.

shall we say, let us say	sagen wir
at 4 o'clock	um vier Uhr
it's all right with me	es ist mir recht

MR. ALLEN	HERR ALLEN
Shall we say at four o'clock? Is that all right with you?	Sagen wir um vier Uhr. Ist Ihnen das recht?

MR. KÖHLER	HERR KÖHLER
Fine.	Ja.

our address (subject or object)	unsere Adresse (nom or acc form)

MR. ALLEN	HERR ALLEN
Our address is 4 Schiller Street.	Unsere Adresse ist Schillerstrasse 4.

to greet	grüssen
give my regards to	grüssen Sie
your wife, Mrs. ... (subject or object)	Ihre Frau Gemahlin (nom or acc form)[6]

MR. KÖHLER	HERR KÖHLER
Please give my regards to Mrs. Allen.	Grüssen Sie bitte Ihre Frau Gemahlin.

remember me	empfehlen Sie mich
to your wife, to Mrs. ...(obj)	Ihrer Frau Gemahlin (dative form)

MR. ALLEN	HERR ALLEN
Thank you, I will. And please remember me to Mrs. Köhler, too.	Danke, und empfehlen Sie mich bitte auch Ihrer Frau Gemahlin.
Til Saturday then. ('Well then, until Saturday!')	Also dann bis Sonnabend.

the man, husband	der Mann
my husband (subject)	mein Mann
the consulate general	das Generalkonsulat

My husband works at the consulate general.	Mein Mann arbeitet im Generalkonsulat.

VII

Let's count:

twenty-one
twenty-two
twenty-three
twenty-four
twenty-five
twenty-six
twenty-seven
twenty-eight
twenty-nine
thirty
thirty-one
thirty-two
and so forth
forty
forty-one
etc.
fifty

VII

Wir zählen:

einundzwanzig
zweiundzwanzig
dreiundzwanzig
vierundzwanzig
fünfundzwanzig
sechsundzwanzig
siebenundzwanzig
achtundzwanzig
neunundzwanzig
dreissig
einunddreissig
zweiunddreissig
und so weiter
vierzig
einundvierzig
usw.
fünfzig

How much is 20 and 30?

20 and 30 is 50.

How much is 18 and 25?

33 and 15?

17 and 19?

14 and 8 and 23?

31 and 16?

Say these numbers: 37, 49, 28, 13, 22, 41, 24.

Wieviel ist 20 und 30?

20 und 30 ist 50.

Wieviel ist 18 und 25?

33 und 15?

17 und 19?

14 und 8 und 23?

31 und 16?

Sagen Sie diese Zahlen: 37, 49, 28, 13, 22, 41, 24.

Notes to the Basic Sentences

[1] Many German nouns are formed as compounds of two or more other nouns. Sometimes the elements are just placed together and written as one word. Sometimes there is a special combining form of the noun which occurs in compounds. Very occasionally compound nouns are hyphenated in German. Note that in every case the specifier of the compound is the same as the specifier of its last element, i.e., Besuchsvisum is a das-word, just as Visum is a das-word. The following compounds occur in this unit:

Besuchsvisum   with the combining form Besuchs-
Visa-Abteilung   with the combining form Visa-
Geschäftsreise   with the combining form Geschäfts-
Staatsangehöriger   with the combining form Staats-

[2] The normal position of the verb in a subordinate clause in German is at the end of the clause.

[3] Note that many German nouns which classify people according to profession, nationality, or membership in a group occur without a specifier.

4   Some German der-nouns end in -e if preceded by the specifier der but end in
    -er if preceded by no specifier or the specifier ein: der Deutsche, ein
    Deutscher, Deutscher (nominative forms); der Angehörige, ein Angehöriger,
    Angehöriger (nominative forms).

5   Samstag is more common in Western and Southern Germany.
    Sonnabend is more common in Northern and Eastern Germany.

6   Ihre Frau Gemahlin is polite, formal usage. A German says 'meine Frau' in
    referring to his own wife, but 'Ihre Frau Gemahlin' in referring to the wife
    of the person he is speaking to, unless he is very well acquainted with the
    family. In that case he would just say 'Ihre Frau'. A lady would normally
    say 'Ihre Frau' in talking to a man, unless the latter is a considerably older
    person or one to whom she owes particular respect because of rank or position.
    In referring to her own husband she would just say 'mein Mann'.

Notes on Pronunciation

A. The German ich-sound

   Whisper English "yes". Prolong the initial sound, as if you were stuttering:
" yyyes" . Whisper the name "Hugh" and prolong the initial sound in the same
way :   " Hhhhugh". Feel the air friction alone, like a long drawn out, whisper-
ed hy- combination. Now try the German words with your instructor. If you have
difficulty with them whisper English "yyyes" and "Hhhhugh" again for a moment
and try to get the air friction sound here distinctly. The same kind of air
friction will occur in all of the following German words:

Practice 1.

ich	König	Milch	leicht
mich	wenig	welch	nicht
weich	wichtig	solch	echt
Pech	endlich	durch	recht

Practice 2.

sicher	Fächer	weichen	München
siechte	nächste	gezeichnet	Häschen
Küche	Löcher	Seuche	Rippchen
Tücher	höchste	leuchte	Söckchen

B. The German ach-sound

    There is no sound in English similar to German -ch in ach. Pronounce
English 'knock.' Listen to the instructor pronounce German nach. Notice
the difference in the final sounds of the two words. In the English word
the back of the tongue is pressed against the back part of the roof of
the mouth stopping the flow of air. If you don't stop the flow of air
entirely but let some of it through by lowering the back part of your
tongue just a little, you should approximate the German sound. This air
friction, or spirant sound is not the same as the one described under A.
It is a lower frequency sound, because it is produced farther back in the
mouth cavity.

Practice 3

doch	Docht	kochen	Tochter
auch	taucht	fauchen	hauchte
nach	macht	lachen	dachte
Tuch	sucht	buchen	suchte
Bruch	Sucht		Buchten

Practice 4 - the <u>ich</u>-sound and the <u>ach</u>-sound compared.

Nacht	Nächte	Loch	Löcher
schwach	Schwäche	Tochter	Töchter
auch	euch	Buch	Bücher
fauchte	feuchte	Sucht	süchtig

Notes on Grammar
(For Home Study)

A. <u>ein</u>-Type Specifiers: <u>ein</u>, <u>kein</u>, <u>mein</u>, <u>sein</u>, <u>ihr</u>, <u>Ihr</u>, <u>unser</u>

I. Forms

1. With <u>der</u>-nouns

Hier ist <u>mein</u> Pass.	Here's <u>my</u> passport.
Ich habe <u>meinen</u> Tabak hier.	I have <u>my</u> tobacco here.
Ich fahre mit <u>meinem</u> Wagen.	I'm going in <u>my</u> car.

With <u>das</u>-nouns

Das ist <u>mein</u> Hotel.	That's <u>my</u> hotel.
Haben Sie <u>mein</u> Gepäck?	Do you nave <u>my</u> luggage?
Er wohnt in <u>meinem</u> Hotel.	He lives at <u>my</u> hotel.

With <u>die</u>-nouns

<u>Meine</u> Heimatstadt ist Berlin.	<u>My</u> home town is Berlin.
Sie kennt <u>meine</u> Frau.	She knows <u>my</u> wife.
Sie kommen aus <u>meiner</u> Heimatstadt.	They come from <u>my</u> home town.

With plural nouns

<u>Meine</u> Eltern kommen aus New York.	<u>My</u> parents come from New York.
Ich habe <u>meine</u> Zigaretten hier.	I have <u>my</u> cigarettes here.
Er wohnt in der Nähe von <u>meinen</u> Eltern.	He lives near <u>my</u> parents.

2. By abstracting the underscored forms of the word <u>mein</u> from the
German sentences above we can set up the following table:

	before <u>der</u>-nouns	before <u>das</u>-nouns	before <u>die</u>-nouns	before plural nouns
NOMINATIVE forms	mein	mein	meine	meine
ACCUSATIVE forms	meinen	mein	meine	meine
DATIVE forms	meinem	meinem	meiner	meinen (-n)

3. The <u>ein</u>-type specifiers include the words <u>ein</u> 'a, an, one' and its
negative converse <u>kein</u> 'not a, not an, not any, not one, no' as well as
the possessive words <u>mein</u> 'my', <u>sein</u> 'his', <u>ihr</u> 'her,their', <u>Ihr</u> 'your'
(the capital is a convention of the writing system), and <u>unser</u> 'our'.
Two other possessive words will be introduced in Unit 11.

Haben Sie <u>einen</u> Ausweis?	Do you have <u>an</u> identification card?
Gibt es hier in der Nähe <u>ein</u> Zigarrengeschäft?	Is there <u>a</u> cigar store near here?
<u>Ihr</u> Antrag wird dann gleich bearbeitet.	<u>Your</u> application will then be processed right away.
<u>Unsere</u> Adresse ist Schillerstrasse 4.	<u>Our</u> address is 4 Schiller Street.
Herr Allen stellt <u>seinem</u> Kollegen Bill Jones Herrn Meyer vor.	Mr. Allen introduces Mr. Meyer to <u>his</u> colleague Bill Jones.
Meine Frau hat <u>ihren</u> Pass noch nicht.	My wife doesn't have <u>her</u> passport yet.

4. Remember that <u>ein</u> occurs only in the singular, but all other <u>ein</u>-type
specifiers have a complete set of forms.

	with <u>der</u>-nouns	with <u>das</u>-nouns	with <u>die</u>-nouns	with plural nouns
Nominative	ein	ein	eine	
Accusative	einen	ein	eine	
Dative	einem	einem	einer	
Nominative	kein	kein	keine	keine
Accusative	keinen	kein	keine	keine
Dative	keinem	keinem	keiner	keinen (-n)
Nominative	sein	sein	seine	seine
Accusative	seinen	sein	seine	seine
Dative	seinem	seinem	seiner	seinen (-n)
Nominative	ihr	ihr	ihre	ihre
Accusative	ihren	ihr	ihre	ihre
Dative	ihrem	ihrem	ihrer	ihren (-n)
Nominative	unser	unser	unsere	unsere
Accusative	unseren	unser	unsere	unsere
Dative	unserem	unserem	unserer	unseren (-n)

5. Compare the underlined forms in the following pairs of sentences:

Ich kenne <u>diesen</u> Mann.	I know this man.
Ich kenne <u>ihren</u> Mann.	I know her husband.
Wohnt er in <u>diesem</u> Hotel?	Does he live in this hotel?
Wohnt er in <u>meinem</u> Hotel?	Does he live in my hotel?
<u>Welche</u> Bank ist das?	Which bank is that?
<u>Unsere</u> Bank ist neben dem Konsulat.	Our bank is next to the consulate.

In Units 1 and 3 we mentioned the correspondence of final sounds in der-type specifiers and the various forms of the pronouns er, es and sie. In the above sentences we see the pattern continued with the ein-type specifiers. In most cases the similarity can be traced through both types of specifiers and the pronouns: keinen-diesen-ihn-den, ihrem-welchem-ihm-dem, unsere-diese-welche, for instance.

6. Compare the underlined forms in the following sentences:

Dieser Autobus fährt nach Schwabing.	This bus goes to Schwabing.
Heute fährt kein Autobus nach Schwabing.	There's no bus going to Schwabing today.
Unser Autobus fährt nach Schwabing.	Our bus goes to Schwabing.
Das ist das Hotel.	That's the hotel.
Ist das Ihr Hotel?	Is that your hotel?
Nein, das ist mein Hotel.	No, that's my hotel.
Ich möchte heute das Visum beantragen.	I'd like to apply for the visa today.
Ich möchte heute mein Visum beantragen.	I'd like to apply for my visa today.
Möchte sie heute ihr Visum beantragen?	Would she like to apply for her visa today?

Note that there is no consistent similarity of final sounds in the underlined forms above. The patterns observed in paragraph 5 do not show up in dieser-kein-unser and das-mein-Ihr. There is then a form of the ein-type specifiers in which the final sound, or ending, found in the der-type specifiers and personal pronouns is lacking. This endingless form occurs as the Nominative form with der-nouns and as the Nominative and Accusative form with das-nouns. The pattern for ein-type specifiers can be summed up in the following pattern chart:

Pattern Chart 2

Nominative	-	-	E	E
Accusative	N	-	E	E
Dative	M	M	R	N (-n)

II. Uses

We have already noted that the ein-type specifiers include ein and kein and the possessives.

1. ein means 'a, an' when unstressed. With slightly increased stress it means 'one'.

Er füllt ein Formular aus.	He's filling out a form.
Füllen Sie nur ein Formular aus!	Just fill out one form.
Muss man ein oder zwei Formulare ausfüllen?	Does one have to fill out one or two forms?

2. kein means 'not a, not an, not any, not one, no'. In English we have an option in many negative statements:

I don't have an identification card. I haven't any identification card.	(Negation of verb)
I have no identification card.	(Negation of noun)

In German there is no equivalent option. In such statements the noun is always negated.

Ich habe keinen Ausweis.   I haven't any identification card.

Er ist kein Deutscher.   He isn't German.
                                    He's no German.

Haben Sie kein Visum?   Don't you have a visa?
                                    Have you no visa?

Wir kennen hier keine   We don't know any Americans here.
Amerikaner.
                                    We know no Americans here.

3. Any of the <u>ein</u>-type specifiers - like the <u>der</u>-type specifiers (noted in
   Unit 3) - can also occur without a following noun, and here they have
   the meanings 'one, not one, not any, mine, his, hers, theirs, yours,
   ours'.

Ich habe Zigarren.   I have some cigars.
Darf ich Ihnen <u>eine</u>   May I offer you <u>one</u>?
anbieten?

Haben Sie Ihren Wagen   Do you have your car here?
hier?
Nein, haben Sie <u>Ihren</u>   No, don't you have <u>yours</u> here either?
auch nicht hier?

III. Special <u>ein</u>-type specifier forms

1. MOST <u>ein</u>-type specifiers have the same form when their noun is understood as they do when it is present, as can be seen in the sentences
   above. Note the following examples, however:

Gibt es hier in der Nähe   Is there a cigar store near here?
ein Zigarrengeschäft?

Hier nebenan ist <u>eins</u>.   There's <u>one</u> next door here.

Ist das Ihr Stadtplan   Is that your map of the city or <u>mine</u>?
oder <u>meiner</u>?
Das ist <u>Ihrer</u>.   That's <u>yours</u>.

The endingless <u>ein</u>-type specifier forms add an ending when they stand
alone: <u>Ihr Stadtplan</u> - <u>Ihrer</u>; <u>ein Zigarrengeschäft</u> - <u>eins</u>. You will
note that the endings added are those of the corresponding <u>der</u>-type
specifier forms, except that the ending - <u>s</u> is added directly to the
stem of the <u>monosyllabic</u> <u>ein</u>-type specifiers: <u>kein-s</u>, for instance, as
compared with <u>unser-es</u>, <u>dies-es</u> and <u>welch-es</u>.

2. These special <u>ein</u>-type specifier forms occur only with <u>der</u>- and <u>das</u>-nouns
   and can be listed as follows:

With <u>der</u>-nouns   einer   keiner   meiner   seiner   ihrer   Ihrer   unserer

With <u>das</u>-nouns   eins   keins   meins   seins   ihrs   Ihrs   unseres

B. Verb Phrases and Word Order

I. We have already spoken about verb phrases which are composed of a FINITE verb
   form and an INFINITIVE form. They have also occurred in this unit:

Herr Köhler <u>will</u> ein   Mr. Köhler wants to apply for a
Besuchsvisum nach Amerika   visitor's visa for America.
<u>beantragen</u>.

Now look at the following examples:

Herr Allen <u>stellt</u> die Herren <u>vor</u>.	Mr. Allen introduces the gentlemen to each other.
<u>Füllen</u> Sie bitte dieses Formular <u>aus</u>.	Please fill out this form.
Ich <u>muss</u> Geld abheben.	I have to get some money.
Herr Köhler <u>hebt</u> gerade Geld von der Bank <u>ab</u>.	Mr. Köhler is just getting some money from the bank.

In these sentences another kind of verb phrase occurs of a FINITE verb (<u>stellt</u>, <u>füllen</u>, <u>hebt</u>) and an ACCENTED ADVERB (<u>vor</u>, <u>aus</u>, <u>ab</u>). In one of the above sentences we have a three-part verb phrase consisting of a FINITE verb (<u>muss</u>), ACCENTED ADVERB (<u>ab-</u>), and INFINITIVE (<u>-heben</u>). Notice that in the writing system, the accented adverb and the infinitive are written as one unit (<u>abheben</u>).

II. You will have seen that in the above sentences, as in earlier examples, the second part of the verb phrase comes at the end of the sentence. We can now summarize our observations about word order in verb phrases up to this point in the following patterns:

1. FINITE VERB ... INFINITIVE   (will ... beantragen)
2. FINITE VERB ... ACCENTED ADVERB   (stellt.. vor)
3. FINITE VERB ... ACCENTED ADVERB plus INFINITIVE (muss ... abheben)

The words <u>gern</u>, <u>lieber</u>, <u>am liebsten</u>

I. We have encountered the word <u>gern</u> several times now. It occurs by itself, with an inflected verb form, and as a part of the verb phrase with <u>möchte (n)</u>. Let us examine these occurrences more closely.

1. By itself <u>gern</u> signifies polite and willing acquiescence in a suggestion, command or question.

Wollen Sie nicht mitkommen?	Don't you want to come along?
Sehr gern.	I'd be very glad to.
Können Sie mir seine Adresse geben? Gerne.	Can you give me his address? Gladly.
Wollen wir heute zusammen in die Stadt fahren? Gerne.	Shall we go down town today? Glad to.
Können wir diesen Stadtplan behalten? Aber gerne.	Can we keep this map of the city? Yes, indeed.

Note that in these examples the alternate form <u>gerne</u> frequently occurs, varying freely with <u>gern</u>.

2. With an inflected verb form <u>gern</u> signifies pleasure in or enjoyment of the action or state expressed.

Ich bin sehr gern hier.	I'm very glad to be here.
Wein trinke ich nicht gern.	I don't like to drink wine.
Da komme ich gern.	I'd be glad to come then.
Gehen Sie gern ins Kino?	Do you enjoy going to the movies?
Er trinkt gern Bier.	He likes (to drink) beer.

As well as expressing acquiescence in a specific suggestion, command or question this is the usual way to say you <u>like</u> doing something in German, describing general attitudes or habits.

3. The verb phrase with <u>möchte(n)</u> expresses a polite request or question. The word <u>gern</u> may or may not occur with it.

Ich möchte gern Zigarren haben.	I'd like to have some cigars.
Was möchten Sie essen?	What would you like to eat?
Vorher möchte ich noch zur Bank gehen.	First I'd like to go to the bank.
Ich möchte ein Visum haben.	I want to get a visa.
Möchten Sie gern ins Kino gehen?	Would you like to go to the movies?

Note that this is everywhere equivalent to the English courtesy formula "would like", and the request expressed is limited and specific.

II. The words <u>lieber</u> and <u>am liebsten</u> do not occur alone but only with an inflected verb form or as part of the verb phrase with <u>möchte(n)</u>.

1. With an inflected verb form <u>lieber</u> and <u>am liebsten</u> express preference or increasing degrees of pleasure or enjoyment.

Ich trinke lieber Würzburger als Pilsner.	I like Würzburger better than Pilsner.
Am liebsten trinke ich ja Löwenbräu.	I like Löwenbräu best of course.
Er raucht lieber Zigarren als Pfeife.	He likes cigars better than a pipe.
Ich gehe am liebsten ins Theater.	I enjoy going to the theater best of all.

2. As part of the verb phrase with <u>möchte(n)</u> the words <u>lieber</u> and <u>am liebsten</u> express preference or intensification in a specific request or question.

Ich möchte lieber Zigarren haben.	I'd rather have some cigars.
Was möchten Sie am liebsten essen?	What would you most like to eat?
Möchten Sie lieber Wein oder Bier trinken?	Would you rather have wine or beer to drink?
Er möchte am liebsten nach Deutschland fahren.	He'd like nothing better than to go to Germany.

SUBSTITUTION DRILL - Part I

This is a drill on the forms of the <u>ein</u>-type specifiers. As in Unit 3 most of the sentence frames are presented with four different substitution groups: <u>der</u>-nouns, <u>das</u>-nouns and <u>die</u>-nouns separately, and then all mixed up together. This drill is designed to build fluent and accurate association of nouns in all gender classes with the appropriate forms of the specifier. If the previous experience and present skill of the students warrant it, very little time need be spent on groups a, b and c. Considerable time should be devoted to group d. in any case, however, until real fluency is achieved.

1. Das ist <u>mein Koffer</u>.

a. Pass - Tabak - Sohn - Parkplatz - Fragebogen	mein Pass - mein Tabak - mein Sohn - mein Parkplatz - mein Fragebogen
b. Hotel - Bier - Gepäck - Geld - Visum	mein Hotel - mein Bier - mein Gepäck - mein Geld - mein Visum
c. Frau - Adresse - Bank - Universität - Strassenbahn	meine Frau - meine Adresse - meine Bank - meine Universität - meine Strassenbahn

d. Parkplatz - Hotel -   mein Parkplatz- mein Hotel - meine
   Universität - Geld - Pass -   Universität - mein Geld - mein Pass -
   Strassenbahn - Gepäck - Sohn -   meine Strassenbahn - mein Gepäck -
   Fragebogen - Bank - Adresse -   mein Sohn - mein Fragebogen - meine
   Tabak - Visum - Frau - Bier   Bank - meine Adresse - mein Tabak -
                                         mein Visum - meine Frau - mein Bier

2. Das sind meine <u>Zigaretten</u>.

     Zigarren - Streichhölzer -   meine Zigarren - meine Streichhölzer -
     Eltern   meine Eltern

3. Ich kenne <u>keinen Amerikaner</u> in
   dieser Stadt.

    a. Polizisten - Konsul - Park -   keinen Polizisten - keinen Konsul -
       Beamten - Herrn Müller   keinen Park - keinen Beamten - keinen
                                      Herrn Müller

    b. Museum - Hotel - Theater - Café -   kein Museum - kein Hotel - kein Theater -
       Geschäft   kein Café - kein Geschäft

    c. Universität - Bank -   keine Universität - keine Bank - keine
       Amerikanerin - Frau Kunze -   Amerikanerin - keine Frau Kunze -
       Ludwigstrasse   keine Ludwigstrasse

    d. Bank - Museum - Universität -   keine Bank - kein Museum - keine
       Amerikaner - Beamten - Hotel -   Universität - keinen Amerikaner - keinen
       Ludwigstrasse - Polizisten -   Beamten - kein Hotel - keine Ludwig-
       Theater - Café - Konsul -   strasse - keinen Polizisten - kein
       Geschäft - Frau Kunze - Park -   Theater - kein Café - keinen Konsul -
       Amerikanerin - Herrn Müller   kein Geschäft - keine Frau Kunze -
                                      keinen Park - keine Amerikanerin -
                                      keinen Herrn Müller

4. Er wohnt in der Nähe von <u>einem
   Flughafen</u>.

    a. Parkplatz - Park - Bahnhof -   einem Parkplatz - einem Park - einem
       Neubau   Bahnhof - einem Neubau

    b. Museum - Hotel - Café - Theater -   einem Museum - einem Hotel - einem
       Zigarrengeschäft   Café - einem Theater - einem
                                      Zigarrengeschäft

    c. Bank - Universität - Botschaft -   einer Bank - einer Universität - einer
       Stadt   Botschaft - einer Stadt

    d. Hotel - Botschaft - Bahnhof -   einem Hotel - einer Botschaft - einem
       Park - Universität - Museum -   Bahnhof - einem Park - einer
       Café - Flughafen - Bank - Park-   Universität - einem Museum - einem
       platz - Zigarrengeschäft -   Café - einem Flughafen - einer Bank -
       Neubau - Stadt - Theater   einem Parkplatz - einem Zigarren=
                                      geschäft - einem Neubau - einer Stadt -
                                      einem Theater

5. Ist das <u>unser Koffer</u>?

    a. Parkplatz - Sohn - Kollege -   unser Parkplatz - unser Sohn - unser
       Wagen - Omnibus   Kollege - unser Wagen - unser Omnibus

    b. Hotel - Gepäck - Geld -   unser Hotel - unser Gepäck - unser
       Formular - Auto   Geld - unser Formular - unser Auto

c. Strassenbahn - Bank - Taxe -   unsere Strassenbahn - unsere Bank -
   Abteilung - Haltestelle   unsere Taxe - unsere Abteilung -
                                            unsere Haltestelle

d. Parkplatz - Hotel - Strassen=   unser Parkplatz- unser Hotel - unsere
   bahnhaltestelle - Geld - Strassen=   Strassenbahnhaltestelle - unser Geld -
   bahn - Gepäck - Wagen - Omnibus -   unsere Strassenbahn - unser Gepäck -
   Taxe - Auto - Sohn - Abteilung -   unser Wagen - unser Omnibus - unsere
   Kollege - Bank - Koffer -   Taxe - unser Auto - unser Sohn - unsere
   Formular   Abteilung - unser Kollege - unsere
                                            Bank - unser Koffer - unser Formular

6. Ich kann _Ihren Koffer_ nicht finden.

   a. Pass- Sohn - Fragebogen - Wagen -   Ihren Pass - Ihren Sohn - Ihren
      Antrag   Fragebogen - Ihren Wagen - Ihren Antrag

   b. Gepäck - Hotel - Visum - Auto -   Ihr Gepäck - Ihr Hotel - Ihr Visum -
      Formular   Ihr Auto - Ihr Formular

   c. Frau - Pfeife - Adresse - Bank -   Ihre Frau - Ihre Pfeife - Ihre Adresse -
      Abteilung   Ihre Bank - Ihre Abteilung

   d. Adresse - Hotel - Formular -   Ihre Adresse - Ihr Hotel - Ihr Formular -
      Bank - Koffer - Antrag - Sohn -   Ihre Bank - Ihren Koffer - Ihren Antrag -
      Pfeife - Fragebogen - Visum -   Ihren Sohn - Ihre Pfeife - Ihren
      Gepäck - Wagen - Frau -   Fragebogen - Ihr Visum - Ihr Gepäck -
      Abteilung - Auto - Pass   Ihren Wagen - Ihre Frau - Ihre Abteilung -
                                            Ihr Auto - Ihren Pass

   e. Zigaretten - Zigarren -   Ihre Zigaretten - Ihre Zigarren - Ihre
      Streichhölzer - Eltern   Streichhölzer - Ihre Eltern

Part II

In the following sentences _ein_-type specifiers occur both with and without
following nouns. Pay particular attention to the _special_ nominative and accusative _ein_-type specifier forms which refer to _der_- and _das_-nouns.

7. Hier ist _ein Koffer_. Dort ist auch
   einer.

          Omnibus - Parkplatz - Stadtplan -   ein Omnibus.einer - ein Parkplatz.einer -
          Wagen - Polizist - Fragebogen -   ein Stadtplan.einer - ein Wagen.einer -
          Herr - Neubau   ein Polizist,einer - ein Fragebogen.
                                              einer - ein Herr.einer - ein Neubau.
                                              einer

8. Haben Sie schon _ein Hotel_, oder
   haben Sie noch _keins_?

          Auto - Glas - Formular - Visum -   ein Auto.keins - ein Glas.keins - ein
          Geschäft   Formular.keins - ein Visum.keins - ein
                                              Geschäft.keins

9. Ist das _sein Koffer_? Nein, es
   ist _unserer_.

          Wagen - Stadtplan - Autobus -   sein Wagen.unserer - sein Stadtplan.
          Parkplatz - Antrag   unserer - sein Autobus.unserer - sein
                                              Parkplatz.unserer - sein Antrag.unserer

10. Ist das <u>Ihr Hotel</u> oder <u>unseres</u>?

      Formular - Gepäck - Geld -
      Bier - Brot

Tape 4B

11. Hat Herr Müller <u>einen Koffer</u>?
    Nein, er hat <u>keinen</u>.

      Pass - Visum - Glas - Wagen -
      Frau - Auto - Zigarre - Stadt=
      plan - Sohn - Geschäft - Pfeife -
      Ausweis - Verabredung -
      Formular

Ihr Formular.unseres - Ihr Gepäck.
unseres - Ihr Geld. unseres - Ihr
Bier.unseres - Ihr Brot.unseres

(End of Tape 4A)

einen Pass.keinen - ein Visum.keins -
ein Glas.keins - einen Wagen.keinen -
eine Frau.keine - ein Atuo.keins -
eine Zigarre.keine - einen Stadtplan.
keinen - einen Sohn.keinen - ein
Geschäft.keins - eine Pfeife.keine -
einen Ausweis.keinen - eine Verabredung.
keine - ein Formular.keins

12. Das ist <u>sein Gepäck</u>. Wo ist <u>Ihrs</u>?

      Bier - Stadtplan - Glas -
      Pfeife - Auto - Parkplatz -
      Pass - Abteilung - Tabak -
      Geld - Antrag - Zigaretten -
      Koffer - Adresse - Ausweis -
      Kaffee - Taxe

sein Bier.Ihrs - sein Stadtplan.Ihrer -
sein Glas.Ihrs - seine Pfeife.Ihre -
sein Auto.Ihrs - sein Parkplatz.Ihrer -
sein Pass.Ihrer - seine Abteilung.
Ihre - sein Tabak.Ihrer - sein Geld.
Ihrs - sein Antrag.Ihrer - seine
Zigaretten.Ihre - sein Koffer.Ihrer -
seine Adresse.Ihre - sein Ausweis.
Ihrer - sein Kaffee.Ihrer - seine
Taxe.Ihre

13. Von <u>welchem</u> Pass spricht er?
    Von <u>seinem</u>.

      Antrag - Formular - Frau -
      Visum - Kollegen - Heimatstadt -
      Geschäft - Pfeife - Neubau -
      Ausweis - Geschäftsreise -
      Besuchsvisum - Adresse

welchem Antrag.seinem - welchem
Formular.seinem - welcher Frau.seiner -
welchem Visum.seinem - welchem Kollegen.
seinem - welcher Heimatstadt.seiner -
welchem Geschäft.seinem - welcher
Pfeife.seiner - welchem Neubau.seinem -
welchem Ausweis.seinem - welcher
Geschäftsreise. seiner - welchem
Besuchsvisum.seinem - welcher Adresse.
seiner

Part III

    In the following sentences make the substitutions indicated, changing other
sentence elements as necessary. Drill for speed, accuracy and fluency.

14. Wo ist <u>mein Geld</u>?

Ihr Mann - seine Eltern - ein Kino -
unsere Koffer - ihr Gepäck - eine
Bank - sein Ausweis - Ihr Pass

15. Hier ist <u>unsere Taxe</u>.

kein Polizist - sein Wagen - keine
Strassenbahnhaltestelle - Ihre Frau -
ein Park - kein Restaurant - mein
Parkplatz - keine Visa-Abteilung

16. Sie hat <u>keine Zigaretten</u>.

keinen Pass - keine Verabredung -
keinen Ausweis - keinen Stadtplan -
kein Geld - kein Auto - keine Eltern -
keinen Mann

17. Er kennt meine Frau.

ihren Mann - einen Polizisten - unsere
Eltern - meinen Sohn - einen Konsul -
ihren Kollegen - einen Diplomaten -
unseren Ober

18. Ich frage einen Polizisten.

seine Frau - Ihren Mann - unsere
Eltern - ihren Bekannten - unseren
Portier - keinen Beamten - meinen
Kollegen - einen Vizekonsul

19. Er arbeitet in einem Hotel.

unserem Café - seinem Geschäft -
meiner Abteilung - einem Konsulat -
ihrem Restaurant - einer Bank

20. Er wohnt in einem Neubau.

ihrer Nähe - unserer Gegend - meinem
Hotel - unserer Stadt - Ihrer Strasse
einem Schloss - meiner Heimatstadt

21. Sie spricht mit einem Herrn.

einem Ober - ihrem Mann - unseren
Eltern - meiner Frau - einem Beamten -
einer Dame - meinem Kollegen

22. Er will ein Visum haben.

einen Pass - ein Formular - eine
Zigarre - keinen Koffer - seine
Pfeife - kein Besuchsvisum - einen
Fragebogen - keine Zigaretten

23. Wir wollen zu meinem Kollegen
gehen.

unserem Bekannten - ihrem Sohn -
seinen Eltern - einem Polizisten -
meiner Frau - ihrem Mann - meiner
Abteilung - unserem Konsul

24. Er trifft einen Bekannten.

ihren Sohn - einen Beamten - meine
Eltern - eine Amerikanerin - eine
Dame - unseren Kollegen - einen
Diplomaten

25. Meine Frau kann sich nicht an
das Klima gewöhnen.

mein Kollege - unser Sohn - ihr
Mann - unsere Eltern - unser Konsul

26. Ich habe keinen Tabak.

eine Zigarre - eine Verabredung -
Ihre Adresse - ein Visum - seinen
Pass - keinen Ausweis - Ihren Antrag

27. Gibt es hier in der Nähe ein
Zigarrengeschäft?

ein Konsulat - einen Neubau - keinen
Park - ein Restaurant - kein Museum -
einen Flughafen - eine Bank - keinen
Markt

28. Was kann ich für Sie tun?

ihn - Ihren Kollegen - sie - ihre
Eltern - Herrn Müller - Frau Meyer -
Ihren Sohn - seine Frau

29. Er bietet ihr eine Zigarette an.

meinem Sohn - dem Diplomaten - seiner
Frau - unserem Kollegen - ihm - dem
Vizekonsul

30. Ich rauche gern.

arbeite - trinke - esse - fahre -
bleibe - komme - frage

31. Sie sind Deutscher, nicht wahr?

Diplomat - Polizist - Amerikaner -
Vizekonsul - Bremer

32. Es passt _mir_ am Sonntag sehr gut.

ihm – meinem Sohn – ihr – uns – seiner
Frau – unseren Eltern – dem Konsul

33. Das Restaurant in der Ludwig‗
strasse gefällt _ihm_ nicht.

ihnen – ihrem Mann – ihr – seinem
Sohn – meiner Frau – Herrn Schulze –
der Dame – meinem Kollegen – unseren
Eltern – mir

34. Er kann sich nicht an _das Klima_
gewöhnen.

diese Gegend – unser Wetter – diese
Zigaretten – sein Auto – diese Idee

VARIATION DRILL

In the following drill your instructor will first read and ask-you to repeat
after him each of the German sentences in the group. Then cover the right hand
side of the page and give the German sentences again, using the English text as
a reminder. Each group drills a particular feature of grammar or syntax:
specifier, verb or noun forms, word order, etc. PLEASE NOTE: that the underlined
German pattern sentence is your model for the structural feature presented.
Form your sentences accordingly.

1. Er will ein Visum beantragen.

He wants to apply for a visa.

a. We're planning to go to Germany.
b. You can go to my colleague.
c. He has to take a business trip.
d. We would like to live in Bavaria.
e. You'll have to go to the customs
   office.
f. I may keep the map of the city.

Wir wollen nach Deutschland fahren.
Sie können zu meinem Kollegen gehen.
Er muss eine Geschäftsreise machen.
Wir möchten in Bayern wohnen.
Sie müssen zum Zoll gehen.

Ich darf den Stadtplan behalten.

2. Er wandert nach Amerika aus.
   Er will nach Amerika auswandern.

He's emigrating to America.
   He's planning to emigrate to America.

a. He introduces the gentlemen.
   Will you please introduce me?
b. He introduces him.
   I still have to introduce you.
c. May I offer you a cigar?
   She offers him a glass of
   beer.
d. Where are you planning to
   emigrate to then?
   He's emigrating to America.
e. Please fill out this questionnaire.
   Must I fill out the form
   right away?
f. He's just withdrawing the money.
   When do you want to withdraw
   your money?

Er macht die Herren bekannt.
   Wollen Sie mich bitte bekannt machen?
Er stellt ihn vor.
   Ich muss Sie noch vorstellen.
Darf ich Ihnen eine Zigarre anbieten?
   Sie bietet ihm ein Glas Bier an.

Wohin wollen Sie denn auswandern?

   Er wandert nach Amerika aus.
Bitte füllen Sie diesen Fragebogen aus.

   Muss ich das Formular gleich
   ausfüllen?
Er hebt gerade das Geld ab.
   Wann wollen Sie Ihr Geld abheben?

3. Sind Sie Bremer?

Are you (originally) from Bremen?

a. Is your wife German?
b. Her husband is a Foreign Service
   Officer, isn't he?
c. He's German, but his colleague
   is an American.
d. His wife is an American.
e. His son is a vice consul in
   Munich.

Ist Ihre Frau Gemahlin Deutsche?
Ihr Mann ist Diplomat, nicht wahr?

Er ist Deutscher, aber sein Kollege
ist Amerikaner.
Seine Frau ist Amerikanerin.
Sein Sohn ist Vizekonsul in München.

4. **Er trinkt nicht gern Wein.**   **He doesn't like (to drink) wine.**

   a. Do you like to go to the theater?   Gehen Sie gern ins Theater?
   b. He likes (smoking) a pipe.   Er raucht gern Pfeife.
   c. Do you enjoy eating at the   Essen Sie gern im Hofbräuhaus?
     'Hofbräuhaus?
   d. I don't like to take the street-   Ich fahre nicht gern mit der Strassen-
     car.   bahn.

5. **Er trinkt lieber Wein als Bier.**   **He likes wine better than beer.**

   a. He likes cigars better than   Er raucht lieber Zigarren als
     cigarettes.   Zigaretten.
   b. I prefer coffee to tea.   Ich trinke lieber Kaffee als Tee.
   c. We like (going to) the theater   Wir gehen lieber ins Theater als ins
     better than the movies.   Kino.
   d. Do you prefer (taking) the bus   Fahren Sie auch lieber mit dem Autobus
     to the streetcar also?   als mit der Strassenbahn?

6. **Er raucht am liebsten Zigaretten.**   **He likes cigarettes the best.**

   a. I like milk best.   Ich trinke am liebsten Milch.
   b. We like Bratwurst best.   Wir essen am liebsten Bratwurst.
   c. She likes driving the best.   Sie fährt am liebsten mit dem Auto.
   d. I like walking the best.   Ich gehe am liebsten zu Fuss.
   e. This is his favorite restaurant.   Er isst am liebsten in diesem
     ('He likes best to eat at this   Restaurant.
     restaurant.')

7. **Woher kommen Sie?**   **Where do you come from?**

   a. Whom do you intend to visit in   Wen wollen Sie in München besuchen?
     Munich?
   b. Who do these cigarettes here   Wem gehören diese Zigaretten hier?
     belong to?
   c. Who works in this section?   Wer arbeitet in dieser Abteilung?
   d. What do you plan to do today?   Was haben Sie heute vor?
   e. Where are you driving today?   Wohin fahren Sie heute?
   f. How's the climate here anyway?   Wie ist eigentlich das Klima hier?
   g. Why are you planning to emigrate?   Warum wollen Sie auswandern?
     ('do you want...')
   h. What bus do you want to take?   Mit welchem Omnibus wollen Sie fahren?
   i. Which form must I fill out?   Welches Formular muss ich ausfüllen?
   j. Which streetcar stops here?   Welche Strassenbahn hält hier?

8. **Gehen Sie gern ins Theater?**   **Do you like to go to the theater?**

   a. He likes to take his car best.   Er fährt am liebsten mit seinem Wagen.
   b. Do you enjoy going to the   Gehen Sie gern ins Museum?
     museum?
   c. My wife likes tea the best.   Meine Frau trinkt am liebsten Tee.
   d. Where do you prefer to live, in   Wo wohnen Sie lieber, in Bremen oder in
     Bremen or in Hamburg?   Hamburg?
   e. He enjoys smoking a pipe.   Er raucht gern Pfeife.
   f. He likes working at the consulate   Er arbeitet lieber im Konsulat als in
     better than at the embassy.   der Botschaft.

9. **Wir möchten gern in die Stadt fahren.**   **We would like to drive down town.**

   a. Would you like to have a map of   Möchten Sie gern einen Stadtplan haben?
     the city?
   b. We would like to live in a new   Wir möchten gern in einem Neubau wohnen.
     building.
   c. I'd like to change this money.   Ich möchte gern dieses Geld wechseln.
   d. Today my husband and I would   Heute möchten mein Mann und ich gern
     like to go to the movies.   ins Kino gehen.
   e. I'd like to take a walk now.   Ich möchte jetzt gern einen Spaziergang
                                          machen.

10. Ich möchte lieber zu Fuss gehen. I'd rather walk.

 a. We'd rather take a taxi than Wir möchten lieber mit einer Taxe als
  our car.   mit unserem Auto fahren.
 b. She'd rather live in Munich Sie möchte lieber in München als in
  than in Bremen.   Bremen wohnen.
 c. Mr. Allen would rather walk Herr Allen möchte lieber zu Fuss gehen
  than take the streetcar.   als mit der Strassenbahn fahren.
 d. He'd rather visit us on   Er möchte uns lieber am Sonnabend
  Saturday than on Sunday.   (Samstag) als am Sonntag besuchen.
 e. Wouldn't you prefer to take Möchten Sie nicht lieber mit dem
  the bus down town?   Omnibus in die Stadt fahren?

11. Ich möchte am liebsten durch den I'd like most to take a walk through
Park gehen.   the park.

 a. I'd like most to have a glass Ich möchte am liebsten ein Glas Bier
  of beer.   trinken.
 b. We'd like most to stay in   Wir möchten am liebsten in München
  Munich.   bleiben.
 c. He'd like most to go to Germany. Er möchte am liebsten nach Deutschland
            fahren.
 d. Mr. Meyer would like a   Herr Meyer möchte am liebsten eine
  cigar best.   Zigarre rauchen.
 e. We'd like most to go to the Am liebsten möchten wir in den
  'Ratskeller'.   Ratskeller gehen.
 f. What would you most like to do? Was möchten Sie am liebsten tun?

VOCABULARY DRILL

  The following vocabulary items have all occurred in the basic sentences of
this unit. A group of four or more sentences illustrates the use of each item.
Repeat the sentences after your instructor; then cover the left-hand side of
the page and give the German again, using the English text as a reminder.

1. ungefähr - "about, approximately"

 a. Wir bleiben ungefähr zwei   We're staying here approximately
  Wochen hier.   two weeks.
 b. Ich habe ungefähr drei Mark I've got about three Marks on me.
  bei mir.
 c. Er kommt in ungefähr vier   He's coming in about four weeks.
  Wochen.
 d. Es kostet ungefähr zehn Mark. It costs approximately ten Marks.

2. bis - "until, to (or)"

 a. Ich bleibe bis drei Uhr.   I'm staying until three o'clock.
 b. Wir bleiben sechs bis acht   We're going to stay six to eight weeks
  Wochen in Deutschland.   in Germany.
 c. Er fährt zwei bis drei Wochen He's going for a visit to America
  auf Besuch nach Amerika.   for two or three weeks.
 d. Er ist von neun bis eins   He's at the consulate from nine until
  im Konsulat.   one.

3. passen (gut) - "to be convenient"

 a. Sein Besuch passt mir heute His visit is not convenient for me
  nicht gut.   today.
 b. Heute passt es meiner Frau sehr It'll be very convenient for my wife
  gut.   today.
 c. Am Sonntag um vier Uhr passt es Sunday at four o'clock is fine for us.
  uns gut.
 d. Heute passt es ihm nicht gut. It's not convenient for him today.
 e. Passt es Ihrem Sohn am Dienstag? Is it convenient for your son on
            Tuesday?

4. <u>um</u> ... <u>Uhr</u> - "at ... o'clock"

   a. Um wieviel Uhr kommen Sie?   What time are you coming?
   b. Ich treffe sie um acht Uhr   I'm meeting her at eight o'clock
      im Café.   at the café
   c. Wir essen um sieben Uhr.   We eat at seven.
   d. Der Autobus fährt um zehn Uhr.   The bus goes at ten o'clock.

5. <u>recht</u> (with dative form of pronoun) - "all right (with someone)"

   a. Ist Ihnen das recht?   Is that all right with you?
   b. Hoffentlich ist es Ihrer Frau   I hope it's all right with your
      auch recht.   wife too.
   c. Das ist uns recht.   That's all right with us.
   d. Ist das dem Konsul nicht recht? Isn't that all right with the consul?
   e. Ich glaube, es ist ihm recht.   I think it's all right with him.

6. <u>grüssen</u> (with accusative form) - "to give one's regards to, to greet"

   a. Grüssen Sie Ihre Frau Gemahlin. Give my regards to your wife.
   b. Bitte grüssen Sie Ihren Sohn.   Please give my regards to your son.
   c. Bitte grüssen Sie Ihre Eltern.   Please give my regards to your parents.
   d. Grüssen Sie Herrn Becker bitte.   Give my regards to Mr. Becker, please.

7. <u>mehr</u> - "more, left (over)"

   a. Ich habe keinen Tabak mehr.   I don't have any tobacco left.
   b. Wir haben heute keine Milch   We don't have any more milk today.
      mehr.
   c. Ich habe leider kein Geld mehr. Unfortunately I don't have any
                                 money left.
   d. Es gibt hier keinen Wein mehr.   There isn't any more wine here.
   e. Ich habe auch keine Zigaretten I don't have any cigarettes left
      mehr.   either.

8. <u>hören</u> - "to hear"

   a. Ich höre, Sie wollen nach   I hear you're planning to go to
      Deutschland fahren.   Germany.
   b. Höre ich nochmal von Ihnen?   Will I hear from you again?
   c. Ich höre, er kommt am Dienstag I hear he's coming on Tuesday
      auf Besuch.   for a visit.
   d. Wir hören oft von ihm.   We hear from him often.

9. <u>machen</u> - "to take (a walk, trip, etc.)"

   a. Sie machen einen Spaziergang   They take a walk through the park.
      durch den Park.
   b. Wir wollen jetzt noch einen   Let's just take a walk now.
      Spaziergang machen.
   c. Möchten Sie mit uns einen   Would you like to take a walk with us?
      Spaziergang machen?
   d. Er macht eine Geschäftsreise   He's going to America on business.
      nach Amerika.   ('... taking a business trip ...')
   e. Sie machen gerade eine Reise   They're just taking a trip through
      durch Deutschland.   Germany.

10 <u>für</u> (with accusative form) - "for"

   a. Was kann ich für Sie tun?   What can I do for you?
   b. Können Sie für mich in die Stadt Can you go down town for me?
      gehen?
   c Er will das Formular für uns   He's willing to fill out the form
      ausfüllen.   for us.
   d. Heben Sie doch bitte das Geld   Please withdraw the money for me.
      für mich ab.
   e. Wir tun das für unseren Sohn.   We're doing that for our son.

11. **bei** (with dative form) - "with, at;   by, beside"

    a. Ich habe keinen Tabak bei mir.   I don't have any tobacco with me.
    b. Meine Koffer sind beim Zoll.   My suitcases are at the customs office.
    c. Er bleibt sechs Wochen bei uns.   He's staying with us (at our house) for six weeks.
    d. Er wohnt bei seinen Eltern.   He lives with his parents (at their house).
    e. Ich arbeite bei der Botschaft.   I work at the embassy.
    f. Das Visum können Sie beim Konsulat in Frankfurt beantragen.   You can apply for the visa at the consulate in Frankfurt.

12. **schade** - "too bad"

    a. Schade, ich habe keinen Tabak mehr.   Too bad; I don't have any tobacco left.
    b. Schade, hier in der Nähe gibt es kein Zigarrengeschäft.   Too bad; there's no cigar store around here.
    c. Schade, aber am Sonntag passt es mir nicht gut.   Too bad, but it's not convenient for me on Sunday.
    d. Schade, wir können nur vier Wochen hier bleiben.   Too bad; we can only stay here four weeks.

13. **aus** (with dative form) - "from, out of"

    a. Er kommt aus Deutschland.   He comes from Germany.
    b. Sie kommen gerade aus dem Restaurant.   They're just coming out of the restaurant.
    c. Kommen Sie um vier Uhr oder um fünf Uhr aus dem Kino?   Will you be coming out of the movies at four or at five o'clock?
    d. Ich glaube, wir kommen um zehn Uhr aus dem Theater.   I think we'll be coming out of the theater at ten o'clock.
    e. Sie kommt aus Berlin.   She comes from Berlin.

                                       (End of Tape 4B)

TRANSLATION DRILL (not recorded)

1. Mr. Köhler is a German.   Herr Köhler ist Deutscher.
2. He's planning to go to America.   Er will nach Amerika fahren.
3. He's obliged to go on business.   Er muss eine Geschäftsreise machen.
4. He goes to the consulate.   Er geht zum Konsulat.
5. There he applies for a visa.   Dort beantragt er ein Visum.
6. At the consulate he meets an acquaintance.   Im Konsulat trifft er einen Bekannten.
7. This (person) is called John Allen.   Dieser heisst John Allen.
8. He asks him, where the visa section is.   Er fragt ihn, wo die Visa-Abteilung ist.
9. Mr. Allen accompanies him to his colleague, Mr. Jones.   Herr Allen geht mit ihm zu seinem Kollegen, Herrn Jones.
10. Mr. Jones is a vice-consul in the visa section.   Herr Jones is Vizekonsul in der Visa-Abteilung.
11. Mr. Allen introduces the gentlemen to each other.   Herr Allen macht die Herren bekannt.
12. Mr. Jones would like to know: Herr Jones möchte wissen:
    a. Does Mr. Köhler want to emigrate?   a. Will Herr Köhler auswandern?
    b. How long does he intend to stay?   b. Wie lange will er bleiben?
    c. Does he have an identification card?   c. Hat er einen Ausweis?
13. Mr. Köhler shows him his passport.   Herr Köhler zeigt ihm seinen Pass.
14. Mr. Jones gives him a form (... a questionnaire).   Herr Jones gibt ihm ein Formular (... einen Fragebogen).

15. Mr. Köhler has to fill that out.   Das muss Herr Köhler ausfüllen.
16. Mr. Allen and Mr. Köhler then talk   Herr Allen und Herr Köhler sprechen
    together.   dann zusammen.
17. Mr. Allen likes it a lot in Bremen.   Herrn Allen gefällt es gut in Bremen.
18. His wife doesn't like the climate   Seiner Frau gefällt das Klima aber
    however.   nicht.
19. She and their son would rather   Sie und ihr Sohn möchten lieber in
    live in Bavaria.   Bayern wohnen.
20. Mr. Köhler can well understand   Herr Köhler kann das gut verstehen.
    that.
21. He is not originally from Bremen.   Er ist kein Bremer.
22. His home town is Berlin.   Seine Heimatstadt ist Berlin.
23. Mr. Allen and Mr. Köhler would   Herr Allen und Herr Köhler möchten
    just like to get something to drink.   noch etwas trinken.
24. Mr. Allen doesn't like wine.   Herr Allen trinkt nicht gern Wein.
25. He prefers Pilsner beer.   Er trinkt lieber Pilsner Bier.
26. Mr. Köhler however likes Würzburger   Herr Köhler trinkt aber lieber
    better.   Würzburger.
27. Unfortunately there's no Löwenbräu   Leider gibt es in diesem Restaurant
    /to be had/ at this restaurant.   kein Löwenbräu.
28. Mr. Allen likes Löwenbräu best.   Herr Allen trinkt Löwenbräu am liebsten.
29. Mr. Köhler likes to smoke a pipe.   Herr Köhler raucht gern Pfeife.
30. Unfortunately he doesn't have   Leider hat er keinen Tabak mehr.
    any tobacco left.
31. He's looking for a cigar store.   Er sucht ein Zigarrengeschäft.
32. There's one next to the restaurant.   Neben dem Restaurant ist eins.
33. Mr. Allen offers him a cigar.   Herr Allen bietet ihm eine Zigarre an.
34. However Mr. Köhler doesn't smoke   Aber Herr Köhler raucht keine
    ('any') cigars.   Zigarren.
35. The Allens live in a new building   Allens wohnen in einem Neubau am Rande
    on the outskirts of town.   der Stadt.
36. Their address is 4 Schiller Street.   Ihre Adresse ist Schillerstrasse 4.
37. Mr. Köhler is supposed to visit   Herr Köhler soll sie am Sonntag
    them on Sunday afternoon at four.   nachmittag um vier besuchen.
38. Unfortunately Sunday is not   Am Sonntag passt es ihm aber leider
    convenient for him, however.   nicht gut.
39. He already has an engagement.   Er hat schon eine Verabredung.
40. Saturday is more convenient for   Am Sonnabend passt es ihm besser.
    him.

RESPONSE DRILL (not recorded)

1. Warum geht Herr Köhler zum   Herr Köhler will ein Visum beantragen.
   Generalkonsulat?
2. Wohin will er fahren?   Er will nach Amerika fahren.
3. Wen trifft er im Konsulat?   Im Konsulat trifft er einen Bekannten,
                                           Herrn Allen.
4. Wo arbeitet Herr Jones?   Herr Jones arbeitet in der Visa-
                                           Abteilung.
5. Warum muss Herr Köhler nach Amerika   Er muss eine Geschäftsreise machen.
   fahren?
6. Wie lange will er dort bleiben?   Er will ungefähr vier bis sechs
                                           Wochen dort bleiben.
7. Ist Herr Köhler Deutscher?   Ja, er ist deutscher Staatsangehöriger.
8. Was muss Herr Köhler ausfüllen?   Er muss ein Formular ausfüllen.
9. Wie gefällt es Herrn Allen in   Es gefällt ihm sehr gut in Bremen.
   Bremen?
10. Warum gefällt es seiner Frau dort   Seine Frau kann sich nicht an das
    nicht so gut?   Klima gewöhnen.
11. Wo möchte sie lieber wohnen?   Sie möchte lieber in Bayern wohnen.
12. Ist Bremen die Heimatstadt von   Nein, seine Heimatstadt ist Berlin.
    Herrn Köhler?
13. Welches Bier trinkt Herr Allen   Herr Allen trinkt gern Pilsner.
    gern?
14. Welches Bier trinkt Herr Köhler   Er trinkt lieber Würzburger.
    lieber?

15. Warum trinkt Herr Allen nicht   In diesem Restaurant gibt es kein
    Löwenbräu?   Löwenbräu.
16. Was raucht Herr Köhler?   Er raucht Pfeife.
17. Warum sucht Herr Köhler ein   Er hat keinen Tabak mehr.
    Zigarrengeschäft?
18. Wo ist ein Zigarrengeschäft?   Neben dem Restaurant ist eins.
19. Was bietet Herr Allen Herrn   Er bietet ihm eine Zigarre an.
    Köhler an?
20. Wen soll Herr Köhler besuchen?   Herr Köhler soll Herrn Allen besuchen.
21. Wo wohnen Allens?   Allens wohnen in einem Neubau.
22. Warum passt es Herrn Köhler am   Herr Köhler hat am Sonntag eine
    Sonntag nicht?   Verabredung.
23. Passt es ihm am Montag besser?   Nein, es passt ihm am Sonnabend
                                            besser.
24. Um wieviel Uhr soll er kommen?   Er soll um vier Uhr kommen.
25. In welcher Strasse wohnen Allens?   Allens wohnen in der Schillerstrasse.

26. Wo beantragt man ein Visum?
27. Wohin fahren Sie?
28. Brauchen Sie ein Visum?
29. Wie ist das Klima hier?
30. Ist Washington Ihre Heimatstadt?
31. Was rauchen Sie lieber, Zigaretten
    oder Zigarren?
32. Wo wohnen Sie hier?
33. Wo möchten Sie am liebsten hinfahren?

CONVERSATION PRACTICE (not recorded)

1

J: Was möchten Sie trinken, Bier oder
   Wein?
M: Ich glaube, ich trinke jetzt lieber
   Kaffee.
J: Ach, trinken Sie nicht gern Bier?
M: Doch, ich trinke Bier sehr gern
   und Wein sogar noch lieber. Aber
   jetzt möchte ich am liebsten
   Kaffee trinken.

2

K: Wollen Sie uns nicht mal besuchen,
   Herr Meyer?
M: Gern; passt es Ihnen am Freitag?
K: Da passt es uns leider nicht;
   wir gehen ins Theater.
   Aber können Sie nicht am Sonnabend
   kommen?
M: Da habe ich schon eine Verabredung.
K: Dann sagen wir Sonntag; ist Ihnen
   das recht?
M: Ja, da passt es mir gut.

3

K: Kennen Sie eigentlich Herrn Jones?
S: Ja. Er arbeitet doch auch im
   Generalkonsulat, nicht wahr?
K: Er ist jetzt in der Visa-Abteilung.
S: Ist seine Frau nicht Deutsche?
K: Nein, sie ist Amerikanerin.
S: Wie lange bleibt Herr Jones noch
   in Bremen?
K: Leider nur noch vier Wochen.
S: Grüssen Sie ihn bitte von mir.

4

A: Ich habe keine Zigaretten bei mir.
   Ist hier in der Nähe ein Zigarren-
   geschäft?
M: Ja, dort auf der anderen Seite der
   Strasse. Aber darf ich Ihnen eine
   Zigarre anbieten?
A: Vielen Dank. Ich rauche nicht gern
   Zigarren.
M: Rauchen Sie auch nicht Pfeife?
A: Doch, aber am liebsten rauche ich
   Zigaretten. Und Sie?
M: Ich rauche lieber Zigarren.

SITUATIONS (not recorded)

At the Consulate

Mr. Keller and his wife wish to visit their son in America. They go to the American Consulate to apply for a visitor's visa. Vice Consul Allen in the Visa Section interviews them, asks for passport, identification, where they are going, etc.

Travel Plans

Mr. Köhler and an acquaintance, Vice Consul Jones, meet in a restaurant near the consulate. They have a beer together and Köhler offers Jones a cigar. The latter thanks him but explains he only smokes a pipe. Köhler also prefers a pipe and Jones offers him his tobacco. He asks Köhler what he's doing in this part of town, and Köhler tells him he is planning a business trip to the U.S. and needs a visa.

FINDER LIST

die	Abteilung	department, section
	als	than
	alt	old
	anbieten	offer
	er bietet ... an	he offers
der	Angehörige	the member (of a family or nation)
der	Antrag	application
	ausfüllen	fill out
	er füllt ... aus	he fills out
	auswandern	emigrate
	er wandert ... aus	he emigrates
der	Ausweis	identification card or paper
	Bayern	Bavaria
	beantragen	apply for
	er beantragt	he applies
	bearbeitet	processed
	bekannt	acquainted
	bekannt machen	introduce
	er macht sie bekannt	he introduces them (to each other)
der	Bekannte	acquaintance
	besser	better
der	Besuch	visit
auf	Besuch	on a visit
das	Besuchsvisum	visitor's visa
	bis	to, up to, until
der	Bremer	man from Bremen
	da	then
	dass	that
der	Deutsche	German
der	Dienstag	Tuesday
der	Donnerstag	Thursday
	empfehlen Sie mich	remember me
das	Formular	form
der	Fragebogen	questionnaire
Ihre	Frau Gemahlin	your wife
der	Freitag	Friday
	für (prep with acc)	for
das	Generalkonsulat	consulate general
das	Geschäft	business, store
die	Geschäftsreise	business trip
	er macht eine Geschäftsreise	he takes a business trip
sich	gewöhnen (an etwas)	to get used (to something)
es	gibt	there is, there are

	gleich	right away
	gleich mal	right
	grüssen	greet
	grüssen Sie	give my regards to
die	Heimat	home
die	Heimatstadt	hometown
die	Herren'	gentlemen (pl)
	hören	hear
	er hört	he hears
das	Klima	climate
der	Kollege	colleague
der	Konsul	consul
	lieber	rather, more preferable
	ich trinke lieber	I like (to drink) better
am	liebsten	best, most preferable
	ich trinke am liebsten	I like (to drink) best
	mal	just
der	Mann	man, husband
der	Mittwoch	Wednesday
der	Montag	Monday
	nächsten	next
	am nächsten Sonntag	next Sunday
	nebenan	next door
der	Neubau	the new building
	Neues	that which is new
es	passt mir	it suits me
die	Pfeife	pipe
am	Rande	on the outskirts
	rauchen	smoke
	recht	
	es ist mir recht	it's all right with me
	sagen	tell
	sagen wir	shall we say, let us say
der	Samstag	Saturday
	schade	bad, too bad
der	Sohn	son
der	Sonnabend	Saturday
der	Sonntag	Sunday
am	Sonntag	on Sunday
der	Staat	state, nation
der	Staatsangehörige	the national, the citizen
der	Tabak	tobacco
	tun	do
	er tut	he does
	um vier Uhr	at four o'clock
	und so weiter	and so forth
	ungefähr	approximately, about
	usw.	etc.
die	Verabredung	engagement
die	Visa-Abteilung	visa section
das	Visum	visa
der	Vizekonsul	vice consul
	vorstellen	introduce
	er stellt ... vor	he introduces
er	wird	he, it will be
die	Woche	week
	Wochen	weeks
	zählen	count
die	Zigarre	cigar
das	Zigarrengeschäft	cigar store
	zu uns	to us, to our house

Tape 5A   HERR ALLEN KLINGELT BEI HERRN WILSON

<u>Basic Sentences</u>

I   I

the apartment   die Wohnung,-en
the floor, the story   der Stock
on the second floor   im ersten Stock[1]
the apartment house   das Etagenhaus,-̈er
of an apartment house   eines Etagenhauses

The Wilsons have an apartment on the   Wilsons haben eine Wohnung im ersten
second floor of an apartment house in Stock eines Etagenhauses in Frankfurt.
Frankfurt.

to ring   klingeln
he rings   er klingelt
at, with   bei
at Mr. Wilson's house (or   bei Herrn Wilson
apartment)

Mr. Allen rings Mr. Wilson's doorbell. Herr Allen klingelt bei Herrn Wilson.
(... 'at Mr. Wilson's apartment.')

open   auf
to open   aufmachen
he opens   er macht ... auf
the door   die Tür,-en

Mr. Wilson opens the door.   Herr Wilson macht die Tür auf.

excuse me   entschuldigen Sie
excuse me   verzeihen Sie
to disturb   stören
he disturbs   er stört

<u>MR. ALLEN</u>   <u>HERR ALLEN</u>

Excuse me for disturbing you,   Entschuldigen Sie, dass ich störe,
Mr. Wilson. ('Excuse that I disturb, Herr Wilson.
Mr. Wilson.')

not at all   durchaus nicht

<u>MR. WILSON</u>   <u>HERR WILSON</u>

You're not disturbing me at all,   Sie stören durchaus nicht, Herr Allen.
Mr. Allen.

to come in   hereinkommen[2]
he comes in   er kommt herein

Won't you come in?   Wollen Sie nicht hereinkommen?

<u>MR. ALLEN</u>   <u>HERR ALLEN</u>

Thank you.   Vielen Dank.

the newspaper came, did come	die Zeitung,-en ist ... gekommen

My paper didn't come today.

Meine Zeitung ist heute nicht gekommen.

to borrow I borrow	sich leihen ich leihe mir

May I borrow yours?

Darf ich mir mal Ihre leihen?

to get (by subscription) he gets	halten er hält

MR. WILSON

HERR WILSON

Yes, indeed. I get two papers, the "Frankfurter Allgemeine" and "Die Welt".

Gern. Ich halte zwei Zeitungen, die "Frankfurter Allgemeine" und "Die Welt".

Which one would you like to have?

Welche möchten Sie haben?

MR. ALLEN

HERR ALLEN

The "Frankfurter Allgemeine", please.

Die "Frankfurter Allgemeine", bitte.

II

II

the place, the seat to sit down ('take a seat') he sits down	der Platz,-̈e Platz nehmen er nimmt ... Platz

MR. WILSON

HERR WILSON

Won't you sit down, Mr. Allen?

Wollen Sie nicht Platz nehmen, Herr Allen?

the minute, the moment	der Augenblick

MR. ALLEN

HERR ALLEN

Thank you, but only for a minute.

Danke, aber nur für einen Augenblick.

the post office the postage stamp to go and get he goes and gets	die Post die Briefmarke,-n holen er holt

I've got to go to the post office and get /some_7 stamps.

Ich muss noch zur Post gehen und Briefmarken holen.

afterward, in a little while by, past	nachher vorbei

MR. WILSON

HERR WILSON

I'm driving by there in a little while. Do you want to ride with me?

Ich fahre nachher dort vorbei. Wollen Sie mitkommen?

MR. ALLEN

HERR ALLEN

I'd be glad to. Are you going down town?

Gern. Fahren Sie in die Stadt?

the hour	die Stunde,-n
in half an hour	in einer halben Stunde
to pick up	abholen
he picks up	er holt ... ab

MR. WILSON

HERR WILSON

Yes, I have to pick up my wife in half an hour.

Ja, ich muss in einer halben Stunde meine Frau abholen.

the aunt	die Tante,-n

She's at her aunt's today.

Sie ist heute bei ihrer Tante.

I knew	ich wusste
relatives	Verwandte

MR. ALLEN

HERR ALLEN

I didn't know that your wife had relatives here.

Ich wusste garnicht, dass Ihre Frau hier Verwandte hat.

the (members of the) family	die Angehörigen
to live	leben
he lives	er lebt

MR. WILSON

HERR WILSON

Yes, my wife's family lives here.

Ja, die Angehörigen meiner Frau leben hier.

III

III

as	wie
the library	die Bibliothek,-en
a fine library	eine schöne Bibliothek

MR. ALLEN

HERR ALLEN

I see you have a fine library, Mr. Wilson. ('As I see, you have...')

Wie ich sehe, haben Sie eine schöne Bibliothek, Herr Wilson.

to read	lesen
he reads	er liest

MR. WILSON

HERR WILSON

Yes, I like to read very much.

Ich lese sehr gern.

the book	das Buch,̈-er
on the way, en route	unterwegs

MR. ALLEN

HERR ALLEN

My books are still on the way unfortunately.

Meine Bücher sind leider noch unterwegs.

one of my books	eins meiner Bücher

MR. WILSON

HERR WILSON

Would you like to borrow one of mine? (...'one of my books')

Möchten Sie sich mal eins meiner Bücher leihen?

MR. ALLEN

Thank you, I would.

    for instance
    the novel
    a good novel
    the author
    by the French author

MR. WILSON

Here's a good novel by the French author Cocteau for instance.

Are you acquainted with the book?

    sometime
MR. ALLEN

No, but I'd like to read it sometime.

    to take along
    he takes along

MR. WILSON

Take it right along with you.

MR. ALLEN

Thank you.

IV

    by chance
    the typewriter

MR. WILSON

Say, Mr. Allen, do you by any chance have a typewriter?

    out of order

Mine is out of order.

MR. ALLEN

I'm sorry, I don't have one.

    a few
    the letter
    the business letter
    to write
    he writes

MR. WILSON

That's too bad. I have to write some business letters.

HERR ALLEN

Danke, gern.

    zum Beispiel, z.B.
    der Roman,-e
    ein guter Roman
    der Schriftsteller,-
    des französischen
    Schriftstellers

HERR WILSON

Hier ist zum Beispiel ein guter Roman des französischen Schriftstellers Cocteau.

Kennen Sie das Buch schon?

    mal
HERR ALLEN

Nein, aber ich möchte es gern mal lesen.

    mitnehmen
    er nimmt ... mit

HERR WILSON

Nehmen Sie es doch gleich mit.

HERR ALLEN

Sehr gern.

IV

    zufällig
    die Schreibmaschine,-n

HERR WILSON

Sagen Sie, Herr Allen, haben Sie zufällig eine Schreibmaschine?

    kaputt

Meine ist kaputt.

HERR ALLEN

Leider habe ich keine.

    einige
    der Brief,-e
    der Geschäftsbrief,-e
    schreiben
    er schreibt

HERR WILSON

Schade. Ich muss einige Geschäftsbriefe schreiben.

the hand
by hand

die Hand,⁻e
mit der Hand

I don't like to write them in longhand.

Die schreibe ich nicht gern mit der Hand.

MR. ALLEN

HERR ALLEN

I think Miss Bruce has one.

Ich glaube, Fräulein Bruce hat eine.

to lend
he lends
surely, certainly

leihen
er leiht
sicher

I'm sure she'll be glad to lend it to you. ('She'll certainly lend it to you gladly.')

Sie leiht sie Ihnen sicher gern.

the secretary
the new secretary

die Sekretärin,-nen
die neue Sekretärin

MR. WILSON

HERR WILSON

Miss Bruce? Isn't she our colleague Smith's new secretary?

Fräulein Bruce? Ist das nicht die neue Sekretärin unseres Kollegen Smith?

the floor, the story
on the third floor

die Etage,-n
in der zweiten Etage[1]

MR. Allen

HERR ALLEN

Yes. She lives here on the third floor.

Ja. Sie wohnt hier in der zweiten Etage

V

V

when
closed, shut
to close
he closes

wann
zu
zumachen
er macht ... zu

MR. ALLEN

HERR ALLEN

When does the post office close actually?

Wann macht die Post eigentlich zu?

we had best go
or else, otherwise
late

wir fahren am besten
sonst
spät

MR. WILSON

HERR WILSON

At five. We'd best go right away or else we'll get there too late.

Um fünf. Wir fahren am besten gleich, sonst kommen wir zu spät.

the circuitous route, the
long way around

der Umweg,-e

MR. ALLEN

HERR ALLEN

Is it really not out of your way?

Ist es auch kein Umweg für Sie?

anyway
the paper
the stationery store

sowieso
das Papier
das Papiergeschäft,-e

MR. WILSON

HERR WILSON

No, I have to go to a stationery store anyway.

Nein, ich muss sowieso noch in ein Papiergeschäft gehen.

to need
he needs
you see (specifying)
the ink
the stationery
the pencil

brauchen
er braucht
nämlich
die Tinte,-n
das Briefpapier
der Bleistift,-e

You see, I need some ink, stationery and pencils.

Ich brauche nämlich Tinte, Briefpapier und Bleistifte.

directly, right
stationery supplies
the stationery store

direkt
die Schreibwaren (pl.)
das Schreibwarengeschäft, -e

MR. ALLEN

HERR ALLEN

There's a stationery store right next to the post office.

Direkt neben der Post ist ein Schreibwarengeschäft.

Where is the wastebasket?
Where are the wastebaskets?
Where is the fountain pen?
Where are the fountain pens?
Where is the house?
Where are the houses?
Where is the mother?
Where are the mothers?
Where is the father?
Where are the fathers?
Where is the brother?
Where are the brothers?
Where is the sister?
Where are the sisters?
Where is the daughter?
Where are the daughters?

Wo ist der Papierkorb?
Wo sind die Papierkörbe?
Wo ist der Füller?
Wo sind die Füller?
Wo ist das Haus?
Wo sind die Häuser?
Wo ist die Mutter?
Wo sind die Mütter?
Wo ist der Vater?
Wo sind die Väter?
Wo ist der Bruder?
Wo sind die Brüder?
Wo ist die Schwester?
Wo sind die Schwestern?
Wo ist die Tochter?
Wo sind die Töchter?

Notes to the Basic Sentences

1 im ersten Stock means literally 'on the first floor'; in der zweiten Etage means literally 'on the second floor'. In Germany as in many European countries the floors are numbered after the ground floor. The first floor is thus the first floor above the ground and is equivalent to our second floor. The second floor in Germany is equivalent to our third floor, and so on.

2 hereinkommen is the normal written form. Most speakers in rapid speech elide the first syllable and actually say 'reinkommen, or er kommt 'rein. You will hear the word pronounced both ways.

Notes on Pronunciation

A. German sch

If you pronounce English 'shown' and then listen carefully to the German schon, you will notice that the first sound of the German word is not quite the same as the English sound. To produce the German sound you will have to round and protrude your lips more than you do for the English sound.

Practice 1

schon	schnitt	Böschung	lutschen	Mensch	losch
Scheck	Schlot	Wäsche	wünschen	falsch	Tisch
Schiff	schrieb	Mischung	fälschen	Klatsch	Fleisch

The same sound occurs in the following words, although here the German writing system uses the symbol s:

Practice 2

Stadt	Spass	streng	springen
steht	Spiel	Strasse	Spross

B. German s

The symbol s is used in the German writing system to represent two more sounds: a voiceless sound as in English 'bus', 'buss' or 'must', and a voiced sound as in English 'housing' or 'busy'. Practice first the voiceless sounds. Notice too, by the way, that German writing may have either s or ss representing this sound.

Practice 3 (voiceless)

des	Busse	wusste	wies	Musse	wüst
Schmiss	Wasser	Liste	Mus	schösse	weist
Hotels	schupse	Mast	Autos	hiessen	grast
Klops	essen	schupst	Boots	Rätsel	lotst

Practice 4 (voiced)

Sohn	besondere	singen	Muse
sende	Thesen	Sieg	Losung

C. German z

We have noted above that the cluster ts occurs in German in such words as Boots and Rätsel. The symbol z is used in the German writing system to represent the same cluster. Practice the following words with your instructor:

    lotsen   Bozen   Rätsel   Brezel   miedst   siezt

This combination of sounds can also occur at the end and at the beginning of a word. Sometimes after a vowel tz is written. Now practice the sounds with your instructor in the following words:

Practice 5

Klotz	Litze	Arzt	zehn	zwei	zusammen
Sitz	Münze	heizt	Zug	Zwerg	Zickzack
März	Heizung	putzt	Ziel	Zwang	Zimmers
ganz	Bolzen	tanzt	Zorn	zwölf	Zeche

Notes on Grammar
(For Home Study)

A. NOUNS and SPECIFIERS

  I. Plural Forms

    1. It is very simple to form the plural of most English nouns; we simply "add an s". There are a few exceptional forms, like feet, and mice and sheep, but generally we have the s-plural.

    2. German, unfortunately for the student, has half a dozen different noun plural forms. Here are some examples from the basic sentences you have memorized:

Die Zigarren kosten zwei Mark.	The cigars cost two marks.
Ich habe nur diese zwei Koffer.	I have only these two suitcases.
Herr Allen stellt die Herren vor.	Mr. Allen introduces the gentlemen.
Meine Bücher sind leider noch unterwegs.	My books are still on the way, unfortunately.
Ich muss einige Briefe schreiben.	I have to write some letters.

    If we now compare the singular forms of the above nouns, we can show what is changed or added to distinguish the plural:

Singular	Plural	
Zigarre	Zigarren	-n has been added to the singular.
Koffer	Koffer	Nothing has been added or changed.
Herr	Herren	-en has been added to the (nominative) singular. (We recall that there is also a non-nominative singular form Herrn with the distinctive ending -n.)
Buch	Bücher	-er has been added to the singular, and there is a change in the stem vowel.

Brief   Briefe   -e has been added to the singular.

An additional common plural form which has not occurred in the basic
sentences is given below:

Auto   Autos   -s has been added to the singular.

3. Note that in some cases a change in the stem vowel has taken place. This
   is similar to the change in the stem vowel of some verbs noted in Unit 2:
   ich fahre, but er fährt. Germans call this kind of sound change UMLAUT,
   and you will frequently hear it referred to by the German term.

4. Note also that there is no differentiation in the plural between
   der-nouns, das-nouns and die-nouns. The plural SPECIFIER forms are the
   same regardless of whether they occur with a der-noun, das-noun or
   die-noun (see Units 3 and 4).

5. We can now re-arrange and expand the list to include all the noun plural
   types of frequent occurrence. We shall add the specifiers and also show
   how the plural is usually indicated in vocabulary listings.

	Singular	Plural	Listed
a) No change from the singular: (often with umlaut of stem vowel)	der Koffer	die Koffer	der Koffer, --
	der Flughafen	die Flughäfen	der Flughafen, ˸-
b) Add -e to the singular: (often with umlaut of stem vowel)	der Brief	die Briefe	der Brief, -e
	der Pass	die Pässe	der Pass, ˸e
c) Add -er to the singular: (often with umlaut of stem vowel)	das Geld	die Gelder	das Geld, -er
	das Buch	die Bücher	das Buch, ˸er
d) Add -en to the (nominative) sing:	die Frau	die Frauen	die Frau, -en
(Some nouns also add -n or -en to form the non-nominative sing)	der Herr	die Herren	der Herr, -n, -en
e) Add -n to the (nominative) sing:	die Zigarre	die Zigarren	die Zigarre,-n
f) Add -s to the singular:	das Auto	die Autos	das Auto, -s

6. An -n is added to the dative plural form of all nouns in groups a), b)
   and c). Nouns in groups d) and e) already have a final -n and nouns in
   group f) do not add an -n.

7. Umlaut of the stem vowel occurs rather haphazardly, so that you are
   going to have to learn the plural for each noun as you encounter it.
   However, in group c) we can say that umlaut will occur with every noun
   whose stem vowel is -a-, -o- or -u-.

8. Nouns with the final syllable -in double the -n- before the plural ending
   -en in group d).

9. A very few foreign words have irregular plural endings. Das Museum
   drops the final -um and replaces it by the -en ending of group d):
   die Museen. Das Visum has the plural die Visen or die Visa. Der Neubau
   inserts a -t- before the -en ending of group d).

10. Here is a list of nouns which have occurred in the first five units
    grouped according to the way their plurals are formed:

a) plural --   plural ⁼-   b) plural -e   plural ⁼e

   der Amerikaner   der Flughafen   der Tag   der Pass
   der Koffer   der Bruder   der Brief   der Bahnhof
   der Füller   der Vater   der Monat   der Platz
   der Wagen   der Bleistift   der Stadtplan
   der Ober   der Besuch   der Sohn
   der Morgen   der Omnibus (Omnibusse) der Spaziergang
   der Wachtmeister   der Wein   der Zoll
   der Ratskeller   der Augenblick   der Parkplatz
   der Fragebogen   der Autobus (Autobusse) der Antrag
   der Bremer   der Dom   der Papierkorb
   der Raucher   der Abend   der Markt
   der Schriftsteller   der Sonntag
                                           der Geschäftsbrief
                                           der Roman
                                           der Pfennig
                                           der Umweg
                                           der Ausweis
   das Essen   die Mutter   das Geschäft   die Stadt
   das Theater   die Tochter   das Jahr   die Hand
                                           das Konsulat
                                           das Brot
                                           das Bier
                                           das Formular
                                           das Papiergeschäft
                                           das Generalkonsulat

c) plural -er   plural ⁼er   d) plural -en

   das Geld   das Buch   der Diplomat   die Frau
                        das Haus   der Herr   die Botschaft
                        das Glas   der Polizist   die Wohnung
                        das Rathaus   der Staat   die Strassenbahn
                        das Schloss   der Neubau   die Bank
                        das Streichholz   (die Neubauten)   die Zeitung
                        das Etagenhaus   das Museum   die Abteilung
                                             (die Museen)   die Tür
                        der Mann   das Visum   die Bibliothek
                                             (die Visen)*   die Amerikanerin
                                                                  die Universität
                                                                  die Verabredung
                                                                  die Gemahlin
                                                                  die Sekretärin

           e) plural -n   f) plural -s

   der Konsul   die Minute   der Park
   der Vizekonsul   die Stunde   der Portier
   der Beamte   die Pfeife   das Auto
   der Bekannte   die Deutsche   das Café
   der Deutsche   die Zigarre   das Kino
   der Kollege   die Zigarette   das Restaurant
   der Angehörige   die Kontrolle   das Hotel
                        die Taxe
   die Dame   die Seite
   die Strasse   die Haltestelle
   die Adresse   die Idee
   die Ecke   die Tante
   die Briefmarke   die Etage
   die Schreib-   die Schwester
     maschine
   die Reise
   die Woche   *   or die Visa

II. Genitive Forms.

1. In addition to the plural in this unit we have encountered some other
   new forms of nouns and specifiers:

   a) Wilsons haben eine   The Wilsons have an apartment on the
      Wohnung im ersten Stock   second floor of an apartment house in
      <u>eines Etagenhauses</u> in   Frankfurt.
      Frankfurt.

   b) Die Angehörigen <u>meiner</u>   My wife's family lives here.
      <u>Frau</u> leben hier.

   c) Möchten Sie sich mal eins   Would you like to borrow one of my
      <u>meiner Bücher</u> leihen?   books?

   d) Hier ist ein Roman <u>des</u>   Here is a novel of the French author
      französischen <u>Schrift-</u>   Cocteau.
      <u>stellers</u> Cocteau.

   e) Ist das nicht die neue   Isn't she our colleague Smith's new
      Sekretärin <u>unseres</u>   secretary?
      <u>Kollegen</u> Smith?

   The underlined forms of the noun and specifier in the above sentences
   are called GENITIVE forms. They indicate possessive relationships --
   the kind of relationships that are designated in English by the -'<u>s</u>
   (or -<u>s</u>') ending, and by the preposition <u>of</u>. The GENITIVE is the fourth
   form, along with Nominative, Accusative and Dative forms, which German
   nouns and specifiers can have. There are no other distinctive forms of
   nouns and specifiers.

2. Let us compare the Genitive forms in the above sentences with the
   corresponding Nominative forms and see what features distinguish them:

Genitive	Nominative	
a) ei<u>nes</u> Etagenhaus<u>es</u>	ein Etagenhaus	The specifier and the noun both have the ending -<u>es</u> added to the Nominative form.
b) mei<u>ner</u> Frau	mei<u>ne</u> Frau	The specifier has the ending -<u>er</u> instead of -<u>e</u>; the noun has the same form as the Nominative.
c) mei<u>ner</u> Bücher	mei<u>ne</u> Bücher	The specifier has the ending -<u>er</u> instead of -<u>e</u>; the noun has the same form as the Nominative.
d) de<u>s</u> Schriftsteller<u>s</u>	de<u>r</u> Schrift-steller	The specifier ends in -<u>s</u> instead of -<u>r</u>; -<u>s</u> is added to the noun.
e) unser<u>es</u> Kolleg<u>en</u>	de<u>r</u> Kollege	The specifier has the ending -<u>es</u> added to the Nominative form; -<u>n</u> is added to the noun.

3. Note that in three cases - a), d) and e) above - the NOUN has a distinct
   Genitive form which differs from the Nominative form. In two cases -
   b) and c) above - the NOUN has the same form.

4. Note that in a), d) and e) the SPECIFIER has the ending -<u>s</u> (or <u>es</u>). In
   b) and c) the SPECIFIER has the ending -<u>er</u>.

5. Let us now summarize what we have observed about Genitive forms:

a) SPECIFIERS with der-nouns and das-nouns in the Genitive have the
   ending -s (or es). Both the der-type and the ein-type Specifiers
   have the same endings: des, dieses, eines, unseres.

b) der-NOUNS and das-NOUNS in the Genitive have the ending -s or
   -es: Hauses, Schriftstellers. A few der-nouns have the ending -n
   or -en: Kollegen, Herrn, Diplomaten, Polizisten, Beamten,
   Bekannten.

c) The SPECIFIERS of die-nouns and plural nouns have the ending -er
   in place of the Nominative ending -e (or -ie): der, dieser, meiner,
   ihrer.

d) die-NOUNS and plural NOUNS in the Genitive have the same form as in
   the Nominative: Frau, Bank, Banken, Bücher, Bleistifte.

6. Here for reference and comparison are some typical Genitive forms:

	Singular	Plural
a) Genitive of der-nouns	des Platzes	der Plätze
	des Omnibusses	der Omnibusse
	dieses Polizisten	dieser Polizisten
	meines Briefes	meiner Briefe
b) Genitive of das-nouns	des Jahres	der Jahre
	des Konsulats	der Konsulate
	dieses Hauses	dieser Häuser
	ihres Buches	ihrer Bücher
c) Genitive of die-nouns	der Dame	der Damen
	dieser Bank	dieser Banken
	unserer Schwester	unserer Schwestern

7. Note that der- and das-nouns ending in the sounds [s], [ts], [z]
   and [š] have the ending -es, as for example des Passes, des Platzes,
   des Hauses and des Tisches. Note also that the writing system requires
   the sound [s] to be written -ss- when non-final: Omnibusses,
   Omnibusse.

8. Otherwise, der- and das-nouns of more than one syllable have -s, as for
   example: des Konsulats, while monosyllabic der- and das-nouns have
   either -s or -es, whichever the speaker prefers; you will hear both
   des Domes and des Doms, des Staats and des Staates.

9. Proper names have an -s (or -es) ending: Peters Haus, Marias Tochter,
   Herrn Meyers Wagen.

10. You will note that the Genitive form of the specifier and noun generally
    follow the noun or pronoun with which a possessive relationship is
    indicated, as in the examples of paragraph 1:

im ersten Stock eines Etagenhauses	on the second floor of an apartment house
die Angehörigen meiner Frau	my wife's family
ein Roman des französischen Schriftstellers	a novel of the French author

Proper names in the Genitive, however, usually <u>precede</u> the noun
designating the thing posessed:

Kennen Sie Peters Frau?	Do you know Peter's wife?
Ist das Herrn Beckers Wagen?	Is that Mr. Becker's car?
Nein, das ist Marias Wagen.	No, that's Mary's car.

11. There is one personal pronoun which has a Genitive form: <u>wer</u>? "who"
has the Genitive form <u>wessen</u>? "whose"

Wessen Auto ist das?	Whose car is that?
Wessen Sohn kennen Sie?	Whose son do you know?

III. Summary of Specifier Forms

1. We have now encountered all the Specifier forms, both the <u>ein</u>-type and
the <u>der</u>-type. The following gives a complete summary of the forms:

		Singular	Plural
a) With	Nom	der Sohn	die Söhne
<u>der</u>-type	Acc	den Sohn	die Söhne
specifiers	Dat	dem Sohn	den Söhnen
	Gen	des Sohnes	der Söhne
	Nom	welches Theater	welche Theater
	Acc	welches Theater	welche Theater
	Dat	welchem Theater	welchen Theatern
	Gen	welches Theaters	welcher Theater
	Nom	diese Wohnung	diese Wohnungen
	Acc	diese Wohnung	diese Wohnungen
	Dat	dieser Wohnung	diesen Wohnungen
	Gen	dieser Wohnung	dieser Wohnungen
b) With	Nom	sein Brief	seine Briefe
<u>ein</u>-type	Acc	seinen Brief	seine Briefe
specifiers	Dat	seinem Brief	seinen Briefen
	Gen	seines Briefes	seiner Briefe
	Nom	<u>seiner</u>	seine	(Referring to
	Acc	seinen	seine	<u>der Brief</u>)
	Dat	seinem	seinen	
	Gen	seines	seiner	
	Nom	ihr Auto	ihre Autos
	Acc	ihr Auto	ihre Autos
	Dat	ihrem Auto	ihren Autos
	Gen	ihres Autos	ihrer Autos
	Nom	<u>ihrs</u>	ihre	(Referring to
	Acc	<u>ihrs</u>	ihre	<u>das Auto</u>)
	Dat	ihrem	ihren	
	Gen	ihres	ihrer	

	Singular	Plural
Nom	unsere Botschaft	unsere Botschaften
Acc	unsere Botschaft	unsere Botschaften
Dat	unserer Botschaft	unseren Botschaften
Gen	unserer Botschaft	unserer Botschaften

	Singular	Plural	
Nom	unsere	unsere	(Referring to
Acc	unsere	unsere	die Botschaft)
Dat	unserer	unseren	
Gen	unserer	unserer	

2. The ein-type specifiers are listed both with and without a following noun. The SPECIAL ein-type specifier forms which occur only when no noun follows the specifier are underlined.

B. REFLEXIVE PRONOUNS

I. In many sentences the object of the verb, the thing or person acted upon, is the same as the subject or actor. We say, for example, in English:

> Mr. Wilson introduced himself. or She thinks a good deal of herself, doesn't she?

The identity of subject and object in English is indicated by adding the suffix -self to the pronoun designating the object. Pronouns of this kind are called REFLEXIVE PRONOUNS.

II. The German Reflexive Pronoun

1. In German, as in English, the subject and object of a verb may be the same. Note the following examples from your basic sentences:

a) Meine Frau kann sich nicht an das Klima gewöhnen.
My wife can't get ('herself') used to the climate.

b) Darf ich mir mal Ihre leihen?
May I borrow ('lend myself') yours?

c) Möchten Sie sich mal eins meiner Bücher leihen?
Would you like to borrow one of my books?

In sentence a) the object of the verb refers to the same person as the subject and has the form sich. In sentence b) the interested bystander or indirect object of the verb is the same person as the subject and has the form mir. In sentence c) the indirect object of the verb is the same person as the subject and has the form sich.

2. German has only one REFLEXIVE PRONOUN, the form sich, meaning 'himself', herself, itself, yourself, yourselves, themselves'. It occurs wherever the subject of the verb is er, sie, Sie, or es or is a noun which can be replaced by er, sie, Sie, or es.

Herr Allen kann sich nicht an das Klima gewöhnen.
Mr. Allen can't get ('himself') used to the climate.

Herr Allen und seine Frau können sich nicht an das Klima gewöhnen.
Mr. Allen and his wife can't get ('themselves') used to the climate.

Können Sie sich nicht an das Klima gewöhnen?
Can't you get ('yourself') used to the climate?

3. The REFLEXIVE PRONOUN <u>sich</u> may function either as the object or as the <u>interested bystander</u> in a sentence. We might say it can have either an Accusative or Dative function. Compare the sentences in 2 above with the following:

Möchten Sie <u>sich</u> ein Buch leihen?	Would you like to borrow ('lend yourself') a book?
Er möchte <u>sich</u> ein Buch leihen.	He would like to borrow ('lend himself') a book.

4. Wherever the subject of the sentence is <u>ich</u> or <u>wir</u> or is a noun which can be replaced by <u>ich</u> or <u>wir</u> German uses the regular pronoun forms <u>mich</u>, <u>mir</u> and <u>uns</u>.

Ich kann <u>mich</u> nicht an das Klima gewöhnen.	I can't get ('myself') used to the climate.
Meine Frau und ich können <u>uns</u> nicht an das Klima gewöhnen.	My wife and I can't get ('ourselves') used to the climate.
Darf ich <u>mir</u> Ihre Zeitung leihen?	May I borrow ('lend myself') your newspaper?
Wir möchten <u>uns</u> gern einige Bücher leihen.	We'd like to borrow ('lend ourselves') some books.

5. The object of a preposition can also refer to the same person as the subject in a sentence.

Er spricht immer nur von <u>sich</u>.	He always talks only about himself.
Ich spreche nicht gern von <u>mir</u>.	I don't like to talk about myself.

6. Whenever the subject of the sentence is <u>er</u>, <u>sie</u>, <u>Sie</u> or <u>es</u> or is a noun which can be replaced by <u>er</u>, <u>sie</u>, <u>Sie</u> or <u>es</u> the REFLEXIVE PRONOUN form <u>sich</u> occurs as a prepositional object referring to the same person as the subject.

7. Wherever the subject of the sentence is <u>ich</u> or <u>wir</u> or is a noun which can be replaced by <u>ich</u> or <u>wir</u> German uses the regular pronoun forms <u>mich</u>, <u>mir</u> and <u>uns</u> after prepositions in order to refer to the same person as the subject.

SUBSTITUTION DRILL - PART I

1. Wo ist <u>der Roman</u>?

a. Brief - Bleistift - Papierkorb - Füller - Vater - Bruder

der Brief - der Bleistift - der Papierkorb - der Füller - der Vater - der Bruder

b. Haus - Buch - Briefpapier - Etagenhaus - Schreibwarengeschäft

das Haus - das Buch - das Briefpapier - das Etagenhaus - das Schreibwarengeschäft

c. Wohnung - Zeitung - Post - Briefmarke - Bibliothek - Schreibmaschine - Tinte - Sekretärin

die Wohnung - die Zeitung - die Post - die Briefmarke - die Bibliothek - die Schreibmaschine - die Tinte - die Sekretärin

(Drill No. 1 continued on next page)

d. Bibliothek - Buch - Tinte -
Briefpapier - Füller - Vater -
Etagenhaus - Papierkorb -
Schreibwarengeschäft - Post -
Brief - Wohnung - Haus -
Sekretärin - Zeitung - Bleistift -
Bruder - Briefmarke - Schreibma-
schine - Roman

die Bibliothek - das Buch - die Tinte -
das Briefpapier - der Füller - der
Vater - das Etagenhaus - der Papierkorb - das Schreibwarengeschäft -
die Post - der Brief - die Wohnung -
das Haus - die Sekretärin - die
Zeitung - der Bleistift - der Bruder -
die Briefmarke - die Schreibmaschine -
der Roman

2. Ich hole <u>den Papierkorb</u>.

Brief - Tinte - Vater - Briefpapier - Zeitung - Schreibmaschine - Füller - Buch - Bleistift - Briefmarke - Schwester

den Brief - die Tinte - den Vater -
das Briefpapier - die Zeitung - die
Schreibmaschine - den Füller - das
Buch - den Bleistift - die Briefmarke - die Schwester

3. Er spricht von <u>dem Roman</u>.

Tochter - Buch - Bibliothek -
Schriftsteller - Wohnung -
Etagenhaus - Brief - Zeitung -
Papiergeschäft

der Tochter - dem Buch - der Bibliothek - dem Schriftsteller - der
Wohnung - dem Etagenhaus - dem Brief -
der Zeitung - dem Papiergeschäft

4. Ich habe nur <u>ein Buch</u>, aber
Herr Keller hat zwei <u>Bücher</u>.

Koffer - Füller - Wagen -
Bruder - Tochter - Bleistift -
Geschäft - Formular - Stadt-
plan - Sohn - Haus - Zeitung -
Schreibmaschine - Pfeife -
Auto - Schwester

Koffer - Füller - Wagen - Brüder -
Töchter - Bleistifte - Geschäfte -
Formulare - Stadtpläne - Söhne -
Häuser - Zeitungen - Schreibmaschinen -
Pfeifen - Autos - Schwestern

5. Das ist <u>mein Bleistift</u>;
Ihre <u>Bleistifte</u> sind dort drüben.

Fragebogen - Brief - Ausweis -
Brot - Formular - Pass - Antrag -
Buch - Glas - Visum - Zeitung -
Briefmarke - Schreibmaschine

Fragebogen - Briefe - Ausweise -
Brote - Formulare - Pässe - Anträge -
Bücher - Gläser - Visa (Visen) -
Zeitungen - Briefmarken - Schreibma-
schinen

PART II

The following is a drill on plural forms. Pay particular attention to
accuracy of pronunciation, but work as rapidly as you can. Drill for fluency.

6. Wo sind die <u>Bleistifte</u>?

Papierkörbe - Adressen - Briefe -
Herren - Cafés - Damen - Geschäfte -
Schreibmaschinen - Fragebogen -
Füller - Briefmarken - Koffer -
Omnibusse - Romane - Ausweise -
Konsulate - Formulare - Pässe -
Anträge

7. Hier sind unsere <u>Zigaretten</u>.

Bücher - Zeitungen - Wagen - Brüder -
Töchter - Schwestern - Tanten -
Parkplätze - Häuser - Gläser - Streich-
hölzer - Diplomaten - Polizisten -
Autos

8. Ich suche die <u>Zeitungen</u>.
   Wo sind sie?

Amerikaner - Frauen - Amerikanerinnen -
Konsuln - Beamten ·· Pfeifen - Taxen -
Tanten - Zigaretten - Briefe - Frage-
bogen - Briefmarken - Pässe - Ausweise -
Sekretärinnen

9. Wir sprechen gerade von den
   <u>Geschäften</u> in Deutschland.

Theatern - Flughäfen - Omnibussen -
Cafés - Bahnhöfen - Städten -
Rathäusern - Schlössern - Kinos -
Etagenhäusern - Diplomaten - Poli-
zisten - Museen - Bibliotheken -
Hotels - Universitäten - Strassen -
Restaurants

10. Wieviele <u>Theater</u> gibt es in
    Deutschland?

Ratskeller - Flughäfen - Dome -
Konsulate - Botschaften - General-
konsulate - Bahnhöfe - Städte -
Schlösser - Diplomaten - Polizisten -
Museen - Banken - Zeitungen - Konsuln

11. Wieviele <u>Restaurants</u> gibt es in
    dieser Stadt?

Parks - Cafés - Kinos - Hotels -
Banken - Theater - Autobusse -
Strassenbahnen - Polizisten -
Strassenbahnhaltestellen - Geschäfte -
Etagenhäuser - Wohnungen - Biblio-
theken - Universitäten

(End of Tape 5A)

Tape 5B

PART III

The following is a drill on genitive forms. Make the substitution indicated
for the element or elements underlined, and make any additional changes required
by the substitution. Drill for accuracy and fluency.

12. Das ist der Wagen des <u>Amerikaners</u>.

a. Diplomaten - Schriftstellers -
   Bruders - Konsuls - Beamten

des Diplomaten - des Schriftstellers -
des Bruders - des Konsuls - des
Beamten

b. Geschäfts - Generalkonsulats -
   Rathauses - Museums - Restaurants - Hotels

des Geschäfts - des Generalkonsulats -
des Rathauses - des Museums - des
Restaurants - des Hotels

c. Botschaft - Mutter - Bank -
   Tochter - Bibliothek -
   Universität- Sekretärin

der Botschaft - der Mutter - der
Bank - der Tochter - der Bibliothek -
der Universität - der Sekretärin

d. Eltern - Brüder - Damen -
   Schwestern - Herren - Söhne

der Eltern - der Brüder - der Damen -
der Schwestern - der Herren - der
Söhne

e. Botschaft - Schriftstellers -
   Damen - Rathauses - Diplomaten -
   Bibliothek - Geschäfts -
   Konsuls - Bank - Schwestern -
   Museums - Tochter - Söhne -
   Beamten - Mutter - Restaurants -
   Eltern - Hotels - Generalkon=
   sulats - Brüder - Universität -
   Bruders - Herren - Amerikaners -
   Sekretärin

der Botschaft - des Schriftstellers -
der Damen - des Rathauses - des
Diplomaten - der Bibliothek - des
Geschäfts - des Konsuls - der Bank -
der Schwestern - des Museums - der
Tochter - der Söhne - des Beamten -
der Mutter - des Restaurants - der
Eltern - des Hotels - des General=
konsulats - der Brüder - der Uni=
versität - des Bruders - der Herren -
des Amerikaners - der Sekretärin

13. Wissen Sie die Adresse <u>des Konsuls</u>?

   a. Schriftstellers - Diplomaten -
       Vizekonsuls - Beamten - Herrn

           des Schriftstellers - des Diplomaten -
           des Vizekonsuls - des Beamten - des
           Herrn

   b. Schreibwarengeschäfts - Kinos -
       Konsulats - Restaurants -
       Etagenhauses - Theaters

           des Schreibwarengeschäfts - des Kinos -
           des Konsulats - des Restaurants -
           des Etagenhauses - des Theaters

   c. Mutter - Bank - Bibliothek -
       Tante - Zeitung - Dame -
       Sekretärin

           der Mutter - der Bank - der Bibliothek -
           der Tante - der Zeitung - der Dame -
           der Sekretärin

   d. Eltern - Brüder - Schwestern -
       Töchter - Söhne

           der Eltern - der Brüder - der
           Schwestern - der Töchter - der Söhne

   e. Bibliothek - Konsulats - Diplo-
       maten - Schwestern - Bank -
       Herrn - Etagenhauses - Beamten -
       Kinos - Töchter - Zeitung -
       Theaters - Eltern - Brüder -
       Schriftstellers - Söhne -
       Konsuls - Tante - Schreibwaren-
       geschäfts - Mutter - Restau-
       rants - Sekretärin - Vizekon-
       suls - Dame

           der Bibliothek - des Konsulats -
           des Diplomaten - der Schwestern -
           der Bank - des Herrn - des Etagen-
           hauses - des Beamten - des Kinos -
           der Töchter - der Zeitung - des
           Theaters - der Eltern - der Brüder -
           des Schriftstellers - der Söhne -
           des Konsuls - der Tante - des
           Schreibwarengeschäfts - der Mutter -
           des Restaurants - der Sekretärin -
           des Vizekonsuls - der Dame

14. Wo ist der Wagen <u>dieses Hotels</u>?

       Frau - Beamten - Geschäfts -
       Amerikanerin - Polizisten -
       Konsuls - Dame - Diplomaten -
       Herrn - Konsulats

           dieser Frau - dieses Beamten - dieses
           Geschäfts - dieser Amerikanerin -
           dieses Polizisten - dieses Konsuls -
           dieser Dame - dieses Diplomaten -
           dieses Herrn - dieses Konsulats

15. Ich gebe Ihnen die Adresse
    <u>eines Diplomaten</u> in München.

       Schriftstellers - Kollegen -
       Dame - Vizekonsuls - Schreib-
       warengeschäfts - Bank -
       Amerikaners - Bibliothek -
       Amerikanerin - Herrn

           eines Schriftstellers - eines
           Kollegen - einer Dame - eines Vize-
           konsuls - eines Schreibwarengeschäfts -
           einer Bank - eines Amerikaners -
           einer Bibliothek - einer Amerikanerin -
           eines Herrn

16. Ist das nicht die Schreibmaschine
    <u>Ihres Bruders</u>?

       Vaters - Schwester - Kollegen -
       Tochter - Sohnes - Tante -
       Mutter - Mannes - Bekannten -
       Frau

           Ihres Vaters - Ihrer Schwester -
           Ihres Kollegen - Ihrer Tochter -
           Ihres Sohnes - Ihrer Tante - Ihrer
           Mutter - Ihres Mannes - Ihres
           Bekannten - Ihrer Frau

17. Möchten Sie die Adresse <u>unseres</u>
    <u>Hotels</u> haben?

       Tante - Konsulats - Botschaft -
       Schwester - Eltern - Konsuls -
       Bank - Sohnes - Kollegen

           unserer Tante - unseres Konsulats -
           unserer Botschaft - unserer Schwester -
           unserer Eltern - unseres Konsuls -
           unserer Bank - unseres Sohnes -
           unseres Kollegen

18. Wir wohnen im Haus <u>meiner Mutter</u>.

unserer Tochter - seiner Schwester -
meines Sohnes - unserer Tante -
seines Bruders - ihres Vaters - eines
Bekannten - ihrer Eltern - meines
Kollegen

19. Haben Sie die Pässe <u>Ihrer Kollegen</u>?

meiner Söhne - seiner Eltern - unserer
Schwestern - meiner Töchter - unserer
Diplomaten

20. Hier ist <u>einer der Bleistifte</u>.

a. Stadtpläne - Söhne - Parkplätze -
   Brüder - Autobusse - Geschäftsbriefe

einer der Stadtpläne - einer der
Söhne - einer der Parkplätze - einer
der Brüder - einer der Autobusse -
einer der Geschäftsbriefe

b. Hotels - Theater - Museen -
   Konsulate - Etagenhäuser

eins der Hotels - eins der Theater -
eins der Museen - eins der Konsulate -
eins der Etagenhäuser

c. Schreibmaschinen - Schwestern -
   Wohnungen - Türen - Bibliotheken - Sekretärinnen

eine der Schreibmaschinen - eine der
Schwestern - eine der Wohnungen -
eine der Türen - eine der Bibliotheken -
eine der Sekretärinnen

d. Museen - Bibliotheken - Brüder -
   Theater - Söhne - Wohnungen -
   Hotels - Konsulate - Park-
   plätze - Schwestern - Etagen-
   häuser - Türen - Autobusse -
   Bleistifte - Schreibmaschinen -
   Stadtpläne - Geschäftsbriefe -
   Sekretärinnen

eins der Museen - eine der Bibliotheken - einer der Brüder - eins der
Theater - einer der Söhne - eine der
Wohnungen - eins der Hotels - eins der
Konsulate - einer der Parkplätze -
eine der Schwestern - eine der
Etagenhäuser - eine der Türen - einer
der Autobusse - einer der Bleistifte -
eine der Schreibmaschinen - einer der
Stadtpläne - einer der Geschäftsbriefe - eine der Sekretärinnen

21. Ich möchte <u>einen der Füller</u> haben.

a. Bleistifte - Stadtpläne -
   Koffer - Papierkörbe -
   Fragebogen

einen der Bleistifte - einen der
Stadtpläne - einen der Koffer - einen
der Papierkörbe - einen der Fragebogen

b. Gläser - Autos - Formulare -
   Häuser - Bücher

eins der Gläser - eins der Autos -
eins der Formulare - eins der Häuser -
eins der Bücher

c. Zeitungen - Pfeifen - Adressen -
   Schreibmaschinen - Briefmarken

eine der Zeitungen - eine der Pfeifen -
eine der Adressen - eine der Schreibmaschinen - eine der Briefmarken

d. Stadtpläne - Pfeifen - Häuser -
   Adressen - Autos - Formulare -
   Koffer - Briefmarken - Bücher -
   Bleistifte - Schreibmaschinen -
   Papierkörbe - Fragebogen -
   Zeitungen - Gläser - Füller

einen der Stadtpläne - eine der
Pfeifen - eins der Häuser - eine der
Adressen - eins der Autos - eins der
Formulare - einen der Koffer - eine
der Briefmarken - eins der Bücher -
einen der Bleistifte - einen der
Schreibmaschinen - einen der Papierkör-
be - einen der Fragebogen - eine der
Zeitungen - eins der Gläser - einen
der Füller

22. **Meine Frau** leiht sich die
Zeitung **ihrer** Tante.

unser Kollege	Unser Kollege leiht sich die Zeitung seiner Tante.
Frau Müller	Frau Müller leiht sich die Zeitung ihrer Tante.
er	Er leiht sich die Zeitung seiner Tante.
seine Frau	Seine Frau leiht sich die Zeitung ihrer Tante.
ihr Mann	Ihr Mann leiht sich die Zeitung seiner Tante.
wir	Wir leihen uns die Zeitung unserer Tante.
Herr Schneider	Herr Schneider leiht sich die Zeitung seiner Tante.

23. **Sie** kann sich nicht an das Klima
gewöhnen.

wir	Wir können uns nicht an das Klima gewöhnen.
seine Töchter	Seine Töchter können sich nicht an das Klima gewöhnen.
ihre Schwester	Ihre Schwester kann sich nicht an das Klima gewöhnen.
ich	Ich kann mich nicht an das Klima gewöhnen.
unser Vater	Unser Vater kann sich nicht an das Klima gewöhnen.
ihr Mann	Ihr Mann kann sich nicht an das Klima gewöhnen.
er	Er kann sich nicht an das Klima gewöhnen.

VARIATION DRILL

The following groups each have five basic variations as indicated in the
pattern sentences. Go through all the variations with each of the nouns
indicated.

1. a. Hier ist ein Polizist.   Brief - Bleistift - Stadtplan
   b. Hier ist einer.
   c. Hier sind die Polizisten.   Buch - Hotel - Kino
   d. Hier ist einer der Polizisten.
   e. Hier ist einer unserer Polizisten. Zeitung - Zigarre - Adresse

2. a. Wo ist ein Füller?   Wagen - Roman - Koffer
   b. Wo ist einer?
   c. Wo sind die Füller?   Restaurant - Geschäft - Café
   d. Wo ist einer der Füller?
   e. Wo ist einer seiner Füller?   Schreibmaschine - Pfeife - Zeitung

3. a. Ich kenne einen Wachtmeister.   Ober - Konsul - Diplomaten
   b. Ich kenne einen.
   c. Ich kenne die Wachtmeister.   Hotel - Museum - Theater
   d. Ich kenne einen der Wachtmeister.
   e. Ich kenne einen unserer Wacht-   Universität - Botschaft - Bank
   meister.

4. a. Das Auto gehört einem Kollegen.   Sohn - Bekannten - Bruder
   b. Das Auto gehört einem.
   c. Das Auto gehört dem Kollegen.   Geschäft - Restaurant - Café
   d. Das Auto gehört einem der
      Kollegen.   Schwester - Tochter - Tante
   e. Das Auto gehört einem meiner
      Kollegen.   (End of Tape 5B)

Tape 6A   VOCABULARY DRILL

1. leben - "to be alive, to live
   (in a larger area)"

   a. Meine Schwestern leben in   My sisters live in Germany.
      Deutschland.
   b. Der Bruder meines Vaters   My father's brother doesn't live here.
      lebt nicht hier.
   c. Leben Ihre Grosseltern noch?   Are your grandparents still living?
   d. Meine Mutter lebt in Frankfurt. My mother lives in Frankfurt.

2. wohnen - "to live, to reside
   (in narrower confines)"

   a. In welcher Etage wohnen Sie?   What floor do you live on?
   b. Er wohnt am Rande der Stadt.   He lives on the outskirts of town.
   c. Sie wohnt bei ihrer Tante.   She lives at her aunt's house.
   d. Meine Eltern wohnen in einem   My parents live in an apartment house.
      Etagenhaus.

3. lesen - "to read"

   a. Lesen Sie gern Romane?   Do you like novels?
   b. Er liest gerade die Zeitung.   He's just reading the newspaper.
   c. Dieses Buch möchte ich gern   This book I'd like to read.
      lesen.
   d. Sie liest gern und viel.   She likes to read, and she reads
                                  a lot.

4. schreiben - "to write"

   a. Entschuldigen Sie, ich muss   Excuse me, I have to write a letter
      jetzt einen Brief schreiben.   now.
   b. Wir schreiben Ihnen bald.   We'll write you soon.
   c. Schreibt er ihr eigentlich?   Does he write to her actually?
   d. Schreiben Sie den Brief mit der Are you writing the letter in
      Hand?   longhand?

5. leihen - "to lend"

   a. Er leiht mir seine Tinte.   He lends me his ink.
   b. Können Sie mir mal Ihren Füller Can you lend me your pen for a
      leihen?   minute?
   c. Welches Buch wollen Sie ihm   Which book do you want to lend him?
      leihen?
   d. Ich leihe Ihnen gern meine   I'll be glad to lend you my type=
      Schreibmaschine.   writer.

6. brauchen - "to need"

     a. Brauchen Sie auch Briefmarken?   Do you need stamps too?
     b. Jetzt brauche ich noch Brief-   Now I just need some stationery.
        papier.
     c. Was brauchen Sie noch, Tinte?   What else do you need, some ink?
     d. Er braucht für diese Reise   He doesn't need a visa for his trip.
        kein Visum.

7. aufmachen - "to open (the door)"

     a. Machen Sie bitte die Tür auf!   Open the door please!
     b. Er macht die Koffer auf.   He opens the suitcases.
     c. Soll ich die Briefe aufmachen?   Shall I open the letters?
     d. Mein Vater macht das Geschäft   My father opens the store.
        auf.

8. abholen - "to pick up"

     a. Ich hole Sie um vier Uhr vom   I'll pick you up at four o'clock
        Bahnhof ab.   from the station.
     b. Er holt uns am Sonntag ab.   He's going to pick us up on Sunday.
     c. Kann ich Sie in einer Stunde   Can I pick you up in an hour?
        abholen?
     d. Wir wollen jetzt unsere Mutter   We want to pick up our mother now.
        abholen.

9. mitnehmen - "to take along
(with one)"

     a. Sie können die Schreibmaschine   You can take the typewriter right
        gleich mitnehmen.   along (with you).
     b. Er nimmt seine Tochter mit.   He's taking his daughter along.
     c. Verzeihen Sie, darf ich diese   Excuse me, may I just take this
        Zeitung mal mitnehmen?   newspaper along (with me)?
     d. Ich nehme Ihre Briefe zur Post mit.   I'll take your letters along (with me)
                                       to the post office.

10. sich leihen - "to borrow"

     a. Er leiht sich drei Bücher.   He borrows three books.
     b. Können wir uns Ihre Schreibma-   Can we borrow your typewriter?
        schine leihen?
     c. Sie will sich eine Zeitung   She wants to borrow a newspaper.
        leihen.
     d. Entschuldigen Sie, kann ich mir   Excuse me, can I just borrow your
        mal Ihren Bleistift leihen?   pencil for a minute?

11. holen - "to (go and) get"

     a. Soll ich Ihnen Briefmarken   Shall I get you some stamps?
        holen?
     b. Holen Sie mir bitte Tinte.   Get me some ink, please.
     c. Er holt gerade eine Zeitung.   He's just gone to get a newspaper.
     d. Darf ich mir jetzt das Buch   May I go and get the book for myself
        holen?   now?

12. sowieso - "anyway"

   a. Wollen Sie mitkommen?
Ich fahre sowieso in die Stadt. — Do you want to come along?
I'm driving down town anyway.

   b. Soll ich Ihnen das Geld
wechseln? Danke, aber ich muss
sowieso noch zur Bank gehen. — Shall I change the money for you?
Thanks, but I have to go to the bank
still anyway.

   c. Können Sie mir Ihre Schreibmaschine leihen? Gern, ich
brauche sie jetzt sowieso nicht. — Can you lend me your typewriter?
Yes indeed, I don't need it now
anyway.

   d. Herr Köhler muss sowieso zur
Post gehen. Er kann Ihnen die
Briefmarken holen. — Mr. Köhler has to go to the post office
anyway. He can get you the stamps.

13. nämlich - "you see"

   a. Geben Sie mir doch bitte Ihren
Bleistift; meiner ist nämlich
kaputt. — Please give me your pencil; mine's
broken, you see.

   b. Ich kann leider nicht kommen;
ich habe nämlich in einer Stunde
eine Verabredung. — I'm sorry, I can't come; you see,
I have an engagement in an hour.

   c. Ich gehe ins Schreibwarengeschäft; ich brauche nämlich
noch Tinte. — I'm going to the stationery store;
I need some ink too, you see.

   d. Wir müssen jetzt gehen, sonst
kommen wir nämlich zu spät. — We'll have to go now; otherwise
we'll be late, you see.

14. direkt - "directly, right"

   a. Ich fahre direkt zum Bahnhof. — I'm going right to the station.

   b. Die Post ist direkt neben dem
Zigarrengeschäft. — The post office is right next to the
cigar store.

   c. Er kommt direkt aus der Stadt. — He's coming directly from town.

   d. Sie können direkt durch den
Park gehen, das ist kein Umweg. — You can go right through the park,
that's not a roundabout route.

15. auf - "open"   zu - "closed"

   a. Die Post ist nur bis 6 auf. — The post office is only open until 6.

   b. Sind die Geschäfte schon zu? — Are the stores closed yet?

   c. Das Museum ist heute nicht auf. — The museum isn't open today.

   d. Die Bank ist leider schon zu. — Unfortunately the bank is already
closed.

TRANSLATION DRILL (not recorded)

1. The Allens and the Wilsons are
Americans. — Allens und Wilsons sind Amerikaner.

2. Mr. Allen and Mr. Wilson are
Foreign Service Officers. — Herr Allen und Herr Wilson sind
Diplomaten.

3. They work at the Consulate General
in Frankfurt. — Sie arbeiten im Generalkonsulat
in Frankfurt.

4. Mrs. Wilson's relatives live in
Germany. — Frau Wilsons Verwandte wohnen in
Deutschland.

5. She still has two brothers and
two sisters. — Sie hat noch zwei Brüder und zwei
Schwestern.

6. Mr. Allen has to go to the post office and get some stamps.

Herr Allen muss zur Post gehen und Briefmarken holen.

7. First, however, he rings Mr. Wilson's doorbell.

Vorher klingelt er aber bei Herrn Wilson.

8. Mr. Wilson opens the door.

Herr Wilson macht die Tür auf.

9. Mr. Allen would like to borrow the "Frankfurter Allgemeine" from Mr. Wilson.

Herr Allen möchte sich von Herrn Wilson die "Frankfurter Allgemeine" leihen.

10. Mr. Wilson gets the "Frankfurter Allgemeine" and "Die Welt".

Herr Wilson hält die "Frankfurter Allgemeine" und "Die Welt".

11. He's glad to lend them to Mr. Allen.

Er leiht sie Herrn Allen gern.

12. The Wilsons have a beautiful library.

Wilsons haben eine schöne Bibliothek.

13. Mr. Allen's books are unfortunately still en route.

Herrn Allens Bücher sind leider noch unterwegs.

14. Mr. Wilson is very willing to lend Mr. Allen some of his books.

Herr Wilson will Herrn Allen gern einige seiner Bücher leihen.

15. Mr. Allen would like to read a novel by ('of') the author Cocteau.

Herr Allen möchte gern einen Roman des Schriftstellers Cocteau lesen.

16. Mr. Wilson has to write some business letters.

Herr Wilson muss einige Geschäftsbriefe schreiben.

17. Unfortunately his typewriter is out of order, and Mr. Allen doesn't have one.

Leider ist seine Schreibmaschine kaputt, und Herr Allen hat keine.

18. But Miss Bruce has one.

Aber Fräulein Bruce hat eine.

19. She's your colleague Smith's new secretary.

Sie ist die neue Sekretärin Ihres Kollegen Smith.

20. Miss Bruce has an apartment on the third floor of the apartment house.

Fräulein Bruce hat eine Wohnung im zweiten Stock des Etagenhauses.

21. The post office is only open until five o'clock.

Die Post ist nur bis fünf Uhr auf.

22. Mr. Allen has to go, or else it will close.

Herr Allen muss gehen, sonst macht sie zu.

23. Mr. Wilson is going down town too.

Herr Wilson fährt auch in die Stadt.

24. He has to pick up his wife, you see.

Er muss nämlich seine Frau abholen.

25. She's at one of her aunts' today.

Sie ist heute bei einer ihrer Tanten.

26. Before that he has to go to a stationery store.

Vorher muss er noch in ein Papier= geschäft gehen.

27. He needs ink, pencils and a pen.

Er braucht Tinte, Bleistifte und einen Füller.

28. He thinks he'd better write his letters in longhand after all.

Er will seine Briefe doch lieber mit der Hand schreiben

29. There's a stationery store next to the post office.

Neben der Post ist ein Papiergeschäft.

30. Mr. Wilson takes Mr. Allen along to the post office.

Herr Wilson nimmt Herrn Allen zur Post mit.

31. It's not out of his way.

Es ist kein Umweg für ihn.

RESPONSE DRILL (not recorded)

1. Wo wohnen Wilsons? — Wilsons wohnen in einem Etagenhaus.
2. In welchem Stock wohnen sie? — Sie wohnen im ersten Stock.
3. Warum geht Herr Allen zu Herrn Wilson? — Herr Allen will sich etwas leihen.
4. Was möchte er sich von ihm leihen? — Er möchte sich eine Zeitung von ihm leihen.
5. Wieviele Zeitungen hält Herr Wilson und welche? — Herr Wilson hält zwei Zeitungen, die "Frankfurter Allgemeine" und "Die Welt."
6. Welche möchte Herr Allen haben? — Herr Allen möchte die "Frankfurter Allgemeine" haben.
7. Wie lange will Herr Allen bei Herrn Wilson bleiben? — Er will nur einen Augenblick bleiben.
8. Warum kann er nur einen Augenblick bleiben? — Er muss noch zur Post gehen.
9. Warum will er zur Post gehen? — Er muss Briefmarken holen.
10. Warum muss Herr Wilson auch in die Stadt fahren? — Herr Wilson muss seine Frau in der Stadt abholen.
11. Bei wem ist seine Frau? — Seine Frau ist bei ihrer Tante.
12. Wann will er sie abholen? — Er will sie in einer halben Stunde abholen.
13. Ist seine Frau Amerikanerin oder Deutsche? — Seine Frau ist Deutsche.
14. Wo wohnen ihre Angehörigen? — Sie wohnen in Frankfurt.
15. Wo sind die Bücher von Herrn Allen? — Sie sind noch unterwegs.
16. Welches Buch möchte er gern mal lesen? — Herr Allen möchte einen Roman von Cocteau lesen.
17. Was möchte sich Herr Wilson von Herrn Allen leihen? — Herr Wilson möchte sich seine Schreibmaschine leihen.
18. Hat er keine Schreibmaschine? — Doch, aber seine Schreibmaschine ist kaputt.
19. Wo wohnt Fräulein Bruce? — Sie wohnt in der zweiten Etage.
20. Wo arbeitet sie? — Sie arbeitet im Konsulat.
21. Wessen Sekretärin ist sie? — Sie ist die Sekretärin von Herrn Smith.
22. Wann macht die Post zu? — Sie macht um fünf Uhr zu.
23. Warum will Herr Wilson in ein Schreibwarengeschäft gehen? — Er braucht Tinte, Briefpapier und Bleistifte.
24. Wo ist das Geschäft? — Das Geschäft ist neben der Post.
25. Will er seine Briefe mit der Hand schreiben? — Ja, Herr Wilson will seine Briefe mit der Hand schreiben.

26. Wo wohnen Ihre Eltern?
27. Ist Ihre Frau Deutsche oder Amerikanerin?
28. Wo leben die Angehörigen Ihrer Frau?
29. Welche Zeitung halten Sie?
30. Lesen Sie lieber Romane oder Zeitungen?
31. Schreiben Sie Ihre Briefe mit der Hand?
32. Wann machen hier die Geschäfte zu?
33. Was gibt es im Schreibwarengeschäft?
34. Wo ist hier die Post?

CONVERSATION PRACTICE (not recorded)

1

A: Ich möchte gern einen Füller haben.
B: Gern. - Wie gefällt Ihnen dieser hier?
A: Zeigen Sie mal; - ja, mit dem kann ich gut schreiben. Ich brauche auch noch zwei Bleistifte und etwas Briefpapier.
B: Hier, bitte.
A: Haben Sie auch Briefmarken?
B: Leider nicht; aber die Post ist gleich nebenan.

3

A. Haben Sie eigentlich Verwandte in Deutschland?
B: Ja, die Eltern meiner Frau leben dort.
A: O, - dann ist Ihre Frau Deutsche? Hat sie noch Brüder und Schwestern?
B: Ja, eine Schwester und zwei Brüder.

2

A: Herr Müller, darf ich mir mal Ihre Schreibmaschine leihen?
B: Brauchen Sie sie gleich?
A: Nein.
B: Ich will nur noch einen Brief schreiben; dann können Sie sie gern haben.
A: Vielen Dank.

4

A: Störe ich, Herr Wilson?
W: Nein, Sie stören durchaus nicht, Herr Allen. Nehmen Sie doch bitte Platz.
A: Danke, nur für einen Augenblick. Ich muss gleich in die Stadt fahren.
W: Fahren Sie auch zur Post?
A: Ja; möchten Sie mitkommen?
W: Sehr gern. Ich brauche nämlich Briefmarken.

SITUATIONS (not recorded)

Im Schreibwarengeschäft

Herr Keller geht in Frau Schulzes Schreibwarengeschäft. Er will einen Füller, sechs Bleistifte und Tinte haben. Frau Schulze kennt ihn gut. Er sagt, seine Schreibmaschine ist kaputt und er muss einige Briefe mit der Hand schreiben. Herr Jones kommt herein, er möchte Briefmarken haben. Die hat Frau Schulze nicht, er muss zur Post in die Stadt fahren. Herr Keller fährt sowieso in die Stadt. Er nimmt Herrn Jones gern mit.

Bei Herrn Schneider

Herr Allen klingelt bei Herrn Schneider in der zweiten Etage. Er möchte sich Herrn Schneiders Schreibmaschine leihen. Er muss nämlich einige Briefe schreiben und seine Schreibmaschine ist noch unterwegs. Herr Schneider will ihm die Schreibmaschine gern leihen, aber will Herr Allen nicht für einen Augenblick hereinkommen? Herr Schneider arbeitet auch im Konsulat und möchte wissen, in welcher Abteilung Herr Allen arbeitet. Er fragt ihn auch woher er kommt, wo seine Heimatstadt ist, usw. Allens gefällt es in Frankfurt sehr gut, und

Herrn Allen gefällt auch seine Arbeit. Dann sagt er Auf Wiedersehen; die Schreibmaschine kann er gleich mitnehmen.

Herr Jones braucht eine Zeitung

Herr Jones klingelt bei seinem Bekannten, Herrn Becker. Er möchte sich eine Zeitung leihen. Herr Becker hat leider keine, er will sich gerade eine holen. Will Herr Jones mitkommen? Unterwegs treffen sie Herrn Keller. Herr Keller zeigt ihnen einige Bücher. Eins der Bücher ist ein Roman von Cocteau. Herr Jones und Herr Becker kennen den Roman nicht. Herr Keller liest sehr viel. Er bietet Herrn Becker eins seiner Bücher an, aber Herr Becker liest nicht gern Romane. Er liest lieber Zeitungen. Herr Jones möchte sich aber gern ein Buch von Herrn Keller leihen.

Narrative (not recorded)

Herr Wilson fährt zum Konsulat. Er will aber vorher noch im Papiergeschäft zwei <u>Kugelschreiber</u>, einen <u>Radiergummi</u> und ein <u>Lineal</u> für seine <u>Kinder kaufen</u>. Er fragt den <u>Verkäufer</u>, wo die <u>Illustrierten</u> sind. Der zeigt sie ihm und Herr Wilson kauft eine für seine Frau. Er trifft Herrn Meyer auf der Strasse. Sie kennen sich gut. Herr Meyer <u>erzählt</u> Herrn Wilson, dass er eine Geschäftsreise nach Amerika machen muss. Er fährt nächsten Monat nach New York. Die Herren fahren zusammen zum Konsulat. Herr Meyer will sich sein Visum dort abholen. Herr Wilson <u>bittet</u> ihn, seine <u>Schwiegereltern</u> in New York zu besuchen. Sie zeigen Herrn Meyer <u>bestimmt</u> gern die Stadt. Er gibt ihm die Adresse und dann <u>verabschieden</u> sich die Herren.

der Kugelschreiber,--	ballpoint	die Illustrierte,-n	picture magazine
der Radiergummi,-s	eraser	erzählen	tell
das Lineal,-e	ruler	bitten	ask
das Kind,-er	child	die Schwiegereltern	parents-in-law
kaufen	buy	bestimmt	certainly
der Verkäufer,--	sales clerk	sich verabschieden	say good-by to each other

FINDER LIST

	abholen	pick up
	er holt ... ab	he picks up
die	Angehörigen (pl)	the members of the family
	auf	open
	aufmachen	open
	er macht ... auf	he opens
der	Augenblick,-e	the minute, the moment
	bei	at
	bei Herrn Wilson	at Mr. Wilson's house
die	Bibliothek,-en	library
	eine schöne Bibliothek	a fine library
der	Bleistift,-e	pencil
	brauchen	need
der	Brief,-e	letter
die	Briefmarke,-n	postage stamp
das	Briefpapier	stationery
der	Bruder,-	brother
das	Buch,-er	book
	direkt	directly, right
	durchaus nicht	not at all
	einige	a few
	entschuldigen Sie	excuse me
die	Etage,-n	floor, story
	in der zweiten Etage	on the third floor
das	Etagenhaus,-er	apartment house
der	Füller,-	pen
ist	gekommen	came, did come
der	Geschäftsbrief,-e	business letter
	halten	get by subscription
	er hält	he gets by subscription
die	Hand,-e	hand
	mit der Hand	by hand
das	Haus,-er	house
	hereinkommen	come in
	er kommt herein	he comes in
	holen	go and get
	kaputt	out of order
	klingeln	ring
	leben	live
	leihen	lend
sich	leihen	borrow
	ich leihe mir	I borrow

	lesen	read
	er liest	he reads
	mitnehmen	take along
	er nimmt ... mit	he takes along
die	Mutter, ¨	mother
	nachher	afterward, in a little while
	nämlich	to be specific
das	Papier	paper
das	Papiergeschäft, -e	stationery store
der	Papierkorb, ¨e	wastepaper basket
der	Platz, ¨e	place, seat
	Platz nehmen	sit down
	er nimmt Platz	he sits down
die	Post	post office
der	Roman, -e	novel
	ein guter Roman	a good novel
	schreiben	write
die	Schreibmaschine, -n	typewriter
die	Schreibwaren (pl)	stationery supplies
das	Schreibwarengeschäft, -e	stationery store
der	Schriftsteller, -	author
	des französischen Schriftstellers	of the French author
die	Schwester, -n	sister
die	Sekretärin, -nen	secretary
	sicher	surely, certainly
	sonst	or else, otherwise
	sowieso	anyway
	spät	late
der	Stock	floor, story
	im ersten Stock	on the second floor
	stören	disturb
die	Stunde, -n	hour
	in einer halben Stunde	in half an hour
die	Tante, -n	aunt
die	Tinte, -n	ink
die	Tochter, ¨	daughter
die	Tür, -en	door
der	Umweg, -e	circuitious route, the long way around
	unterwegs	on the way, en route
der	Vater, ¨	father
	Verwandte (pl)	relatives
	verzeihen Sie	excuse me
	vorbei	by, past
	wann	when
	wie	as
die	Wohnung, -en	apartment
ich	wusste	I know
die	Zeitung, -en	newspaper
	zu	closed, shut
	zufällig	by chance
	zumachen	to close
	er macht ... zu	he closes
	zum Beispiel, z.B.	for instance, e.g.

TELEPHONGESPRÄCHE

Basic Sentences

I

I

the telephone	das Telephon,-e
the Economic Section	die Wirtschaftsabteilung,-en
·of the American Consulate	des amerikanischen
General	Generalkonsulats

The telephone rings in the Economic
Section of the American Consulate
General.

Das Telephon klingelt in der Wirtschaftsabteilung des amerikanischen
Generalkonsulats.

to take off	abnehmen
the receiver	der Hörer,-
to answer	sich melden

The secretary lifts up the receiver
and answers.

Die Sekretärin nimmt den Hörer ab
und meldet sich.

SECRETARY

SEKRETÄRIN

American Consulate General.

Amerikanisches Generalkonsulat.

the Certina Company

die Certina G.m.b.H.[1]

MR. BAUER

HERR BAUER

This is the Certina Company, Bauer
speaking.

Hier Certina G.m.b.H., Bauer.

May I speak to Mr. Wilson, please?

Kann ich bitte Herrn Konsul Wilson
sprechen?

| at the moment | im Augenblick |
| the office | das Büro,-s |

SECRETARY

SEKRETÄRIN

I'm sorry, Mr. Wilson is not in the
office at the moment.

Der Herr Konsul ist leider im
Augenblick nicht im Büro.

important	wichtig
the conference	die Konferenz,-en
at an important conference	in einer wichtigen Konferenz

He's at an important conference right
now.

Er ist gerade in einer wichtigen
Konferenz.

to come back

zurückkommen

MR. BAUER

HERR BAUER

Do you know when he'll be back?

Wissen Sie, wann er zurückkommt?

indefinite

unbestimmt

SECRETARY

SEKRETÄRIN

I really can't say.

Das ist unbestimmt.

to tell, to give a message

ausrichten

Can I give him a message?	Kann ich ihm etwas ausrichten?

I'd like him to	er möchte [2]
soon	bald
possible	möglich
as soon as possible	sobald wie möglich
to call up	anrufen

MR. BAUER

HERR BAUER

Yes. Please tell him I'd like him to call me as soon as possible.	Ja; sagen Sie ihm doch bitte, er möchte mich sobald wie möglich anrufen.

it is about, the matter at hand is	es handelt sich um (plus acc)
urgent	dringend
the matter	die Angelegenheit,-en

It's about a very urgent matter.	Es handelt sich um eine dringende Angelegenheit.

to reach	erreichen
to be reached	zu erreichen

SECRETARY

SEKRETÄRIN

How can he reach you? ('How are you to be reached?')	Wie sind Sie zu erreichen?

under, at	unter
the number	die Nummer,-n

MR. BAUER

HERR BAUER

At 77 94 51.	Unter der Nummer 77 94 51.[3]

whole, entire	ganz
the afternoon	der Nachmittag,-e
the whole afternoon	den ganzen Nachmittag

I'll be in my office all afternoon.	Ich bin den ganzen Nachmittag in meinem Büro.

II

II

In the afternoon.	Nachmittags.

to connect	verbinden

MR. WILSON

HERR WILSON

Mr. Bauer, please.	Verbinden Sie mich bitte mit Herrn Bauer.

to call	rufen

SWITCHBOARD

ZENTRALE

I'm ringing.	Ich rufe.

MR. BAUER

HERR BAUER

Bauer speaking.	Hier Bauer.

MR. WILSON	HERR WILSON

This is Mr. Wilson.

Hier Wilson.

    a little while ago
    at my home or office
    called

    vorhin
    bei mir
    angerufen

You called my office a little while
ago Mr. Bauer.

Sie haben vorhin bei mir angerufen,
Herr Bauer.

    about what

    worum

What can I do for you, Mr. Bauer?
('What is the matter at hand, Mr.
Bauer?')

Worum handelt es sich?

    about
    the import regulations
    the new import regulations

    um (prep with acc)
    die Einfuhrbestimmungen
    die neuen Einfuhrbe-
    stimmungen

MR. BAUER	HERR BRAUER

It's about the new import regulations.

Um die neuen Einfuhrbestimmungen.

    exact
    the information
    exact information
    about it, about them

    genau
    die Auskunft, ⁀e
    eine genaue Auskunft
    darüber

I need exact information about them.

Ich brauche eine genaue Auskunft
darüber.

    to fear, to be afraid
    on the telephone
    a bit
    involved, complicated
    a bit complicated

    fürchten
    telephonisch
    etwas
    umständlich
    etwas umständlich

MR. WILSON	HERR WILSON

I'm afraid that would be a bit
complicated on the telephone.

Ich fürchte, das ist telephonisch
etwas umständlich.

    to where I am
    to my office

    zu mir
    zu mir ins Büro

Can't you come to my office?

Können Sie nicht zu mir ins Büro
kommen?

MR. BAUER	HERR BAUER

I'd be glad to. When would it be
convenient for you?

Gern, wann passt es Ihnen?

    tomorrow
    early
    tomorrow morning
    between

    morgen
    früh
    morgen früh
    zwischen

MR. WILSON	HERR WILSON

The best time would be tomorrow
morning between 10 and 11.

Am besten morgen früh zwischen
10 und 11.

I will be	ich werde ... sein

MR. BAUER — **HERR BAUER**

Fine! I'll be at your office at ten-thirty, Mr. Wilson.

Gut! Ich werde um zehn Uhr dreissig bei Ihnen sein, Herr Konsul.

obliged	verbindlich
much obliged	verbindlichen Dank
the telephone call	der Anruf,-e

I'm very much obliged for your call.

Verbindlichen Dank für Ihren Anruf.

nothing	nichts
to thank	danken
nothing to be thanked for	nichts zu danken

MR. WILSON — **HERR WILSON**

Don't mention it, Mr. Bauer.

Nichts zu danken, Herr Bauer.

I'll see you tomorrow then.

Ich sehe Sie dann also morgen.

III

the conversation	das Gespräch,-e
the long distance call	das Ferngespräch,-e
to place (a telephone call)	anmelden
to dial	wählen

Mr. Wiegand would like to place a long distance call and dials zero zero.

Herr Wiegand möchte ein Ferngespräch anmelden und wählt Null Null.

the office	das Amt,-̈er
the long distance office	das Fernamt,-̈er

LONG DISTANCE — **FERNAMT**

Long distance Munich, Operator 6.

Fernamt München, Platz 6.

the placing (of a telephone call)	die Anmeldung,-en
the person-to-person call	die Voranmeldung,-en
person-to-person	mit Voranmeldung

MR. WIEGAND — **HERR WIEGAND**

This is Munich 38 22 55.
I'd like Wiesbanden 3 38 79 please, person-to-person for Mrs. Gisela Wiegand.

Hier München 38 22 55.
Bitte Wiesbaden 3 38 79 mit Voranmeldung für Frau Gisela Wiegand.

to spell	buchstabieren
the name	der Name,-ns,-n[4]

LONG DISTANCE — **FERNAMT**

Please spell your name.

Buchstabieren Sie den Namen bitte.

MR. WIEGAND — **HERR WIEGAND**

W - i - e - g - a - n - d.

Wilhelm-Ida-Emil-Gustav-Anton-Nordpol-Dora.

to repeat	wiederholen

LONG DISTANCE	FERNAMT

Repeating:
Wiesbaden 3 38 79 person-to-person
for Mrs. Gisela Wiegand. That's
W - i - e - g - a - n - d.

Ich wiederhole:
Wiesbaden 3 38 79 mit Voranmeldung
für Frau Gisela Wiegand. (Wilhelm-
Ida-Emil-Gustav-Anton-Nordpol-Dora.)

Your number is 38 22 55.

Für 38 22 55.

to hang up	auflegen

MR. WIEGAND	HERR WIEGAND

Shall I hang up?

Soll ich auflegen?

the telephone set
on the phone, on the wire

der Apparat,-e
am Apparat

LONG DISTANCE	FERNAMT

No, hold on please.
I'm ringing.

Nein, bleiben Sie bitte am Apparat.
Ich rufe.

the party

der Teilnehmer,-

Your party is on the wire now.
Go ahead please.

Teilnehmer ist jetzt am Apparat.
Bitte sprechen.

IV   IV

Buchstabier-Tafel

A – Anton	G – Gustav	O – Otto	U – Ulrich
Ä – Ärger	H – Heinrich	Ö – Ökonom	Ü – Übermut
B – Berta	I – Ida	P – Paula	V – Viktor
C – Cäsar	J – Julius	Q – Quelle	W – Wilhelm
CH – Charlotte	K – Kaufmann	R – Richard	X – Xanthippe
D – Dora	L – Ludwig	S – Samuel	Y – Ypsilon
E – Emil	M – Martha	Sch – Schule	Z – Zacharias
F – Friedrich	N – Nordpol	T – Theodor	

to spell   buchstabieren

Spell the following names: Buchstabieren Sie folgende Namen:

Wilhelmy, Prokosch, Massenhausen, Dreisörner, Pfettrach,
Jemgung, Qualitz, Marxgrün, Vechta, Räderloh, Chalupka

Let's count: Wir zählen:

sixty	sechzig
seventy	siebzig
eighty	achtzig
ninety	neunzig
a hundred	hundert

Say these numbers: Sagen Sie diese Zahlen:

62, 84, 96, 73, 88, 65, 91, 76, 67, 89

Give the following telephone numbers: Geben Sie folgende Telefonnummern:

Berlin 72 43 61, München 8 29 15, Frankfurt 33 17 45, Bremen 1 63 26

Mühldorf 21 00, Rosenheim 5 49, Erding 69, Ingolstadt 3-1 93

Notes to the Basic Sentences

[1] G.m.b.H. is the abbreviation for Gesellschaft mit beschränkter Haftung, meaning "limited liability company". It is similar to the abbreviations "Inc." and "Ltd." with which you are familiar.

[2] möchte(n) is often used to express a request or polite command to a third person indicated by the subject of the sentence:

> Sie möchten Ihre Frau anrufen, Herr Konsul.
>
> Your wife wants you to call her, Mr. Wilson.

> Rufen Sie meine Frau an und sagen Sie ihr, sie möchte um 5 Uhr kommen.
>
> Call up my wife and tell her to come at 5 o'clock.

[3] German telephone numbers are usually written in two-digit groups: 77 94 51. They are spoken both by decades and by digits, i.e., for this number you will hear both: siebenundsiebzig vierundneunzig einundfünfzig and sieben sieben neun vier fünf eins.

[4] The forms of this noun in the singular are: der Name, den Namen, dem Namen, des Namens; its plural is regular.

Notes on Pronunciation

A. Some difficult clusters

In Unit 4 we presented the ich-sound and the ach-sound after and between vowels and in combination with certain consonants. Unit 5 dealt with the ts-cluster in initial, final and inter-vocalic position. These sounds also occur in complex clusters, as the following examples show. Practice them with your instructor.

Practice 1

nicht	durch	gänzlich	wenigsten	acht	lachst
nichts	Furcht	herzlich	nächsten	achtzehn	machst
rechts	furchtbar	weichlich	höchste	achtzig	buchst
sechzehn	fürchten	rechtzeitig	möglichst	Hochzeit	lochst

B. Review of vowel contrasts

Up to now we dealt with the German sounds which are most different from English sounds. By way of review we will drill the most difficult of these sounds again, starting with the contrasts between -o- and -ö- and between -u- and -ü-.

Practice 2

grosse – Grösse	Tochter – Töchter
schon – schön	offen – Löffel
Ofen – Öfen	fordere – fördere

Practice 3

Tute	-	Tüte	Mutter	- Mütter
Huhn	-	kühn	rucken	- Rücken
Tour	-	Tür	Hunde	- Büde

Practice 4

Söhne	-	Sühne	Götter	- Mütter
töte	-	Tüte	Köche	- Küche
Föhre	-	führe	schösse	- Schüsse

(End of Tape 6A)

Notes on Grammar
(For Home Study)

A. ADJECTIVES

I. Adjectives have occurred in a number of sentences in the first five units:

München ist eine <u>schöne</u> Stadt.	Munich is a <u>beautiful</u> city.
Das Essen ist dort sehr <u>gut</u>.	The food is very <u>good</u> there.
In welcher Gegend ist das <u>amerikanische</u> Konsulat?	What part of town is the <u>American</u> Consulate in?
Er trifft einen <u>alten</u> Bekannten.	He meets an <u>old</u> acquaintance.
Hier ist ein <u>guter</u> Roman.	Here's a <u>good</u> novel.

Note that some of these adjectives have endings: <u>schön-e</u>, <u>amerikanisch-e</u>, <u>alt-en</u>, <u>gut-er</u>; while some do not: <u>gut</u>, <u>interessant</u>. The adjectives without endings are commonly called Predicate Adjectives; they are often seperated by a verb from the noun or pronoun they modify. The adjectives with endings are commonly called Attributive Adjectives. They occur in a SPECIFIER-ADJECTIVE-NOUN sequence: <u>das amerikanische Konsulat,</u> <u>ein guter Roman.</u>

II. Predicate adjectives NEVER HAVE ENDINGS. They may occur either before or after the noun or pronoun they modify. Here are some further examples.

Meine Schreibmaschine ist <u>kaputt</u>.	My typewriter is <u>out of order</u>.
Die Wirtschaftsabteilung ist nicht sehr <u>gross</u>.	The Economic Section is not very <u>large</u>.
Sehr <u>schön</u> ist diese neue französische Briefmarke.	(A) very <u>beautiful</u> (specimen) is this new French stamp.

III. Adjectives are also used as adverbs in German. Like predicate adjectives they NEVER HAVE ENDINGS:

Ich verstehe Sie <u>gut</u>.	I understand you <u>well</u>.
Sprechen Sie bitte <u>langsam</u>.	Please speak <u>slowly</u>.
Er spricht <u>ausgezeichnet</u> deutsch.	He speaks German <u>excellently</u>.

IV. Attributive adjectives in SPECIFIER-ADJECTIVE-NOUN sequences ALWAYS HAVE
    ENDINGS.

  1. After <u>der</u>-type specifiers the adjective endings are <u>-e</u> or <u>-en</u>:

     Nom   Der <u>neue</u> Vizekonsul wohnt in diesem Etagenhaus.
     Acc   Den <u>neuen</u> Vizekonsul kenne ich noch nicht.
     Dat   Meine Sekretärin spricht mit dem <u>neuen</u> Vizekonsul.
     Gen   Kennen Sie die Frau des <u>neuen</u> Vizekonsuls?

     Nom   Dieses <u>grosse</u> Hotel gehört meinem Vater.
     Acc   Dieses <u>grosse</u> Hotel kenne ich nicht.
     Dat   In diesem <u>grossen</u> Hotel wohnt Herr Becker.
     Gen   Der Portier dieses <u>grossen</u> Hotels zeigt es Ihnen.

     Nom   Wo ist hier die <u>amerikanische</u> Botschaft?
     Acc   Ich suche die <u>amerikanische</u> Botschaft.
     Dat   Sie arbeitet in der <u>amerikanischen</u> Botschaft.
     Gen   Eine Sekretärin der <u>amerikanischen</u> Botschaft wohnt in
           der Schubertstrasse.

     Nom   Wieviel kosten die <u>neuen</u> Bleistifte?
     Acc   Brauchen Sie schon die <u>neuen</u> Bleistifte?
     Dat   Schreiben Sie mit den <u>neuen</u> Bleistiften?
     Gen   Geben Sie mir bitte einen der <u>neuen</u> Bleistifte.

  2. After <u>ein</u>-type specifiers the adjective endings are <u>-e</u>, <u>-en</u>, <u>-er</u> or <u>-es</u>:

     Nom   Das ist ein <u>amerikanischer</u> Schriftsteller.
     Acc   Ich kenne einen <u>amerikanischen</u> Schriftsteller.
     Dat   Er spricht mit einem <u>amerikanischen</u> Schriftsteller.
     Gen   Sie ist die Frau eines <u>amerikanischen</u> Schriftstellers.

     Nom   Ist das Ihr <u>neues</u> Auto?
     Acc   Haben Sie schon Ihr <u>neues</u> Auto?
     Dat   Fahren Sie mit Ihrem <u>neuen</u> Auto?
     Gen   Ist die Tür Ihres <u>neuen</u> Autos schon kaputt?

     Nom   Frau Keller ist meine <u>neue</u> Sekretärin.
     Acc   Kennen Sie meine <u>neue</u> Sekretärin?
     Dat   Sprechen Sie mit meiner <u>neuen</u> Sekretärin!
     Gen   Das ist die Schreibmaschine meiner <u>neuen</u> Sekretärin.

     Nom   Unsere <u>alten</u> Kollegen fahren jetzt nach Amerika.
     Acc   Wir besuchen unsere <u>alten</u> Kollegen in Berlin.
     Dat   Wir möchten mit unseren <u>alten</u> Kollegen im Hofbräuhaus essen.
     Gen   Die Büros unserer <u>alten</u> Kollegen sind im ersten Stock.

  3. The noun is not always present in a sequence; it may be <u>understood</u>
     from the context. In any case the form of the adjective remains the same.

     Fahren Sie mit dem alten   Are you going in the old car or in
     Wagen oder mit dem neuen?   the new one?
     Wissen Sie seine neue   Do you know his new address?
     Adresse?
     Ich habe hier nur seine   I only have his old one here.
     alte.
     Ist das ein altes Buch   Is that an old book or a new one?
     oder ein neues?

     Notice that we usually substitute the pronoun "one" in English for the
     noun that is omitted.

4. If there is more than one adjective in a sequence, they all have the same form:

Hier ist ein guter neuer Roman.	Here's a good new novel.
Wer wohnt in diesem schönen alten Haus?	Who lives in this beautiful old house?
Das ist eine alte amerikanische Briefmarke.	That's an old American stamp.

5. Except for the number "one", which is the specifier ein, and ordinal numbers like "first", "second", etc., which will be dealt with later on, the numerals have NO ENDINGS and do not affect the forms of adjectives in a SPECIFIER-ADJECTIVE-NOUN sequence at all:

Das sind <u>meine</u> zwei <u>alten Kollegen</u>.	Those are <u>my</u> two <u>old colleagues</u>.
Wo sind <u>unsere</u> drei <u>neuen Bleistifte</u>?	Where are <u>our</u> three <u>new pencils</u>?

V. Attributive adjectives are sometimes used as nouns. Their forms are the same as those outlined above.

Im Konsulat trifft er einen alten <u>Bekannten</u>.	In the consulate he meets an old acquaintance.
Ja, die <u>Angehörigen</u> meiner Frau leben hier.	Yes, (the members of) my wife's family live here.

These nouns may refer to either men or women, but their forms change accordingly, and also depending on whether they are preceded by an <u>ein</u>-type specifier or a <u>der</u>-type specifier.

Er ist ein alter <u>Bekannter</u> von mir.	He's an old acquaintance of mine.
Sie ist eine alte <u>Bekannte</u> von mir.	She's an old acquaintance of mine.
Der <u>Bekannte</u> meiner Schwester kommt aus Berlin.	My sister's (gentleman) friend comes from Berlin.
Die <u>Bekannte</u> Ihres Bruders ist sehr nett.	Your brother's (lady) friend is very nice.
Die <u>Bekannten</u> meiner Eltern fahren heute nach Bonn.	My parents' friends are driving to Bonn today.

Here is a list of similar nouns which have occurred thus far:

		Referring to Men	Referring to Woman	Plural
(a)	With <u>der</u>-type specifier	der Beamte		die Beamten
		der Deutsche	die Deutsche	die Deutschen
		der Angehörige	die Angehörige	die Angehörigen
		der Staatsangehörige	die Staatsangehörige	die Staatsange-hörigen
		der Verwandte	die Verwandte	die Verwandten
(b)	With <u>ein</u>-type specifier	ein Beamter		unsere Beamten
		ein Deutscher	eine Deutsche	keine Deutschen
		ein Angehöriger	eine Angehörige	meine Angehörigen
		ein Staatsange-höriger	eine Staatsange-hörige	keine Staatsange-hörigen
		ein Verwandter	eine Verwandte	ihre Verwandten

B. TIME EXPRESSIONS

    I. We have encountered several references to time thus far:

Ich war <u>zwei Monate</u> in Bonn.	I was in Bonn for two months.
<u>In zehn Minuten</u> sind Sie da.	You'll be there in ten minutes.
Kommen Sie <u>am nächsten</u> Sonntag zu uns.	Come and see us next Sunday.
Konsul Wilson ist leider <u>im Augenblick</u> nicht im Büro.	I'm sorry, Mr. Wilson is not in the office at the moment.
Ich bin <u>den ganzen Nachmittag</u> in meinem Büro.	I'll be in my office all afternoon.

        1. Time reference can be given by a prepositional phrase with <u>in</u> or <u>an</u> followed by a Dative form of the noun.

        2. Time reference can be given by an Accusative form of the noun or specifier-adjective-noun phrase.

        3. Prepositional phrases or noun phrases referring to time <u>precede</u> phrases referring to place.

C. QUESTION-WORD PRONOUNS WITH PREPOSITIONS

    I. When a question-word pronoun in a prepositional phrase refers to a human being, the regular pronoun form is used.

Mit wem spricht er?	Who is he talking to?
Zu wem soll ich gehen?	Who am I supposed to go to?
Für wen tun Sie das?	Who are you doing that for?

Conversational English usually ends the sentence with the preposition, although formal and literary usage permit placing it at the beginning: For whom are you doing that? Note that German however always requires the sequence of preposition first, followed by object form (accusative or dative) of the pronoun.

    II. When an inanimate object is referred to, a question-word pronoun in a prepositional phrase may be replaced by the special form <u>wo-</u>.

Um was handelt es sich? or	
Worum handelt es sich?	What is it about?
Wovon spricht sie?	What is she speaking of?
Womit schreiben Sie lieber, mit dem Füller oder mit der Schreibmaschine?	What do you prefer to write with, pen or typewriter?

This is similar to the replacement of the pronoun by <u>da-</u> in such forms as <u>daneben</u>, <u>damit</u>, <u>davon</u>, etc., as noted in Unit 3. If the preposition begins with a vowel the special combining form is <u>wor-</u> (<u>wor</u>um, <u>wor</u>auf, <u>wor</u>an, etc.)

SUBSTITUTION DRILL - Part I

    This is a drill on the <u>forms</u> of the adjectives in specifier-adjective-noun sequences. As in Unit 3, 4 and 5 the sequences are presented .systematically by <u>der</u>-nouns, <u>das</u>-nouns and <u>die</u>-nouns first and then at random. Drill for accuracy, fluency and speed.

1. Ist das <u>der neue Wagen</u>?

    a. Ober - Kollege - Konsul -   der neue Ober - der neue Kollege -
       Apparat - Füller   der neue Konsul - der neue Apparat -
                                   der neue Füller

b. Büro - Telephon - Generalkonsulat - Haus - Geschäft

   das neue Büro - das neue Telephon -
   das neue Generalkonsulat - das neue
   Haus - das neue Geschäft

c. Abteilung - Nummer - Wohnung -
   Adresse - Sekretärin

   die neue Abteilung - die neue Nummer -
   die neue Wohnung - die neue Adresse -
   die neue Sekretärin

d. Telephon - Wagen - Wohnung -
   Konsul - Geschäft - Haus -
   Kollege - Adresse - Füller -
   Nummer - Abteilung - Generalkon-
   sulat - Apparat - Büro - Ober -
   Sekretärin

   das neue Telephon - der neue Wagen -
   die neue Wohnung - der neue Konsul -
   das neue Geschäft - das neue Haus -
   der neue Kollege - die neue Adresse -
   der neue Füller - die neue Nummer -
   die neue Abteilung - das neue Generalkonsulat - der neue Apparat - das neue
   Büro - der neue Ober - die neue
   Sekretärin

2. Er kennt <u>den alten Portier</u>.

a. Beamten - Schriftsteller -
   Polizisten - Herrn Becker -
   Markt - Park

   den alten Beamten - den alten Schriftsteller - den alten Polizisten - den
   alten Herrn Becker - den alten Markt -
   den alten Park

b. Theater - Haus - Schloss -
   Museum - Hotel

   das alte Theater - das alte Haus - das
   alte Schloss - das alte Museum - das
   alte Hotel

c. Universität - Dame - Bibliothek -
   Stadt - Frau

   die alte Universität - die alte Dame -
   die alte Bibliothek - die alte Stadt -
   die alte Frau

d. Bibliothek - Polizisten -
   Schloss - Beamten - Frau -
   Hotel - Stadt - Schriftsteller -
   Markt - Dame - Park - Museum -
   Theater - Universität - Portier

   die alte Bibliothek - den alten Polizisten - das alte Schloss - den alten
   Beamten - die alte Frau - das alte
   Hotel - die alte Stadt - den alten
   Schriftsteller - den alten Markt -
   die alte Dame - den alten Park - das
   alte Museum - das alte Theater - die
   alte Universität - den alten Portier

3. Er geht zu <u>dem alten Bahnhof</u>.

a. Flughafen - Parkplatz - Ratskeller

   zu dem alten Flughafen - zu dem alten
   Parkplatz - zu dem alten Ratskeller

b. Hotel - Büro - Theater - Museum -
   Rathaus

   zu dem alten Hotel - zu dem alten
   Büro - zu dem alten Theater - zu dem
   alten Museum - zu dem alten Rathaus

c. Universität - Botschaft - Bibliothek - Bank

   zu der alten Universität - zu der
   alten Botschaft - zu der alten Bibliothek - zu der alten Bank

d. Bahnhof - Hotel - Museum - Flug-
   hafen - Rathaus - Bibliothek -
   Büro - Ratskeller - Bank -
   Theater - Botschaft - Parkplatz -
   Universität

   zu dem alten Bahnhof - zu dem alten
   Hotel - zu dem alten Museum - zu dem
   alten Flughafen - zu dem alten Rathaus -
   zu der alten Bibliothek - zu dem alten
   Büro - zu dem alten Ratskeller - zu
   der alten Bank - zu dem alten Theater -
   zu der alten Botschaft - zu dem alten
   Parkplatz - zu der alten Universität

4. Hier ist ein guter Bleistift.

   a. Füller – Koffer – Roman –   ein guter Füller – ein guter Koffer –
   Parkplatz – Wein   ein guter Roman – ein guter Parkplatz –
         ein guter Wein

   b. Buch – Theater – Restaurant –   ein gutes Buch – ein gutes Theater –
   Café – Geschäft   ein gutes Restaurant – ein gutes
         Café – ein gutes Geschäft

   c. Universität – Bibliothek –   eine gute Universität – eine gute
   Schreibmaschine – Zigarre –   Bibliothek – eine gute Schreibmaschine –
   Zeitung   eine gute Zigarre – eine gute Zeitung

   d. Schreibmaschine – Bleistift –   eine gute Schreibmaschine – ein guter
   Geschäft – Füller – Universität –   Bleistift – ein gutes Geschäft – ein
   Koffer – Zeitung – Restaurant –   guter Füller – eine gute Universität –
   Parkplatz – Roman – Zigarre –   ein guter Koffer – eine gute Zeitung –
   Buch – Café – Wein – Theater –   ein gutes Restaurant – ein guter
   Bibliothek   Parkplatz – ein guter Roman – eine
         gute Zigarre – ein gutes Buch – ein
         gutes Café – ein guter Wein – ein
         gutes Theater – eine gute Bibliothek

5. Ich suche einen guten Wagen.

   a. Füller – Roman – Wein –   einen guten Füller – einen guten
   Bleistift – Stadtplan   Roman – einen guten Wein – einen
         guten Bleistift – einen guten
         Stadtplan

   b. Buch – Hotel – Auto – Café –   ein gutes Buch – ein gutes Hotel –
   Restaurant   ein gutes Auto – ein gutes Café –
         ein gutes Restaurant

   c. Zeitung – Universität – Biblio-   eine gute Zeitung – eine gute Uni-
   thek – Sekretärin – Schreibma-   versität – eine gute Bibliothek –
   schine   eine gute Sekretärin – eine gute
         Schreibmaschine

   d. Roman – Universität – Wagen –   einen guten Roman – eine gute Universi-
   Auto – Hotel – Füller –   tät – einen guten Wagen – ein gutes
   Zeitung – Restaurant – Wein –   Auto – ein gutes Hotel – einen guten
   Sekretärin – Café – Stadtplan –   Füller – eine gute Zeitung – ein
   Buch – Schreibmaschine – Blei-   gutes Restaurant – einen guten Wein –
   stift – Bibliothek   eine gute Sekretärin – ein gutes
         Café – einen guten Stadtplan – ein
         gutes Buch – eine gute Schreibmaschine –
         einen guten Bleistift – eine gute
         Bibliothek –

6. Hier ist die Adresse eines alten
   Bekannten.

   a. Kollegen – Schriftstellers –   eines alten Kollegen – éines alten
   Beamten – Diplomaten – Konsuls   Schriftstellers – eines alten Beamten –
         eines alten Diplomaten – eines alten
         Konsuls

   b. Dame – Amerikanerin – Tante –   einer alten Dame – einer alten Ameri-
   Universität – Sekretärin   kanerin – einer alten Tante – einer
         alten Universität – einer alten Sekre-
         tärin

(Drill No. 6 continued on the next page.)

c. Beamten - Amerikanerin -
   Bekannten - Dame - Kollegen -
   Tante - Sekretärin - Schriftstellers - Universität - Diplomaten - Konsuls

eines alten Beamten - einer alten
Amerikanerin - eines alten Bekannten -
einer alten Dame - eines alten Kollegen -
einer alten Tante - einer alten Sekretärin - eines alten Schriftstellers -
einer alten Universität - eines alten
Diplomaten - eines alten Konsuls

7. Können Sie mir die Adresse _eines_
   guten Geschäfts geben?

   a. Hotels - Restaurants - Cafés

   eines guten Hotels - eines guten
   Restaurants - eines guten Cafés

Part II

In the following drill various adjectives which have occurred up to this
point are employed, in both predicate and attributive function.

8. Unser Auto ist nicht _alt_.

   kaputt - schön - gross - neu - gut

9. Diese Auskunft ist _gut_.

   genau - neu - wichtig - besser -
   dringend

10. Die Einfuhrbestimmungen sind _neu_.

    besser - gut - alt - wichtig

11. Sie haben vorhin _bei mir_ angerufen.

    uns - ihm - ihnen - ihr - Ihnen -
    dem Diplomaten - meiner Tante -
    seinen Eltern - ihrem Bruder - unserer
    Schwester - meiner Sekretärin

12. _Ich_ habe _meine_ Zigaretten nicht
    bei _mir_.

   wir

   Wir haben unsere Zigaretten nicht bei
   uns.

   Herr Müller

   Herr Müller hat seine Zigaretten nicht
   bei sich.

   meine Frau

   Meine Frau hat ihre Zigaretten nicht
   bei sich.

   sie (pl)

   Sie haben ihre Zigaretten nicht bei
   sich.

   Ihr Mann

   Ihr Mann hat seine Zigaretten nicht
   bei sich.

   Fräulein König

   Fräulein König hat ihre Zigaretten
   nicht bei sich.

   sie (sg)

   Sie hat ihre Zigaretten nicht bei sich.

13. Das sind die _alten Füller_.

   amerikanisch- Konsuln   ... die amerikanischen Konsuln
   französisch- Bücher   ... die französchen Bücher
   deutsch- Zigaretten   ... die deutschen Zigaretten
   alt- Zeitungen   ... die alten Zeitungen
   wichtig- Nummern   ... die wichtigen Nummern
   neu- Bleistifte   ... die neuen Bleistifte
   schön- Geschäfte   ... die schönen Geschäfte

14. Das sind <u>seine grossen neuen Autos</u>.

    unser- schön- alt- Restaurants   ... unsere schönen alten Restaurants
    mein- alt- kaputt- Füller   ... meine alten kaputten Füller
    ihr- neu- französisch- Bücher   ... ihre neuen französischen Bücher
    unser- gross- amerikanisch-   ... unsere grossen amerikanischen
    Wagen   Wagen
    ihr- schön- deutsch- Romane   ... ihre schönen deutschen Romane

15. Er spricht mit <u>den neuen Vize-
konsuln</u>.

    französisch- Schriftstellern   ... den französischen Schriftstellern
    nett- Amerikanern   ... den netten Amerikanern
    wichtig- Beamten   ... den wichtigen Beamten
    alt- Deutschen   ... den alten Deutschen
    nett- Sekretärinnen   ... den netten Sekretärinnen
    amerikanisch- Kollegen   ... den amerikanischen Kollegen
    deutsch- Diplomaten   ... den deutschen Diplomaten

16. Das ist <u>das neue grosse Kino</u>.

    alt- deutsch- Zeitung   ... die alte deutsche Zeitung
    neu- amerikanisch- Konsul   ... der neue amerikanische Konsul
    berühmt- alt- Universität   ... die berühmte alte Universität
    gross- neu- Hotel   ... das grosse neue Hotel
    berühmt- alt- Rathaus   ... das berühmte alte Rathaus
    kaputt- alt- Schreibmaschine   ... die kaputte alte Schreibmaschine
    nett- alt- Herr   ... der nette alte Herr

17. Er zeigt uns die <u>guten deutschen
Zigarren</u>.

    schön- alt- Bücher   ... die schönen alten Bücher
    neu- amerikanisch- Zeitungen   ... die neuen amerikanischen Zeitungen
    gut- französisch- Weine   ... die guten französischen Weine
    neu- gut- Schreibmaschinen   ... die neuen guten Schreibmaschinen
    berühmt- alt- Briefmarken   ... die berühmten alten Briefmarken

18. Sie kennen <u>unsere netten deutschen
Cafés</u>.

    kein- alt- französisch- Romane   ... keine alten französischen Romane
    unser- berühmt- alt- Schlösser ... unsere berühmten alten Schlösser
    ihr- neu- gross- Abteilungen   ... ihre neuen grossen Abteilungen
    sein- schön- gross- Geschäfte ... seine schönen grossen Geschäfte
    unser- wichtig- neu- Fragebogen ... unsere wichtigen neuen Fragebogen
    ihr- nett- neu- Wohnungen   ... ihre netten neuen Wohnungen
    unser- umständlich- deutsch-   ... unsere umständlichen deutschen
    Geschäftsbriefe   Geschäftsbriefe

19. Das ist <u>unser altes deutsches Hotel</u>.

    ein- wichtig- amerikanisch-   ... ein wichtiger amerikanischer
    Schriftsteller   Schriftsteller
    ihr- schön- neu- Schreibmaschine ... ihre schöne neue Schreibmaschine
    unser- berühmt- alt- Universität ... unsere berühmte alte Universität
    sein- alt- kaputt- Füller   ... sein alter kaputter Füller
    unser- gross- alt- Wohnung   ... unsere grosse alte Wohnung
    ihr- nett- neu- Sekretärin   ... ihre nette neue Sekretärin
    sein- gut- neu- Roman   ... sein guter neuer Roman
    ein- neu- französisch- Zeitung ... eine neue französische Zeitung

20. Er hat <u>einen neuen deutschen Wagen</u>.

    schön- gross- Wohnung   ... eine schöne grosse Wohnung
    alt- kaputt- Telephon   ... ein altes kaputtes Telephon
    gut- deutsch- Schreibmaschine   ... eine gute deutsche Schreibmaschine
    schön- französisch- Namen   ... einen schönen französischen Namen
    gross- neu- Büro   ... ein grosses neues Büro
    nett- alt- Sekretärin   ... eine nette alte Sekretärin
    neu- amerikanisch- Füller   ... einen neuen amerikanischen Füller
    nett- amerikanisch- Kollegen   ... einen netten amerikanischen Kollegen

21. Zeigen Sie mir <u>einen der kaputten Füller</u>.

    französisch- Zeitungen   ... eine der französischen Zeitungen
    neu- Fragebogen   ... einen der neuen Fragebogen
    deutsch- Romane   ... einen der deutschen Romane
    neu- Büros   ... eins der neuen Büros
    amerikanisch- Briefmarken   ... eine der amerikanischen Briefmarken
    gross- Etagenhäuser   ... eins der grossen Etagenhäuser
    alt- Wagen   ... einen der alten Wagen

22. Sie wohnen in <u>einem grossen neuen Hotel</u>.

    schön- französisch- Stadt   ... einer schönen französischen Stadt
    gross- amerikanisch- Etagenhaus ... einem grossen amerikanischen Etagenhaus
    schön- alt- Park   ... einem schönen alten Park
    nett- deutsch- Haus   ... einem netten deutschen Haus
    gross- neu- Wohnung   ... einer grossen neuen Wohnung
    schön- gross- Neubau   ... einem schönen grossen Neubau

23. Es handelt sich um <u>eine seiner neuen Sekretärinnen</u>.

    unser- deutsch- Schriftsteller ... einen unserer deutschen Schriftsteller
    Ihr- neu- Formulare   ... eins Ihrer neuen Formulare
    unser- dringend- Konferenzen   ... eine unserer dringenden Konferenzen
    unser- amerikanisch- Vizekonsuln ... einen unserer amerikanischen Vizekonsuln
    Ihr- neu- Einfuhrbestimmungen   ... eine Ihrer neuen Einfuhrbestimmungen
    sein- wichtig- Briefe   ... einen seiner wichtigen Briefe
    ihr- deutsch- Geschäfte   ... eins ihrer deutschen Geschäfte

CONVERSION DRILL

In the following sentences convert the underlined nouns to the plural as indicated, making any other necessary changes.

1. Hier ist der schöne <u>Park</u>.   Hier sind die schönen Parks.
2. Wo ist mein neuer <u>Bleistift</u>?   Wo sind meine neuen Bleistifte?
3. Hier wohnt unser guter <u>Bekannter</u>. Hier wohnen unsere guten Bekannten.
4. Er kennt den französischen <u>Roman</u>. Er kennt die französischen Romane.
5. Sie liest die amerikanische <u>Zeitung</u>. Sie liest die amerikanischen Zeitungen.
6. Ihre nette <u>Verwandte</u> besucht uns heute. Ihre netten Verwandten besuchen uns heute.
7. Wie gefällt Ihnen die grosse <u>Wohnung</u>? Wie gefallen Ihnen die grossen Wohnungen?
8. Hier ist kein deutscher <u>Beamter</u>. Hier sind keine deutschen Beamten.
9. Dieser schöne <u>Koffer</u> gehört mir nicht. Diese schönen Koffer gehören mir nicht.
10. Hier gibt es keinen grossen <u>Parkplatz</u>. Hier gibt es keine grossen Parkplätze.

11. Mein amerikanischer <u>Kollege</u> ist <u>Vizekonsul</u>.

Meine amerikanischen Kollegen sind Vizekonsuln.

12. Er spricht mit der <u>Sekretärin</u> der neuen <u>Abteilung</u>.

Er spricht mit den Sekretärinnen der neuen Abteilungen.

13. Wollen Sie das nicht der netten <u>Amerikanerin</u> zeigen?

Wollen Sie das nicht den netten Amerikanerinnen zeigen?

14. Hier ist die neue <u>Schreibmaschine</u> meiner <u>Schwester</u>.

Hier sind die neuen Schreibmaschinen meiner Schwestern.

15. Kennen Sie das nette <u>Buch</u> dieses <u>Schriftstellers</u>?

Kennen Sie die netten Bücher dieser Schriftsteller?

16. Ich kann mit diesem kaputten <u>Füller</u> nicht schreiben.

Ich kann mit diesen kaputten Füllern nicht schreiben.

17. Ist das der neue <u>Pfennig</u>?

Sind das die neuen Pfennige?

VARIATION DRILL

1. <u>Mit wem spricht Herr Wiegand gerade?</u>

<u>Who is Mr. Wiegand just talking to?</u>

   a. To whom may I go in this matter?

Zu wem darf ich in dieser Angelegenheit gehen?

   b. Who would you like to talk to?

Mit wem möchten Sie sprechen?

   c. Who does this young man work for?

Für wen arbeitet dieser junge Mann?

   d. Who is it about?

Um wen handelt es sich denn?

   e. Who are you speaking of actually?

Von wem sprechen Sie eigentlich?

2. <u>Wovon spricht die neue Sekretärin?</u>

<u>What is the new secretary talking about?</u>

   a. What are you writing with, pencil or pen ('ink')?

Womit schreiben Sie, mit Bleistift oder mit Tinte?

   b. What do you need this information for?

Wofür brauchen Sie diese Auskunft?

   c. What does he mention ('write of') in his letter?

Wovon schreibt er in seinem Brief?

   d. What is it about?

Worum handelt es sich?

3. <u>Hoffentlich ist diese Auskunft genau.</u>

<u>I hope this information is accurate.</u>

   a. I hope the book is good.

Hoffentlich ist das Buch gut.

   b. Is the typewriter new?

Ist die Schreibmaschine neu?

   c. Unfortunately the fountain pen is broken.

Leider ist der Füller kaputt.

   d. Is the conference important?

Ist die Konferenz wichtig?

4. <u>Dieses Formular ist neu.</u>

<u>This form is new.</u>

   a. The office is unfortunately not very large.

Das Büro ist leider nicht sehr gross.

   b. The park is very beautiful

Der Park ist sehr schön.

   c. This apartment is very nice.

Diese Wohnung ist sehr nett.

   d. This long distance call is urgent.

Dieses Ferngespräch ist dringend.

5. <u>Dieser Brief ist sehr wichtig.</u>

<u>This letter is very important.</u>

   <u>Das ist ein wichtiger Brief.</u>

<u>This is an important letter.</u>

   a. The book is very good. I'm reading a good book.

Das Buch ist sehr gut. Ich lese ein gutes Buch.

   b. Is the palace famous? That is a famous palace.

Ist das Schloss berühmt? Das ist ein berühmtes Schloss.

   c. The telephone call is urgent. You have an urgent telephone call.

Der Anruf ist dringend. Sie haben einen dringenden Anruf.

(Drill No. 5 is continued on the next page.)

d. His information is very
accurate.
   Seine Auskunft ist sehr genau.

I need ('an') accurate
information.
   Ich brauche eine genaue Auskunft.

e. This pencil is broken
unfortunately.
   Dieser Bleistift ist leider kaputt.

I can't write with this broken
pencil.
   Ich kann mit diesem kaputten Bleistift
nicht schreiben.

6. <u>Die deutsche Sekretärin legt gerade
den Hörer auf.</u>
   <u>The German secretary ist just hanging
up (the receiver).</u>

a. The nice American vice consul
is not coming back today.
   Der nette amerikanische Vizekonsul
kommt heute nicht zurück.

b. The new vice consul in the visa
section places a call to
Wiesbaden.
   Der neue Vizekonsul der Visa-Abteilung
meldet ein Gespräch nach Wiesbaden an.

c. The American officer lifts off
the receiver.
   Der amerikanische Beamte nimmt den
Hörer ab.

d. My German friend doesn't like
to call me up at the office.
   Mein deutscher Bekannter ruft mich nicht
gern im Büro an.

7. <u>Das Telephon klingelt im
amerikanischen Generalkonsulat.</u>
   <u>The telephone rings in the
American Consulate General.</u>

a. They live in a nice new
building.
   Sie wohnen in einem schönen Neubau.

b. He works at ('in') the American
Embassy.
   Er arbeitet in der amerikanischen
Botschaft.

c. We live in an old apartment
house.
   Wir wohnen in einem alten Etagenhaus.

d. You'll reach him in the new
visa section.
   Sie erreichen ihn in der neuen Visa-
Abteilung.

e. She works in our new office.
   Sie arbeitet in unserem neuen Büro.

8. <u>Hier ist die Adresse des neuen
Konsuls.</u>
   <u>Here's the new consul's address.</u>

a. I'm going in an old friend's
car.
   Ich fahre mit dem Wagen eines alten
Bekannten.

b. She's the wife of the American
vice consul.
   Sie ist die Frau des amerikanischen
Vizekonsuls.

c. That's the information of a
German official.
   Das ist die Auskunft eines deutschen
Beamten.

d. She's the secretary of our new
department.
   Sie ist die Sekretärin unserer neuen
Abteilung.

e. We'll talk to the wife of the
famous writer.
   Wir sprechen mit der Frau des
berühmten Schriftstellers.

9. <u>Kennen Sie den amerikanischen
Generalkonsul?</u>
   <u>Do you know the American Consul General?</u>

a. Do you need the exact address
of Mr. Allen?
   Brauchen Sie die genaue Adresse von
Herrn Allen?

b. Is she looking for the old
secretary of the Economic
Section?
   Sucht sie die alte Sekretärin der
Wirtschaftsabteilung?

c. Is she connecting the French
official with the customs office
or the Economic Section?
   Verbindet sie den französischen Beamten
mit dem Zoll oder mit der Wirtschaftsabteilung?

d. Is he going to give her the exact
information?
   Gibt er ihr die genaue Auskunft?

e. Are you going to call up the
American Foreign Service Officer?
   Rufen Sie den amerikanischen Diplomaten
an?

(End of Tape 6B)

10. Sie schreibt ihrem Kollegen
    einen wichtigen Brief.

    a. I'll show the official my
       American passport.
    b. He's taking a nice German pen
       along for his (gentleman)
       relative.
    c. She's giving her (lady)
       relative an English novel.
    d. He'll lend your (lady) friend
       his new typewriter.

11. Er bleibt das ganze Jahr in
    Frankfurt.

    a. He's in an important con-
       ference all afternoon.
    b. We still have to work in the
       office for an hour.
    c. He has to live one month in a
       ('the') hotel.
    d. We're staying in Munich for a
       week.
    e. I can only stay a moment
       unfortunately.

12. Er will uns am nächsten Montag
    besuchen.

    a. We're going to Germany in one
       week.
    b. I intend to go and eat in an
       hour.
    c. She's coming to Bonn next
       Tuesday.
    d. I'm going to the post office
       in half an hour.
    e. They're going to America in
       two months.

She's writing her colleague an
important letter.

Ich zeige dem Beamten meinen amerikanischen Pass.
Er nimmt seinem Verwandten einen
schönen deutschen Füller mit.

Sie gibt ihrer Verwandten einen
englischen Roman.
Er leiht Ihrer Bekannten seine neue
Schreibmaschine.

He's going to stay in Frankfurt the
whole year.

Er ist den ganzen Nachmittag in einer
wichtigen Konferenz.
Wir müssen noch eine Stunde im Büro
arbeiten.
Er muss einen Monat im Hotel wohnen.

Wir bleiben eine Woche in München.

Ich kann leider nur einen Augenblick
bleiben.

He wants to visit us next Monday.

Wir fahren in einer Woche nach
Deutschland.
Ich will in einer Stunde essen gehen.

Sie kommt am nächsten Dienstag nach
Bonn.
Ich gehe in einer halben Stunde
zur Post.
Sie fahren in zwei Monaten nach
Amerika.

VOCABULARY DRILL

1. verbinden - "to connect"

    a. Können Sie mich mit der
       deutschen Botschaft verbinden?
    b. Sie verbindet ihn mit dem
       Vizekonsul.
    c. Verbinden Sie mich bitte mit
       Nummer 77 10 81.
    d. Sie verbindet ihn mit dem
       Generalkonsulat.

Can you connect me with the German
Embassy?
She connects him with the vice-consul.

Please connect me with Number 77 10 81.

She connects him with the consulate
general.

2. sobald wie möglich - "as soon as possible"

    a. Kommen Sie bitte so bald wie
       möglich.
    b. Ich schreibe ihm sobald wie
       möglich.
    c. Er kommt so bald wie möglich
       zu Ihnen.
    d. Wir sollen sobald wie möglich
       anrufen.
    e. Die Konferenz muss sobald wie
       möglich sein.

Come as soon as you can, please.

I'll write him as soon as possible.

He's coming to see you as soon as he
can.
We're supposed to call as soon as
possible.
The conference has to be as soon as
possible.

3. <u>anrufen</u> - "to call up"

   a. Die Sekretärin ruft nachher   The secretary will call again in a
       wieder an.   little while.
   b. Rufen Sie mich bitte im Büro   Call me up at the office please.
       an.
   c. Sie will das Fernamt anrufen.   She wants to call long distance.
   d. Bitte rufen Sie die Wirtschafts-   Please call the Economic Section.
       abteilung an.

4. <u>es handelt sich um</u> (plus acc) - "the matter at hand is, it is about"

   a. Worum handelt es sich?   What's it about?
   b. Es handelt sich um eine wichtige   It's about an important /⎯piece of_/
       Auskunft.   information.
   c. Handelt es sich um die neuen   Is it about the new import
       Einfuhrbestimmungen?   regulations?
   d. Es handelt sich um das Fernge-   It's about the long distance telephone
       spräch mit der Certina G.m.b.H.   conversation with the Certina Company.
   e. Jetzt handelt es sich um den   The matter at hand now is the letter
       Brief von Konsul Wilson.   from Consul Wilson.

5. <u>telephonisch</u> - "on the telephone, by telephone"

   a. Ich möchte gern eine telephoni-   I'd like to have some information
       sche Auskunft haben.   by telephone.
   b. Sprechen Sie doch telephonisch   Talk to him on the telephone.
       mit ihm.
   c. Warum sagen Sie es ihm nicht   Why don't you tell it to him on
       telephonisch?   the telephone?
   d. Er will morgen telephonisch   He's planning to talk to the consul
       mit dem Konsul sprechen.   on the telephone tomorrow.

6. <u>wählen</u> - "to dial"

   a. Wählen Sie 66 73 58.   Dial 66 73 58.
   b. Er wählt die Nummer seines   He dials his colleague's number.
       Kollegen.
   c. Welche Nummer muss ich wählen?   Which number do I have to dial?
   d. Wählen Sie Null, dann meldet   Dial zero; then long distance will
       sich das Fernamt.   answer.
   e. Sie wählt die Nummer des   She dials the number of the American
       amerikanischen Konsulats.   Consulate.

7. <u>anmelden</u> - "to place"

   a. Ich möchte ein dringendes   I'd like to place an urgent call.
       Gespräch anmelden.
   b. Melden Sie bitte ein Gespräch   Please place a call to Frankfurt.
       nach Frankfurt an.
   c. Sie meldet ein Gespräch an.   She's placing a call.
   d. Wir wollen das Gespräch jetzt   We don't want to place the call yet.
       noch nicht anmelden.
   e. Er meldet ein Gespräch mit   He's placing a person-to-person call.
       Voranmeldung an.

8. <u>sich melden</u> - "to answer"

   a. Die Sekretärin meldet sich.   The secretary answers.
   b. Im Konsulat meldet sich keiner.   No one answers at the consulate.
   c. Meldet sich Bremen immer noch   Does Bremen still not answer?
       nicht?
   d. Die Sekretärin der Wirtschafts-   The secretary of the Economic Section
       abteilung meldet sich.   answers.

9. <u>wiederholen</u> - "to repeat"

   a. Die Sekretärin wiederholt   The secretary repeats his number.
      seine Nummer.
   b. Können Sie bitte die Auskunft   Can you repeat the information
      wiederholen?   please?
   c. Er wiederholt seine Adresse.   He repeats his address.
   d. Wiederholen Sie Ihren Namen   Please repeat your name.
      bitte.

10. <u>ausrichten</u> - "to give (someone) a message, to tell (someone something)"

   a. Darf ich ihm etwas ausrichten?   May I give him a message?
   b. Können Sie ihm ausrichten, er   Can you tell him I'd like him to
      möchte sobald wie möglich   come as soon as possible?
      kommen.
   c. Was kann ich Herrn Schulze   What can I tell Mr. Schulze?
      ausrichten?
   d. Richten Sie ihm das bitte aus.   Please tell him that.
   e. Er richtet es ihr gerne aus.   He'll be glad to give her the message.

TRANSLATION DRILL (not recorded)

1. In the Economic Section of the consulate general in Düsseldorf the telephone rings.
   In der Wirtschaftsabteilung des Generalkonsulats in Düsseldorf klingelt das Telephon.

2. A secretary answers.
   Eine Sekretärin meldet sich.

3. Mr. Bauer is on the telephone.
   Herr Bauer ist am Apparat.

4. He would like to speak to Consul Wilson.
   Er möchte mit Herrn Konsul Wilson sprechen.

5. But unfortunately Consul Wilson is not in his office at the moment.
   Aber leider ist Konsul Wilson im Augenblick nicht in seinem Büro.

6. His secretary says he is at an important conference.
   Seine Sekretärin sagt, er ist in einer wichtigen Konferenz.

7. She doesn't know when he's coming back either.
   Sie weiss auch nicht, wann er zurückkommt.

8. Mr. Bauer would like Consul Wilson to call him as soon as possible.
   Konsul Wilson möchte Herrn Bauer sobald wie möglich anrufen.

9. Mr. Bauer will be in his office all afternoon.
   Herr Bauer ist den ganzen Nachmittag in seinem Büro.

10. He can be reached at 77 94 51.
   Er ist unter der Nummer 77 94 51 zu erreichen.

11. The secretary gives the consul the message that Mr. Bauer would like him to call him.
   Die Sekretärin richtet dem Konsul aus, er möchte Herrn Bauer anrufen.

12. In the afternoon between four and five o'clock Consul Wilson calls back.
   Am Nachmittag zwischen vier und fünf Uhr ruft Konsul Wilson zurück.

13. He asks Mr. Bauer what he can do for him ('what the matter at hand is').
   Er fragt Herrn Bauer, worum es sich handelt.

14. Mr. Bauer would like exact information.
   Herr Bauer möchte eine genaue Auskunft haben.

15. It's about the new import regulations.
   Es handelt sich um die neuen Einfuhrbestimmungen.

16. But that is somewhat complicated on the telephone.
   Aber das ist telephonisch etwas umständlich.

17. Mr. Bauer is supposed to come to Consul Wilson's office tomorrow morning between ten and eleven o'clock.
   Herr Bauer soll morgen früh zwischen zehn und elf Uhr zu Konsul Wilson ins Büro kommen.

18. That suits Mr. Bauer very well.
   Das passt Herrn Bauer sehr gut.

19. Mr. Wiegand would like to talk to Mrs. Gisela Wiegand in Wiesbaden.
   Herr Wiegand möchte mit Frau Gisela Wiegand in Wiesbaden sprechen.

20. He dials zero and long distance answers.	Er wählt Null und das Fernamt meldet sich.
21. He places a person-to-person call.	Er meldet ein Gespräch mit Voranmeldung an.
22. He gives ('says') his number and than the number of the /‾other‾/ party.	Er sagt seine Nummer und dann die Nummer des Teilnehmers.
23. Then he has to spell his name.	Dann muss er seinen Namen buchstabieren.
24. Long distance repeats what he says.	Das Fernamt wiederholt was er sagt.
25. Mr. Wiegand is not to hang up.	Herr Wiegand soll den Hörer nicht auflegen.
26. Long distance is ringing.	Das Fernamt ruft.
27. Now the party is on the line.	Jetzt ist der Teilnehmer am Apparat.
28. Will you give him a message please?	Wollen Sie ihm bitte etwas ausrichten?
29. Please take the receiver off the hook.	Nehmen Sie bitte den Hörer ab.
30. Shall I hang up again?	Soll ich wieder auflegen?
31. Please connect me with the French Embassy.	Verbinden Sie mich bitte mit der französischen Botschaft.
32. Tomorrow morning I plan to call the American Consulate.	Morgen früh will ich das amerikanische Konsulat anrufen.
33. We're visiting a (gentleman) relative of my wife's.	Wir besuchen einen Verwandten meiner Frau.
34. He'd like to talk to an official in the Economic Section.	Er möchte mit einem Beamten in der Wirtschaftsabteilung sprechen.
35. My relatives like it in Germany very much.	Meinen Verwandten gefällt es sehr gut in Deutschland.
36. Here is my new telephone number.	Hier ist meine neue Telephonnummer.
37. The house belongs to an American Foreign Service Officer.	Das Haus gehört einem amerikanischen Diplomaten.

RESPONSE DRILL (not recorded)

1. Wo klingelt das Telephon?	Das Telephon klingelt im amerikanischen Generalkonsulat.
2. Wer meldet sich?	Eine Sekretärin meldet sich.
3. Wer ruft das Generalkonsulat an?	Herr Bauer ruft an.
4. Mit wem will Herr Bauer sprechen?	Er will mit Herrn Konsul Wilson sprechen.
5. In welcher Abteilung arbeitet Konsul Wilson?	Er arbeitet in der Wirtschaftsabteilung.
6. Mit wem spricht Herr Bauer?	Er spricht mit Konsul Wilsons Sekretärin.
7. Wo ist Herr Wilson?	Herr Wilson ist in einer wichtigen Konferenz.
8. Wann kommt er zurück?	Das ist unbestimmt.
9. Was soll Konsul Wilson tun, wenn er zurückkommt?	Er soll Herrn Bauer anrufen.
10. Wo arbeitet Herr Bauer?	Herr Bauer arbeitet bei der Certina G.m.b.H.
11. Wie ist Herr Bauer zu erreichen?	Er ist unter der Nummer 77 94 51 zu erreichen.
12. Wie lange bleibt Herr Bauer in seinem Büro?	Er bleibt den ganzen Nachmittag in seinem Büro.
13. Wann ruft Konsul Wilson zurück?	Herr Wilson ruft am Nachmittag zurück.
14. Was möchte Herr Bauer von Konsul Wilson wissen?	Er möchte etwas über die neuen Einfuhrbestimmungen wissen.
15. Gibt ihm Herr Wilson die Auskunft gleich?	Nein, das ist telephonisch etwas umständlich.
16. Wann kann er zu Konsul Wilson kommen?	Er kann morgen früh zwischen zehn und elf Uhr zu ihm ins Büro kommen.

17. Was macht Herr Wiegand?	Er ruft das Fernamt an.
18. Warum ruft er das Fernamt an?	Er will ein Gespräch mit Voranmeldung anmelden.
19. Mit wem möchte er sprechen?	Er möchte mit Frau Gisela Wiegand sprechen.
20. Wo wohnt Frau Wiegand?	Frau Wiegand wohnt in Wiesbaden.

21. Wie meldet man in München ein Ferngespräch an?
22. Was müssen Sie dem Fernamt sagen?
23. Was macht das Fernamt dann?
24. Buchstabieren Sie bitte Ihren Namen.

CONVERSATION PRACTICE (not recorded)

1

M: Hier Müller.
J: Hier Jones. Kann ich bitte mit Fräulein Müller sprechen?
M: Fräulein Müller ist leider im Augenblick nicht hier. Kann ich ihr etwas ausrichten?
J: Nein danke, ich rufe in einer Stunde wieder an.

2

K: Bitte Düsseldorf 58 64 22, mit Voranmeldung für Herrn Peter König.
F: Ihre Nummer bitte?
K: 24 23 21.
F: Bleiben Sie am Apparat. Ich rufe.

3

A: Wirtschaftsabteilung, Allen.
S: Guten Tag, Herr Allen. Hier Certina G.m.b.H., Schmidt. Kann ich Sie einen Augenblick stören?
A: Sie stören nicht, Herr Schmidt. Worum handelt es sich?
S: Um die neuen Zollbestimmungen. Ich möchte gern eine genaue Auskunft darüber haben. Kann ich um zwei Uhr zu Ihnen ins Büro kommen?
A: Um zwei Uhr muss ich leider zu einer Konferenz gehen. Können Sie vielleicht um vier Uhr kommen?
S: Gern. Vielen Dank und Auf Wiedersehen.
A: Auf Wiedersehen, Herr Schmidt.

SITUATIONS

Anruf im Konsulat

Frau Schmidt will ihre Verwandten in Amerika besuchen. Sie ruft im amerikanischen Generalkonsulat in Frankfurt an. Sie möchte wissen: Kann sie bald ein Besuchsvisum bekommen? Der amerikanische Vizekonsul sagt ihr, sie möchte am nächsten Tag zu ihm ins Büro kommen. Frau Schmidt fragt, wann es ihm passt. Er sagt, am besten zwischen zehn und elf Uhr. Sie braucht ihren Pass und ihre Ausweise. Dann kann sie das Visum beantragen.

Ferngespräch mit Stuttgart

Herr Jones wohnt in München. Er möchte am Samstag seine deutschen Bekannten in Stuttgart besuchen und ruft sie vorher an. Leider weiss er ihre Telephonnummer nicht, aber er hat die Adresse. Er wählt Null und das Fernamt meldet sich. Herr Jones sagt, er möchte mit Herrn oder Frau Walter Müller in Stuttgart, Ludwigstrasse 4 sprechen. Das Fernamt sagt ihm die Nummer und verbindet ihn. Frau Müller ist leider am Samstag nicht da. Aber am Sonntag passt es ihnen gut.

Narrative

Ortsgespräche: In allen <u>grösseren</u> <u>Orten</u> der Bundesrepublik können Sie die
gewünschte Nummer <u>selbst</u> wählen.

Ferngespräche: Zwischen vielen Orten hat man "Selbstwählferndienst". Wo es
den noch nicht gibt, müssen Sie das Ferngespräch beim Fernamt
anmelden. Nur <u>über</u> das Fernamt können Sie auch diese drei
<u>Arten</u> von Gesprächsverbindungen haben:

V - Gespräche: Sie sagen gleich bei der Anmeldung dem Fräulein vom Fernamt
den <u>Namen</u> der Person, die Sie sprechen wollen. Das Gespräch
zählt dann <u>erst</u>, <u>wenn</u> die gewünschte Person am Apparat ist.

X P - Gespräche: Das sind Ferngespräche mit Personen <u>ohne</u> <u>Fernsprechanschluss</u>.
Die gewünschte Person <u>wird</u> dann an einen <u>öffentlichen</u>
Fernsprecher <u>gerufen</u>.

R - Gespräche: Die <u>Gebühren</u> dieser Gespräche <u>bezahlt</u> die gewünschte <u>Sprechstelle</u>,
wenn die Person, die sich dort meldet, damit <u>einverstanden</u> ist.

	grösseren	fairly large
der	Ort,-e	place, locality
	gewünschte	desired
	selbst	yourself, himself, themselves
	über	via
die	Art,-en	kind
	erst	only, not until
	wenn	when
	ohne	without
der	Fernsprechanschluss	telephone connection
	wird ... gerufen	is called
die	Gebühr,-en	charge
	bezahlen	pay
die	Sprechstelle,-n	station
	mit etwas einverstanden sein	be in agreement with something

FINDER LIST

	abnehmen	take off
	achtzig	eighty
das	Amt,-̈er	office
die	Angelegenheit,-en	matter
	anmelden	place (a telephone call)
die	Anmeldung,-en	the placing (of a telephone call)
der	Anruf,-e	call
	anrufen	call up
	er hat ... angerufen	he has called up
der	Apparat,-e	telephone set
	am Apparat	on the phone, on the wire
	auflegen	hang up
im	Augenblick	at the moment
die	Auskunft,-̈e	information
	eine genaue Auskunft	exact information
	ausrichten	tell, to give a message
	bald	soon
	bei mir	at my place, home or office
	buchstabieren	spell
das	Büro,-s	office
die	Certina G.m.b.H.	the Certin Company

	danken	thank
	darüber	about it, about them
	dringend	urgent
die	Einfuhrbestimmungen	import regulations
	erreichen	reach
	zu erreichen	to be reached
	etwas	a bit
das	Fernamt, ̈er	long distance office
das	Ferngespräch,-e	long distance call
	früh	early
	morgen früh	tomorrow morning
	fürchten	fear, be afraid
	ganz	whole, entire
	genau	exact
das	Gespräch,-e	conversation, call
es	handelt sich um	it is about, the matter at hand is
der	Hörer,-	receiver
	hundert	a hundred
die	Konferenz,-en	conference
sich	melden	answer
er	möchte	I'd like him to
	möglich	possible
	sobald wie möglich	as soon as possible
	morgen	tomorrow
der	Nachmittag,-e	afternoon
	den ganzen Nachmittag	the whole afternoon
	nachmittags	in the afternoon
der	Name,-ns,-n	name
	neunzig	ninety
	nichts	nothing
die	Nummer,-n	number
	rufen	call
	sechzig	sixty
die	Sekretärin,-nen	secretary
	siebzig	seventy
der	Teilnehmer,-	party
das	Telephon,-e	telephone
	telephonisch	on the telephone, by telephone
	um (prep with acc)	about
	umständlich	involved, complicated
	unbestimmt	indefinite
	unter	under, at
	verbinden	connect
	verbindlich	obliged
	verbindlichen Dank	much obliged
die	Voranmeldung,-en	person-to-person call
	mit Voranmeldung	person-to-person
	vorhin	a little while ago
	wählen	dial
ich	werde ... sein	I will be
	wichtig	important
	wiederholen	repeat
die	Wirtschaftsabteilung,-en	Economic Section
	worum	about what
	zu mir	to where I am
	zu mir ins Büro	to my office
	zurückkommen	come back
	zwischen	between

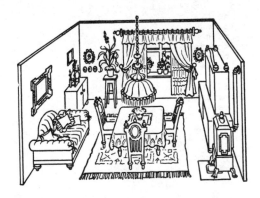 

BEIM EINRICHTEN

Basic Sentences

<table>
<tr><td colspan="2" align="center">I</td><td colspan="2" align="center">I</td></tr>
<tr>
<td>to move in
he moves in</td>
<td></td>
<td>einziehen
er zieht ... ein</td>
<td></td>
</tr>
</table>

to move in
he moves in

einziehen
er zieht ... ein

The Beckers are moving into their new house.

Beckers ziehen in ihr neues Haus ein.

to help
he helps me
the arranging (of the furniture)
in the process of arranging the furniture

helfen
er hilft mir
das Einrichten

beim Einrichten

Mr. and Mrs. Keller are helping them arrange the furniture.

Herr und Frau Keller helfen ihnen beim Einrichten.

the living room
to arrange (the furniture)
he arranges

das Wohnzimmer,-
einrichten
er richtet ... ein

MR. BECKER

HERR BECKER

The only thing left now is the living room.

Jetzt müssen wir nur noch das Wohnzimmer einrichten.

the room
other
to stand
all, everything
in place

das Zimmer,-
anderen
stehen
alles
an Ort und Stelle

Everything's in place in the other rooms.

In den anderen Zimmern steht schon alles an Ort und Stelle.

to begin, to start
he begins
the carpet, the rug

anfangen
er fängt ... an
der Teppich,-e

MRS. BECKER

FRAU BECKER

Good, let's begin with the rug.

Gut, fangen wir mit dem Teppich an.

to lay, to put
the middle

legen
die Mitte

We'll lay it in the middle of the room.

Den legen wir in die Mitte des Zimmers.

II

II

little
the table
to put (down)

klein
der Tisch,-e
hinstellen[3]

MR. KELLER

Where shall we put the little table?

    to fit
    in front of
    both
    the easy-chair

MR. BECKER

It will look good in front of the two easy-chairs.

    the sofa
    the wall
    to put, to place

We can place the sofa over against the wall there.

    the lamp
    the floor lamp
    to go, to belong (in a certain place)

MR. KELLER

And where does the floor lamp go?

    between
    the smoking table
    the bookcase

MR. BECKER

Put it between the smoking table and the bookcase, please.

    the desk
    to match, to go (with)
    the furniture

MR. KELLER

The new desk matches your furniture very well.

Where's it supposed to go?

    for the time being, temporarily
    the window

MR. BECKER

Let's put it in front of the big window for the time being.

HERR KELLER

Wo sollen wir den kleinen Tisch hinstellen?

    passen[4]
    vor (two-way prep)
    beide
    der Sessel

HERR BECKER

Der passt gut vor die beiden Sessel.

    das Sofa,-s
    die Wand,¨e
    stellen

Das Sofa können wir dort an die Wand stellen.

    die Lampe
    die Stehlampe,-n
    hinkommen

HERR KELLER

Und wo kommt die Stehlampe hin?

    zwischen (two-way prep)
    der Rauchtisch,-e
    der Bücherschrank,¨e

HERR BECKER

Stellen Sie sie doch bitte zwischen den Rauchtisch und den Bücherschrank.

    der Schreibtisch,-e
    passen (zu etwas)
    die Möbel (pl)

HERR KELLER

Der neue Schreibtisch passt sehr gut zu Ihren Möbeln.

Wo soll er stehen?

    vorläufig

    das Fenster,-

HERR BECKER

Stellen wir ihn doch vorläufig vor das grosse Fenster.

III

the blanket, the cover	die Decke,-n
the wool blanket	die Wolldecke,-n

MRS. KELLER

Where shall I put the blankets?

FRAU KELLER

Wo soll ich die Wolldecken hinlegen?

for the moment	erst mal
over, above	über (two-way prep)
the chair	der Stuhl,-̈e
the back of the chair	die Stuhllehne,-n

MRS. BECKER

Just put them over the back of the
chair for the moment please.

FRAU BECKER

Legen Sie sie doch bitte erst mal
über die Stuhllehne.

the quilt	die Steppdecke,-n
to lie	liegen
the bedroom	das Schlafzimmer,-
the bed	das Bett,-en

The quilts are already in the bedroom
on our beds.

Die Steppdecken liegen schon im
Schlafzimmer auf unseren Betten.

the linen	die Wäsche
to unpack	auspacken
he unpacks	er packt ... aus

MRS. KELLER

Shall I unpack the linen now?

FRAU KELLER

Soll ich jetzt die Wäsche auspacken?

in the meantime	inzwischen
the china, dishes	das Geschirr
to bother (about something),	sich kümmern (um etwas)
to take care (of something)	
he takes care (of something)	er kümmert sich (um etwas)

MRS. BECKER

Yes, that'll be fine, and then I can
take care of dishes in the meantime.

FRAU BECKER

Ja gut, dann kann ich mich inzwischen
um das Geschirr kümmern.

IV

the picture	das Bild,-er
could	könnten
to hang	hängen

MR. BECKER

I think, we could hang the big
picture over the sofa.

HERR BECKER

Das grosse Bild könnten wir eigentlich
über das Sofa hängen.

the crate with the pictures	die Bilderkiste,-n
at all, anyhow	überhaupt

165

MR. KELLER	HERR KELLER

Is the crate with the pictures here yet anyhow?

Ist die Bilderkiste überhaupt schon da?

to bring up, to bring in	heraufbringen
he brings in	er bringt ... herauf
the crate	die Kiste,-n

MR. BECKER	HERR BECKER

No, but the men are just bringing two big crates in.

Nein, aber die Männer bringen gerade zwei grosse Kisten herauf.

with them, among them	dabei
in among them, along with them	mit dabei

MR. KELLER	HERR KELLER

Perhaps it's in among them.

Vielleicht ist sie mit dabei.

the packing	die Verpackung
the thing	die Sache,-n
neat, tidy, well done	ordentlich

MR. KELLER	HERR KELLER

They really did a good job of packing your things. ('The packing of your things was really well done.')

Die Verpackung Ihrer Sachen war wirklich sehr ordentlich.

right, quite	recht
satisfied	zufrieden

MR. BECKER	HERR BECKER

I'm quite satisfied with it.

Ich bin auch recht zufrieden damit.

the people	die Leute
the packer	der Packer,-
the effort, pains	die Mühe
I take pains, I make an effort	ich gebe mir Mühe
given, taken	gegeben

The people took a lot of trouble.

Die Leute haben sich Mühe gegeben.

V

V

to arrive	ankommen
he arrives	er kommt ... an
the freight	das Frachtgut,-̈er

MRS. BECKER	FRAU BECKER

I hope the freight arrives soon.

Hoffentlich kommt das Frachtgut bald an.

MR. BECKER	HERR BECKER

I'll just give them a quick call.

Ich will gleich mal anrufen.

the telephone book	das Telephonbuch,-̈er
Where's the telephone book?	Wo ist das Telephonbuch?
the radiator; the heating plant	die Heizung,-en
under	unter (two-way prep)
MRS. BECKER	FRAU BECKER
It's there on the radiator under the newspapers.	Es liegt dort auf der Heizung unter den Zeitungen.
Is the furnace all right, by the way?	Ist eigentlich die Heizung in Ordnung?
to hope	hoffen
the workman	der Handwerker,-
at any rate, in any case	jedenfalls
yesterday	gestern
they were here	sie sind ... dagewesen
MR. BECKER	HERR BECKER
I hope so. At any rate the workmen were here yesterday.	Ich hoffe. Die Handwerker sind jedenfalls gestern dagewesen.

VI

to think (that something is thus and so)	finden
to look, appear	aussehen
he looks, he appears	er sieht ... aus
really	richtig
cozy, comfortable, inviting	gemütlich
MR. KELLER	HERR KELLER
I think it looks really comfortable /here/ now.	Ich finde, jetzt sieht es schon richtig gemütlich aus.
at last	endlich
to sit down	sich hinsetzen[5]
he sits down	er setzt sich ... hin
MR. BECKER	HERR BECKER
Yes! Why don't we sit down for a change?	Ja! Wollen wir uns nicht endlich mal hinsetzen?
well	na
first	erst
empty	leer
to clear away	wegschaffen
he clears away	er schafft ... weg
MR. KELLER	HERR KELLER
Well, first we still have to get rid of the empty crates and trunks.	Na, erst müssen wir aber noch die leeren Kisten und Koffer wegschaffen.
clean	sauber
to clean up	saubermachen
he cleans up	er macht ... sauber

<u>MRS. KELLER</u>

And clean up a bit!

     the basement, the cellar
     to carry
     he carries

<u>MR. BECKER</u>

The men can carry the crates down
to the cellar.

     to bring, to take (something
     somewhere)
     the attic

We'd best take the trunks right up to
the attic.

     after that

<u>MRS. BECKER</u>

But after that we're going to eat
something.

            VII

     to sit

<u>MR. BECKER</u>

Where shall we sit?

     the kitchen table
     to sit down
     he sits down

<u>MRS. BECKER</u>

We can sit down right here at the
kitchen table.

     easy, simple
     easiest, simplest

That's the easiest /thing_7.

     such, like that
     the kitchen

<u>MRS. KELLER</u>

I'd like to have a kitchen like that
too!

     such
     the refrigerator
     combined
     the range
     the gas range
     the electric range

<u>FRAU KELLER</u>

Und etwas sauber machen!

     der Keller,-
     tragen
     er trägt

<u>HERR BECKER</u>

Die Männer können die Kisten in den
Keller tragen.

     bringen

     der Boden,¨

Die Koffer bringen wir am besten
gleich auf den Boden.

     danach

<u>FRAU BECKER</u>

Danach essen wir aber etwas!

            VII

     sitzen

<u>HERR BECKER</u>

Wo wollen wir denn sitzen?

     der Küchentisch
     sich setzen[5]
     er setzt sich

<u>FRAU BECKER</u>

Wir können uns doch gleich hier an
den Küchentisch setzen.

     einfach
     am einfachsten

Das ist am einfachsten.

     solch
     die Küche

<u>FRAU KELLER</u>

Solch eine Küche möchte ich auch
haben!

     so
     der Kühlschrank,¨e
     kombiniert
     der Herd
     der Gasherd
     der Elektroherd

MR. KELLER	HERR KELLER

Yes, with such a large refrigerator and combination gas and electric range.

Ja, mit so grossem Kühlschrank und kombiniertem Gas- und Elektroherd.

especially	besonders
much, many	viel
built-in	eingebaut
the cupboard	der Schrank, ̈e

MRS. KELLER	FRAU KELLER

And I like the many built-in cupboards especially well.

Und mir gefallen besonders die vielen eingebauten Schränke!

VIII

VIII

the garden	der Garten, ̈
behind	hinter (two-way prep)
to look at something	sich etwas ansehen
I look at	ich sehe mir ... an

MRS. BECKER	FRAU BECKER

We have a big yard behind the house. Do you want to take a look at it?

Wir haben einen grossen Garten hinter dem Haus. Wollen Sie sich den mal ansehen?

ideal	ideal
the child	das Kind, -er
the playing	das Spielen[1]
for playing	zum Spielen

MRS. KELLER	FRAU KELLER

Yes, I'd like to. --- My, it's an ideal place for the children to play.

Gern. --- Der ist ja ideal für die Kinder zum Spielen!

the suburb	der Vorort, -e
nicer	schöner
quiet	ruhig
quieter	ruhiger

MRS. BECKER	FRAU BECKER

It's really much nicer and quieter here in the suburbs than in the city.

Hier im Vorort ist es wirklich viel schöner und ruhiger als in der Stadt.

by the way	übrigens
to rent (from someone)	mieten
he rents (for himself)	er mietet (sich)

MRS. KELLER	FRAU KELLER

We're planning to rent a house soon too, by the way.

Wir wollen uns übrigens auch bald ein Haus mieten.

to move	ziehen
the neighborhood	die Nachbarschaft

MRS. BECKER	FRAU BECKER

Why don't you move to our neighborhood?

Warum ziehen Sie nicht in unsere Nachbarschaft?

to rent (to someone)	vermieten
he rents (to someone)	er vermietet
for rent	zu vermieten

There are still some nice houses for rent here.

Hier sind noch einige nette Häuser zu vermieten.

the rent	die Miete,-n
outside, out here	draussen

MRS. KELLER

FRAU KELLER

How are the rents out here?

Wie sind die Mieten hier draussen?

not at all	garnicht
high	hoch

MRS. BECKER

FRAU BECKER

They're not high at all.

Sie sind garnicht so hoch.

IX

IX

a thousand

tausend

Let's count from a hundred to a thousand.

Zählen wir von hundert bis tausend.

a hundred and one	hunderteins
a hundred and two	hundertzwei
a hundred and three	hundertdrei
a hundred and ten	hundertzehn
a hundred and twenty	hundertzwanzig
a hundred and fifty	hundertfünfzig
a hundred and seventy-five	hundertfünfundsiebzig
two hundred	zweihundert
three hundred	dreihundert
five hundred	fünfhundert
a thousand and one	tausendeins
sixteen hundred	sechzehnhundert
following	folgend
(the) following numbers	folgende Zahlen

Give the following numbers in German:

Sagen Sie folgende Zahlen auf deutsch:

390, 578, 722, 333, 1480, 699, 1145, 1565, 1910, 616

Notes to the Basic Sentences

[1] The infinitive form of many verbs can be used as a noun in German. It is always a <u>das</u>-noun. English has similar nouns, like <u>playing</u>, <u>working</u>, <u>speaking</u>, etc., but often uses the infinitive in equivalent sentences.

[2] This adjective always has an ending of some kind, in this case the ending that the specifier-adjective-noun sequence <u>den anderen Zimmern</u> requires. There is no endingless citation form, but regular adjective endings are added to the stem <u>ander-</u>.

[3] The verb <u>stellen</u> "to put" is complemented either by a prepositional phrase such as <u>an die Wand</u> or by the word <u>hin</u>. It does not occur without a complement, however.

4 This is actually the same verb as was encountered in Unit 4 in the form
es passt mir "it suits me, it's convenient for me" and as occurs later on
in this unit with the preposition zu, meaning "to match, to go (with)".
Because of the divergent English equivalents in different situations the
verb is listed separately each time. In this sentence the implication is
that the table will end up in front of the two chairs when it has been
put there; in its grammatical influence on the syntactic environment
(vor die beiden Sessel, accusative) it is equivalent to the verb stellen
"to put".

5 The verb sich setzen "to sit down" is usually complemented by a prepositional
phrase such as an den Tisch or by the word hin.

Notes on Pronunciation

A. Vowels in Syllables Not Having Primary Stress

Up to now we have given our attention to the vowels occurring in stressed
syllables. Most of the items presented for pronunciation practice have been
one or two syllables in length, although German words of six or more syllables
occur. While only one syllable receives primary stress, vowels in syllables
not having primary stress retain the same sound quality and length which they
have when stressed. Practice the following words with your instructor, making
sure that your imitation of all vowel sounds in each word is accurate:

Practice 1

Umweg	Amerika	Konsulat
Autobus	Museum	Amerikanerin
Schreibmaschine	politisch	Universität
Heimatstadt	Verabredung	Sekretärin
Wiedersehen	Spaziergang	Bibliothek

B. Review

Continuing the review of difficult pronunciation features begun in Unit 6
here are two troublesome vowel contrasts: short -a- and short -o-, and long -i-
and long -e-:

Practice 2

Kasten	- kosten	sieht	-	seht
lachen	- lochen	Wiesen	-	Wesen
Tanne	- Tonne	liegen	-	legen

An important and often difficult consonant contrast is that between the ich-
or ach-sounds on the one hand and the k-sound on the other:

Practice 3

Augenblick	- wahrscheinlich	backen	- machen
sickert	- sichert	Doktor	- Tochter
direkt	- recht	Akt	- acht
drückte	- Süchte	druckt	- Sucht

The following items provide additional practice in post-vocalic r and post-vocalic l:

Practice 4

Tier	wird		viel	hilft
		für		
mehr	Herz		Mehl	Welt
		führt		
Paar	hart		mal	halb
		höher		
vor	Dorf		wohl	Golf
		hört		
Kur	Durst		Pfuhl	Schuld

The following provides review in the practice of pre-vocalic r:

Practice 5

Papiere	zufrieden	höre
leere	reden	Grösse
Jahre	rauchen	führe
bohre	Büro	berühmt
Fuhre	rufen	grüsse

(End of Tape 7A)

Notes on Grammar (not recorded)
(For Home Study)

A. ADJECTIVES - THE ADJECTIVE-NOUN SEQUENCE

  I. In Unit 6 we discussed attributive adjectives in specifier-adjective-noun
     sequences. Attributive adjectives are not always preceded by specifiers
     however; they also occur in ADJECTIVE-NOUN sequences. Note the following
     examples from the basic sentences of this and preceding units:

Amerikanisches General-   American Consulate General.
konsulat.
Ich muss <u>einige</u> Geschäfts-   I have to write <u>some</u> business letters.
briefe schreiben.
Ja, mit so <u>grossem</u> Kühl-   Yes, with such a <u>large</u> refrigerator
schrank und <u>kombiniertem</u>   and <u>combination</u> gas and electric
Gas- und Elektroherd   range.

II. Attributive adjectives in ADJECTIVE-NOUN sequences ALWAYS HAVE ENDINGS.

1. The adjective endings are -<u>e</u>, -<u>em</u>, -<u>en</u>, -<u>er</u> or -<u>es</u>:

Nom <u>Amerikanischer</u> Tabak ist gut.
Acc Ich rauche gern <u>amerikanischen</u> Tabak.
Dat Ich rauche nur Zigaretten mit <u>amerikanischem</u> Tabak.

Nom Hier ist <u>deutsches</u> Geld.
Acc Haben Sie <u>deutsches</u> Geld?
Dat Was können wir hier mit <u>deutschem</u> Geld tun?

Nom Ist das hier <u>gute</u> Tinte?
Acc Hier haben Sie <u>gute</u> Tinte.
Dat Mit <u>guter</u> Tinte kann man gut schreiben.

Nom Hier sind <u>grosse</u> Sessel.
Acc Ich suche <u>grosse</u> Sessel.
Dat Ich habe ein Wohnzimmer mit <u>grossen</u> Sesseln.

2. No genitive forms are listed for the ADJECTIVE-NOUN sequence, as they occur only very rarely. Note that the adjective endings of the nominative, accusative and dative forms correspond throughout to the endings of the <u>der</u>-type specifiers.

3. Preceding adverbs or numerals do not affect the forms of the adjectives in ADJECTIVE-NOUN sequences:

Die Männer bringen gerade   The men are just bringing two big
zwei <u>grosse</u> Kisten herauf.   crates in.
Heute ist wirklich <u>schönes</u>   It's really nice weather today.
Wetter.

4. The noun is not always present in a sequence when it can be understood from the context. The form of the adjective is the same whether the noun is present or not:

Haben Sie deutsches Geld?   Do you have any German money?
Nein, ich habe nur   No, I only have American /̄ money_/.
<u>amerikanisches</u>.

Brauchen Sie einen grossen   Do you need a large rug for the
Teppich für das Wohnzimmer?   living-room? No, I'd like to have
Nein, ich möchte zwei <u>kleine</u> two small ones for the bedroom.
für das Schlafzimmer haben.

Trinken Sie lieber deutschen   Do you like German or French wine
oder französischen Wein?   better? I like French /̄ wine_/
Ich trinke lieber   better.
<u>französischen</u>.

Notice that we usually repeat the noun in English.

5. If there is more than one adjective in an ADJECTIVE-NOUN sequence, all
   have the same endings:

Hier sind noch <u>einige</u> <u>nette</u> Häuser zu vermieten.	There are still some nice houses for rent here.
Eine Küche mit so <u>vielen</u> <u>eingebauten</u> Schränken ist doch schön.	A kitchen with so many built-in cupboards really is nice.
Trinken Sie gern <u>gutes</u> <u>deutsches</u> Bier?	Do you like good German beer?

III. Adjectives used as nouns often occur without a preceding specifier.

   1. Their endings are the same as those outlined above:

Ist sie Amerikanerin oder <u>Deutsche</u>?	Is she an American or a German?
Sie sind <u>Deutscher</u>, nicht wahr?	You're German, aren't you?
Ich wusste nicht, dass Ihre Frau hier <u>Verwandte</u> hat.	I didn't know that your wife has relatives here.

   2. Note that adjectives used as nouns may be preceded by other adjectives.
   Both then have the same ending:

Ist sie <u>deutsche Staatsangehörige</u>?	Is she a German citizen?
Er ist <u>amerikanischer Beamter</u>.	He's an American official.
Meine Frau hat <u>nette Verwandte</u> in Berlin.	My wife has nice relatives in Berlin.
Wir haben <u>gute Bekannte</u> in Frankfurt.	We have good friends in Frankfurt.

   3. Note carefully the distinction <u>in form</u> between adjectives used as nouns
   when they are preceded by a specifier and when they are not:

Das ist <u>der amerikanische Beamte</u>.	That's the American official.
Morgen besuchen wir <u>die netten Verwandten</u> meiner Frau in Berlin.	Tomorrow we're going to visit my wife's nice relatives in Berlin.
Wir treffen <u>unsere guten Bekannten</u> in Frankfurt.	We're meeting our good friends in Frankfurt.

IV. Adjectives in ADJECTIVE-NOUN sequences and in SPECIFIER-ADJECTIVE-NOUN
    sequences:

   1. Compare the following sentences:

Das ist <u>guter französischer</u> Wein.	That's good French wine.
Das ist <u>ein guter französischer</u> Wein.	That's a good French wine.
Wo ist <u>der gute</u> französische Wein?	Where's the good French wine?

Das ist <u>gutes</u> <u>deutsches</u> Geschirr.	That's good German dinnerware.
Das ist <u>ihr</u> <u>gutes</u> <u>deutsches</u> Geschirr.	That's her good German dinnerware.
Wo ist <u>das</u> <u>gute</u> <u>deutsche</u> Geschirr?	Where's the good German dinnerware?

You will note that there is no difference in the form of adjectives
in adjective-noun sequences and in sequences with the <u>endingless</u> <u>ein</u>-type
specifiers. There <u>is</u> a difference between the form of <u>these</u> adjectives
and adjectives in a specifier-adjective-noun sequence where the specifier
also has an ending.

B. AN IRREGULAR ADJECTIVE - <u>hoch</u>

I. The adjective <u>hoch</u> has occurred in this unit only as a predicate adjective:

Die Mieten sind hier garnicht so hoch.	The rents here are not high at all.

II. As an attributive adjective the stem form <u>hoh</u>- with regular adjective
endings occurs:

Wir haben hier sehr <u>hohe</u> Mieten.	We have very high rents here.
Das ist ein ganz <u>hohes</u> Etagenhaus.	That's quite a high apartment building.

C. SUMMARY OF TWO-WAY PREPOSITIONS

I. In Unit 3 it was noted that certain prepositions when followed by a dative
form indicate where someone or something is to be found and when followed
by an accusative form indicate where someone or something that is in
motion is going to end up. We have now encountered the total inventory
of TWO-WAY PREPOSITIONS, nine in all. Let us review some of the sentences
in which they have occurred:

Das Sofa können wir dort <u>an</u> die Wand stellen.	We can place the sofa over against the wall there.
Die Steppdecken liegen <u>auf</u> unseren Betten.	The quilts are on our beds.
Wir haben einen grossen Garten <u>hinter</u> dem Haus.	We have a big yard behind the house.
Den Teppich legen wir <u>in</u> die Mitte des Zimmers.	We'll lay the carpet in the middle of the room.
Rechts <u>neben</u> dem Schloss ist die Universität.	Next to the palace on the right is the university.
Das grosse Bild könnten wir <u>über</u> das Sofa hängen.	We could hang the big picture above the sofa.
Das Telephonbuch liegt dort <u>unter</u> den Zeitungen.	The telephone book is there under the newspapers.
Stellen wir den Schreibtisch <u>vor</u> das grosse Fenster.	Let's put the desk in front of the big window.
Stellen Sie die Lampe <u>zwischen</u> den Rauchtisch und den Bücherschrank.	Put the lamp between the smoking table and the bookcase.

1. Note that there is a close link between the TWO-WAY PREPOSITION and the verbs in these sentences. In the sentences where a dative form follows the preposition verbs which indicate or describe a static situation occur. liegen, haben, ist. In the sentences where an accusative form follows the preposition verbs indicating action or motion occur: stellen, legen, hängen.

2. It is important to note however that two-way prepositions may be followed by an accusative form in a sentence where the verb by itself does not necessarily indicate motion. In association WITH THE ACCUSATIVE object of a two-way preposition the verb ALWAYS IMPLIES MOTION.

> Der Tisch passt gut vor   The table fits the picture in front
> die beiden Sessel.   of the two easy-chairs (and therefore
>   should end up in that location).

3. Likewise a DATIVE FORM following a two-way preposition ALWAYS IMPLIES A STATIC RELATIONSHIP, nonchanging, even when the verb is a verb of action or motion:

> Das grosse Bild hängt dort   The big picture is hanging there
> über dem Sofa.   above the sofa.
>
> Das grosse Bild können wir   We can hang the big picture above the
> über das Sofa hängen.   sofa.

D. VERBS - legen, liegen, stehen and stellen

I. In English we generally use the forms "is" and "are" to describe the location of a person or an object, and a form of the verb "to put" in describing the act of placing an object in a certain location. We can, however, make implicit reference to the shape of the object and to the position it is in:

> My brief-case is there on   My brief-case is lying there on the
> the table.   table.
> You can put your brief-case   You can lay your brief-case on the
> on the table there.   table there.
>   OR
> His gun is over against the   His gun is standing over against the
> wall there.   wall there.
> He puts his gun over against   He stands his gun up against the wall
> the wall there.   there.

II. German usually makes more frequent reference to position than English. The verbs liegen and stehen, like English "to lie" and "to stand", besides giving the location of an object or a person, clearly imply his, or its position. In German also, however, the verb forms ist and sind occur with a location:

Die Steppdecken liegen auf   The quilts are (lying) on our beds.
unseren Betten.
Der neue Schreibtisch steht   The new desk is (standing) in front
vor dem Fenster.   of the window.
                            but

Das Buch ist auf dem Tisch.   The book is on the table.
Das Buch liegt auf dem   The book is located on the table and
Tisch.   is lying flat.
Das Bild ist auf dem   The picture is on the desk.
Schreibtisch.
Das Bild steht auf dem   The picture is located on the desk
Schreibtisch.   but is in a standing frame or propped
                                     up against something.

III. German has no non-specifying verb corresponding to the English verb
     "to put" and always describes the act of placing some object in a certain
     location in terms of its final position there, whether lying or standing,
     by using the verbs legen and stellen.

Wir können das Sofa an die   We can put the sofa up against the
Wand stellen.   wall, where it is to stand.
Wo soll ich die Wolldecken   Where shall I put the woolen blankets,
hinlegen?   i.e., where shall I leave them lying?

E. VERBS - REVIEW OF PRESENT

We have added more than fifty verbs to the inventory since the outline of
the present tense was given in Unit 2. At that time two main patterns and
one subsidiary pattern were noted, those of kommen, geben and arbeiten, as
well as the irregular verb patterns. By way of review we present here a
reference list of the verbs added in Units 3 - 7.

   1. These verbs follow the pattern illustrated by komm-e, komm-t,
      komm-en:

brauchen	hoffen	liegen	sitzen
bringen	gewöhnen	machen	stehen
buchstabieren	grüssen	(packen)	stellen
danken	(heben)	auspacken	stören
erreichen	abheben	parken	suchen
fragen	holen	passen	trinken
freuen	hören	rauchen	wählen
(füllen)	leben	rufen	wiederholen
ausfüllen	legen	schreiben	zählen
hängen	leihen	setzen	ziehen

   2. These verbs follow the pattern illustrated by geb-e, gib-t,
      geb-en, in which a different stem occurs in the er-form.

anfangen	fängt ... an	nehmen	nimmt
helfen	hilft	sehen	sieht
lesen	liest	tragen	trägt

177

3. These verbs follow the subsidiary pattern illustrated bei <u>arbeit-e</u>, <u>arbeit-e-t</u>, <u>arbeit-en</u>, in which a connecting vowel -e- occurs before the <u>er-</u>form ending. Note that all have stems ending in -t- or -d-.

anbieten	bietet ... an	vermieten	vermietet
finden	findet	melden	meldet
fürchten	fürchtet	ausrichten	richtet ... aus
mieten	mietet	einrichten	richtet ... ein

4. A few verbs follow a second subsidiary pattern. An example is <u>auswander-n</u>, in which the <u>wir-</u>form ending is -n instead of -en. We have encountered only four other verbs which follow this pattern.

      klingel-n   kümmer-n   tu-n   wechsel-n

5. Please note that a number of verbs which differ from the above only in having additional accented adverbs associated with them have not been listed separately, since their forms and endings remain the same.

Tape 7B   SUBSTITUTION DRILL - Part I

This first part of the drill is concerned with the <u>forms</u> of adjectives in ADJECTIVE-NOUN sequences and is designed to provide a maximum of natural sequences for repetition. These should be gone over rapidly but accurately, until all sentences can be given correctly with unhesitating fluency at conversational speed. The instructor will first give complete sentences for repetition, then will cue with the adjective-noun sequences, finally with the adjectives or nouns alone where appropriate.

1. Wieviel kostet <u>deutscher</u> Wein?

französischer Wein – amerikanischer Wein – guter Wein

2. Wieviel kostet <u>guter Kaffee</u>?

gutes Bier – guter Tee – gutes Briefpapier – gute Wäsche – guter Tabak – guter Wein

3. Ihm gehören viele <u>neue</u> Häuser.

viele kleine Häuser – viele schöne Häuser – viele alte Häuser – viele grosse Häuser – viele andere Häuser

4. Haben Sie gute deutsche <u>Bücher</u>?

gute deutsche Romane – gute deutsche Bilder – gute deutsche Zigarren – gute deutsche Teppiche – gute deutsche Zeitungen

5. Ich suche noch einige andere <u>Bilder</u>.

einige andere Romane – einige andere Stühle – einige andere Möbel – einige andere Bücher – einige andere Zeitungen

6. Ich suche <u>guten Wein</u>.

gutes Briefpapier – guten Tabak – gutes Geschirr – gute Wäsche – guten Kaffee – gutes Bier

7. Hier ist <u>schönes Briefpapier</u>.

... amerikanisch___ Tabak	... amerikanischer Tabak
... kaputt___ Geschirr	... kaputtes Geschirr
... französisch___ Wein	... französischer Wein
... sauber___ Wäsche	... saubere Wäsche
... deutsch___ Bier	... deutsches Bier
... wichtig___ Frachtgut	... wichtiges Frachtgut

8. Haben Sie <u>deutschen Wein</u>?

... amerikanisch___ Bier	... amerikanisches Bier
... englisch___ Tee	... englischen Tee
... neu___ Wäsche	... neue Wäsche
... wichtig___ Frachtgut	... wichtiges Frachtgut
... gut___ Tabak	... guten Tabak
... schön___ Briefpapier	... schönes Briefpapier

9. Dort steht eine Kiste mit
<u>französischem Wein</u>.

... wichtig___ Frachtgut	... wichtigem Frachtgut
... deutsch___ Bier	... deutschem Bier
... neu___ Wäsche	... neuer Wäsche
... amerikanisch___ Tabak	... amerikanischem Tabak
... neu___ Geschirr	... neuem Geschirr

10. In diesem Haus sind <u>schöne
neue Möbel</u>.

... einig___ berühmt___ Bilder	... einige berühmte Bilder
... viel___ kaputt___ Stühle	... viele kaputte Stühle
... alt___ hoh___ Schränke	... alte hohe Schränke
... gut___ klein___ Teppiche	... gute kleine Teppiche
... gross___ neu___ Tische	... grosse neue Tische

Part II

In this part of the drill both adjective-noun sequences and specifier-
adjective-noun sequences are presented. Pay careful attention to the differences.

11. Diese Stadt hat viele <u>schöne Parks</u>.   viele saubere Strassen - viele schöne
Gärten - viele grosse Neubauten -
viele schöne Vororte

12. Diese Stadt hat keine <u>schönen Parks</u>.   keine sauberen Strassen - keine schönen
Gärten - keine grosse Neubauten -
keine schönen Vororte

13. Hier gibt es <u>schöne Bilder</u>.   grosse Tische - neue Sessel - gute
Romane - alte Möbel

14. Hier gibt es keine <u>schönen Bilder</u>.   keine grossen Tische - keine neuen
Sessel - keine guten Romane - keine
alten Möbel

15. Haben Sie einige <u>schöne Bilder</u>?   einige grosse Tische - einige neue
Sessel - einige gute Romane - einige
alte Möbel

16. Wir haben keine guten Bücher.

    ... viel___ neu___ Möbel   ... viele neue Möbel
    ... kein___ gross___ Fenster   ... keine grossen Fenster
    ... drei schön___ Teppiche   ... drei schöne Teppiche
    ... einig___ französisch___   ... einige französische Zeitungen
         Zeitungen
    ... kein___ neu___ Anträge   ... keine neuen Anträge

17. Das ist eine Stadt mit schönen Parks.

    ... ein___ berühmt___ Dom   ... einem berühmten Dom
    ... viel___ gross___ Geschäften   ... vielen grossen Geschäften
    ... neu___ gross___   ... neuen grossen Etagenhäusern
         Etagenhäusern
    ... ein___ berühmt___ alt___   ... einem berühmten alten Museum
         Museum
    ... viel___ gut___ Restaurants   ... vielen guten Restaurants
    ... ein___ sehr schön___   ... einer sehr schönen Universität
         Universität

18. Das ist ein Haus mit einem kleinen Garten.

    ... klein___ Garten   ... kleinem Garten
    ... gross___ Keller   ... grossem Keller
    ... ein___ schön___ Boden   ... einem schönen Boden
    ... ausgezeichnet___ neu___   ... ausgezeichneter neuer Heizung
         Heizung
    ... ein___ schön___ gross___   ... einer schönen grossen Küche
         Küche
    ... viel___ eingebaut___   ... vielen eingebauten Schränken
         Schränken

19. In dieser Stadt sind schöne Parks.

    ... viel__ gross__ Geschäfte   ... viele grosse Geschäfte
    ... ein__ berühmt__ Dom   ... ein berühmter Dom
    ... fünf neu__ Etagenhäuser   ... fünf neue Etagenhäuser
    ... ein__ berühmt__ alt__   ... ein berühmtes altes Museum
         Museum
    ... einig__ gut__ Restaurants   ... einige gute Restaurants
    ... ein__ sehr schön__   ... eine sehr schöne Bibliothek
         Bibliothek
    ... gross__ Parkplätze   ... grosse Parkplätze
    ... ein__ schön__ Park   ... ein schöner Park

20. Diese Stadt hat schöne Parks.

    ... viel__ gross__ Geschäfte   ... viele grosse Geschäfte
    ... ein__ berühmt__ Dom   ... einen berühmten Dom
    ... fünf neu__ Etagenhäuser   ... fünf neue Etagenhäuser
    ... ein__ berühmt__ alt__   ... ein berühmtes altes Museum
         Museum
    ... einig__ gut__ Restaurants   ... einige gute Restaurants
    ... ein__ sehr schön__   ... eine sehr schöne Bibliothek
         Bibliothek
    ... gross__ Parkplätze   ... grosse Parkplätze
    ... ein__ schön__ Park   ... einen schönen Park

Part III

This part of the drill is concerned with two-way prepositions. Some
sentences require dative forms, and some sentences require accusative forms.

21. Er stellt einen Stuhl <u>vor den
Schreibtisch.</u>

neben die Tür - auf den Teppich -
hinter den Tisch - zwischen die
Betten - in den Garten - an die Wand

22. <u>Vor dem Schreibtisch</u> steht ein
Stuhl.

neben der Tür - auf dem Teppich -
hinter dem Tisch - zwischen den
Betten - im Garten - an der Wand

23. Der Papierkorb steht <u>hinter dem
Sofa.</u>

vor der Tür - zwischen den Stühlen -
neben dem Rauchtisch - im Wohnzimmer -
unter dem Schreibtisch - hinter der
Stehlampe

24. Ich stelle den Papierkorb <u>hinter
das Sofa.</u>

vor die Tür - zwischen die Stühle -
neben den Rauchtisch - ins Wohnzimmer -
unter den Schreibtisch - hinter die
Stehlampe

25. Legen Sie bitte das Buch <u>neben die
Schreibmaschine.</u>

unter die Lampe - auf den Tisch -
ins andere Zimmer - hinter das
Telephonbuch - neben die Zeitungen

26. Das Buch liegt <u>neben der Schreib=
maschine.</u>

unter der Lampe - auf dem Tisch -
im anderen Zimmer - hinter dem
Telephonbuch - neben den Zeitungen

27. Der Brief liegt <u>unter den
Zeitungen.</u>

zwischen den Büchern - neben der
Schreibmaschine - im Schrank - hinter
der Lampe - auf dem Küchentisch

28. Sie legt den Brief <u>unter die
Zeitungen.</u>

zwischen die Bücher - neben die
Schreibmaschine - in den Schrank -
hinter die Lampe - auf den Küchentisch

29. Das Bild hängt <u>über dem Sofa.</u>

zwischen den Fenstern - neben der Tür -
über dem Schreibtisch - im Wohnzimmer -
an der Wand - in der Bibliothek

30. Soll ich das Bild <u>über das Sofa</u>
hängen?

zwischen die Fenster - neben die Tür -
über den Schreibtisch - ins Wohnzimmer -
an die Wand - in die Bibliothek

VARIATION DRILL

1. <u>Wir setzen uns in das grosse</u>   <u>We'll sit down in the big living</u>
   <u>Wohnzimmer.</u>   <u>room.</u>

   a. Let's carry the suitcases up to   Wir wollen die Koffer auf den Boden
      the attic.   tragen.
   b. He's putting the chair behind   Er stellt den Stuhl hinter den
      the desk.   Schreibtisch.
   c. Please sit down beside my son.   Setzen Sie sich bitte neben meinen
                                             Sohn.
   d. She's putting the woolen blanket   Sie legt die Wolldecke über die
      over the back of the chair.   Stuhllehne.
   e. He's putting the letters under   Er legt die Briefe unter seine
      his newspaper.   Zeitung.
   f. The kitchen table goes between   Der Küchentisch kommt zwischen den
      the refrigerator and the range.   Kühlschrank und den Herd.

2. <u>Wir wohnen neben der alten Post.</u>   <u>We live next to the old post office.</u>

   a. He works in another office.   Er arbeitet in einem anderen Büro.
   b. On the corner a policeman is   An der Ecke steht ein Polizist.
      standing.
   c. I'll park behind your car.   Ich parke hinter Ihrem Wagen.
   d. Above the desk there's a big   Über dem Schreibtisch hängt ein grosses
      picture.   Bild.
   e. The taxi is just stopping in   Die Taxe hält gerade vor seinem Haus.
      front of his house.

3. <u>Stellen Sie den Papierkorb bitte</u>   <u>Please put the wastepaper basket</u>
   <u>unter den Schreibtisch.</u>   <u>under the desk.</u>

   a. Hang this picture above the   Hängen Sie dieses Bild über das grosse
      large sofa.   Sofa.
   b. Please drive your car ⌊around⌋   Fahren Sie bitte Ihren Wagen hinter
      behind the house.   das Haus.
   c. She puts the little table beside   Sie stellt den kleinen Tisch neben
      her easy-chair.   ihren Sessel.
   d. We're moving to ('into') another   Wir ziehen in eine andere Stadt.
      city.
   e. Drive ⌊up⌋ onto this parking   Fahren Sie doch auf diesen Parkplatz.
      lot.
   f. He sits down in front of the   Er setzt sich vor das grosse Fenster.
      big window.

4. <u>Die Zeitung liegt hinter der Lampe.</u>   <u>The newspaper is behind the lamp.</u>

   a. The pictures are still in the   Die Bilder sind noch in der grossen
      big crate.   Kiste.
   b. My car stops at the corner there.   Mein Wagen hält dort an der Ecke.
   c. He's sitting behind his   Er sitzt hinter seinem Bekannten.
      friend.
   d. The blanket is lying over the   Die Wolldecke liegt über der
      back of the chair.   Stuhllehne.
   e. The bus stops in front of the   Der Autobus hält vor der neuen Bank.
      new bank.
   f. The big easy-chair is between   Der grosse Sessel steht zwischen dem
      the bookcase and the smoking   Bücherschrank und dem Rauchtisch.
      table.

5. Das ist ein Zimmer mit vielen
   neuen Möbeln.

    a. We're staying with nice German
      relatives.
      b. They work in large new offices.
      c. He introduces him to a few
      American gentlemen.
      d. I don't like to live in old,
      small hotels.

6. Wir haben gute französische
   Zeitungen.

    a. Get me /̲ some̲_/ other good
      stationery.
      b. He has /̲ some̲_/ old famous
      stamps.
      c. We still need /̲ some̲_/ other
      good carpets.
      d. I hope we can find /̲ some̲_/
      good German wine there.

7. Der grosse Schreibtisch steht auf
   dem Teppich.

    a. The freight is still in the
      cellar.
      b. Are you going to put the new
      floor lamp in the corner or-
      next to the easy chair?
      c. Put the new sofa there against
      the wall, please.
      d. Our car is behind the house.
      e. Are the books already in the
      book-case?
      f. Put the typewriter on the table
      next to the lamp.

8. Er legt den Füller und das
   Briefpapier auf den Schreibtisch.

    a. Where do you want to put the
      carpet?
      b. The rug is already in the
      living room.
      c. The letter is under your new
      book.
      d. Put the passport in your desk.

    e. The woolen blankets are in the
      bedroom on our beds.

That's a room with a lot of nice
furniture.

Wir wohnen bei netten deutschen
Verwandten.
Sie arbeiten in grossen neuen Büros.
Er macht ihn mit einigen
amerikanischen Herren bekannt.
Ich wohne nicht gern in alten kleinen
Hotels.

We have /̲ some̲_/ good French
newspapers.

Holen Sie mir bitte anderes gutes
Briefpapier.
Er hat alte berühmte Briefmarken.

Wir brauchen noch andere gute Teppiche.

Hoffentlich können wir dort guten
deutschen Wein finden.

The big desk is on the rug.

Das Frachtgut steht noch im Keller.

Stellen Sie die neue Stehlampe in die
Ecke oder neben den Sessel?

Stellen Sie das neue Sofa bitte dort
an die Wand.
Unser Wagen steht hinter dem Haus.
Stehen die Bücher schon im Bücherschrank?
Stellen Sie die Schreibmaschine
auf den Tisch neben die Lampe.

He puts the fountain pen and the
stationery on the desk.

Wo wollen Sie den Teppich hinlegen?

Der Teppich liegt schon im Wohnzimmer.

Der Brief liegt unter Ihrem neuen
Buch.
Legen Sie den Pass in Ihren
Schreibtisch.
Die Wolldecken liegen im Schlafzimmer
auf unseren Betten.

9. Stellen Sie den Papierkorb unter den Tisch.

Put the wastebasket under the table.

a. In front of the window is a small desk.

Vor dem Fenster steht ein kleiner Schreibtisch.

b. Next to the sofa is an easy-chair.

Neben dem Sofa steht ein Sessel.

c. He's putting the round table in front of the sofa.

Er stellt den runden Tisch vor das Sofa.

d. Where shall I put the chair?

Wo soll ich den Stuhl hinstellen?

e. On the desk is a pretty lamp.

Auf dem Schreibtisch steht eine schöne Lampe.

10. Die Kinder liegen schon im Bett.

The children are already in bed.

a. The questionnaires are on my desk.

Die Fragebogen liegen auf meinem Schreibtisch.

b. The secretary puts the forms in the consul's office.

Die Sekretärin legt die Formulare ins Büro des Konsuls.

c. The quilt is on a chair in our bedroom.

Die Steppdecke liegt auf einem Stuhl in unserem Schlafzimmer.

d. The new paper is on the table by the door.

Die neue Zeitung liegt auf dem Tisch neben der Tür.

e. Put the book on my desk please.

Legen Sie das Buch bitte auf meinen Schreibtisch.

11. Stellen Sie das Sofa an die Wand und die Stehlampe daneben.

Put the sofa over against the wall and the floor lamp next to it.

a. I'll put the little table beside the easy chair and the smoking table in front of it.

Den kleinen Tisch stelle ich neben den Sessel und den Rauchtisch davor.

b. Does the floor lamp go beside the smoking table? No, behind it.

Kommt die Stehlampe neben den Rauchtisch? Nein, dahinter.

c. Put the chair in front of the desk please and the wastebasket under it.

Stellen Sie den Stuhl bitte vor den Schreibtisch und den Papierkorb darunter.

d. We'll put the sofa over against the wall and hang the picture above it.

Das Sofa stellen wir an die Wand und das Bild hängen wir darüber.

e. In the bedroom there are two beds (standing) and between them there is a chair.

Im Schlafzimmer stehen zwei Betten und dazwischen steht ein Stuhl.

12. Ist der Koffer bei meinem anderen Gepäck? Ja, er ist auch dabei.

Is the suitcase with my other luggage? Yes, it's / there / along with it.

a. Mr. Becker is going to America soon; did you know that? ('Do you know that already?') Yes, he talks about it a lot.

Herr Becker fährt bald nach Amerika, wissen Sie das schon? Ja, er spricht viel davon.

b. The typewriter is not good, but I can still write with ('on') it.

Die Schreibmaschine ist nicht gut, aber ich kann darauf noch schreiben.

c. I'd like to buy a house, but I don't have any money for it.

Ich möchte ein Haus kaufen, aber ich habe kein Geld dafür.

d. I like your new suit, and your necktie goes well with it too.

Ihr neuer Anzug gefällt mir gut, und die Krawatte passt auch gut dazu.

VOCABULARY DRILL

1. einziehen - "to move in"

   a. Wann ziehen Sie hier ein?   When are you moving in here?
   b. Sie zieht heute ein.   She's moving in today.
   c. Wir wollen bald einziehen.   We're planning to move in soon.
   d. Ich glaube, Sie können noch   I believe you can't move in yet.
      nicht einziehen.

2. ziehen - "to move"

   a. Wir ziehen nächste Woche in   We're moving into our new house
      unser neues Haus.   next week.
   b. Er zieht heute in die Wohnung   He's moving into the apartment next
      nebenan.   door today.
   c. Wann wollen Sie in Ihr neues   When are you planning to move into
      Haus ziehen?   your new house?
   d. Kellers ziehen bald in eine   The Kellers are moving to a new
      andere Wohnung.   ('different') apartment soon.

3. einrichten - "to arrange, set up (the furniture);
                 to fix up (the place of dwelling)"

   a. Morgen richten wir unser neues   We're setting up the furniture in
      Haus ein.   our new house tomorrow.
   b. Heute richten wir die anderen   We'll fix up the other rooms today.
      Zimmer ein.
   c. Sie richtet ihr Zimmer mit   She's fixing up her room with new
      neuen Möbeln ein.   furniture.
   d. Wann wollen Sie Ihre Wohnung   When do you intend to fix up your
      einrichten?   apartment?

4. auspacken - "to unpack"

   a. Wir müssen noch die Kisten   We still have to unpack the crates.
      auspacken.
   b. Sie packt gerade ihren grossen   She's just unpacking her big suitcase.
      Koffer aus.
   c. Wollen wir die neue Wäsche   Shall we unpack the new linens
      gleich auspacken?   right away?
   d. Bitte packen Sie jetzt das gute   Please unpack the good dinnerware
      Geschirr aus.   now.

5. ankommen - "to come, to get (to a destination); to arrive"

   a. Hoffentlich kommt der Brief   I hope the letter gets there soon.
      bald an.
   b. Die neuen Sessel sollen heute   The new easy-chairs are supposed
      ankommen.   to come today.
   c. Wann kommt das Frachtgut hier   When does the freight get here?
      an?
   d. Ich glaube, die Kisten kommen   I believe the crates won't get here
      heute noch nicht an.   today.

6. <u>aussehen</u> - "to look, to appear to be"

    a. Wie sieht Ihr neues Haus aus?   What does your new house look like?
    b. Ihre neuen Möbel sehen wirklich   Your new furniture really looks
        sehr schön aus.   very nice.
    c. Ihr Wagen sieht noch ganz   Your car looks almost new.
        neu aus.
    d. Diese Wohnung sieht sehr sauber   This apartment looks very clean.
        aus.

7. <u>sich etwas ansehen</u> - "to look at something"

    a. Darf ich mir mal Ihre schönen   May I take a look at your beautiful
        Bilder ansehen?   pictures?
    b. Heute wollen wir uns einige   We want to look at some new furniture
        neue Möbel ansehen.   today.
    c. Sie sehen sich gerade unseren   They're just taking a look around
        Garten an.   our yard.
    d. Er sieht sich die kleine   He's looking at the little typewriter.
        Schreibmaschine an.

8. <u>helfen</u> (plus dative) - "to help (someone)"

    a. Können wir Ihnen beim Einrichten   Can we help you set up the furniture?
        helfen?
    b. Sie hilft ihm heute im Büro.   She's helping him at the office today.
    c. Helfen Sie bitte der Sekretärin   Please help the secretary in the
        in der Visa-Abteilung.   visa section.
    d. Sie hilft ihrem Vater heute im   She's helping her father in the store
        Geschäft.   today.

9. <u>passen</u> (plus prep with acc) - "the right (or a good) place for ... is ..."

    a. Der neue Sessel passt gut dort   That's a good place for the new easy-
        in die Ecke.   chair, there in the corner.
    b. Die alten Möbel passen nicht in   This room is not the right place for
        dieses Zimmer.   the old furniture.
    c. Der kleine Tisch passt gut neben   That's a good place for the little
        den Sessel.   table, beside the easy-chair.
    d. Passt diese grosse Lampe auf den   Is that the right place for this big
        Schreibtisch?   lamp, on the desk?

10. <u>passen zu</u> (dat) - "to go with, to match"

    a. Dieser neue Schreibtisch passt   This new desk goes well with the
        gut zu den Möbeln.   furniture.
    b. Die grossen Sessel passen nicht   The big easy-chairs don't match the
        zu dem kleinen Sofa.   little sofa.
    c. Diese Stühle passen sehr gut zu   These chairs match the table very
        dem Tisch.   well.
    d. Der Bücherschrank soll zu den   The bookcase is supposed to match
        Möbeln passen.   the furniture.

11. **tragen** - "to carry

    a. Er trägt die Bücher zur   He's carrying the books to the library.
       Bibliothek.
    b. Tragen Sie die grossen Koffer   Carry the big suitcases to the attic
       bitte auf den Boden.   please.
    c. Die Männer tragen einige grosse The men are carrying a few large
       Kisten in den Keller.   crates to the cellar.
    d. Sie können die Wolldecken erst   You can carry the blankets into the
       mal ins Schlafzimmer tragen.   bedroom for the moment.

12. **(sich) mieten** - "to rent (for oneself)"

    a. Ich muss ein anderes Zimmer   I have to rent a different room.
       mieten.
    b. Kellers mieten ein Haus in   The Kellers are renting a house in
       unserer Nachbarschaft.   our neighborhood.
    c. Er will sich in Bonn einen   He's planning to rent a car in Bonn.
       Wagen mieten.
    d. Wir wollen uns in München eine We're planning to rent a large
       Wohnung mieten.   apartment in Munich.

13. **vermieten** - "to rent (out)"

    a. Er will das Zimmer im zweiten   He's planning to rent out the room
       Stock vermieten.   on the third floor.
    b. Sind hier viele grosse   Are there many large apartments for
       Wohnungen zu vermieten?   rent here?
    c. Herr Becker kann sein Haus   Mr. Becker is unfortunately not able
       leider nicht vermieten.   to rent his house.
    d. Herr Schulze will uns sein   Mr. Schulze wants to rent us his
       Haus vermieten.   house.

14. **sich (hin)setzen** - "to sit (down)"

    a. Setzen Sie sich bitte in diesen Please sit in this easy-chair.
       Sessel.
    b. Jetzt können wir uns endlich   Now we can sit down at last.
       hinsetzen.
    c. Wir setzen uns an den   We're going to sit at the kitchen
       Küchentisch.   table.
    d. Wollen Sie sich nicht hinsetzen? Don't you want to sit down?
    e. Ich setze mich auf das Sofa.   I'll sit on the sofa.
    f. Wo können wir uns hinsetzen?   Where can we sit?
    g. Er setzt sich an den Schreib-   He sits down at the desk.
       tisch.

15. **sitzen** - "to be seated"

    a. Er sitzt den ganzen Tag an   He sits at his desk all day.
       seinem Schreibtisch.
    b. Ich glaube, sie sitzt neben   I think she's sitting beside her
       ihrem Vater.   father.
    c. Wir wollen heute im Garten   Why don't we sit /out_7 in the yard
       sitzen.   today.
    d. Sie sitzt auf ihrem Stuhl   She's sitting in her chair beside
       neben dem Fenster.   the window.

                                          (End of Tape 7B)

TRANSLATION (not recorded)

1. The Beckers have a new house in a suburb of Cologne.	Beckers haben ein neues Haus in einem Vorort von Köln.
2. Behind the house there's a beautiful yard.	Hinter dem Haus ist ein schöner Garten.
3. It's /an/ ideal /place/ for the children to play.	Der ist ideal für die Kinder zum Spielen.
4. Their friends, Mr. and Mrs. Keller, want to rent a house for themselves soon too.	Ihre Bekannten, Herr und Frau Keller, wollen sich auch bald ein Haus mieten.
5. Perhaps they'll move into the Becker's neighborhood.	Vielleicht ziehen sie in die Nachbarschaft von Beckers.
6. There are still a few nice houses for rent there.	Dort sind noch einige nette Häuser zu vermieten.
7. And the rent isn't very high either.	Und die Miete ist auch nicht sehr hoch.
8. The Beckers are moving into their house today.	Heute ziehen Beckers in ihr Haus.
9. The furnace is all right now too.	Die Heizung ist jetzt auch in Ordnung.
10. Mr. and Mrs. Keller are helping the Beckers arrange the furniture.	Herr und Frau Keller helfen Beckers beim Einrichten.
11. They only have the living-room left to fix up.	Sie müssen nur noch das Wohnzimmer einrichten.
12. In the other rooms the furniture is already in place.	In den anderen Zimmern stehen die Möbel schon an Ort und Stelle.
13. They begin with the carpet.	Sie fangen mit dem Teppich an.
14. They put it in the middle of the room.	Sie legen ihn in die Mitte des Zimmers.
15. Then they put the round table in front of the two easy-chairs.	Dann stellen sie den runden Tisch vor die beiden Sessel.
16. They put the large sofa over against the wall.	Das grosse Sofa stellen sie an die Wand.
17. That's a good place for it.	Es passt gut dorthin.
18. The floor lamp is supposed to be between the smoking table and the bookcase.	Zwischen dem Rauchtisch und dem Bücherschrank soll die Stehlampe stehen.
19. The Beckers have a new desk.	Beckers haben einen neuen Schreibtisch.
20. It matches the other furniture well.	Der passt gut zu den anderen Möbeln.
21. They put it in front of the big window for the time being.	Sie stellen ihn vorläufig vor das grosse Fenster.
22. A few crates are still in the moving van.	Einige Kisten sind noch im Möbelwagen.
23. The men are just bringing two crates into the house.	Die Männer bringen gerade zwei Kisten ins Haus.
24. I hope the crate with the pictures is one of them.	Hoffentlich ist die Bilderkiste mit dabei.
25. They want to hang the big picture over the sofa.	Sie wollen das grosse Bild über das Sofa hängen.
26. The things are very well packed.	Die Verpackung der Sachen ist sehr ordentlich.
27. Mr. Becker is very well satisfied with it.	Herr Becker ist sehr zufrieden damit.
28. Unfortunately the freight isn't there yet.	Leider ist das Frachtgut noch nicht da.
29. Mr. Becker intends to call right away.	Herr Becker will gleich anrufen.
30. But now he can't find the telephone book.	Aber jetzt kann er das Telephonbuch nicht finden.
31. Mrs. Becker looks /for it/ and finds it.	Frau Becker sucht und findet es.
32. It's under the newspapers.	Es liegt unter den Zeitungen.

33. Then Mrs. Becker takes care of the good dinnerware.
Dann kümmert sich Frau Becker um das gute Geschirr.

34. Mrs. Keller intends to unpack the linen in the meantime.
Frau Keller will inzwischen die Wäsche auspacken.

35. She lays the new woolen blankets over the back of the chair.
Sie legt die neuen Wolldecken über die Stuhllehne.

36. The quilts are already on the beds in the bedroom.
Die Steppdecken liegen schon im Schlafzimmer auf den Betten.

37. The empty crates and suitcases are still in the rooms.
In den Zimmern stehen noch die leeren Kisten und Koffer.

38. They have to get rid of them.
Die müssen sie wegschaffen.

39. The men are to carry the crates to the cellar.
Die Männer sollen die Kisten in den Keller tragen.

40. Mr. Becker and Mr. Keller take the suitcases to the attic.
Herr Becker und Herr Keller bringen die Koffer auf den Boden.

41. Mrs. Keller wants to clean up a bit.
Frau Keller will etwas saubermachen.

42. Now everything looks quite cozy.
Jetzt sieht alles ganz gemütlich aus.

43. At last they can relax in a chair.
Endlich können sie mal sitzen.

44. They sit down at the kitchen table and eat something.
Sie setzen sich an den Küchentisch und essen etwas.

45. The kitchen is very nice, with /_a_/ combination gas and electric range, large refrigerator and many built-in cupboards.
Die Küche ist sehr schön, mit kombiniertem Gas- und Elektroherd, grossem Kühlschrank und vielen eingebauten Schränken.

RESPONSE DRILL

1. Was machen Beckers?
Sie ziehen in ihr neues Haus ein.

2. Wer hilft ihnen beim Einrichten?
Herr und Frau Keller helfen ihnen beim Einrichten.

3. Welches Zimmer richten sie ein?
Sie richten das Wohnzimmer ein.

4. Warum richten sie nicht auch die anderen Zimmer ein?
In den anderen Zimmern steht schon alles an Ort und Stelle.

5. Wohin legen sie den Teppich?
Sie legen ihn in die Mitte des Zimmers.

6. Was stellen sie vor die Sessel?
Sie stellen den kleinen Tisch vor die Sessel.

7. Wo steht das Sofa?
Das Sofa steht an der Wand.

8. Wohin stellen sie die Stehlampe?
Sie stellen sie zwischen den Rauchtisch und den Bücherschrank.

9. Haben Beckers einen alten Schreibtisch?
Nein, sie haben einen neuen.

10. Wo soll der Schreibtisch stehen?
Er soll vor dem grossen Fenster stehen.

11. Wohin soll Frau Keller die Wolldecken legen?
Sie soll sie über die Stuhllehne legen.

12. Wo liegen die Steppdecken?
Die Steppdecken liegen im Schlafzimmer auf den Betten.

13. Um was kümmert sich Frau Becker?
Sie kümmert sich um das Geschirr.

14. Was macht Frau Keller inzwischen?
Sie packt die Wäsche aus.

15. Wo soll das grosse Bild hinkommen?
Sie wollen es über das Sofa hängen.

16. Wer trägt die Kisten ins Haus?
Die Männer tragen sie ins Haus.

17. Wie ist die Verpackung?
Die Verpackung ist gut und Beckers sind sehr zufrieden damit.

18. Ist die Heizung in Ordnung?
Ja; die Handwerker sind jedenfalls dagewesen.

19. Wie sieht jetzt alles aus?
Jetzt sieht alles richtig gemütlich aus.

20. Was machen sie mit den leeren Kisten und Koffern?
Die Koffer bringen sie auf den Boden und die Männer tragen die leeren Kisten in den Keller.

21. Was wollen Frau Becker und Frau Keller machen?
Sie wollen etwas sauber machen.

(This drill is continued on next page.)

22. Wohin setzen sie sich später?

Sie setzen sich an den Küchentisch und essen etwas.

23. Wie ist die Küche?

Die Küche ist sehr schön.

24. Warum gefällt Frau Keller die Küche so gut?

Es ist eine Küche mit grossem Kühlschrank, kombiniertem Gas- und Elektroherd und vielen eingebauten Schränken.

25. Wo ist der Garten?

Er ist hinter dem Haus.

26. Für wen ist der Garten ideal?

Er ist ideal für die Kinder zum Spielen.

27. Warum wohnt Frau Becker gern im Vorort?

Im Vorort ist es viel ruhiger als in der Stadt.

28. Was wollen Kellers bald tun?

Sie wollen sich bald ein Haus mieten.

29. Wo sind noch nette Häuser zu vermieten?

In der Nachbarschaft von Beckers sind noch einige nette Häuser zu vermieten.

30. Wie sind die Mieten?

Sie sind garnicht sehr hoch.

31. Wo wohnen Sie?
32. Wieviele Zimmer haben Sie?
33. Was für Möbel stehen in Ihrem Wohnzimmer?
34. Wo stehen diese Möbel
35. Was steht und liegt auf Ihrem Schreibtisch?

CONVERSATION PRACTICE (not recorded)

1

A: Wo soll dieser kleine Tisch stehen?
B: Dort neben dem Bücherschrank.
A: Und die Lampe hier?
B: Stellen Sie die doch bitte zwischen die zwei Fenster.
A: Soll der Sessel dort in der Ecke stehen oder neben der Tür?
B: Ich finde, der passt gut dort in die Ecke.

2

D: Wie hoch sind hier eigentlich die Mieten für neue Wohnungen?
A: Hier in der Stadt sind sie sehr hoch.
D: Ich brauche eine Wohnung mit grossen Zimmern.
A: In unserer Nachbarschaft sind einige nette Häuser zu vermieten. Wollen Sie sich die nicht mal ansehen?
D: Ja, wir möchten auch lieber im Vorort wohnen.

3

A: Wo soll ich die Zeitungen hinlegen?
C: Die können Sie auf den kleinen Tisch legen. Das Telephonbuch liegt auch dort.
A: Kann ich jetzt die Bücher aus= packen?
C: Ja, bitte. Und stellen Sie sie doch gleich in den Bücherschrank.

4

C: Wo sollen wir die Kisten hinstellen?
D: Wieviele Kisten sind es denn?
C: Vier grosse und zwei kleine.
D: Stellen Sie bitte die grossen hier ins Wohnzimmer und die zwei kleinen in die Küche.

5

B: Verzeihung, ist hier ein Zimmer zu vermieten?
C: Ich habe zwei Zimmer zu vermieten, ein grosses und ein kleines.
B: Kann ich mir das grosse Zimmer mal ansehen?
C: Aber gern. Hier rechts, bitte.

SITUATIONS

Johnsons mieten ein Haus

Herr und Frau Johnson sehen sich im
Vorort von Stuttgart ein Haus an. Es
gehört Herrn Meyer, und der möchte es
vermieten. Johnsons brauchen ein
grosses Haus. Sie haben vier kleine
Kinder. Herr Meyer zeigt ihnen die
Zimmer. Das Haus gefällt Johnsons
sehr gut. Die Küche ist sehr gross,
hat aber leider keinen Kühlschrank
und nur einen alten Herd. Herr Meyer
will aber einen neuen Kühlschrank
in die Küche stellen. Dann zeigt er
den Garten hinter dem Haus. Herr
Johnson möchte wissen, wie hoch die
Miete ist. Herr Meyer sagt 400.-- DM.
Johnsons mieten das Haus.

Wo stehen die Möbel?

Der Lehrer stellt einen Stuhl neben,
vor und hinter den Tisch, oder in die
Ecke, vor die Tür und an die Wand.
Der Lehrer stellt den Papierkorb unter
den Schreibtisch, legt sein Buch auf
den Tisch, unter die Zeitung, auf den
Stuhl usw. Die Studenten sagen, was
der Lehrer mit dem Stuhl und den
anderen Sachen macht und wo der Stuhl
und die anderen Sachen stehen oder
liegen.
Der eine Student sagt, welche Möbel
in seiner Wohnung stehen und wo.
Der andere malt (draws) an die Tafel
(blackboard), wie die Wohnung
aussieht.

NARRATIVE

Wissen Sie schon, dass Smiths heute umziehen? Wohin? Nun, ich glaube nach
Chicago. Sie wollen wissen, was sie mit den Möbeln machen? Die Herrenzimmer-
und Esszimmermöbel wollen sie verkaufen, auch das neue Klavier. Sie nehmen nur
die Teppiche, Bilder, Bücher und ihre Betten mit. Warum? Ja, so ein Umzug ist
doch furchtbar teuer und in Chicago können sie sich ja wieder neue Möbel kaufen.
Frau Smith möchte sowieso gern ein Ecksofa im dänischen Stil haben. Sie verstehen
das nicht? Ja, ist denn das in Deutschland anders als hier? Erzählen Sie mal.
Hier ist zum Beispiel die Familie Schröder aus Hamburg. Herr Schröder
arbeitet schon ein Jahr in München und nun hat er endlich eine Wohnung gefunden
und seine Familie kann umziehen. Es ist zwar nur eine kleine Etagenwohnung
aber er muss dafür schon 3000.-- DM Baukostenzuschuss zahlen. Es ist ja so
schwer eine Wohnung zu finden. Heute kommt nun also der Möbelwagen. Alle
Möbel kommen mit, sogar der alte Schrank und der kleine Schreibtisch von Onkel
Fritz, der auf dem Boden stand. Das sind alte Familienstücke und daran hängt
man doch! Die neue Wohnung ist klein, aber irgendwo wird man schon einen Platz
dafür finden. Man kann die Sachen ja zuerst auch auf den Boden stellen. Und
vielleicht geht der Traum vom 'Eigenheim' doch mal in Erfüllung.

umziehen	move	zahlen	pay
das Herrenzimmer	study	schwer	difficult
verkaufen	sell	das Familienstück	heirloom
das Klavier	piano	daran hängt man doch	of course one
der Umzug	move		is attached to them
teuer	expensive	irgendwo	somewhere
kaufen	buy	der Traum	dream
anders	different	das Eigenheim	home of one's
erzählen	tell		own
die Familie	family	in Erfüllung gehen	come true
zwar	to be sure		
der Baukostenzuschuss	option paid to		
apartment builder by	future tenants		

FINDER LIST

	alles	all, everything
	anderen	other
	anfangen	begin, start
	ankommen	arrive
	ansehen	
	sich etwas ansehen	look at something
	auspacken	unpack
	aussehen	look, appear
	beide	both
	besonders	especially
das	Bett,-en	bed
das	Bild,-er	picture
die	Bilderkiste,-n	crate with the pictures
der	Boden,ᐞ	attic
	bringen	bring, take (something somewhere)
der	Bücherschrank,ᐞe	bookcase
	dabei	with them, among them
	dagewesen	been there
	danach	after that
die	Decke,-n	blanket, cover
	draussen	outside, out here
	einfach	easy, simple
am	einfachsten	the easiest, simplest
	eingebaut	built-in
das	Einrichten	arranging (of the furniture)
	einrichten	arrange (the furniture)
	einziehen	move in
der	Elektroherd	electric range
	endlich	at last
	erst	first
	erst mal	for the moment
das	Fenster,-	window
	finden	think (that something is thus and so)
	folgend	following
	folgende Zahlen	(the) following numbers
das	Frachtgut,ᐞer	freight
	garnicht	not at all
der	Garten,ᐞ	garden
der	Gasherd	gas range
	gegeben	given, taken
	gemütlich	cozy, comfortable, inviting
das	Geschirr	china, dishes
	gestern	yesterday
der	Handwerker,-	workman
	hängen	hang
die	Heizung,-en	radiator; heating plant
	helfen	help
	heraufbringen	bring up, bring in
der	Herd,-e	range
	hinkommen	go, belong in a certain place
	hinter (two-way prep)	behind
sich	hinsetzen	sit down
	hinstellen	put (down)
	hoch	high
	hoffen	hope
	ideal	ideal
	inzwischen	in the meantime
	jedenfalls	at any rate, in any case
der	Keller,-	basement, cellar
das	Kind,-er	child
die	Kiste,-n	crate
	klein	little
	kombiniert	combined
	könnten	could

die	Küche,-n	kitchen
der	Küchentisch,-e	kitchen table
der	Kühlschrank,-̈e	refrigerator
sich	kümmern (um etwas)	bother (about something), take care (of something)
die	Lampe,-n	lamp
	leer	empty
	legen	lay, put
die	Leute	people
	liegen	lie
die	Miete,-n	rent
sich	mieten	rent
die	Mitte	middle
die	Möbel (pl)	furniture
die	Mühe	effort, pains
	ich gebe mir Mühe	I make an effort, I take pains
	na	well
die	Nachbarschaft	neighorhood
	ordentlich	neat, tidy
an	Ort und Stelle	in place
der	Packer,-	packer
	passen	fit
	passen (zu etwas)	match, go (with)
der	Rauchtisch,-e	smoking table
	recht	right, quite
	richtig	really
	ruhig	quiet
die	Sache,-n	thing
	sauber	clean
	saubermachen	clean up
	er macht ... sauber	he cleans up
das	Schlafzimmer,-	bedroom
	schöner	nicer
der	Schrank,-̈e	cupboard
der	Schreibtisch,-e	desk
der	Sessel,-	easy-chair
sich	setzen	sit down
	sitzen	sit
	so	such
das	Sofa,-s	sofa
	solch	such, like that
das	Spielen	playing
	stehen	stand
die	Stehlampe,-n	floor lamp
	stellen	put, place
die	Steppdecke,-n	quilt
der	Stuhl,-̈e	chair
die	Stuhllehne,-n	back of the chair
	Tausend	a thousand
das	Telephonbuch,-̈er	telephone book
der	Teppich,-e	carpet, rug
der	Tisch,-e	table
	tragen	carry
	über (two-way prep)	over, above
	überhaupt	at all, anyhow
	übrigens	by the way
	unter (two-way prep)	under
	vermieten	rent (to someone)
die	Verpackung	packing
	viel	much, many
	vor (two-way prep)	in front of
	vorläufig	temporarely, for the time being
der	Vorort,-e	suburb
die	Wand,-̈e	wall
die	Wäsche	linen
	wegschaffen	to clear away

das	Wohnzimmer,-	living-room
die	Wolldecke,-n	wool blanket
	ziehen	move
das	Zimmer,-	room
	zufrieden	satisfied
	zwischen (two-way prep)	between

„Den nehme ich!"

Tape 8A   BEIM EINKAUFEN

                               Basic Sentences

                 I   I

the person   die Person,-en
the sales clerk   der Verkäufer,-

Cast of characters: Mr. Becker,   Personen: Herr Becker, Herr Wilson,
Mr. Wilson, a sales clerk.   ein Verkäufer.

the errand, purchase   die Besorgung,-en
to do errands, to go   Besorgungen machen
shopping

MR. BECKER   HERR BECKER

I have to do some shopping.   Ich muss einige Besorgungen machen.
Do you want to come along?   Wollen Sie mitkommen?

to buy   kaufen

MR. WILSON   HERR WILSON

What are you planning to buy?   Was wollen Sie denn kaufen?

a couple, a few   ein paar[1]
the shirt   das Hemd,-en
the soft-collar shirt   das Sporthemd,-en

MR. BECKER   HERR BECKER

A few (soft-collar) shirts.   Ein paar Sporthemden.

MR. WILSON   HERR WILSON

What store are you going to?   In welches Geschäft gehen Sie?

usually   gewöhnlich

MR. BECKER   HERR BECKER

I usually buy ⌐my things⌐ at   Ich kaufe gewöhnlich bei Schwarz
Schwarz and Co.   und Co.

reasonable, inexpensive   preiswert
the men's ready-made   das Herrenkonfektions-
clothing store   geschäft,-e

It's an inexpensive men's clothing   Das ist ein preiswertes Herren-
store.   konfektionsgeschäft.

MR. WILSON   HERR WILSON

Well, I'll be glad to come along then.   Ja, da komme ich gern mit..

the suit   der Anzug,-̈e
the summer   der Sommer,-
the summer suit   der Sommeranzug,-̈e

I'd like to look at a couple of summer suits.	Ich möchte mir mal ein paar Sommeranzüge ansehen
Do you buy your suits there too?	Kaufen Sie Ihre Anzüge auch dort?

rather, pretty
the selection

ziemlich
die Auswahl

MR. BECKER

HERR BECKER

Yes, you'll have a pretty large selection there.	Ja, Sie haben dort eine ziemlich grosse Auswahl.

I suppose, you suppose
light-weight

wohl
leicht

MR. WILSON

HERR WILSON

How much do you suppose a light-weight suit costs?	Wieviel kostet wohl ein leichter Anzug?

all
the price range

allen
die Preislage,-n

MR. BECKER

HERR BECKER

You'll find them in all price ranges.	Die finden Sie in allen Preislagen.

to spend

ausgeben

About how much do you want to spend?	Wieviel wollen Sie ungefähr ausgeben?

approximately, around

etwa

MR. WILSON

HERR WILSON

Around two hundred marks.	Etwa zweihundert Mark.

at the moment
to be able to afford something
I can afford it

augenblicklich
sich etwas leisten können

ich kann es mir leisten

I can't afford any more at the moment.	Mehr kann ich mir augenblicklich nicht leisten.

suitable
something suitable

passend
etwas Passendes[2]

MR. BECKER

HERR BECKER

In that price range you'll certainly find something suitable.	In der Preislage finden Sie sicher etwas Passendes.

II	II

In the store.

Im Geschäft.

SALES CLERK

VERKÄUFER

Good day, gentlemen.

Guten Tag, meine Herren.

What would you like? ('What may it be?')

Was darf's sein?

white
colored

weiss
farbig

MR. BECKER

HERR BECKER

Can you show me a few white and a few colored (soft-collar) shirts?

Können Sie mir ein paar weisse und ein paar farbige Sporthemden zeigen?

long
short
the sleeve

lang
kurz
der Ärmel,-

SALES CLERK

VERKÄUFER

Glad to. With long or short sleeves?

Gern; mit langen oder kurzen Ärmeln?

MR. BECKER

HERR BECKER

Long.

Mit langen.

SALES CLERK

VERKÄUFER

How do you like these here?

Wie gefallen Ihnen diese hier?

the quality

die Qualität,-en

Very good quality!

Sehr gute Qualität!

bad, poor

schlecht

MR. BECKER

HERR BECKER

Not bad. How much do they cost?

Nicht schlecht; wieviel kosten sie?

SALES CLERK

VERKÄUFER

The white one costs twenty-five fifty.

Das weisse kostet fünfundzwanzig Mark fünfzig.

striped
cheap
cheaper

gestreift
billig
billiger

The striped one is somewhat cheaper.

Das gestreifte ist etwas billiger.

MR. BECKER

HERR BECKER

Give me one striped one and two white ones please.

Geben Sie mir bitte ein gestreiftes und zwei weisse.

something else in addition
the underwear
some underwear

sonst noch etwas
die Unterwäsche
etwas Unterwäsche[3]

the pair
the sock

das Paar
die Socke,-n

SALES CLERK

VERKÄUFER

Will there be anything else? ('May
it be something else in addition?')

Darf es sonst noch etwas sein?

Perhaps some underwear or a pair of
socks?

Vielleicht etwas Unterwäsche oder ein
Paar Socken?

the necktie

die Krawatte,-n

MR. BECKER

HERR BECKER

No, but let me see some neckties,
please.

Nein, aber zeigen Sie mir bitte noch
einige Krawatten.

solid colored
figured

einfarbig
gemustert

SALES CLERK

VERKÄUFER

Solid colors or figured? ('Solid
colored ones or figured ones?')

Einfarbige oder gemusterte?

MR. BECKER

HERR BECKER

Figured ones.

Gemusterte.

bright, loud

auffällig

SALES CLERK

VERKÄUFER

Is this one too bright for you?

Ist Ihnen diese hier zu auffällig?

Tt goes well with your suit.

Sie passt gut zu Ihrem Anzug.

MR. BECKER

HERR BECKER

Yes, I like it.

Ja, die gefällt mir.

green
in addition
along with it

grün
dazu
mit dazu

And put this green one in along with
it, too.

Und legen Sie diese grüne noch mit
dazu.

That's all then.

Das ist dann alles.

SALES CLERK

VERKÄUFER

Thank you very much.

Vielen Dank.

the slip
the sales slip

der Zettel,-
der Kassenzettel,-

Here's your sales slip.

Hier ist Ihr Kassenzettel.

to pay
the cashier's desk or window

bezahlen
die Kasse,-n

Please pay there at the cashier's
window.

Bezahlen Sie bitte dort an der Kasse.

to get
downstairs

bekommen
unten

MR. WILSON

HERR WILSON

Are the suits downstairs here too?
('Does one get suits downstairs here
too?')

Bekommt man Anzüge auch hier unten?

SALES CLERK

VERKÄUFER

No, on the second floor.

Nein, im ersten Stock.

the elevator

der Fahrstuhl, ̈e

The elevator is there to the right.

Der Fahrstuhl ist dort rechts.

III

III

SALES CLERK

VERKÄUFER

What can I show you?

Was darf ich Ihnen zeigen?

I'd like to have, I'm
interested (in having)

ich hätte gern

MR. WILSON

HERR WILSON

I'm interested in a light-weight suit.

Ich hätte gern einen leichten Anzug.

particular, certain
the wish

bestimmt
der Wunsch, ̈e

SALES CLERK

VERKÄUFER

Certainly; do you have something
particular in mind? ('Do you have a
particular wish?')

Bitte sehr; haben Sie einen bestimmten
Wunsch?

grey
the show window

grau
das Schaufenster,-

MR. WILSON

HERR WILSON

You have a grey suit in the show
window, right at the door.

Sie haben einen grauen Anzug im
Schaufenster, gleich an der Tür.

I like that one quite well.

Der gefällt mir ganz gut.

to mean
light grey

meinen
hellgrau

SALES CLERK

VERKÄUFER

Do you mean the light grey one?

Meinen Sie den hellgrauen?

similar

ähnlich

MR. WILSON

HERR WILSON

Yes, do you have one like that here
perhaps? ('Perhaps you have a similar
one here?')

Ja; vielleicht haben Sie einen
ähnlichen hier?

the size	die Grösse,-n

SALES CLERK

VERKÄUFER

I'm sorry, I don't have the grey one in your size any more.

Den grauen habe ich leider nicht mehr in Ihrer Grösse.

the color	die Farbe,-n
a different color, another color	eine andere Farbe

Would another color be all right? ('May it also be a different color?')

Darf es auch eine andere Farbe sein?

brown	braun

MR. WILSON

HERR WILSON

Yes, the brown one looks very nice, too.

Ja, der braune sieht auch sehr gut aus.

what, what kind of	was für
the material	der Stoff,-e

What kind of ('a') material is that?

Was für ein Stoff ist das?

pure, all	rein
the wool	die Wolle

SALES CLERK

VERKÄUFER

All wool, ('an') excellent quality.

Reine Wolle, eine ausgezeichnete Qualität.

the summer clearance sale	der Sommerschlussverkauf,¨e

And now very reasonable in the summer clearance sale.

Und jetzt im Sommerschlussverkauf sehr preiswert.

the coat, jacket	die Jacke,-n
to try on	anprobieren

MR. WILSON

HERR WILSON

I'll just try the coat on.

Ich will die Jacke mal anprobieren.

the mirror	der Spiegel,-

SALES CLERK

VERKÄUFER

Certainly; there's a mirror over there.

Bitte, da drüben ist ein Spiegel.

the cut	der Schnitt,-e
to fit	sitzen

MR. WILSON

HERR WILSON

I like the cut, and the coat fits well too.

Der Schnitt gefällt mir und die Jacke sitzt auch gut.

How much does the suit cost?

Wieviel kostet der Anzug?

expensive	teuer[4]

SALES CLERK	VERKÄUFER

It's not at all expensive, only a hundred and sixty-five marks.

Er ist garnicht teuer, nur hundert-fünfundsechzig Mark.

to wrap up	einpacken

MR. WILSON	HERR WILSON

All right; wrap it up for me [then] please.

Gut, packen Sie ihn mir bitte ein.

Notes to the Basic Sentences

[1] ein paar corresponds to the English "a couple" in the loose sense of quantity meaning "two or more but pobably less than ten".

[2] etwas Passendes. An adjective after etwas or nichts may function as a das-noun. In the writing system it is therefore usually capitalized, and it has the endings of the adjective-noun sequence or the adjective standing alone referring to a das-noun.

[3] etwas Unterwäsche. Etwas may be followed by a singular noun without a specifier; it functions in this case as an indefinite quantity word.

[4] teuer is the form of the adjective as a predicate, when it has no ending. When endings are added the stem often appears as teur-, and the forms teures, teure, teuren, occur along with teueres, teuere, teueren, etc.

Notes on Pronunciation

A. German ng and nk

    The English words "singer" and "finger" both contain the same nasal sound, a kind of hum through the nose made with the tongue in the position for g. In the first word the nasal sound occurs alone before the following vowel. In the second word we actually have a cluster of ng plus g. We might write "fing-ger" to represent the sounds more accurately. This cluster never occurs in German; only the nasal sound alone occurs between vowels. Practice the following words with your instructor:

Practice 1

bringe	Finger	Klingel
senge	Hunger	Angel
Lunge	Sänger	Bengel

    The English words "bank" and "banker" contain the same nasal sound, but it is followed here by k. We might write "bangk" and "bangker" to represent this cluster more accurately. The same cluster occurs in German, but it is represented in the writing system by both ng and nk. Many speakers pronounce final ng and ng before voiceless consonants as if it were followed by k; other speakers pronounce only a very short nasal sound without the following k. Follow the pronunciation your instructor gives you for these words:

Practice 2

sinke	Wink	Ring	rings	links
lenke	Geschenk	eng	längst	lenkst
Funke	Trunk	jung	jüngst	dankst
danke	Bank	lang	langsam	tunkst

B. Final -b, -d and -s

Final stops and spirants are always <u>voiceless</u> in German. There is nothing like English "had" or "beg" or "was". In the writing system the symbols <u>b</u>, <u>d</u> and <u>s</u> indicate sounds which are voiced at the beginning of words and syllables but voiceless at the end of words and syllables.

Practice 3

Sack	was	Bonn	ob
Süden	als	Leibe	Leib
also	Hotels	Grabes	Grab
Unsinn	preiswert	lobe	Lobgesang

Dose	Jod	gut	Bug
Bades	Bad	Tage	Tag
Süden	Südseite	Sieges	Sieg
leide	leidlich	schweige	schweigsam

Notice also that German, unlike English, may thus have <u>long vowels</u> followed by voiceless consonants.

C. Final -m and -n

English vowels followed by an <u>n</u> or an <u>m</u> tend to be nasalized. There is an anticipation of the nasal consonant during the pronunciation of the vowel. Compare the sounds in English "ban" and "bad" or "on" and "ought", for example, and see if you can hear and feel the difference. The nasalization of vowels does not occur in German in this way. There is, rather, a separation between vowel articulation and articulation of the following <u>m</u> and <u>n</u>. It is almost as if there were two syllables, a vowel syllable and a separate <u>m</u>-syllable or <u>n</u>-syllable with a distinct but very brief hum on the <u>m</u> or <u>n</u>. Practice the following words with your instructor taking care not to nasalize the vowels but to articulate the final nasals separately and distinctly:

Practice 4

lahm	Plan
Lehm	zehn
intim	Wien
Atom	Lohn
Ruhm	Huhn

D. Unstressed final -en

In normal speech the unstressed ending -en often is not pronounced as a full, separate syllable but only as a hum-like extension of the preceding consonant. The same thing takes place in English when you say "wooden" or "broken" at conversational speed. You leave your tongue in the position for <u>d</u> or <u>k</u> while you open your nose and hum for a split second. By this kind of assimilation final -en in German is actually only an /n/, hummed briefly, after <u>d</u>, <u>t</u> or <u>n</u>; after <u>b</u>, <u>p</u> or <u>m</u> it is an /m/; after <u>g</u>, <u>k</u> or <u>ng</u> it is actually a short hum on /ng/.

Practice 5

$[$ -n $]$	$[$ -m $]$	$[$ -ng $]$
eingeladen	ausgeben	gegen
Boden	bleiben	liegen
vermieten	Aktenmappen	umgezogen
arbeiten	tippen	Wolldecken
ihnen	Stehlampen	Socken
wohnen	kommen	bringen
Strassenbahnen	zusammen	Zeitungen

Notes on Grammar

(For Home Study)

A.   Specifiers and Adjectives

I. In the last five units we have presented the forms and patterns of
specifiers and adjectives in sequences and standing alone. A few additional
items we have encountered should also be noted. Here are examples:

Das ist <u>alles</u>.   That's everything.
Die finden Sie in <u>allen</u>   You'll find them in all price ranges.
Preislagen.

Können Sie mir <u>ein paar</u>   Can you show me a few white shirts?
weisse Hemden zeigen?

<u>Was für</u> ein Stoff ist das?   What kind of material is that?

In der Preislage finden Sie   In that price range you'll certainly
sicher <u>etwas</u> Passendes.   find something suitable.

1. <u>All-</u> is a <u>der</u>-type specifier. In the singular it usually occurs with
the endings <u>-es</u> or <u>-em</u> and usually stands alone or is followed only by
an adjective. In the plural it occurs both alone and as part of the
regular specifier-adjective-noun sequence.

Haben Sie alles?   Do you have everything?
Ich bin mit allem   I'm satisfied with everything.
zufrieden.
Alles andere kaufe ich   I'll buy everything else tomorrow.
morgen.
Nicht alle deutschen   Not all German cars are small.
Wagen sind klein.
In allen grossen Städten   In all large cities you'll find a
finden Sie einige gute   few good hotels.
Hotels.

2. The fixed phrases <u>ein paar</u> and <u>was für</u> are NOT specifiers. They are
indeclinable modifiers like the numbers. They are invariable; that is,
they have no endings or variations in form. <u>Ein paar</u> has indefinite
plural reference, and adjectives following it have the forms of the
adjective-noun sequence noted in Unit 7. <u>Was für</u> has both plural and
singular reference. In the singular it is usually followed by a form
of the specifier <u>ein</u>, in the plural by the adjective-noun sequence.
<u>Was für</u> may function both to introduce a question: "What kind of ...?"
or to introduce an exclamation: "What ... !

Hier sind ein paar leichte Sommeranzüge.	Here are a couple of light-weight summer suits.
Ich habe nur ein paar grüne Krawatten.	I only have a couple of green neckties.
Das sind Briefe von ein paar alten Freunden in Deutschland.	Those are letters from a couple of old friends in Germany.
Was für Anzüge sind das, Sommeranzüge?	What kind of suits are those, summer suits?
Was für schöne und preiswerte Anzüge sind das!	What good and inexpensive suits those are!
Was für ein guter Stoff ist das!	What good material that is!
Mit was für einem Füller schreiben Sie?	What kind of a pen are you writing with?
In was für ein Geschäft gehen wir, in ein Herrenkonfektionsgeschäft?	What kind of a store are we going to, a men's ready-made clothing store?

3. The quantity words <u>etwas</u> and <u>nichts</u> likewise are NOT specifiers, and adjectives following them have the forms of the adjective-noun sequence or of the adjective standing alone.

Ich möchte gern etwas Kaltes trinken.	I'd like something cold to drink.
Haben Sie etwas Ähnliches hier?	Do you have something similar here?
Es gibt nichts Neues.	There's nothing new.
Ich habe nichts Bestimmtes vor.	I don't have anything particular planned.

Note that an adjective standing <u>alone</u> after one of these words has indefinite reference, and its forms are those of an adjective referring to a <u>das</u>-noun. The adjective itself functions as a noun, and it is usually capitalized in the writing system.

II. Some confusion arises in phrases with <u>alle</u>, <u>viele</u>, <u>einige</u>, <u>ein paar</u> and <u>was für</u>. Here is a summary presentation of specifier-adjective-noun sequences and adjective-noun sequences involving these words.

1. Specifier-adjective-noun sequences:

Sind das <u>meine deutschen Bücher</u>?	Are those my German books?
<u>Welche deutschen Bücher</u> sind das?	Which German books are those?
Nicht <u>alle deutschen Bücher</u> sind so teuer.	Not all German books are so expensive.
<u>Was für ein deutsches Buch</u> ist denn das?	What kind of a German book is that?

2. Adjective-noun sequences:

Sind das <u>deutsche Bücher</u>?	Are those German books?
Hier sind ein paar <u>deutsche Bücher</u>.	Here are a couple of German books.
Was für <u>deutsche Bücher</u> sind denn das?	What kind of German books are those?
<u>Viele deutsche Bücher</u> sind für uns wichtig.	Many German books are important for us.
<u>Einige deutsche Bücher</u> sind sehr teuer.	Some German books are very expensive.

Remember! <u>Alle</u> is a specifier. <u>Viele</u> and <u>einige</u> are adjectives.
<u>Ein paar</u> and <u>was für</u> are indeclinable modifiers and not part of the
specifier-adjective-noun or adjective-noun sequences.

B. Adjectives with Dative

I. We have only one or two examples of an adjective which is followed or
preceded by a dative form of the noun or pronoun.

Das ist mir recht.	That's all right with me.
Ist Ihnen das recht?	Is that all right with you?

II. A number of adjectives may be accompanied or COMPLEMENTED in this way
by a dative form of a noun or pronoun.

Dieser Anzug ist dem anderen sehr ähnlich.	This suit is very similar to the other one.
Der Mann ist mir bekannt.	The man is known to me.
Das ist mir ganz neu.	That's a new one on me.
Das ist seinem Bruder nicht möglich.	That's not possible for his brother (i.e., his brother can't do that.)
Machen Sie mir die Schreibmaschine nicht kaputt!	Don't wreck the typewriter on me!

III. A still greater number of adjectives are COMPLEMENTED by a dative form
when they are also accompanied by a modifier such as <u>zu</u>.

Das ist unseren Studenten zu einfach.	That's too simple for our students.
Diese Arbeit ist mir zu viel.	This job is too much for me.
Der Brief ist mir zu wichtig dafür.	The letter is too important to me for that.
Der Mantel ist Ihnen garnicht zu gross.	The coat isn't at all too big for you.
Der Anzug ist mir zu klein.	The suit is too small for me.
Herr Keller ist meiner Schwester zu alt.	Mr. Keller is too old for my sister's taste.
Am Sonnabend Nachmittag dann, oder ist Ihnen das zu unbestimmt?	On Saturday afternoon then, or is that too indefinite for you?

Note that the adjective is complemented in English by a phrase with a
preposition, usually "to" or "for". The prepositional phrase may occur
in German as a complement to some adjectives also.

Diese Jacke ist zu klein für mich.	This suit-coat is too small for me.
Er ist viel zu alt für meine Schwester.	He's much too old for my sister.
Die Arbeit ist zu viel für meine Frau.	The work is too much for my wife.

C. WORD ORDER

I. In Unit 3 we observed that the FINITE VERB FORM is the SECOND ELEMENT of a
German statement. Here are some more examples illustrating this basic
German word order pattern taken from the basic sentences of Units 4 - 8.

Die finden Sie in allen Preislagen.	You'll find them in all price ranges.
Wein trinke ich nicht gern.	I don't care for wine.
Der neue Schreibtisch passt sehr gut zu Ihren Möbeln.	The new desk matches your furniture very well.
Die Angehörigen meiner Frau leben hier.	My wife's family lives hier.
Hier im Vorort ist es wirklich viel schöner und ruhiger als in der Stadt.	It's really much nicer and quieter here in the suburbs than in the city.
In den anderen Zimmern steht schon alles an Ort und Stelle.	Everything's in place in the other rooms.
Den grauen habe ich leider nicht mehr in Ihrer Grösse.	I'm sorry, I don't have the grey one in your size any more.
Wie ich sehe, haben Sie eine schöne Bibliothek.	(As) I see you have a fine library.

Note that the FIRST ELEMENT of these sentences may be as short as a pronoun or a noun alone, or as long as a complete specifier-adjective-noun sequence. It may have the nominative, accusative or dative form. It may be a prepositional phrase or a phrase consisting of a noun or specifier-adjective noun sequence plus another noun or sequence in the genitive form. It may also be a separate clause with its own subject and verb. Notice, too, how often German word order differs from the pattern: Subject-Verb-Object, which is basic in English.

II. The words ein, einige, viele usually do not begin a sentence which gives a location, anwering the question "where?". The following examples from the basic sentences illustrate this point.

Direkt neben der Post ist ein Schreibwarengeschäft.	There's a stationery store right next to the post office.
Da drüben ist ein Spiegel.	There's a mirror over there.
Hier nebenan ist eins.	There's one next door here.
Hier sind noch einige nette Häuser zu vermieten.	There are still some nice houses for rent here.

Notice that English likewise avoids beginning sentences with the indefinite article or the words "some" and "a few". Try re-phrasing the English sentences on the right above so as to begin with "one" or "some" or "a" and notice how awkward and unnatural these sentences sound.

III. THE FINITE VERB FORM is the SECOND ELEMENT also in statements which are preceded by an introductory phrase containing a verb such as finden, fürchten, glauben, sagen. Note the following examples:

Ich fürchte, das ist telephonisch etwas umständlich.	I'm afraid that's a bit complicated on the telephone.
Ich höre, Sie wollen nach Amerika fahren.	I hear you're planning to go to America.
Ich glaube, Fräulein Bruce hat eine.	I think Miss Bruce has one.
Sagen Sie ihm doch bitte, er möchte mich sobald wie möglich anrufen.	Please tell him I'd like him to call me as soon as possible.
Ich finde, jetzt sieht es schon richtig gemütlich aus.	I think it looks really comfortable here now.

These examples actually represent in each case two separate statements. The first statement is thus not an element of the second; in each one separately the basic word order pattern is observed.

D. COMPOUND NOUNS

I. English has many compound nouns like <u>newspaper</u>, <u>fireman</u>, <u>outpost</u>, etc.,
   which the writing system treats as single units. We have others like
   <u>letter</u>-paper, <u>Minute Man</u>, <u>lookout post</u>, <u>after-effect</u>, etc., which, although
   they are the same sort of compounds, are written as two units, sometimes
   completely separate and sometimes connected by a hyphen. In German,
   compound nouns are of very common occurrence and not infrequently contain
   four or five or even more elements. They are almost all written as single
   units and hence often look rather formidable. They may turn out to be more
   difficult than <u>automobileinsurancesalesman</u>, however.

II. Let us examine some typical German compound nouns which we have encountered
    in the last few units and see what they are composed of:

           1) das Papiergeschäft   = das Papier + das Geschäft
           2) die Schreibmaschine   = schreib-   + die Maschine
           3) der Nachmittag   = nach   + der Mittag
           4) der Neubau   = neu   + der Bau

   Notice that the FINAL ELEMENT of each of these words is a noun. This is
   just like English, as the examples in the paragraph above show. Notice
   also that each of these compounds is a <u>der</u>-noun, a <u>das</u>-noun or a <u>die</u>-noun
   according to whether its FINAL ELEMENT is a <u>der</u>-noun, a <u>das</u>-noun or a
   <u>die</u>-noun. PRECEDING ELEMENTS may be: 1) another NOUN, 2) a PREPOSITION,
   or 4) an ADJECTIVE. Let us examine these types of compound nouns in turn.

1. Compounds made up of NOUN + NOUN

           der Sommer,-   + der Anzug,¨e   = der Sommeranzug,¨e
           das Papier,-e   + das Geschäft,-e   = das Papiergeschäft,-e
           die Heimat   + die Stadt,¨e   = die Heimatstadt,¨e
           die Bahn,-en   + der Hof,¨e   = der Bahnhof,¨e
           der Sport   + das Hemd,-en   = das Sporthemd,-en
           das Blei   + der Stift,-e   = der Bleistift,-e

   Notice that <u>das</u>-nouns may combine with <u>der</u>-nouns and <u>die</u>-nouns as well
   as with <u>das</u>-nouns, and <u>der</u>-nouns may combine with <u>die</u>-nouns and <u>das</u>-nouns
   as well as with <u>der</u>-nouns, etc., BUT IT IS ALWAYS THE FINAL ELEMENT that
   determines whether the compound as a whole is a <u>der</u>-noun, a <u>das</u>-noun or
   a <u>die</u>-noun. A compound noun also has the same plural as its final
   element. What are the component parts of the following compound nouns?

           der Autobus   das Briefpapier   die Stuhllehne
           der Stadtplan   das Telephonbuch   die Briefmarke

2. Compounds made up of VERB STEM + NOUN

           park- (parken)   + der Platz   = der Parkplatz
           schau- (schauen)   + das Fenster   = das Schaufenster
           schreib- (schreiben) + die Maschine = die Schreibmaschine

   Here are some more compounds of the same type. What are their
   component parts?

           der Rauchtisch   das Wohnzimmer   die Stehlampe
           der Fahrstuhl   das Schlafzimmer   die Schreibwaren (pl)

3. Compounds made up of a PREPOSITION + NOUN

           nach   + der Mittag   = der Nachmittag
           bei   + das Spiel   = das Beispiel
           vor   + die Anmeldung   = die Voranmeldung

Here are a few more compounds of this type. Although some of them are new you will have no difficulty in recognizing their component parts.

der Vorort	das Hinterhaus	die Unterwäsche
der Umweg	die Nebenstrasse	die Zwischenzeit

4   Compounds made up of an ADJECTIVE + NOUN

neu	+ der Bau	= der Neubau
fern	+ das Gespräch	= das Ferngespräch
gross	+ die Stadt	= die Grosstadt

The following are a few more examples of this type of compound:

der Kühlschrank	das Fernamt	die Kleinstadt

III. Many nouns and verbs have special forms or plural forms when they occur as <u>non-final</u> elements in compounds. The following compounds contain such special forms:

Staats- (der Staat)	+ der Angehörige	= der Staatsangehörige
Wirtschafts- (die Wirtschaft)	+ die Abteilung	= die Wirtschafts- abteilung
Etagen- (die Etage)	+ das Haus	= das Etagenhaus
Frage- (fragen)	+ der Bogen	= der Fragebogen
Elektro- (elektrisch)	+ der Herd	= der Elektroherd

In the following compounds identify both the special combining form of the first element and the form the element has when not combined.

der Bücherschrank	das Zigarrengeschäft	die Geschäftsreise
der Küchentisch	das Besuchsvisum	die Bilderkiste
der Kassenzettel	das Konfektionsgeschäft	die Visa-Abteilung

IV. As mentioned in paragraph I, German compound nouns frequently have more than two elements. The following examples have occurred in our basic sentences up to this point. Can you break them down into their component elements?

            das Herrenkonfektionsgeschäft   der Sommerschlussverkauf

V. Compounding is an active process in the language, and you will often hear and see compounds which no dictionary lists. Since the meaning of the whole compound is usually the sum of its parts (cf. <u>Geschäftsbrief</u>, <u>Schreibwarengeschäft</u>), you will usually be able to figure out the meaning of a new compound with little or no difficulty. In a few cases, of course, the English equivalent may not be apparent at all (cf. <u>Fahrstuhl</u>, <u>Vorort</u>), but words of this kind are almost always listed in the dictionary.

SUBSTITUTION DRILL

This is in part a review of the noun, specifier and adjective sequences you have already had. Some new items are included, but the patterns are all familiar ones. Aim for maximum speed and fluency WITH ABSOLUTE ACCURACY. Procedure is as outlined in Unit 7, including occasional spot translations to English and back to German.

1. Brauchen Sie noch ein paar Krawatten?

Hemden - Stühle - Bleistifte - Gläser - Briefmarken

2. Ich brauche noch etwas Stoff.

Geld - Wäsche - Milch - Geschirr - Papier

3. Was für Teppiche wollen Sie kaufen?

Wäsche - Wein - Socken - Briefpapier - Hemden - Möbel

4. Was für einen Stoff möchten Sie?

Anzug - Buch - Jacke - Koffer - Krawatte - Roman - Zeitung - Tabak

einen Anzug - ein Buch - eine Jacke - einen Koffer - eine Krawatte - einen Roman - eine Zeitung - einen Tabak

5. Sind das alle deutschen Zeitungen?

neu - englisch - alt - französisch -

neuen - englischen - alten - französischen

6. Hier sind ein paar alte Bücher.

deutsch - neu - klein - schön - gut - bekannt

deutsche - neue - kleine - schöne - gute - bekannte

7. Was für ein schönes grosses Zimmer ist das!

Küche - Kühlschrank - Bibliothek - Wagen - Bild - Herd - Fenster

eine schöne grosse Küche - ein schöner grosser Kühlschrank - eine schöne grosse Bibliothek - ein schöner grosser Wagen - ein schönes grosses Bild - ein schöner grosser Herd - ein schönes grosses Fenster

8. Hier gibt's nichts Neues.

gut - ähnlich - preiswert - teuer - ander-

Gutes - Ähnliches - Preiswertes - Teueres - Anderes

9. Wollen Sie etwas Anderes haben?

ähnlich - preiswert - passend - einfarbig - gemustert - teuer - gestreift

Ähnliches - Preiswertes - Passendes - Einfarbiges - Gemustertes - Teueres - Gestreiftes

10. Wieviel kostet die graue Krawatte?

```
... d__ weiss__ Stoff?
... d__ deutsch__ Buch?
... d__ gross__ Lampe?
... d__ braun__ Tisch?
... d__ gestreift__ Sporthemd?
... d__ grün__ Koffer?
```

```
... der weisse Stoff?
... das deutsche Buch?
... die grosse Lampe?
... der braune Tisch?
... das gestreifte Sporthemd?
... der grüne Koffer?
```

11. Haben Sie <u>keinen grauen Anzug</u> in
    meiner Grösse?

      ... kein__ gestreift__ Jacke ...   ... keine gestreifte Jacke ...
      ... kein__ billig__ Hemd ...   ... kein billiges Hemd ...
      ... kein__ farbig__ Socken ...   ... keine farbigen Socken ...
      ... kein__ braun__ Anzug ...   ... keinen braunen Anzug

12. Wie gefällt Ihnen <u>mein neues Bild</u>?

      ... sein__ hellgrau__ Anzug?   ... sein hellgrauer Anzug?
      ... unser__ deutsch__ Auto?   ... unser deutsches Auto?
      ... mein__ eingebaut__ Bücher-   ... mein eingebauter Bücherschrank?
      schrank?
      ... unser__ alt__ Bibliothek?   ... unsere alte Bibliothek?
      ... ihr__ ander__ Roman?   ... ihr anderer Roman?

13. <u>Dieses weisse Hemd</u> kaufe ich mir.

      ... dies__ gross__ Koffer ...   ... diesen grossen Koffer ...
      ... dies__ alt__ Bild ...   ... dieses alte Bild ...
      ... dies__ gemustert__ Stoff ... ... diesen gemusterten Stoff ...
      ... dies__ grün__ Jacke ...   ... diese grüne Jacke ...
      ... dies__ preiswert__ Geschirr ... ... dieses preiswerte Geschirr ...

14. Ich kenne hier <u>ein gutes Geschäft</u>.

      ... ein__ alt__ Schloss.   ... ein altes Schloss.
      ... ein__ schön__ Bibliothek.   ... eine schöne Bibliothek.
      ... ein__ deutsch__ Café.   ... ein deutsches Café.
      ... ein__ gross__ Parkplatz.   ... einen grossen Parkplatz.
      ... ein__ ausgezeichnet__ Hotel. ... ein ausgezeichnetes Hotel.

15. Sind Sie mit <u>Ihrem neuen Wagen</u>
    zufrieden?

      ... sein__ lang__ Brief ...   ... seinem langen Brief ...
      ... Ihr__ neu__ Heizung ...   ... Ihrer neuen Heizung ...
      ... dies__ alt__ Kühlschrank ...   ... diesem alten Kühlschrank ...
      ... unser__ neu__ Einfuhr-   ... unseren neuen Einfuhrbestimmungen
      bestimmungen ...
      ... d__ teur__ Elektroherd ...   ... dem teuren Elektroherd ...
      ... Ihr__ deutsch__ Geschirr ...   ... Ihrem deutschen Geschirr ...

16. <u>Ihr grüner Wagen</u> sieht sehr gut aus.

      ... sein__ deutsch__ Auto ...   ... sein deutsches Auto ...
      ... ihr__ eingebaut__ Bücher-   ... ihr eingebauter Bücherschrank ...
      schrank ...
      ... sein__ einfarbig__ Krawatte ... ... seine einfarbige Krawatte ...
      ... unser__ neu__ Rathaus ...   ... unser neues Rathaus ...

17. Ich möchte mir einige <u>neue Möbel</u>
    kaufen.

      ... passend__ Gläser ...   ... passende Gläser ...
      ... leicht__ Zigarren ...   ... leichte Zigarren ...
      ... gross__ Papierkörbe ...   ... grosse Papierkörbe ...
      ... gut__ Bilder ...   ... gute Bilder ...
      ... preiswert__ Koffer ...   ... preiswerte Koffer ...
      ... deutsch__ Bücher ...   ... deutsche Bücher ...

                                     (End of Tape 8A)

18. Zeigen Sie mir bitte <u>einen der
    braunen Anzüge.</u>

    ... ein__ d__ schön__ Krawatten.   ... eine der schönen Krawatten.
    ... ein__ d__ weiss__ Hemden.   ... eins der weissen Hemden.
    ... ein__ d__ grau__ Anzüge.   ... einen der grauen Anzüge.
    ... ein__ d__ neu__ Jacken.   ... eine der neuen Jacken.
    ... ein__ d__ deutsch__ Bücher.   ... eins der deutschen Bücher.
    ... ein__ d__ englisch__ Stoffe.   ... einen der englischen Stoffe.

19. Die Krawatte passt gut zu <u>Ihrem
    neuen Anzug.</u>

    ... sein__ farbig__ Hemd.   ... seinem farbigen Hemd.
    ... Ihr__ braun__ Anzug.   ... Ihrem braunen Anzug.
    ... mein__ grau__ Jacke.   ... meiner grauen Jacke.
    ... dies__ einfarbig__ Stoff.   ... diesem einfarbigen Stoff.

20. Wie ist die Qualität <u>dieses
    hellgrauen Stoffes?</u>

    ... dies__ neu__ Unterwäsche?   ... dieser neuen Unterwäsche?
    ... dies__ einfarbig__ Teppichs?   ... dieses einfarbigen Teppichs?
    ... dies__ grün__ Socken?   ... dieser grünen Socken?
    ... dies__ farbig__ Sporthemdes?   ... dieses farbigen Sporthemdes?
    ... dies__ gemustert__ Krawatte?   ... dieser gemusterten Krawatte?
    ... dies__ deutsch__ Hemden?   ... dieser deutschen Hemden?

21. Ich möchte mir gern <u>ein paar gute
    Anzüge</u> ansehen.

    ... ein paar deutsch__ Bücher ...   ... deutsche Bücher ...
    ... ein paar gestreift__ Hemden ...   ... gestreifte Hemden ...
    ... ein paar einfarbig__ Krawat-   ... einfarbige Krawatten ...
        ten ...
    ... ein paar alt__ Briefmarken ...   ... alte Briefmarken ...
    ... ein paar leicht__ Koffer ...   ... leichte Koffer ...
    ... ein paar weiss__ Wolldecken ...   ... weisse Wolldecken ...

22. Wie gefällt Ihnen <u>die neue Jacke
    Ihrer Frau?</u>

    ... d__ alt__ Rathaus unser__   ... das alte Rathaus unserer Stadt?
        Stadt?
    ... d__ grau__ Sommeranzug mein__   ... der graue Sommeranzug meines
        Mannes?   Mannes?
    ... d__ auffällig__ Krawatte   ... die auffällige Krawatte meines
        mein__ Bruders?   Bruders?
    ... d__ neu__ Wohnung mein__   ... die neue Wohnung meiner Eltern?
        Eltern?
    ... d__ gestreift__ Jacke Ihr__   ... die gestreifte Jacke Ihrer Frau?
        Frau?

23. Wieviel kosten <u>weisse Hemden?</u>

    ... gut__ Socken?   ... gute Socken?
    ... englisch__ Zigaretten?   ... englische Zigaretten?
    ... gestreift__ Sporthemden?   ... gestreifte Sporthemden?
    ... amerikanisch__ Wagen?   ... amerikanische Wagen?
    ... deutsch__ Möbel?   ... deutsche Möbel?

24. <u>Alle neuen Wohnungen</u> sind teuer.

      Alle englisch__ Stoffe ...   ... englischen Stoffe ...
      Alle amerikanisch__ Autos ...   ... amerikanischen Autos ...
      Alle berühmt__ Briefmarken ...   ... berühmten Briefmarken ...
      Alle gut__ Wolldecken ...   ... guten Wolldecken ...

25. Hier gibt es <u>viele grosse Geschäfte</u>.

    ... viele klein__ Parks.   ... kleine Parks.
    ... viele schön__ Neubauten.   ... schöne Neubauten.
    ... viele teur__ Hotels.   ... teure Hotels.
    ... viele schlecht__ Strassen.   ... schlechte Strassen.
    ... viele gross__ Schaufenster. ... grosse Schaufenster.
    ... viele neu__ Etagenhäuser.   ... neue Etagenhäuser.

26. Wir haben <u>keine grossen Teppiche</u>.

    ... keine gut__ Kinos.   ... guten Kinos.
    ... keine deutsch__ Wagen.   ... deutschen Wagen.
    ... keine amerikanisch__ Schreib- ... amerikanischen Schreibmaschinen.
      maschinen.
    ... keine einfarbig__ Krawatten. ... einfarbigen Krawatten.
    ... keine gestreift__ Hemden.   ... gestreiften Hemden.

27. Ich bin mit allen <u>neuen Möbeln</u> zufrieden.

    ... englisch__ Stoffen ...   ... englischen Stoffen ...
    ... gestreift__ Sporthemden ... ... gestreiften Sporthemden ...
    ... gemustert___ Teppichen ...   ... gemusterten Teppichen ...
    ... einfarbig__ Krawatten ...   ... einfarbigen Krawatten ...

28. Wir kommen mit ein paar <u>ameri-kanischen Diplomaten</u>.

    ... englisch__ Freunden.   ... englischen Freunden.
    ... alt__ Herren.   ... alten Herren.
    ... deutsch__ Bekannten.   ... deutschen Bekannten.
    ... französisch__ Beamten.   ... französischen Beamten.

29. Kennt Herr Becker nicht ein paar <u>junge Deutsche</u>?

    ... amerikanisch__ Beamte?   ... amerikanische Beamte?
    ... französisch__ Diplomaten? ... französische Diplomaten?
    ... nett__ Bremer?   ... nette Bremer?
    ... deutsch__ Schriftsteller?   ... deutsche Schriftsteller?

30. Ich möchte gern <u>einige weisse Hemden</u> haben.

    ... ein paar einfarbig__   .. ein paar einfarbige Krawatten ...
      Krawatten ...
    ... all__ französisch__   .. alle französischen Zeitungen ...
      Zeitungen ...
    ... dies__ klein__ Bilder ...   ... diese kleinen Bilder ...
    ... einig__ deutsch__   ... einige deutsche Briefmarken ...
      Briefmarken ...
    ... ein paar gut__ Wolldecken ... ... ein paar gute Wolldecken ...
    ... kein__ grün__ Socken ...   ... keine grünen Socken ...

EXPANSION DRILL

The following sentences are provided for practice in expanding a given sentence frame by the addition of a descriptive modifier. The tutor gives the adjective for the group and then reads the first sentence. The student repeats the sentence after the tutor as given and then repeats it once more, expanding it to include the form of the adjective required in that particular sentence. The same procedure is followed for all the sentences in the group.

1. neu

a. Wir wollen zu dem Restaurant gehen.
b. Gefällt Ihnen dieses Restaurant?
c. Wir suchen ein Restaurant.
d. Die Restaurants sind nicht weit von hier.
e. Sprechen Sie von den Restaurants?
f. Hier gibt es viele Restaurants.
g. Hier in der Nähe sind ein paar Restaurants.

Wir wollen zu dem neuen Restaurant gehen.
Gefällt Ihnen dieses neue Restaurant?
Wir suchen ein neues Restaurant.
Die neuen Restaurants sind nicht weit von hier.
Sprechen Sie von den neuen Restaurants?
Hier gibt es viele neue Restaurants.
Hier in der Nähe sind ein paar neue Restaurants.

2. grün

a. Hier ist eine Krawatte.
b. Geben Sie mir bitte die Krawatte.
c. Das passt gut zu Ihrer Krawatte.
d. Gefallen Ihnen diese Krawatten?
e. Ich möchte einige Krawatten haben.
f. Alle Krawatten sind mir zu auffällig.
g. Was für Krawatten haben Sie?

Hier ist eine grüne Krawatte.
Geben Sie mir bitte die grüne Krawatte.
Das passt gut zu Ihrer grünen Krawatte.
Gefallen Ihnen diese grünen Krawatten?
Ich möchte einige grüne Krawatten haben.
Alle grünen Krawatten sind mir zu auffällig.
Was für grüne Krawatten haben Sie?

3. braun

a. Das ist meine Jacke.
b. Die Krawatte passt gut zu meiner Jacke.
c. Ich suche eine Jacke.
d. Wollen Sie mal eine der Jacken anprobieren?
e. Im Schaufenster sind einige Jacken.
f. Alle Jacken hier gefallen mir nicht.
g. Was für eine Jacke wollen Sie sich kaufen, eine ___ ?

Das ist meine braune Jacke.
Die Krawatte passt gut zu meiner braunen Jacke.
Ich suche eine braune Jacke.
Wollen Sie mal eine der braunen Jacken anprobieren?
Im Schaufenster sind einige braune Jacken.
Alle braunen Jacken hier gefallen mir nicht.
Was für eine Jacke wollen Sie sich kaufen, eine braune?

4. grau

a. Wo ist der Anzug?
b. Ist das Ihr Anzug?
c. Zeigen Sie mir bitte einen Anzug.
d. Das Sporthemd passt gut zu meinem Anzug.
e. Was für ein schönen Anzug haben Sie!
f. Er hat einige Anzüge.
g. Ich habe ein paar Anzüge.

Wo ist der graue Anzug?
Ist das Ihr grauer Anzug?
Zeigen Sie mir bitte einen grauen Anzug.
Das Sporthemd passt gut zu meinem grauen Anzug.
Was für einen schönen grauen Anzug haben Sie!
Er hat einige graue Anzüge.
Ich habe ein paar graue Anzüge.

In the following groups a different adjective is indicated for each sentence.

5. a. Ist das Ihr Teppich? (neu)　　　　　Ist das Ihr neuer Teppich?
   b. Ich suche meinen Teppich.　　　　　Ich suche meinen kleinen Teppich.
      (klein)
   c. Wie gefällt Ihnen die Farbe　　　　Wie gefällt Ihnen die Farbe meines
      meines Teppichs? (gross)　　　　　grossen Teppichs?
   d. Gehört Ihnen dieser Teppich?　　　Gehört Ihnen dieser einfarbige
      (einfarbig)　　　　　　　　　　　Teppich?
   e. Er hat viele Teppiche. (alt)　　　Er hat viele alte Teppiche.
   f. Ich habe auch ein paar Teppiche.　Ich habe auch ein paar gemusterte
      (gemustert)　　　　　　　　　　　Teppiche.
   g. Was für ein Teppich ist das,　　　Was für ein Teppich ist das, ein
      ein ___? (deutsch)　　　　　　　　deutscher?

6. a. Das ist Stoff. (hellgrau)　　　　　Das ist hellgrauer Stoff.
   b. Wie ist die Qualität dieses　　　　Wie ist die Qualität dieses gestreiften
      Stoffes? (gestreift)　　　　　　　Stoffes?
   c. Gefällt Ihnen dieser Stoff?　　　　Gefällt Ihnen dieser englische Stoff?
      (englisch)
   d. Ich suche einen Stoff.　　　　　　Ich suche einen einfarbigen Stoff.
      (einfarbig)
   e. Einige Stoffe gefallen mir　　　　Einige gemusterte Stoffe gefallen mir
      sehr gut. (gemustert)　　　　　　sehr gut.
   f. Ich möchte ein paar Stoffe　　　　Ich möchte ein paar gute Stoffe haben.
      haben. (gut)
   g. Was für einen Stoff haben Sie　　　Was für einen preiswerten Stoff haben
      da? (preiswert)　　　　　　　　　Sie da?

7. a. Arbeiten Sie in dem Geschäft?　　　Arbeiten Sie in dem alten Geschäft?
      (alt)
   b. Kennen Sie das Geschäft?　　　　　Kennen Sie das kleine Geschäft?
      (klein)
   c. Ich suche ein Geschäft.　　　　　Ich suche ein deutsches Geschäft.
      (deutsch)
   d. Ich kenne hier alle Geschäfte.　　Ich kenne hier alle grossen Geschäfte.
      (gross)
   e. Es gibt hier nicht viele　　　　　Es gibt hier nicht viele ähnliche
      Geschäfte. (ähnlich)　　　　　　Geschäfte.
   f. Er will mir einige Geschäfte　　　Er will mir einige preiswerte Geschäfte
      zeigen. (preiswert)　　　　　　　zeigen.
   g. Was für Geschäfte gibt es hier?　　Was für neue Geschäfte gibt es hier?
      (neu)
   h. Wir haben hier ein paar　　　　　Wir haben hier ein paar gute Geschäfte.
      Geschäfte. (gut)
   i. Was für ein Geschäft ist denn　　　Was für ein amerikanisches Geschäft
      das? (amerikanisch)　　　　　　　ist denn das?

TRANSFORMATION DRILL

The following is an exercise in controlling German word order patterns.

1. Sie haben heute einen netten Anzug
   im Schaufenster.

   a. Im Schaufenster ...   Im Schaufenster haben Sie heute einen
                                           netten Anzug.
   b. Heute ...   Heute haben Sie einen netten Anzug im
                                           Schaufenster.
   c. Einen netten Anzug ...   Einen netten Anzug haben Sie heute im
                                           Schaufenster.
   d. Sie ...   Sie haben heute einen netten Anzug im
                                           Schaufenster.

2. Ich habe die graue Jacke leider
   nicht mehr in Ihrer Grösse.

   a. Leider ...   Leider habe ich die graue Jacke nicht
                                           mehr in Ihrer Grösse.
   b. Die graue Jacke ...   Die graue Jacke habe ich leider nicht
                                           mehr in Ihrer Grösse.
   c. In Ihrer Grösse ...   In Ihrer Grösse habe ich die graue
                                           Jacke leider nicht mehr.
   d. Ich ...   Ich habe die graue Jacke leider nicht
                                           mehr in Ihrer Grösse.

3. Ich kann mir augenblicklich nicht
   mehr leisten.

   a. Augenblicklich ...   Augenblicklich kann ich mir nicht
                                           mehr leisten.
   b. Mehr ...   Mehr kann ich mir augenblicklich nicht
                                           leisten.
   c. Ich ..   Ich kann mir augenblicklich nicht
                                           mehr leisten.

4. Jetzt möchte ich mir auch noch
   einige Krawatten ansehen.

   a. Ich ...   Ich möchte mir jetzt auch noch einige
                                           Krawatten ansehen.
   b. Einige Krawatten ...   Einige Krawatten möchte ich mir jetzt
                                           auch noch ansehen.
   c. Jetzt ...   Jetzt möchte ich mir auch noch einige
                                           Krawatten ansehen.

5. Der Konsul wohnt jetzt in dem
   grossen Haus.

   a. In dem grossen Haus ...   In dem grossen Haus wohnt jetzt der
                                           Konsul.
   b. Jetzt ...   Jetzt wohnt der Konsul in dem grossen
                                           Haus.
   c. Wohnt ... ?   Wohnt der Konsul jetzt in dem grossen
                                           Haus?
   d. Ja, der Konsul ...   Ja, der Konsul wohnt jetzt in dem
                                           grossen Haus.

6. Wir wollen heute ins Kino gehen.

    a. Heute ...   Heute wollen wir ins Kino gehen.
    b. In welches ...   In welches Kino wollen wir heute gehen?
    c. Wohin ...   Wohin wollen wir heute gehen?
    d. Wo ...   Wo wollen wir heute hingehen?
    e. Ins Kino ...   Ins Kino wollen wir heute gehen.

7. Diese braune Krawatte passt
wirklich sehr gut zu Ihrem Anzug.

    a. Zu Ihrem Anzug ...   Zu Ihrem Anzug passt diese braune
                              Krawatte wirklich sehr gut.
    b. Wirklich sehr gut ...   Wirklich sehr gut passt diese braune
                              Krawatte zu Ihrem Anzug.
    c Diese braune Krawatte ...   Diese braune Krawatte passt wirklich
                              sehr gut zu Ihrem Anzug.

8. Jetzt müssen wir die Bilder über
das Sofa hängen.

    a. Müssen ...?   Müssen wir jetzt die Bilder über das
                              Sofa hängen?
    b. Die Bilder ...   Die Bilder müssen wir jetzt über das
                              Sofa hängen.
    c. Über das Sofa ...   Über das Sofa müssen wir jetzt die
                              Bilder hängen.
    d. Wir ...   Wir müssen jetzt die Bilder über das
                              Sofa hängen.

9. Ich kaufe meine Anzüge gewöhnlich
hier in diesem Geschäft.

    a. Hier in diesem Geschäft ... Hier in diesem Geschäft kaufe ich
                              gewöhnlich meine Anzüge.
    b. Meine Anzüge ...   Meine Anzüge kaufe ich gewöhnlich
                              in diesem Geschäft.
    c. Ich ...   Ich kaufe meine Anzüge gewöhnlich
                              in diesem Geschäft.
    d. Gewöhnlich ...   Gewöhnlich kaufe ich meine Anzüge
                              in diesem Geschäft.

10. Bezahlen Sie diese Sachen bitte
da vorne an der Kasse.

    a. Bitte ...   Bitte bezahlen Sie diese Sachen da
                              vorne an der Kasse.
    b. Da vorne an der Kasse ...   Da vorne an der Kasse bezahlen Sie
                              bitte diese Sachen.
    c. Diese Sachen ...   Diese Sachen bezahlen Sie bitte da
                              vorne an der Kasse.
    d. Bezahlen ...   Bezahlen Sie diese Sachen bitte da
                              vorne an der Kasse.

11. In dieser Farbe haben wir leider
augenblicklich nichts Ähnliches.

    a. Leider ...   Leider haben wir in dieser Farbe
                              augenblicklich nichts Ähnliches.
    b. Wir ...   Wir haben in dieser Farbe leider
                              augenblicklich nichts Ähnliches.
    c. Augenblicklich ...   Augenblicklich haben wir leider nichts
                              Ähnliches in dieser Farbe.
    d. In dieser Farbe ...   In dieser Farbe haben wir augenblicklich
                              leider nichts Ähnliches.

12. Ich glaube, das ist keine genaue
    Auskunft.

    Das ...   Das ist keine genaue Auskunft, glaube
                                           ich.

    Ich finde, das ist eine gute
    Qualität.

    Das ...   Das ist eine gute Qualität, finde ich.

    Ich glaube, er macht eine
    Geschäftsreise.

    Er ...   Er macht eine Geschäftsreise, glaube
                                           ich.

    Unser Haus ist in einer idealen
    Gegend, finden wir.

    Wir ...   Wir finden, unser Haus ist in einer
                                           idealen Gegend.

    Wir können uns das nicht leisten,
    glaube ich.

    Ich ...   Ich glaube, wir können uns das nicht
                                           leisten.

    Diese Bestimmung ist sehr wichtig,
    finde ich.

    Ich ...   Ich finde, diese Bestimmung ist sehr
                                           wichtig.

VARIATION DRILL

1. Geben Sie mir bitte ein paar   Give me a couple of solid-color and
   einfarbige und ein paar gemusterte   a couple of figured neckties, please.
   Socken.

   a. I'm looking for solid-color and   Ich suche einfarbige und gemusterte
      figured socks.   Socken.
   b. Show me a few light-weight and   Zeigen Sie mir bitte einige leichte
      reasonably priced jackets.   und preiswerte Jacken.
   c. He has many new and beautiful   Er hat viele neue und schöne Sachen.
      things.
   d. Do you have striped and /plain_7   Haben Sie gestreifte und weisse
      white soft-collar shirts?   Sporthemden?
   e. My wife would like to look at a   Meine Frau möchte sich ein paar lange
      couple of long and a couple of   und ein paar kurze Jacken ansehen.
      short jackets.
   f. They have a lot of small rugs   Sie haben viele kleine Teppiche und
      and a couple of big ones.   ein paar grosse.

2. Unsere beiden alten Wagen fahren   Both our old cars still run quite well.
   noch ganz gut.

   a. All the new shirts are unfortu-   Alle neuen Hemden sind mir leider zu
      nately too small for me.   klein.
   b. How do you like my new striped   Wie gefallen Ihnen meine neuen
      (soft-collar) shirts?   gestreiften Sporthemden?
   c. I don't like all the other   Alle anderen Farben gefallen mir nicht.
      colors.

(This drill is continued on next page.)

d. These light-weight suits are also very reasonable.

Diese leichten Anzüge sind auch sehr preiswert.

e. No new cars are really cheap.

Keine neuen Autos sind wirklich billig.

f. All the good suits in this store are too expensive for me.

Alle guten Anzüge in diesem Geschäft sind mir zu teuer.

3. **Hier gibt es keine grossen Geschäfte, nur kleine.**

There aren't any big stores here, only small ones.

a. I know a lot of American restaurants here but only a couple of German ones.

Ich kenne hier viele amerikanische Restaurants, aber nur ein paar deutsche.

b. He doesn't read any English newspapers but all the German ones.

Er liest keine englischen Zeitungen, aber alle deutschen.

c. I can show you a lot of good materials but unfortunately no English ones.

Ich kann Ihnen viele gute Stoffe zeigen, aber leider keine englischen.

d. Do you have only striped, soft collar shirts, no solid-color ones?

Haben Sie nur gestreifte Sporthemden und keine einfarbigen?

e. We don't know any French wines, but $/$ we do know$/$ all the German ones.

Wir kennen keine französischen Weine, aber alle deutschen.

f. I have a few brown jackets here in your size but no green ones.

Ich habe einige braune Jacken in Ihrer Grösse, aber keine grünen.

4. **Er will mir etwas Nettes kaufen.**

He wants to buy something nice for me.

a. Do you have something suitable in this price range?

Haben Sie etwas Passendes in dieser Preislage?

b. I'll be glad to show you something else in addition.

Ich zeige Ihnen gern noch etwas Anderes.

c. In this color unfortunately we don't have anything similar.

In dieser Farbe haben wir leider nichts Ähnliches.

d. I hope he doesn't give us anything expensive.

Hoffentlich gibt er uns nichts Teueres.

e. I can't find anything good here.

Ich kann hier nichts Gutes finden.

5. **Ist Ihnen das recht?**

Is that all right with you?

a. That's all right with him.

Das ist ihm recht.

b. That's very important to us.

Das ist uns sehr wichtig.

c. Do you know about that?

Ist Ihnen das bekannt?

d. I'm unfortunately not able to.

Das ist mir leider nicht möglich.

6. **Diese neuen Einfuhrbestimmungen sind dem Konsul nicht bekannt.**

The consul doesn't know about these new import regulations.

a. My father doesn't know about the book.

Das Buch ist meinem Vater nicht bekannt.

b. My wife is unfortunately not able to make the visit.

Dieser Besuch ist meiner Frau leider nicht möglich.

c. The telephone call is very important to the vice-consul.

Das Telephongespräch ist dem Vize-konsul sehr wichtig.

d. German newspapers are not very much like American ones.

Die deutschen Zeitungen sind den amerikanischen nicht sehr ähnlich.

7. **Dieser Anzug ist mir leider zu gross.**

This suit is too big for me unforunately.

a. Is this tie too loud for you?

Ist Ihnen diese Krawatte zu auffällig?

b. The sleeves of this shirt are much too long for me.

Die Ärmel dieses Hemdes sind mir viel zu lang.

c. His (suit) coat is too short for him.

Seine Jacke ist ihm zu kurz.

d. The weather is too unpleasant ('bad') for us today.

Das Wetter ist uns heute zu schlecht.

8. **Dieser Anzug ist zu gross für mich.**   **This suit is too big for me.**

   a. This big car is too expensive   Dieser grosse Wagen ist zu teuer
      for us.   für uns.
   b. I think the house is too small   Ich glaube, das Haus ist zu klein
      for you.   für Sie.
   c. Here in the suburbs it's too   Hier im Vorort ist es zu ruhig für
      quiet for me.   mich.
   d. Isn't this apartment too large   Ist diese Wohnung nicht zu gross
      for him?   für ihn?

9. **Ich möchte mir ein kleines Haus
   kaufen.**   **I'd like to buy a little house.**

   a. He can't afford a new car now.   Er kann sich jetzt kein neues Auto
                                               leisten.
   b. I want to take a look at another   Ich will mir eine andere Wohnung
      apartment.   ansehen.
   c. He's going to buy a light grey   Heute kauft er sich einen hellgrauen
      suit today.   Anzug.
   d. She wouldn't like to rent a large   Sie möchte sich kein grosses Zimmer
      room.   mieten.
   e. I want to borrow a book.   Ich will mir ein Buch leihen.

10. **Was für neue Möbel haben Sie denn?**   **What (kind of) new furniture do you
                                                have?**

   a. Which new stores do you know   Welche neuen Geschäfte kennen Sie
      here?   hier?
   b. What (kind of) German books do   Was für deutsche Bücher lesen Sie?
      you read?
   c. What (kind of) grey suits do   Was für graue Anzüge meinen Sie?
      you mean?
   d. Which striped shirts would you   Welche gestreiften Hemden möchten Sie
      like (to have)?   haben?
   e. Which famous authors are you   Welche berühmten Schriftsteller kennen
      familiar with?   Sie?
   f. What (kind of) old letters are   Was für alte Briefe suchen Sie?
      you looking for?
   g. Which old letters are you   Welche alten Briefe suchen Sie?
      looking for?

11. **Von welchen neuen Büchern sprechen
    Sie?**   **Which new books are you talking about?**

   a. What old people is he talking   Mit was für alten Leuten spricht er
      to there, anyway?   denn da?
   b. What German book are you talking   Von was für einem deutschen Buch
      about?   sprechen Sie?
   c. Which American officials do you   Mit welchen amerikanischen Beamten
      want to talk to?   wollen Sie sprechen?
   d. What new cars is he talking   Von was für neuen Wagen spricht er
      about anyway?   denn?
   e. Which German restaurants were   In welchen deutschen Restaurants
      you at?   waren Sie?
   f. What kind of an official does   Mit was für einem Beamten will er
      he want to talk to?   sprechen?
   g. Which official does he want to   Mit welchem Beamten will er sprechen?
      talk to?

12. **Er liest gerade eine deutsche Zeitung.**   **He's just reading a German newspaper.**

    a. He's carrying the empty suitcases to the attic.
        Er trägt die leeren Koffer auf den Boden.

    b. She reads lots of French novels.
        Sie liest viele französische Romane.

    c. He probably doesn't see them.
        Er sieht sie wahrscheinlich nicht.

    d. She's carrying her typewriter to the other room.
        Sie trägt ihre Schreibmaschine in das andere Zimmer.

    e. He's not going to take the grey jacket.
        Er nimmt die graue Jacke nicht.

13. **Ich hoffe, die Männer tragen die Kisten bald in den Keller.**   **I hope the men carry the crates /down / to the cellar soon.**

    a. I hope the people take /some_/
        Ich hoffe, die Leute geben sich Mühe.

    b. We think the Meyers are satisfied with their new apartment.
        Wir glauben, Meyers sind mit ihrer neuen Wohnung zufrieden.

    c. They say they're not familiar with Munich yet.
        Sie sagen, sie kennen München noch nicht.

    d. My impression is ('I find'), the store is not very good.
        Ich finde, das Geschäft ist nicht sehr gut.

                (End of Tape 8B)

Tape 9A   VOCABULARY DRILL

1. kaufen - "to buy"

    a. Kaufen Sie doch eine gute Qualität.
        Buy a good one! ('Buy a good quality!')

    b. Bei Schwarz und Co. kann man sehr preiswert kaufen.
        You can buy /things_/ very reasonably at Schwarz & Co.

    c. Ich will mir einen neuen Wagen kaufen.
        I want to buy a new car.

    d. In diesem Geschäft kaufen wir gewöhnlich unsere Anzüge.
        This is the store where we usually buy our suits. ('In this store we usually buy ...')

2. ausgeben (für) - "to spend (for)"

    a. Ich will jetzt kein Geld ausgeben.
        I don't want to spend any money now.

    b. Für Bücher gebe ich viel Geld aus.
        I spend a lot for books.

    c. Er gibt immer viel Geld für seine Anzüge aus.
        He always spends a lot of money for his suits.

    d. Wieviel wollen Sie für die Jacke ausgeben?
        How much do you want to spend for the jacket?

    e. Für eine gute Qualität müssen Sie mehr ausgeben.
        For a good quality /item_/ you have to spend more.

3. bekommen - "to get ('obtain or receive')"

    a. Heute bekommen wir keine Zeitung.
        We won't get a newspaper today.

    b. Wo kann man gute Möbel bekommen?
        Where can you get good furniture?

    c. In dieser Preislage bekommen Sie dort keinen Anzug.
        You won't get a suit there in this price range.

    d. Leider können Sie das nicht in reiner Wolle bekommen.
        I'm sorry you can't get an all wool one. (' ... get that in all wool.')

4. **einpacken** - "to wrap (up)"

a. Bitte packen Sie den Spiegel gut ein!	Please wrap the mirror well!
b. Er packt gerade die Socken ein.	He's just wrapping the socks.
c. Ich muss jetzt die Hemden einpacken.	I have to wrap up the shirts now.
d. Packen Sie mir bitte das Geschirr ein.	Wrap up the china for me please.
e. Der Verkäufer kann Ihnen die Wäsche und die Wolldecken zusammen einpacken.	The sales clerk can wrap the linen and the blankets together ∠in one package∠.

5. **meinen** - "mean ('intend to say')"

a. Meinen Sie das gestreifte Hemd da drüben?	Do you mean the striped shirt over there?
b. Welchen Anzug meinen Sie, den hellgrauen?	Which suit do you mean, the light grey one?
c. Wie meinen Sie das eigentlich?	What do you mean by that (actually)?
d. Wen meinen Sie, Herrn Müller?	Who do you mean, Mr. Müller?

6. **ungefähr, etwa** - "about, approximately"

a. In unserem Konsulat arbeiten ungefähr 30 Beamte.	Approximately 30 staff people work at our consulate.
b. Er hat etwa 20 Krawatten.	He has about twenty neckties.
c. Sie müssen für ein Sporthemd ungefähr 25 Mark ausgeben.	You'll have to spend about 25 marks for a (soft-collar) shirt.
d. Wir bleiben etwa drei Jahre in Deutschland.	We're going to stay in Germany approximately three years.

7. **sich leisten können** - "to be able to afford"

a. Ich kann mir leider noch keinen neuen Wagen leisten.	Unfortunately I can't afford a new car yet.
b. Diesen teuren Anzug kann er sich nicht leisten.	He can't afford this expensive suit.
c. Wir können uns kein grosses Haus leisten.	We can't afford a large house.
d. Können Sie sich das leisten?	Can you afford that?
e. Dieses Jahr können wir uns auch einen neuen Wagen leisten.	This year we'll be able to afford a new car too.

8. **sitzen** - "to fit, to hang"

a. Diese braune Jacke sitzt sehr gut.	This brown (suit) coat fits very well.
b. Ihre Krawatte sitzt nicht richtig.	Your tie needs to be adjusted. ('Your tie doesn't fit right.')
c. Dieser Anzug sitzt nicht.	This suit doesn't quite fit.
d. Sein neuer Anzug sitzt schlecht.	His new suit doesn't hang well.

9. **bezahlen** - "pay ∠for∠"

a. Ich möchte den Anzug gern gleich bezahlen.	I'd like to pay for the suit right away.
b. Bezahlen Sie die Hemden bitte an der Kasse.	Please pay for the shirts at the cashier's.
c. Wieviel muss ich noch bezahlen?	How much do I owe you? ('How much do I still have to pay?')
d. Für einen guten Wagen müssen Sie viel bezahlen.	You have to pay a lot for a good car.

10. <u>noch ein</u> / <u>ein ander-</u> - "another (in addition) / another (different)"

a. Können Sie mir noch eine Jacke geben? Ich brauche zwei.

Can you give me another jacket? I need two.

b. Können Sie mir eine andere Jacke zeigen? Diese sitzt nicht richtig.

Can you show me another jacket? This one doesn't fit right.

c. Zeigen Sie mir bitte noch einen dieser Stoffe, sie gefallen mir gut.

Show me another one of these materials; I like them.

d. Darf ich Ihnen einen anderen Stoff geben, die Qualität von diesem ist nicht so gut.

May I give you a different material? The quality of this one is not so good.

e. Ich möchte gern noch einen Anzug anprobieren.

I'd like to try on another suit.

f. Möchten Sie lieber einen anderen Anzug anprobieren?

Would you rather try on a different suit?

g. Ich glaube, wir brauchen noch einen Stuhl, hier sind nur fünf.

I think we need another chair, there are only five here.

h. Bringen Sie bitte einen anderen Stuhl, dieser ist kaputt.

Bring another chair please; this one is broken.

11. <u>hätte(n) gern</u> - "want, be looking for"

a. Ich hätte gern einen hellgrauen Anzug.

I want a light grey suit.

b. Herr Becker hätte gern eine gemusterte Krawatte.

Mr. Becker is looking for a figured necktie.

c. Wir hätten gern einen neuen Wagen.

We want a new car.

d. Ich hätte gern einen kombinierten Gas- und Elektroherd.

I'm looking for a combination gas and electric range.

e. Er hätte gern ein deutsches Buch.

He wants a German book.

12. <u>all-</u> "all, everything"

a. Er will mir alles in dieser Stadt zeigen.

He's going to show me everything in this city.

b. Geben Sie mir bitte von allem etwas.

Give me some of everything please.

c. Ist das alles, oder darf ich Ihnen sonst noch etwas zeigen?

Is that all, or may I show you something else?

d. Ich möchte gern alles sehen.

I'd like to see everything.

TRANSLATION DRILL (not recorded)

1. Mr. Becker wants to go down town and do some shopping.

Herr Becker will in die Stadt fahren und einige Besorgungen machen.

2. He's planning to go to a men's ready-made clothing store too.

Er will auch in ein Herrenkonfektions-geschäft gehen.

3. He needs a few soft-collar shirts.

Er braucht ein paar Sporthemden.

4. Mr. Wilson would like to come along and take a look at a few suits.

Herr Wilson möchte gern mitkommen und sich einige Anzüge ansehen.

5. The suits are very reasonable now in the summer clearance sale.

Die Anzüge sind jetzt im Sommerschluss-verkauf sehr preiswert.

6. He doesn't want to spend more than two hundred marks.

Er möchte nicht mehr als zweihundert Mark ausgeben.

7. He can't afford any more at the moment.

Mehr kann er sich augenblicklich nicht leisten.

8. However, in that price range he'll surely be able to find something suitable at Schwarz and Co.

Aber in der Preislage kann er sicher etwas Passendes bei Schwarz und Co. finden.

9. Mr. Becker usually buys his suits there too.	Herr Becker kauft seine Anzüge gewöhnlich auch dort.
10. It's a good but ('and') reasonable store, and one has a large selection there.	Es ist ein gutes und preiswertes Geschäft und man hat dort eine grosse Auswahl.
11. The two gentlemen go there together.	Die beiden Herren gehen zusammen dorthin.
12. In the show window right at the door they see a light grey suit.	Im Schaufenster gleich an der Tür sehen sie einen hellgrauen Anzug.
13. Mr. Wilson likes it very much.	Der gefällt Herrn Wilson sehr gut.
14. They go right to the second floor in the elevator.	Sie fahren gleich mit dem Fahrstuhl in den ersten Stock.
15. Unfortunately they don't find the grey suit in Mr. Wilson's size any more.	Leider finden sie den grauen Anzug nicht mehr in Herrn Wilsons Grösse.
16. The sales clerk shows him a brown suit like it ('a similar brown suit').	Der Verkäufer zeigt ihm einen ähnlichen braunen Anzug.
17. The quality is excellent, all wool.	Die Qualität ist ausgezeichnet, reine Wolle.
18. Mr. Wilson tries on the coat of the brown suit.	Herr Wilson probiert die Jacke des braunen Anzugs an.
19. It fits very well, and he likes the cut.	Sie sitzt sehr gut und der Schnitt gefällt ihm.
20. The suit only costs a hundred and sixty-five marks.	Der Anzug kostet nur hundertfünfundsechzig DM.
21. Mr. Wilson buys the suit, and the sales clerk wraps it up.	Herr Wilson kauft den Anzug und der Verkäufer packt ihn ein.
22. Then Mr. Becker takes a look at some shirts.	Dann sieht sich Herr Becker einige Hemden an.
23. He buys a striped soft-collar shirt with long sleeves and two white shirts.	Er kauft sich ein gestreiftes Sporthemd mit langen Ärmeln und zwei weisse Hemden.
24. The material the shirts are made of ('of the shirts') is good.	Der Stoff der Hemden ist gut.
25. The striped shirt is somewhat cheaper than the white ones.	Das gestreifte Hemd ist etwas billiger als die weissen.
26. The sales clerk would like to show Mr. Becker something else (in addition).	Der Verkäufer möchte Herrn Becker gern noch etwas anderes zeigen.
27. But Mr. Becker doesn't need any underwear or socks now.	Aber Herr Becker braucht jetzt keine Unterwäsche oder Socken.
28. He would like to take a look at a few neckties, however.	Er möchte sich aber gern noch einige Krawatten ansehen.
29. The sales clerk shows him solid color and figured ones.	Der Verkäufer zeigt ihm einfarbige und gemusterte.
30. Mr. Becker finds a figured one.	Herr Becker findet eine gemusterte.
31. This one goes well with his suit.	Diese passt gut zu seinem Anzug.
32. He likes a green tie very well, too.	Eine grüne Krawatte gefällt ihm auch sehr gut.
33. He takes both.	Er nimmt beide.
34. The sales clerk gives him a sales slip.	Der Verkäufer gibt ihm einen Kassenzettel.
35. Mr. Becker pays for the shirts and ties at the cashier's window.	Herr Becker bezahlt die Hemden und Krawatten an der Kasse.

RESPONSE DRILL (not recorded)

1. Warum will Herr Becker in die Stadt fahren?

   Er muss einige Besorgungen machen.

2. Was will er sich denn kaufen?

   Er will sich ein paar Sporthemden kaufen.

3. In welchem Geschäft kauft er gewöhnlich?

   Er kauft gewöhnlich bei Schwarz und Co.

4. Was für ein Geschäft ist das?

   Das ist ein Herrenkonfektionsgeschäft.

5. Wer fährt mit Herrn Becker in die Stadt?

   Herr Wilson fährt mit ihm in die Stadt.

6. Warum fährt er mit?

   Er will sich ein paar Sommeranzüge ansehen.

7. Wieviel Geld will Herr Wilson ungefähr für einen Anzug ausgeben?

   Er will etwa zweihundert Mark dafür ausgeben.

8. Was für Hemden will sich Herr Becker kaufen?

   Er will sich Sporthemden kaufen.

9. Wieviele kauft er sich?

   Er kauft sich drei Sporthemden.

10. Wieviel kostet das weisse Hemd?

    Das weisse Hemd kostet fünfundzwanzig Mark fünfzig.

11. Wie ist die Qualität der Hemden?

    Die Qualität der Hemden ist sehr gut.

12. Was möchte ihm der Verkäufer gern noch zeigen?

    Er möchte ihm gern noch etwas Unterwäsche und ein Paar Socken zeigen.

13. Was sieht sich Herr Becker dann noch an?

    Er sieht sich noch einige Krawatten an.

14. Was für eine Krawatte möchte er haben?

    Er möchte eine gemusterte Krawatte haben.

15. Wieviele Krawatten kauft er sich?

    Er kauft sich zwei Krawatten, eine gemusterte und eine grüne.

16. Was gibt ihm dann der Verkäufer?

    Er gibt ihm den Kassenzettel.

17. Wo bezahlt Herr Becker?

    Er bezahlt an der Kasse.

18. In welchem Stock gibt es Anzüge?

    Im ersten Stock.

19. Wie kommen die beiden Herren in den ersten Stock?

    Sie fahren mit dem Fahrstuhl in den ersten Stock.

20. Was für einen Anzug möchte Herr Wilson haben?

    Er möchte einen hellgrauen Sommeranzug haben.

21. Welcher Anzug gefällt ihm gut?

    Ein grauer Anzug im Schaufenster gefällt ihm gut.

22. Was für einen Anzug zeigt ihm der Verkäufer?

    Er zeigt ihm einen ähnlichen braunen.

23. Was für ein Stoff ist es?

    Der Stoff ist sehr gut, reine Wolle.

24. Was probiert Herr Wilson an?

    Er probiert die Jacke an.

25. Wie sitzt die Jacke?

    Die Jacke sitzt sehr gut.

26. Wie teuer ist der Anzug?

    Der Anzug kostet nur hundertfünfundsechzig Mark.

27. Warum ist der Anzug jetzt gerade so preiswert?

    Es ist Sommerschlussverkauf.

28. Was macht der Verkäufer?

    Der Verkäufer packt den Anzug ein.

29. Wo kaufen Sie Ihre Anzüge?

30. Was für eine Farbe hat die Krawatte von Herrn ...

31. Wieviel kostet ein gutes, weisses Sporthemd?

32. Wo ist hier ein preiswertes und gutes Herrenkonfektionsgeschäft?

33. Was wollen Sie sich heute kaufen?

34. In welche Geschäfte gehen Sie?

CONVERSATION PRACTICE (not recorded)

1

A: Wieviel kostet dieses weisse
   Sporthemd?
B: Das kostet sechzehn Mark fünfzig.
A: Und das gestreifte hier?
B: Das kostet nur zwölf Mark achtzig.
A: Bitte geben Sie mir ein weisses
   und zwei gestreifte.

2

A: Wo ist hier ein gutes Möbel-
   geschäft?
B: Was wollen Sie sich denn kaufen?
A: Einen grossen Schreibtisch, ein
   Sofa und vielleicht auch zwei
   Sessel.
B: Ich glaube, da gehen Sie am besten
   zu Schäfer und Co.
A: Ist das ein sehr teures Geschäft?
B: Nein, durchaus nicht.

3

A: Wo kann ich hier einen guten
   Sommeranzug bekommen?
B: Bei Schwarz und Co. haben Sie eine
   reiche Auswahl.
A: Kaufen Sie Ihre Sachen auch dort?
B: Ja, gewöhnlich kaufe ich sie dort
   oder in dem grossen Konfektions-
   geschäft in der Schubertstrasse.

4

A: Was darf ich Ihnen zeigen?
B: Ich möchte gern ein Sporthemd
   haben.
A: In welcher Farbe und Grösse?
B: In weiss. Die Grösse weiss ich
   leider nicht genau.
A: Wie gefällt Ihnen dieses hier?
B: Ganz gut. Wieviel kostet es denn?
A: Es ist sehr preiswert, - es kostet
   nur zehn Mark fünfzig.
B: Gut, geben Sie mir bitte drei
   davon.

5

A: Ich möchte gern ein Paar Socken
   haben.
V: Gern; lange oder kurze?
A: Kurze, bitte.
V: Welche Farbe, - haben Sie einen
   bestimmten Wunsch?
A: Nein; aber sie müssen einfarbig
   sein, vielleicht grau oder grün.
V: Hier sind gute Socken, reine Wolle.
A: Ja, die gefallen mir auch.
   Packen Sie bitte drei Paar ein.
V: Hier ist Ihr Kassenzettel.
   Bitte bezahlen Sie dort an der
   Kasse.

SITUATIONS (not recorded)

Im Damenkonfektionsgeschäft

Herr und Frau Jones machen Besorgunge
Im Schaufenster eines Damenkonfek-
tionsgeschäfts sieht Frau Jones eine
nette Jacke. Sie möchte gern etwas
Ähnliches haben. Sie gehen in das
Geschäft und die Verkäuferin fragt si
was sie haben möchte. Frau Jones sac
die Jacke im Schaufenster gefällt ihr
gut. Hoffentlich kann sie sie in
ihrer Grösse bekommen. Die Verkäuferin zeigt ihr eine ähnliche
Jacke. Frau Jones will sie anprobieren. Leider passt sie ihr nicht. Si
probiert noch einige andere Jacken ar
aber sie gefallen Frau Jones nicht gu
Leider hat das Geschäft keine grosse
Auswahl. Frau Jones kauft nichts.

Im Herrenkonfektionsgeschäft

Herr Jones will sich einige Sporthemden und Krawatten kaufen. Er geht
in ein Geschäft und der Verkäufer
zeigt ihm Hemden in allen Farben,
gemusterte und einfarbige. Herr Jones
nimmt vier Hemden. Dann sieht er sich
die Krawatten an. Er sucht eine
gemusterte Krawatte. Endlich findet
er eine. Die passt auch zu seinem
hellgrauen Anzug. Der Verkäufer gibt
ihm den Kassenzettel und Herr Jones
geht zur Kasse und bezahlt.

Im Möbelgeschäft

Jones' wollen sich neue Möbel kaufen.
Sie fragen Herrn Schmidt, wo ein
gutes Möbelgeschäft ist. Herr Schmidt
sagt ihnen, er kauft gern bei Schneider und Co. Das ist ein gutes altes
Geschäft in der Bahnhofstrasse. Herr
und Frau Jones gehen dorthin und
sehen sich Wohnzimmer-Möbel an. Sie
kaufen sich einen Schreibtisch, einen
grossen Sessel, einen Bücherschrank,
vier Stühle, ein Sofa, eine Stehlampe
und einen kleinen Rauchtisch. Dann
zeigt ihnen der Verkäufer noch einige
schöne Teppiche. Aber die Teppiche
sind sehr teuer und Herr und Frau
Jones wollen sich noch keinen kaufen.

Wieviel kostet es?

Sie kommen gerade aus der Stadt und
erzählen den anderen Herren in Ihrer
Klasse, was Sie sich kaufen wollen
und wieviel alles kostet.
Die Herren nehmen einen Bleistift und
schreiben die Zahlen auf das Papier.
Dann fragen Sie: "Wieviel kostet
alles zusammen?"

NARRATIVE (not recorded)

Herr und Frau Jones machen einen Spaziergang durch das Geschäftszentrum
Düsseldorfs. Die Schaufensterauslagen gefallen ihnen sehr gut und Frau Jones
bleibt lange vor dem Schaufenster eines Damenmodengeschäfts stehen. Ihr gefallen
die schönen Kleider, Pullover, Strickjacken und Blusen. Die Handschuhe,
Handtaschen und Strümpfe harmonieren mit der Kleidung.

Herr Jones interessiert sich mehr für die Herrenmode. Sie ist in Deutschland etwas konservativer als in Amerika. Hellgelbe Socken, feuerrote Pullover
oder schreiend-bunte Krawatten findet man nicht sehr oft. Viele Herren kaufen
ihre Anzüge auch heute noch beim Schneider. Man kann aber auch sehr gute Anzüge
von der Stange kaufen. Die Bedienung in den Geschäften ist gewöhnlich sehr
höflich und aufmerksam. Die Verkäufer haben eine lange Ausbildungszeit.
Soviele Ausverkäufe wie in Amerika gibt es in Deutschland nicht. Ausverkäufe
sind gesetzlich geregelt. Aber in allen Städten gibt es einen Sommerschluss-
verkauf und einen Winterschlussverkauf.

Herr und Frau Jones gehen auch in ein Schuhgeschäft. Die Schuhe in den
Schaufenstern sind nicht numeriert. Im Geschäft müssen sie dem Verkäufer sagen,
was sie haben wollen. Dieser zeigt ihnen dann mehrere Paar Schuhe, und Herr
Jones findet auch bald etwas, was ihm gefällt.

das Geschäfts-
  zentrum
	- the business
	  district
		schreiend-bunt	- screaming loud

die Auslage	- the display	der Schneider	- the tailor
die Mode	- the fashion	die Stange	- the (clothing) rack
das Kleid	- the dress	die Bedienung	- the service
die Strickjacke	- the cardigan	höflich	- courteous
die Bluse	- the blouse	aufmerksam	- attentive
der Handschuh	- the glove	die Ausbildungs-	- the training
die Handtasche	- the handbag	zeit	period
der Strumpf	- the stocking	der Ausverkauf	- the (special)
die Kleidung	- the clothing		sale
hellgelb	- bright yellow	gesetzlich	- by law
		geregelt	- regulated
feuerrot	- fiery red	numeriert	- numbered
		mehrere	- several

FINDER LIST

	ähnlich	similar
	allen	all
	anprobieren	try on
der	Anzug, ⁼e	suit
der	Ärmel, -	sleeve
	auffällig	bright, loud
	augenblicklich	at the moment
	ausgeben	spend
die	Auswahl	selection
	bekommen	get
die	Besorgung, -en	errand, purchase
	Besorgungen machen	do errands, go shopping
	bestimmt	particular, certain
	bezahlen	pay
	billig	cheap
	billiger	cheaper
	braun	brown
	dazu	in addition
	mit dazu	along with it
	einfarbig	solid colored
	ein paar	a couple, a few
	einpacken	wrap up
	etwa	approximately, around
der	Fahrstuhl, ⁼e	elevator
die	Farbe, -n	color
	eine andere Farbe	a different color, another color
	farbig	colored
	gemustert	figured
	gestreift	striped
	gewöhnlich	usually
	grau	grey
die	Grösse, -n	size
	grün	green
ich	hätte gern	I'd like to have, I'm interested (in having)
	hellgrau	light grey
das	Hemd, -en	shirt
das	Herrenkonfektionsgeschäft, -e	men's ready-made clothing store
die	Jacke, -n	coat, jacket
die	Kasse, -n	cashier's desk or window
der	Kassenzettel, -	sales slip
	kaufen	buy
die	Krawatte, -n	necktie
	kurz	short
	lang	long
	leicht	light-weight
sich		
etwas	leisten	to be able to afford something
	ich kann es mir leisten	I can afford it
	meinen	mean
das	Paar	pair
	passend	suitable
etwas	Passendes	something suitable
die	Person, -en	person, character
die	Preislage, -n	price range
	preiswert	reasonable, inexpensive
die	Qualität, -en	quality
	rein	pure, all
das	Schaufenster, -	show window
	schlecht	bad, poor
der	Schnitt, -e	cut
	sitzen	fit
die	Socke, -n	sock

der	Sommer,-	summer
der	Sommeranzug,¨e	summer suit
der	Sommerschlussverkauf,¨e	summer clearance sale
	sonst noch etwas	something else in addition
der	Spiegel,-	mirror
das	Sporthemd,-en	soft-collar shirt
der	Stoff,-e	material
	teuer	expensive
	unten	downstairs
die	Unterwäsche	underwear
der	Verkäufer,-	salesclerk
	was für	what, what kind of
	weiss	white
	wohl	I suppose, you suppose
die	Wolle	wool
der	Wunsch,¨e	wish
der	Zettel,-	slip
	ziemlich	rather, pretty

EINE FAHRT IN DIE BERGE

Basic Sentences

I

I

the place	der Ort,-e
the Volkswagen	der Volkswagen,-
the 'Autobahn', the parkway	die Autobahn,-en
Southern Germany	Süddeutschland

Place: In a Volkswagen on the Autobahn in Southern Germany.

Ort: In einem Volkswagen auf der Autobahn in Süddeutschland.

the time	die Zeit,-en
the weekend	das Wochenende,-n
July	der Juli
in July	im Juli

Time: A weekend in July.

Zeit: Ein Wochenende im Juli.

the (married) couple	das Ehepaar,-e
the friend	der Freund,-e

Cast of Characters: The American couple, Mr. and Mrs. Wilson, and their German friends, Mr. and Mrs. Becker.

Personen: Das amerikanische Ehepaar, Herr und Frau Wilson, und ihre deutschen Freunde, Herr und Frau Becker.

to look forward to	sich freuen auf (plus acc)
the Alps	die Alpen

MRS. WILSON

FRAU WILSON

I'm looking forward to the Alps.

Ich freue mich schon auf die Alpen.

the luck	das Glück
to be lucky	Glück haben

I hope we'll be lucky as far as the weather's concerned.

Hoffentlich haben wir Glück mit dem Wetter.

cold	kalt
not as cold as	nicht so kalt wie

MRS. BECKER

FRAU BECKER

Today it's not as cold as yesterday.

Heute ist es nicht so kalt wie gestern.

warm	warm
warmer	wärmer
last, previous	vorigen

MRS. WILSON

FRAU WILSON

Yes, it's warmer than ⌐it was⌐ all last week.

Ja, es ist wärmer als in der ganzen vorigen Woche.

that way, like that	so

I hope it stays that way.

Hoffentlich bleibt es so.

II

highest	höchste
the mountain	der Berg,-e

MRS. WILSON

The Zugspitze <u>is</u> the highest mountain in Germany, isn't it?

almost	fast
meters	Meter

MR. BECKER

Yes, it's almost 10 000 feet high.

every, each	jeder
every summer	jeden Sommer
the (range of) mountains	das Gebirge,-

MRS. WILSON

Do you go to the mountains every summer?

last	letzt
last summer	letzten Sommer
the Baltic Sea	die Ostsee[2]

MR. BECKER

No, last summer for example we were on the Baltic.

the winter	der Winter,-
quite often	öfters[3]
the skiing	das Skilaufen
for skiing	zum Skilaufen

But in the winter we quite often go to the mountains to ski.

MRS. WILSON

To the Alps?

the Black Forest	der Schwarzwald
near, close	nah
closer	näher

MR. BECKER

Yes, or to the Black Forest; it's closer for us.

to ski	Ski laufen
he skis	er läuft ... Ski

MRS. WILSON

My husband and I like to ski too.

II

FRAU WILSON

Die Zugspitze ist doch der höchste Berg Deutschlands, nicht wahr?

HERR BECKER

Ja, sie ist fast dreitausend Meter[1] hoch.

FRAU WILSON

Fahren Sie jeden Sommer ins Gebirge?

HERR BECKER

Nein; letzten Sommer waren wir zum Beispiel an der Ostsee.

Aber im Winter fahren wir öfters in die Berge zum Skilaufen.

FRAU WILSON

In die Alpen?

HERR BECKER

Ja, oder in den Schwarzwald; der ist für uns näher.

FRAU WILSON

Mein Mann und ich laufen auch gern Ski.

where we live	bei uns zu Hause
little, not much	wenig
the snow	der Schnee

Where we live there's not much snow in the winter, unfortunately.

Bei uns zu Hause gibt es leider wenig Schnee im Winter.

III

III

<u>MR. BECKER</u>

<u>HERR BECKER</u>

What's the climate like in your country anyway?

Wie ist eigentlich das Klima in Ihrer Heimat?

I have heard	ich hörte
hot	heiss
hotter	heisser

I've heard it's hotter in the summer-time than /¯it is_7 here.

Ich hörte, in den Sommermonaten ist es heisser als hier.

moist, humid	feucht
more humid	feuchter

<u>MR. WILSON</u>

<u>HERR WILSON</u>

That's right, and more humid too.

Das stimmt; und auch feuchter!

the rain	der Regen
much rain	viel Regen

<u>MR. BECKER</u>

<u>HERR BECKER</u>

Do you have much rain?

Haben Sie viel Regen?

the humidity (of the air)	die Luftfeuchtigkeit

<u>MR. WILSON</u>

<u>HERR WILSON</u>

No, but the humidity is very high.

Nein, aber die Luftfeuchtigkeit ist sehr hoch.

the season	die Jahreszeit,-en
nicest, most beautiful	am schönsten

<u>MR. BECKER</u>

<u>HERR BECKER</u>

What season is nicest where you live?

Welche Jahreszeit ist bei Ihnen am schönsten?

the fall	der Herbst
longer	länger

<u>MR. WILSON</u>

<u>HERR WILSON</u>

The fall; it's longer and warmer than /¯it is_7 here.

Der Herbst; er ist länger und wärmer als hier.

the spring	der Frühling,-e

The spring is much too short unfortunately.

Der Frühling ist leider viel zu kurz.

IV

fast	schnell
faster	schneller

MR. BECKER

Now we can go a little faster again.

IV

HERR BECKER

Jetzt können wir wieder etwas schneller fahren.

less	weniger
the traffic	der Verkehr
less traffic	weniger Verkehr
down	unten
the valley	das Tal,¨er

There's less traffic here than down in the valley.

Hier ist weniger Verkehr als unten im Tal.

cool	kühl
cooler	kühler
up	oben

MR. WILSON

But it's also cooler up here.

HERR WILSON

Aber es ist auch kühler hier oben.

(future auxiliary)	werden
he will, he's going to	er wird
the overcoat	der Mantel,¨
to put on	anziehen
I put something on	ich ziehe etwas an
I'm cold, chilly	mir ist kalt[4]

MR. WILSON

I'm going to put my coat on; I'm cold.

HERR WILSON

Ich werde meinen Mantel anziehen, mir ist kalt.

to freeze	frieren

Aren't you freezing, Mr. Becker?

Frieren Sie nicht, Herr Becker?

thick, heavy	dick
thicker, heavier	dicker
the sweater, pullover	der Pullover,-
to have on	anhaben
he has it on	er hat es an

MR. BECKER

No, but I have a heavier sweater on than you, too.

HERR BECKER

Nein, ich habe aber auch einen dickeren Pullover an als Sie.

V

V

the tire	der Reifen,-
the flat tire	die Reifenpanne,-n
I need it	es fehlt mir
we needed it	es hat uns gefehlt

MR. BECKER	HERR BECKER
A flat!!! That's all we needed!!!	Reifenpanne!!! Das hat uns gerade noch gefehlt!!!

<table>
<tr><td>it would have
to be ... !
when
the filling station</td><td>ausgerechnet

wenn
die Tankstelle,-n</td></tr>
</table>

MRS. BECKER	FRAU BECKER
And it would have to be when there's no gas station nearby, too!	Und ausgerechnet dann, wenn keine Tankstelle in der Nähe ist!

<table>
<tr><td>all right then
just, simply
myself, himself,
ourselves etc.</td><td>na ja
eben
selbst</td></tr>
</table>

MR. BECKER	HERR BECKER
All right then, we'll just have to change the tire ourselves.	Na ja, da müssen wir eben selbst den Reifen wechseln.

<table>
<tr><td>the photograph</td><td>die Aufnahme,-n</td></tr>
</table>

MRS. BECKER	FRAU BECKER
Meanwhile I'll take a couple of pictures.	Inzwischen werde ich ein paar Aufnahmen machen.

<table>
<tr><td>the view
wonderful</td><td>die Aussicht
wunderbar</td></tr>
</table>

The view's wonderful from up here.	Die Aussicht von hier ist wunderbar.

<table>
<tr><td>the camera</td><td>der Photoapparat,-e</td></tr>
</table>

Where's the camera?	Wo ist der Photoapparat?

<table>
<tr><td>the briefcase</td><td>die Aktenmappe,-n</td></tr>
</table>

MR. BECKER	HERR BECKER
In the briefcase, I think.	In der Aktenmappe, glaube ich.

VI

<table>
<tr><td>the cloud
the sky</td><td>die Wolke,-n
der Himmel,-</td></tr>
</table>

MR. WILSON	HERR WILSON
Just look at those dark clouds in the sky.	Sehen Sie mal diese dunklen Wolken am Himmel!

<table>
<tr><td>to rain
it's raining</td><td>regnen
es regnet</td></tr>
</table>

It's probably going to rain soon.	Es wird wahrscheinlich bald regnen.

the radio	das Radio,-s
to turn on	anstellen
he turns on	er stellt ... an

MR. BECKER

| | HERR BECKER |

I'll turn the radio on. · Ich werde das Radio anstellen.

| the news | die Nachrichten |

Maybe we can hear the news. · Vielleicht können wir die Nachrichten hören.

| the weather report | der Wetterbericht,-e |

RADIO

RADIO

Now we present the weather report: · Wir bringen Ihnen jetzt den Wetterbericht.

at noon	mittags
heavy, severe	schwer
the thunderstorm	das Gewitter,-
the Lower Alps	die Voralpen
later	später
sunny, fair	sonnig

At noon a severe thunderstorm ⌐is expected⌐ in the Lower Alps; later fair and warmer again. · Mittags schweres Gewitter in den Voralpen, später wieder sonnig und wärmer.

| to hurry | sich beeilen |
| I hurry | ich beeile mich |

MR. BECKER

HERR BECKER

We'll have to hurry then. · Da müssen wir uns aber beeilen.

| we were planning | wir wollten |
| to eat lunch | zu Mittag essen |

We were planning to eat lunch in Garmisch. · Wir wollten doch in Garmisch zu Mittag essen.

Notes to the Basic Sentences

[1] **Meter.** Since one meter very nearly equals 40 inches, the simplest way of calculating an equivalent number of feet is to multiply by 10 and divide by 3.

[2] **die Ostsee.** The Baltic coast north of Lübeck is part of the Federal Republic. Many of the formerly well-known resorts however are in Eastern Germany.

[3] **öfters** is a variant form of **öfter**, the comparative of the adverb **oft** (see page 236). **Öfters** means "fairly often, quite often, while **öfter** means literally "more often", and implies a comparison.

[4] The occurrence of a dative form with an adjective is already familiar in such expressions as: **Das ist mir recht** and **Ist Ihnen diese** (**Krawatte**) **zu auffällig**? The construction **mir ist kalt** is an impersonal one which has no actual grammatical subject.

Notes on Grammar
(For Home Study)

A.   COMPARISON OF ADJECTIVES AND ADVERBS

I. Three 'degrees' of intensity

Three different degrees of intensity are expressed by adjectives and adverbs. We noted this in Unit 4, where the adverbs <u>gern</u>, <u>lieber</u> and <u>am liebsten</u> were discussed. The same difference in degree is shown by a number of adjective and adverb forms occurring in the present unit:

Es ist nicht so kalt wie gestern.	It's not as cold as yesterday.
Jetzt können wir schneller fahren.	Now we can go faster.
Welche Jahreszeit ist am schönsten?	What season is the nicest one?

II. Positive, Comparative and Superlative Forms

The forms of adjectives and adverbs corresponding to the different degrees of intensity are called POSITIVE, COMPARATIVE and SUPERLATIVE. Note the similarity of German and English forms:

Positive:	kalt	schnell	schön	cold	fast	nice
Comparative:	kält-er	schnell-er	schön-er	cold-er	fast-er	nice-r
Superlative:	kält-est	schnell-st	schön-st	cold-est	fast-est	nice-st

The suffixes <u>-er</u> and <u>-est</u> (or <u>-st</u>) are added to the basic, or positive form of the adjective or adverb to make the comparative and superlative. In addition to this <u>some</u> monosyllabic German adjectives and adverbs change or 'umlaut' their stem vowels in the comparative and superlative forms.

1. Relatively few adjectives and adverbs have umlaut in their comparative and superlative forms, but those which are umlauted are of rather frequent occurrence. Here is a complete list of the adjectives and adverbs encountered up to this point in which umlaut takes place. A few show other irregularities which will be pointed out later.

alt	gross	hoch	kurz	lang	nah	oft	warm

2. English also uses the words <u>more</u> and <u>most</u> to indicate comparative and superlative degree, especially with words of several syllables. German however, uses ONLY the suffixes:

Positive:	praktisch	umständlich	practical	complicated
Comparative:	praktisch-er	umständlich-er	more practical	more complicated
Superlative:	praktisch-st	umständlich-st	most practical	most complicated

3. The superlative suffix is usually <u>-st</u>, but it is <u>-est</u> after <u>s</u> (heiss-est), <u>t</u> (kält-est) or <u>z</u> (kürz-est). It may be either <u>-st</u> or <u>-est</u> after vowels (neu-st, neu-est).

III. Stem-lengtheners versus Endings

The comparative and superlative suffixes are NOT ENDINGS. They are STEM-LENGTHENERS, to which endings are added when the comparative and superlative forms occur as attributive adjectives, i.e. as part of an adjective-noun or specifier-adjective-noun phrase:

Die Zugspitze ist der höch-st-e Berg Deutschlands.	The Zugspitze is the highest mountain in Germany.
Ich habe einen dick-er-en Pullover an.	I have a heavier sweater on.

If you remember that STEM-LENGTHENER and ENDING are BOTH present in some phrases you will not be confused by such examples as the following:

Das ist ein schwer-er Wagen.	(Ending only)
Das ist ein schwer-er-er Wagen.	(Stem-lengthener + ending)
Das ist unser neu-er Teppich.	(Ending only)
Das ist unser neu-st-er Teppich.	(Stem-lengthener + ending)
Hier ist eine teuer-e Lampe.	(Full stem with ending)
Hier ist eine teur-er-e Lampe.	(Short stem with stem lengthener + ending)

IV. Predicate Adjectives and Adverbs

Positive and Comparative forms occurring as predicate adjectives or adverbs have no endings. Superlative forms, however, occur in a special predicate phrase:

Dieses Haus ist klein.	This house is small.
Dieses Haus ist klein-er.	This house is smaller.
Dieses Haus ist am klein-st-en.	This house is / the / smallest.
Dieses Haus ist das klein-st-e Haus von allen.	This is the smallest house of all.
Unser Wagen fährt schnell.	Our car is going fast.
Unser Wagen fährt schnell-er.	Our car is going faster.
Unser Wagen fährt am schnell-st-en.	Our car is going / the / fastest.

The superlative of most adjectives never appears in the stem form only. When it is attributive it has the regular adjective endings; when it is a predicate adjective or an adverb it has the special phrase form. Note that English also very often uses a phrase with 'the'.

V. Irregular Comparison

A few adjectives and adverbs are quite irregular in their comparative and superlative formation. The following is a complete list of those encountered up to this point:

Positive:	gern	gross	gut	hoch	nah	viel
Comparative:	lieber	grösser	besser	höher	näher	mehr
Superlative:	liebst	grösst	best	höchst	nächst	meist

VI. The complete comparison

1. A complete comparison may contain a comparative form of the adjective or adverb and a phrase introduced by als 'than' or, in the negative, nicht so plus the positive form of the adjective or adverb and a phrase introduced by wie 'as'.

Der Herbst ist länger und wärmer als hier.	The fall is longer and warmer than / it is / here.
Heute ist es nicht so kalt wie gestern.	Today it's not as cold as yesterday.
Hier ist weniger Verkehr als unten im Tal.	There's less traffic here than down in the valley.
Hier ist nicht so viel Verkehr wie unten im Tal.	There's not as much traffic here as down in the valley.

Note that phrases following als and wie have the same case forms as the phrases with which they are being compared and prepositions are repeated:

Der Vater ist natürlich älter als sein Sohn.	(Both are Nominative forms)
Der Sohn ist nicht so alt wie sein Vater.	(Both are Nominative forms)
Ich trinke lieber diesen Wein als den französischen.	(Both are Accusative forms)
Sie kommen schneller mit dem Auto als mit der Strassenbahn in die Stadt.	(Preposition mit occurs twice)

2. A complete comparison may also contain a superlative form plus a genitive form or a phrase introduced by the prepositions in or von:

Die Zugspitze ist der höchste Berg Deutschlands.	The Zugspitze is the highest mountain in Germany ('Germany's highest mountain').
Der Everest ist der höchste Berg in der ganzen Welt.	Everest is the highest mountain in the whole world.
Von allen Städten Amerikas hat Washington das heisseste und feuchteste Wetter in den Sommermonaten.	Of all the cities in America Washington has the hottest and most humid weather in the summer months.

B.   QUANTITY ADJECTIVES

I. Quantity adjectives in German have endings only under certain conditions.

1. Viel 'much, many' and wenig 'not much, few have endings when they occur in the plural:

| Er kennt viele Deutsche, aber er spricht nur mit wenigen. | He knows many Germans but he only talks to a few. |

2. Viel and wenig have endings when they occur AFTER A SPECIFIER:

| Mir gefallen die vielen eingebauten Schränke. | I like the many built-in cupboards. |
| Mit seinem wenigen Geld kann er sich kein Auto leisten. | With the little money he has he can't afford a car. |

3. Viel and wenig usually DO NOT have endings in the singular when they occur WITHOUT A SPECIFIER:

Haben Sie viel Regen?	Do you have much rain?
Bei uns zu Hause gibt es leider wenig Schnee im Winter.	Where we live there's not much snow in the winter, unfortunately.
Ich habe nicht viel Zeit.	I don't have much time.

However, there is one fixed expression where an ending occurs: Vielen Dank.

II. Comparative forms of the quantity adjectives do not have endings.

The comparative forms mehr 'more' and weniger 'less' NEVER have endings:

Sie hat sicher mehr Geld als ich.	She certainly has more money than I.
Hat sie weniger Zeit als der Konsul?	Does she have less time than the consul?
Wir haben hier weniger Verkehr als in der Stadt.	We have less traffic here than in town.
Er hat mehr Bücher als ich.	He has more books than I.
In Deutschland gibt es weniger Tankstellen als in Amerika.	In Germany there are fewer gas stations than in America.

VERBS.   THE FUTURE PHRASE.

I. In Units 2 and 3 we noted that the verbs dürfen, können, müssen, sollen and wollen and the special forms möchte and möchten occur together with an infinitive in German to form a verb phrase. These verbs, which help to make up verb phrases, are called AUXILIARY VERBS. We have now encountered one more such verb. Notice the similarity in the way it is used.

Jetzt können wir wieder etwas schneller fahren.	Now we can go a little faster again.
Ich werde mir meinen Mantel anziehen.	I'm going to put my coat on.
Wir müssen eben den Reifen wechseln.	We'll just have to change the tire.
Inzwischen werde ich ein paar Aufnahmen machen.	Meanwhile I'll take a couple of pictures.
Es wird wahrscheinlich bald regnen.	It's probably going to rain soon.

The verb phrase consisting of a form of the auxiliary werden plus an infinitive is used to refer to future time and is known as the FUTURE PHRASE.

II. Future time is indicated by other devices in German also.

1. The Present Tense form of the verb, often with a time expression:

In welches Geschäft gehen Sie?	What store are you going to?
Wo kommt die Stehlampe hin?	Where does the floor lamp go?
In zehn Minuten sind Sie da.	You'll be there in ten minutes.
Hoffentlich kommt das Frachtgut bald an.	I hope the freight arrives soon.
Ich fahre nachher dort vorbei.	I'm driving by there in a little while.

Note that English also may use a Present Tense form of the verb ('arrives'), but just as frequently uses a phrase consisting of 'will' or "'ll" plus an infinitive, or a phrase with the '-ing' form of the verb.

2. A verb phrase with the auxiliaries sollen or wollen, often with a time expression:

Ich will gleich mal anrufen.	I'll just give them a quick call.
Wo sollen wir den kleinen Tisch hinstellen?	Where shall we put the little table?
Wir wollen essen gehen.	We're planning to go and eat.
Soll ich auflegen?	Shall I hang up?
Ich will nach Schwabing fahren.	I'm planning to go to Schwabing.
Er soll in zehn Minuten kommen.	He's supposed to be coming in ten minutes.
Wie lange wollen Sie bleiben?	How long do you intend to stay?

Notice however that although future time is indicated in every case, something else is also implied. The sentences with wollen indicate the desire, plan or intention of the subject. The sentences with sollen express a desire, intention or opinion of someone other than the subject of the sentence, i.e., someone 'wants' or 'expects' the subject to do something, or, in questions, the subject is inquiring about the desire or expectation of another person with regard to his contemplated action.

D. SPECIFIERS: jeder

Jeder 'each, every' should be added to the list of der-type specifiers presented in Unit 3. It has the same endings and functions in the same way as der, dieser and welcher.

Jeder deutsche Photoapparat kostet in Deutschland weniger als in Amerika.

Every German camera costs less in Germany than in America.

E. TIME EXPRESSIONS

I. Noun phrases in time expressions are of two main types: prepositional phrases and independent noun phrases.

1. Prepositional phrases with an and in have the dative form; prepositional phrases with für have the accusative form:

Kommen Sie doch mal am nächsten Sonntag zu uns!
Why don't you come to see us next Sunday?

In den Sommermonaten ist es heisser als hier.
In the summer months it's hotter than it is here.

Ich muss in einer halben Stunde meine Frau abholen.
I have to pick up my wife in half an hour.

Wollen Sie nicht Platz nehmen? Danke, aber nur für einen Augenblick.
Won't you sit down? Thanks, but only for a minute.

2. Independent noun phrases usually have the accusative form:

Fahren Sie jeden Sommer ins Gebirge?
Do you go to the mountains every summer?

Letzten Sommer waren wir an der Ostsee.
Last summer we were on the Baltic.

Ich bin den ganzen Nachmittag in meinem Büro.
I'll be in my office all afternoon.

II. The names of the months are nearly always preceded by a form of the specifier in German. All are der-words.

Ein Wochenende im Juli.
A weekend in July.

Der Mai ist immer schön.
May is always lovely.

Wir fahren im August nach Deutschland.
We're going to Germany in August.

Here is the complete list:

der Januar	der Juli
der Februar	der August
der März	der September
der April	der Oktober
der Mai	der November
der Juni	der Dezember

SUBSTITUTION DRILL - Part I

1. Wir haben viel <u>Regen</u>.

Schnee - Besuch - Gepäck - Zeit

2. Ich habe nur wenig <u>Geld</u>.

Zeit - Hunger - Durst - Gepäck -
Tabak - Tinte - Briefpapier

3. Sie hat mehr <u>Zeit</u> als ich.

Geld - Gepäck - Geschirr - Besuch -
Durst - Hunger

4. Er trinkt wenig <u>Bier</u>.

Wasser - Tee - Kaffee - Wein - Milch

5. Er hat weniger <u>Gepäck</u> als ich.

Geld - Zeit - Besuch - Tabak -
Briefpapier

6. Wem gehört <u>das</u> viele <u>Geld</u>?

Geschirr - Gepäck - Papier - Wäsche -
Tabak - Stoff

7. Er trinkt viel <u>Bier</u>.

Wasser - Tee - Kaffee - Wein - Milch

8. Hier gibt es <u>mehr Schnee</u> als bei
Ihnen zu Hause.

mehr Regen - weniger Geschäfte - mehr
Parkplätze - weniger Cafés - mehr
Taxen - weniger Gewitter

9. Hier ist es nicht so <u>heiss</u> wie
in Berlin.

kalt - feucht - warm - kühl - schön -
ruhig

10. <u>Mein Vater</u> wird morgen nach Berlin
fahren.

meine Eltern - ich - sie - sein
Bruder - Herr und Frau Wilson -
ihre Schwester

11. <u>Ich</u> will <u>meine</u> Jacke anziehen.

er - sie (sg) - Sie - meine Schwester -
Ihre Frau

12. <u>Wir</u> wollen <u>unsere</u> Mäntel anziehen.

sie - meine Brüder - Herr Becker und
Herr Wilson - die Damen

13. <u>Mir</u> ist kalt.

•ihm - ihr - uns - ihnen - meiner Frau -
Ihrer Mutter - unseren Eltern.

14. Ist <u>Ihnen</u> zu warm

                    Ihrer Tochter - ihnen - ihm - seinen
                    Eltern

15. Wir freuen uns auf <u>die Alpen</u>.

                    Berge - Gebirge - Besuch - Sommer -
                    Frühling - Mai - Brief - Reise

16. Er stellt <u>das Radio</u> an.

                    Heizung - Elektroherd - Gasherd

                              (End of Tape 9A)

Tape 9B   SUBSTITUTION DRILL - Part II

1. Er fährt jetzt <u>schneller</u>.

    langsam - gut - ruhig - weit -
    schlecht   langsamer - besser - ruhiger -
                              weiter - schlechter

2. Dieses Haus ist am <u>grössten</u>.

    klein - schön - alt - gemütlich -
    neu - billig - hoch   am kleinsten - am schönsten - am
                              ältesten - am gemütlichsten - am
                              neusten - am billigsten - am höchsten

3. Der Herbst ist hier die <u>schönste</u>
Jahreszeit.

    lang - kurz - warm - kalt - kühl   längste - kürzeste - wärmste -
                              kälteste - kühlste

4. Hier ist es <u>heisser</u> als in Berlin.

    kalt - feucht - warm - kühl -
    schön - ruhig   kälter - feuchter - wärmer - kühler -
                              schöner - ruhiger

5. Wo ist es am <u>schönsten</u>?

    warm - kalt - heiss - kühl -
    ruhig - preiswert   am wärmsten - am kältesten - am
                              heissesten - am kühlsten - am ruhig-
                              sten - am preiswertesten

6. Er kauft sich den <u>teuersten Anzug</u>.

    den guten Mantel - die schöne
    Krawatte - den kurzen Roman - das
    billige Hemd - die warme Jacke -
    das gute Briefpapier - die schöne
    Lampe - den grossen Teppich   den besten Mantel - die schönste
                              Krawatte - den kürzesten Roman - das
                              billigste Hemd - die wärmste Jacke -
                              das beste Briefpapier - die schönste
                              Lampe - den grössten Teppich

7. Ihr Haus ist <u>grösser</u> als <u>meins</u>.

    schön (unser) - klein (sein) - alt
    (ihr) - neu (mein) - gemütlich
    (unser)   schöner als unseres - kleiner als
                              seins - älter als ihrs - neuer als
                              meins - gemütlicher als unseres

8. Das ist unser <u>billigster</u> Wagen
   hier in Deutschland.

   gut - leicht - gross - teuer -   bester - leichtester - grösster -
   klein   teuerster - kleinster

9. Er hat ein <u>grösseres</u> Zimmer als
   sein Bruder.

   schön - klein - gemütlich - ruhig - schöneres - kleineres - gemütlicheres -
   nett - gut   ruhigeres - netteres - besseres

10. Er arbeitet in dem <u>grössten</u>
    Geschäft der Stadt.

    alt - schön - gut - neu - teuer   ältesten - schönsten - besten -
                                        neusten - teuersten

11. Das sind unsere <u>schönsten</u> Hemden.

    preiswert - gut - einfach - teuer - preiswertesten - besten - einfachsten -
    neu - billig   teuersten - neusten - billigsten

12. Wir kaufen uns eine <u>grössere</u> Lampe.

    billig - klein - schön - gut -   billigere - kleinere - schönere -
    einfach - nett   bessere - einfachere - nettere

13. Ist das Ihr <u>kleinstes</u> Auto?

    neu - gut - teuer - preiswert -   neustes - bestes - teuerstes -
    billig - gross - leicht   preiswertestes - billigstes - grösstes
                                         leichtestes

14. Das sind die <u>schönsten</u> Tage.

    heiss - kurz - kalt - feucht -   heissesten - kürzesten - kältesten -
    kühl - lang - warm - ruhig   feuchtesten - kühlsten - längsten -
                                         wärmsten - ruhigsten

15. Ich nehme <u>das kleinere Zimmer</u>.

    (preiswert) Wagen - (dick) Woll-   den preiswerteren Wagen - die dickere
    decke - (alt) Wein - (gut) Akten-   Wolldecke - den älteren Wein - die
    tasche - (gross) Hemd - (gut)   bessere Aktentasche - das grössere
    Briefpapier   Hemd - das bessere Briefpapier

16. Kennen Sie <u>das neuste Buch</u> von ihm?

    (berühmt) Roman - (klein) Tochter - den berühmtesten Roman - die kleinste
    (alt) Schwester - (gross) Geschäft - Tochter - die älteste Schwester - das
    (neu) Kollege   grösste Geschäft - den neusten
                                         Kollegen

17. Hier ist ein Bild <u>der ältesten
    Stadt</u>.

    (berühmt) Museum - (schön) Universi- des berühmtesten Museums - der schön-
    tät - (hoch) Dom - (neu) Auto -   sten Universität - des höchsten Doms -
    (alt) Rathaus   des neusten Autos - des ältesten
                                         Rathauses

18. Er arbeitet in <u>einer schöneren
Bibliothek</u> als ich.

(gross) Neubau - (klein) Hotel -
(gut) Theater - (alt) Geschäft -
(neu) Bank - (klein) Büro -
(wichtig) Abteilung

einem grösseren Neubau - einem kleine-
ren Hotel - einem besseren Theater -
einem älteren Geschäft - einer neueren
Bank - einem kleineren Büro - einer
wichtigeren Abteilung

19. Das ist <u>der grösste Tisch</u> in
diesem Geschäft.

(preiswert) Wein - (teuer) Akten-
tasche - (gut) Briefpapier

der preiswerteste Wein - die teuerste
Aktentasche - das beste Briefpapier

20. Diese Stadt hat <u>bessere Restaurants</u>
als Bremen.

(schön) Parks - (alt) Häuser -
(preiswert) Hotels - (klein) Ge-
schäfte - (gross) Etagenhäuser

schönere Parks - ältere Häuser -
preiswertere Hotels - kleinere Ge-
schäfte - grössere Etagenhäuser

21. Ich gehe heute in <u>ein besseres
Restaurant</u>.

(alt) Bibliothek - (nett) Café -
(gross) Bank - (preiswert) Ge-
schäft - (klein) Neubau

eine ältere Bibliothek - ein netteres
Café - eine grössere Bank - ein preis-
werteres Geschäft - einen kleineren
Neubau

CONVERSION DRILL

The following drill contains positive and negative comparisons. The positive
sentences are on the left, and the negative comparisons are on the right. Cover
the right-hand side of the page and read sentence on the left out loud, then
convert it to a negative comparative statement. After the whole drill has been
completed in this way, cover the left-hand side of the page, read a sentence out
loud and then convert it to a positive comparison.

1. Oben in den Bergen ist es heute
windiger als unten im Tal.

Oben in den Bergen ist es heute nicht
so windig wie unten im Tal.

2. Hier ist es kühler als in Süddeutsch-
land.

Hier ist es nicht so kühl wie in
Süddeutschland.

3. Im Sommer ist es in Washington
heisser als in Frankfurt.

Im Sommer ist es in Washington nicht
so heiss wie in Frankfurt.

4. Ihre Schreibmaschine ist besser als
meine.

Ihre Schreibmaschine ist nicht so gut
wie meine.

5. Hier ist weniger Verkehr als auf
der Autobahn.

Hier ist nicht so wenig Verkehr wie
auf der Autobahn.

6. Das weisse Hemd gefällt mir besser
als das farbige.

Das weisse Hemd gefällt mir nicht so
gut wie das farbige.

7. Ist denn der Dom in Köln grösser
als der in Frankfurt?

Ist denn der Dom in Köln nicht so gross
wie der in Frankfurt?

8. Finden Sie diesen Stoff besser als
den anderen da?

Finden Sie diesen Stoff nicht so gut
wie den anderen da?

9. Diese Zeitung ist interessanter als
die Frankfurter Allgemeine.

Diese Zeitung ist nicht so interessant
wie die Frankfurter Allgemeine.

10. Dieser Brief ist augenblicklich
dringender und wichtiger als Ihr
Ferngespräch.

Dieser Brief ist augenblicklich nicht
so dringend und wichtig wie Ihr Fern-
gespräch.

11. Das Material dieses blauen Anzugs
ist leichter als das des grauen.

Das Material dieses blauen Anzugs ist
nicht so leicht wie das des grauen.

12. Wir fahren lieber mit der Strassen-
bahn als mit dem Autobus.

Wir fahren nicht so gern mit der
Strassenbahn wie mit dem Autobus.

(continued on the next page)

13. Er will mehr von dem deutschen
    Wein als von dem französischen
    kaufen.

    Er will nicht so viel von dem deutschen
    Wein wie von dem französischen kaufen.

14. Unsere Küche ist gemütlicher als
    das Wohnzimmer.

    Unsere Küche ist nicht so gemütlich
    wie das Wohnzimmer.

15. In den neuen Etagenhäusern sind
    die Mieten höher als in den alten.

    In den neuen Etagenhäusern sind die
    Mieten nicht so hoch wie in den alten.

16. Wir sehen den Wagen des Konsuls
    öfter als den des Botschafters.

    Wir sehen den Wagen des Konsuls nicht
    so oft wie den des Botschafters.

17. In dieser Stadt gibt es mehr
    Omnibusse als Strassenbahnen.

    In dieser Stadt gibt es nicht so viele
    Omnibusse wie Strassenbahnen.

VARIATION DRILL

1. **Hier gibt es wenig Schnee im
   Winter.**

   **There's not much ('little') snow here
   in the winter.**

   a. Is there much rain in the spring
      where you live?
      Gibt es beiIhnen viel Regen im Frühling?
   b. Unfortunately I have but little
      time.
      Ich habe leider nur wenig Zeit.
   c. Do you have much work?
      Haben Sie viel Arbeit?
   d. We unfortunately have little
      luck with the weather.
      Wir haben leider wenig Glück mit dem
      Wetter.
   e. He doesn't have much tobacco.
      Er hat nicht viel Tabak.
   f. She has few dishes but lots of
      linen!
      Sie hat wenig Geschirr aber viel
      Wäsche.

2. **Heute ist es nicht so heiss wie
   gestern.**

   It's not as hot today as yesterday.

   a. It doesn't rain as much here
      as where we live.
      Hier regnet es nicht so viel wie bei
      uns zu Hause.
   b. The humidity is not as high
      here as in Washington.
      Die Luftfeuchtigkeit ist hier nicht so
      hoch wie in Washington.
   c. I don't like the brown coat as
      well as the gray one.
      Der braune Mantel gefällt mir nicht so
      gut wie der graue.
   d. This little range here is not
      as practical as the big combi-
      nation one.
      Dieser kleine Herd hier ist nicht so
      praktisch wie der grosse kombinierte.
   e. This store is not as reasonable
      as the other one.
      Dieses Geschäft ist nicht so preiswert
      wie das andere.

3. **Hier ist es wärmer als im Gebirge.**

   It's warmer here than in the mountains.

   a. My sister is older than my
      brother.
      Meine Schwester ist älter als mein
      Bruder.
   b. The brown suit is more expensive
      than the gray one.
      Der braune Anzug ist teurer als der
      graue.
   c. In our country ('homeland') it's
      hotter in the summer than
      ⎾it is⏋ in Germany.
      In unserer Heimat ist es im Sommer
      heisser als in Deutschland.
   d. I like this wine better than the
      other one.
      Ich trinke diesen Wein lieber als den
      anderen.
   e. In Frankfurt there's less snow
      than in Munich.
      In Frankfurt gibt es weniger Schnee
      als in München.

4. **Der Frühling ist bei uns am
   schönsten.**

   **The spring is the nicest ⎾season⏋
   where we live.**

   a. Which season is the warmest one
      where you live?
      Welche Jahreszeit ist bei Ihnen zu
      Hause am wärmsten?
   b. I really like this coat best.
      Dieser Mantel gefällt mir wirklich am
      besten.

c. I think the gray jacket is the   Ich glaube, die graue Jacke ist am
   shortest one.   kürzesten.
d. This part of town is the quietest   Diese Gegend ist am ruhigsten.
   one.
e. He says this picture is the most   Er sagt, dieses Bild ist am berühmtesten.
   famous one.
f. Which car is the largest one   Welcher Wagen ist denn am grössten?
   then?

5. Kennen Sie den höchsten Berg in   Are you familiar with the highest
   Amerika?   mountain in America?

a. That's the best book of the   Das ist das beste Buch des Jahres.
   year.
b. She's going to buy (herself) the   Sie kauft sich den preiswertesten
   least expensive coat.   Mantel.
c. He has the biggest house in our   Er hat das grösste Haus in unserer
   neighborhood.   Nachbarschaft.
d. We live in the quietest part of   Wir wohnen in der ruhigsten Gegend
   the city.   der Stadt.
e. Are you familiar with his best-   Kennen Sie sein bekanntestes Buch?
   known book?
f. I'm just reading her most   Ich lese gerade ihren berühmtesten
   famous novel.   Roman.

6. Fahren Sie bitte etwas schneller.   Please drive a little faster.

a. Stay here a little longer!   Bleiben Sie doch etwas länger hier!
b. Make the coat a bit shorter   Machen Sie den Mantel bitte etwas
   please.   kürzer.
c. Please speak a bit slower.   Sprechen Sie bitte etwas langsamer.
d. Please come a bit earlier   Kommen Sie morgen bitte etwas früher.
   tomorrow.
e. Please call (up) a little later.   Rufen Sie bitte etwas später an.

7. Haben Sie vielleicht einen preiswer-   Do you perhaps have a less expensive
   teren Mantel als den im Schaufenster?   coat than the one in the window?

a. That's a much higher building   Das ist ein viel höheres Gebäude als
   than the new building on the   der Neubau am Markt.
   market place.
b. Lon't you have any better   Haben Sie keinen besseren Stoff als
   material than this?   diesen?
c. That's a larger car than ours.   Das ist ein grösserer Wagen als unserer.
d. These are better shirts than   Das sind bessere Hemden als die teuren
   the expensive ones at Schwarz   bei Schwarz und Co.
   and Co.
e. I believe there is no more   Ich glaube, es gibt kein teureres
   expensive radio than this big   Radio als dieses grosse hier.
   one here.

8. Wir kaufen weniger englische als   We buy fewer English /̅books 7̅ than
   deutsche Bücher.   German books.

a. We have more acquaintances here   Wir haben hier mehr Bekannte als
   than real friends.   richtige Freunde.
b. I don't see him as often as   Ich sehe ihn nicht so oft wie seinen
   /̅I see 7̅ his brother.   Bruder.
c. This rug goes ('fits') better in   Dieser Teppich passt besser vor den
   front of the desk than in front   Schreibtisch als vor das Sofa.
   of the sofa.
d. In Bonn people don't drink as   In Bonn trinkt man nicht so viel
   much French as German wine.   französischen wie deutschen Wein.
e. We buy German beer more often   Wir kaufen deutsches Bier öfter als
   than French wine.   französischen Wein.

9. **Ich werde jetzt ein paar Aufnahmen machen.**   <u>I'm going to take a few pictures now.</u>

a. My new secretary is not going to come today.
Meine neue Sekretärin wird heute nicht kommen.

b. When are you going to go to Germany?
Wann werden Sie denn nach Deutschland fahren?

c. We'll change the tire right away ourselves.
Wir werden den Reifen gleich selbst wechseln.

d. He'll surely write to you soon.
Er wird Ihnen sicher bald schreiben.

e. I hope it's not going to rain today.
Hoffentlich wird es heute nicht regnen.

10. **Wir werden wahrscheinlich im Juli an die Ostsee fahren.**   <u>We'll probably go to the Baltic in July.</u>

a. His parents are supposed to come to /‾see‾/ him in August.
Seine Eltern sollen im August zu ihm kommen.

b. In February we're going to go to the Black Forest to ski ('for skiing').
Im Februar werden wir in den Schwarzwald zum Skilaufen fahren.

c. Are you planning to go to Germany in September or October?
Wollen Sie im September oder im Oktober nach Deutschland fahren?

d. Her sister is supposed to come to America in March.
Ihre Schwester soll im März nach Amerika kommen.

e. My brother wants to visit us in May.
Mein Bruder will uns im Mai besuchen.

f. We'll be home in December.
Wir werden im Dezember zu Hause sein.

11. **Er arbeitet den ganzen Tag in seinem Büro.**   <u>He works in his office all day.</u>

a. She's going to stay two years in Germany.
Sie bleibt zwei Jahre in Deutschland.

b. Are you going to be in your office all afternoon?
Sind Sie den ganzen Nachmittag in Ihrem Büro?

c. I was in Berlin /‾for‾/ one whole month.
Ich war einen ganzen Monat in Berlin.

d. We're going to stay a whole week in Southern Germany.
Wir bleiben eine ganze Woche in Süddeutschlannd.

12. **Beckers fahren jeden Sommer an die Ostsee.**   <u>The Beckers go to the Baltic every summer.</u>

a. Mr. Müller was in America last year.
Herr Müller war letztes Jahr in Amerika.

b. Last week we were in the Black Forest.
Vorige Woche waren wir im Schwarzwald.

c. Please come and see us next week-end.
Bitte besuchen Sie uns nächstes Wochenende.

d. This winter I'm going to the mountains to ski.
Diesen Winter fahre ich ins Gebirge zum Skilaufen.

e. He buys (himself) a different car every year.
Er kauft sich jedes Jahr ein anderes Auto.

13. **Ich werde Sie in den nächsten Tagen anrufen.**   <u>I'll call you in the /‾course of the‾/ next few days.</u>

a. I won't be home on Tuesday.
Ich werde am Dienstag nicht zu Hause sein.

b. I'll come, but just for a minute.
Ich werde kommen, aber nur für einen Augenblick.

c. This Saturday unfortunately we won't be able to come.
An diesem Sonnabend werden wir leider nicht kommen können.

d. I'll certainly write the letter in the course of the next week.
In der nächsten Woche werde ich bestimmt den Brief schreiben.

e. On that day I'll probably be able to come.
An dem Tag werde ich wahrscheinlich kommen können.

14. Der Frühling ist hier leider viel zu kurz.

The spring is much too short here unfortunately.

   a. The humidity is too high here in the summer.
   b. This sweater is too small.
   c. It's too cool up in the mountains today.
   d. Mr. Becker drives much too fast.
   e. The weather is too bad today.

Die Luftfeuchtigkeit ist hier im Sommer zu hoch.
Dieser Pullover ist zu klein.
Oben in den Bergen ist es heute zu kühl.
Herr Becker fährt viel zu schnell.
Das Wetter ist heute zu schlecht.

15. Der Sommer ist mir hier zu heiss.

The summer is too warm for me here.

   a. Is the coat too expensive for you?
   b. It's too cool for us here in the mountains.
   c. I hope it's not too cold for him here.
   d. The trip to the mountains is too far for her.

Ist Ihnen der Mantel zu teuer?
Hier in den Bergen ist es uns zu kühl.
Hoffentlich ist es ihm hier nicht zu kalt.
Die Fahrt ins Gebirge ist ihr zu weit.

16. Mir ist kalt, ich ziehe meinen Mantel an.

I'm cold; I'm going to put my coat on.

   a. Open the window, please; we're very warm.
   b. I think he's cold; he doesn't have a sweater on.
   c. I'm very warm; I intend to put on a lighter jacket.
   d. We're cold - you too?

Machen Sie bitte das Fenster auf, uns ist sehr warm.
Ich glaube, ihm ist kalt, er hat keinen Pullover an.
Mir ist sehr warm; ich will eine leichtere Jacke anziehen.
Uns ist kalt, - Ihnen auch?

(End of Tape 9B)

Tape 10A

VOCABULARY DRILL

1. sich freuen auf - "to look forward to"

   a. Wir freuen uns auf die Alpen.
   b. Er freut sich auf den Besuch seiner Eltern.
   c. Ich freue mich auf Ihren Brief.
   d. Freuen Sie sich auf Deutschland?

   e. Meine Frau freut sich auf das Skilaufen im Schwarzwald.

We're looking forward to the Alps.
He's looking forward to the visit of his parents.
I'm looking forward to your letter.
Are you looking forward to /your trip to / Germany?
My wife is looking forward to (the) skiing in the Black Forest.

2. unten / oben - "up / down"

   a. Oben in den Bergen gibt es noch viel Schnee.
   b. Unten im Tal ist es viel wärmer als hier.
   c. Hier oben im Gebirge ist es ziemlich kühl.
   d. Wohnen Sie in den Bergen oder unten in der Stadt?

Up in the mountains there's still a lot of snow.
Down in the valley it's much warmer than here.
Up here in the mountains it's pretty cool.
Do you live in the mountains or down in the city?

3. anziehen - "to put on, to wear"

   a. Er zieht seinen warmen Pullover an.
   b. Heute ziehe ich meinen neuen Mantel an.

He's putting on his warm sweater.
I'm going to wear my new coat today.

(Continued on the next page.)

c. Ich glaube, wir müssen
   heute warme Jacken anziehen.
d. Ziehen Sie den Pullover
   oder die Jacke an?

I think we'll have to put on warm
jackets today.
Are you going to wear your sweater
or your jacket?

4. **vorig- / letzt-** - "last, past"

a. Heute ist es wärmer als in den
   letzten Tagen.
b. Es ist dieses Jahr heisser als
   im vorigen Jahr.
c. Letztes Jahr war ich im Schwarzwald.
d. Vorigen Sonntag war er bei uns.
e. Heute ist es nicht so heiss wie
   vorige Woche.
f. Dieses Wochenende ist es wärmer
   als letztes Wochenende.

Today it's warmer than ⎾it's been⏌
in the last few days.
It's hotter this year than in the
year past.
Last year I was in the Black Forest.

Last Sunday he was at our house.
Today it's not as hot as ⎾it was⏌
last week.
It's warmer this week-end than last
week-end.

5. **anhaben** - "to have on"

a. Er hat einen wärmeren Mantel an
   als ich.
b. Was für einen Anzug hat er heute
   an?
c. Sie haben heute einen schönen
   Pullover an!
d. Haben Sie eine neue Jacke an?

He has a warmer coat on than I.

What kind of a suit does he have on
today?
You have a handsome sweater on today!

Is that a new jacket you have on?

6. **ausgerechnet** - "it would have to (be) ...!"

a. Ausgerechnet heute muss es
   regnen!
b. Sie will ausgerechnet heute
   abend kommen.
c. Ausgerechnet jetzt stellt er
   das Radio an.
d. Der Sommerschlussverkauf fängt
   ausgerechnet morgen an.
e. Warum fragen Sie ausgerechnet
   mich!

It would have to be today that it rains!

It would have to be this evening that
she wants to come!
He would have to turn the radio on
now!
The summer clearance sale would have
to begin tomorrow!
Why do I have to be the one you ask!

7. **anstellen** - "to turn on"

a. Stellen Sie bitte das Radio an,
   wir möchten den Wetterbericht
   hören.
b. Soll ich jetzt das Radio
   anstellen?
c. Ich werde die Heizung anstellen,
   es ist kalt hier.
d. Sie stellt den Elektroherd an.
e. Sie stellt gerade den Gasherd
   an.

Turn the radio on please; we'd like
to hear the weather report.

Shall I turn the radio on now?

I'll turn on the furnace; it's cold
here.
She turns on the electric range.
She's just turning on the gas-stove.

8. **sich beeilen** - "to hurry (up)"

a. Sie müssen sich beeilen, die
   Geschäfte machen um sechs Uhr zu.
b. Hoffentlich beeilt er sich!
c. Beeilen Sie sich!
d. Wir beeilen uns schon, wir
   können nicht viel schneller
   arbeiten.

You'll have to hurry; the stores close
at six o'clock.
I hope he hurries!
Hurry up!
We're hurrying all right; we can't
work much faster.

9. <u>zu Mittag essen</u> - "to eat lunch"

    a. Wann essen wir heute zu Mittag?   When are we eating lunch today?
    b. Wo wollen Sie zu Mittag essen?   Where do you want to eat lunch?
    c. Essen Sie immer in diesem   Do you always eat lunch at this
       Restaurant zu Mittag?   restaurant?
    d. Er isst gewöhnlich im Hof-   He usually eats lunch at the Hofbräu-
       bräuhaus zu Mittag.   haus.

TRANSLATION DRILL (not recorded)

1. Two couples, a German one and an American one, are traveling to Southern Germany in a Volkswagen.

Zwei Ehepaare, ein deutsches und ein amerikanisches, fahren mit dem Volkswagen nach Süddeutschland.

2. On the Autobahn there is a lot of traffic and the automobiles are traveling very fast.

Auf der Autobahn ist viel Verkehr und die Autos fahren sehr schnell.

3. The Wilsons and the Beckers are very fortunate with the weather.

Wilsons und Beckers haben grosses Glück mit dem Wetter.

4. It is not as cold as in the last /few_/ days.

Es ist nicht so kalt wie in den letzten Tagen.

5. Mrs. Wilson is very much looking forward to the Alps.

Frau Wilson freut sich schon sehr auf die Alpen.

6. She'd like to see the highest mountain, the Zugspitze.

Sie möchte gern den höchsten Berg, die Zugspitze, sehen.

7. The Zugspitze is almost ten thousand feet high.

Die Zugspitze ist fast dreitausend Meter hoch.

8. Last year the Beckers were on the Baltic in the summer.

Letztes Jahr waren Beckers im Sommer an der Ostsee.

9. In the winter they quite often travel to the mountains, to the Alps or the Black Forest.

Im Winter fahren sie öfters ins Gebirge, in die Alpen oder in den Schwarzwald.

10. They like to ski.

Sie laufen gern Ski.

11. The Wilsons like skiing too.

Wilsons laufen auch gern Ski.

12. Unfortunately, where they live there's but little snow in the winter.

Leider gibt es bei ihnen zu Hause nur wenig Schnee im Winter.

13. In the summer it's very hot, and the humidity is very high.

Im Sommer ist es sehr heiss und die Luftfeuchtigkeit ist sehr hoch.

14. The fall is the nicest time of year in the Wilsons' (home) country.

Der Herbst ist in Wilsons Heimat die schönste Jahreszeit.

15. Unfortunately the spring is shorter there than in Germany.

Leider ist der Frühling dort kürzer als in Deutschland.

16. Mr. Becker is driving a bit faster again now.

Herr Becker fährt jetzt wieder etwas schneller.

17. There's not as much traffic up in the mountains as down in the valley.

Oben in den Bergen ist nicht so viel Verkehr wie unten im Tal.

18. It's getting pretty cool, however, and Mr. Wilson wants to put on his coat.

Es wird aber ziemlich kühl und Herr Wilson will seinen Mantel anziehen.

19. He's cold.

Ihm ist kalt.

20. Mr. Becker is not freezing.

Herr Becker friert nicht.

21. He has a warmer sweater on than Mr. Wilson.

Er hat einen wärmeren Pullover an als Herr Wilson.

22. They have a flat tire!

Sie haben eine Reifenpanne!

23. That was all they needed.

Das hat ihnen gerade noch gefehlt.

24. There's no gas station nearby either.

In der Nähe ist auch keine Tankstelle.

25. The two men change the tire themselves.

Die beiden Herren wechseln den Reifen selbst.

26. Mrs. Becker looks for the camera.

Frau Becker sucht den Photoapparat.

27. It's in the briefcase.

Er ist in der Aktenmappe.

28. The view is wonderful, and she'd like to take a couple of pictures.

Die Aussicht ist wunderbar und sie möchte ein paar Aufnahmen machen.

(Continued on the next page.)

29. They see a lot of dark clouds in the sky.	Sie sehen viele dunkle Wolken am Himmel.
30. It's probably going to rain soon.	Wahrscheinlich wird es bald regnen.
31. Mr. Becker would like to hear the weather report.	Herr Becker möchte den Wetterbericht hören.
32. He turns on the radio.	Er stellt das Radio an.
33. He's lucky; the radio /¯station_7 is just presenting the news and the weather report.	Er hat Glück, das Radio bringt gerade die Nachrichten und den Wetterbericht.
34. In the afternoon sunny and warmer; later, severe thunder storms in the Alps.	Nachmittags sonnig und wärmer, später schwere Gewitter in den Alpen.
35. The men hurry very much.	Die Herren beeilen sich sehr.
36. The Beckers and the Wilsons have planned to eat lunch in Garmisch.	Beckers und Wilsons haben vor, in Garmisch zu Mittag zu essen.

RESPONSE DRILL (not recorded)

1. Wohin fahren die beiden Ehepaare, Wilsons und Beckers?	Sie fahren nach Süddeutschland.
2. An welchem Tag und in welchem Monat fahren sie?	Sie fahren an einem Wochenende im Juli.
3. Mit was für einem Wagen fahren sie?	Sie fahren mit einem Volkswagen.
4. Wie ist das Wetter?	Das Wetter ist gut. Es ist nicht so kalt wie gestern und viel wärmer als in der ganzen vorigen Woche.
5. Wie heisst der höchste Berg Deutschlands?	Er heisst Zugspitze.
6. Wie hoch ist die Zugspitze?	Die Zugspitze ist fast dreitausend Meter hoch.
7. Wo waren Beckers letzten Sommer?	Letzten Sommer waren Beckers an der Ostsee.
8. Wann fahren Beckers öfters ins Gebirge?	Im Winter fahren sie öfters ins Gebirge.
9. Warum fahren sie im Winter gern in die Berge?	Sie laufen gern Ski.
10. Laufen Wilsons auch Ski? Gibt es bei ihnen zu Hause viel Schnee im Winter?	Ja, sie laufen auch gern Ski, aber leider gibt es bei ihnen zu Hause wenig Schnee.
11. Wie ist das Klima in Wilsons Heimat?	In den Sommermonaten ist es sehr heiss und die Luftfeuchtigkeit ist hoch.
12. Welche Jahreszeit ist dort am längsten und schönsten?	Der Herbst ist dort die längste und schönste Jahreszeit.
13. Warum kann Herr Becker jetzt wieder schneller fahren?	Oben in den Bergen ist weniger Verkehr als unten im Tal.
14. Warum zieht Herr Wilson seinen Mantel an?	Ihm ist kalt.
15. Friert Herr Becker auch? Was hat Herr Becker an?	Nein, er friert nicht. Er hat einen dicken Pullover an.
16. Warum müssen die beiden Herren den Reifen wechseln?	Sie haben eine Reifenpanne und es gibt keine Tankstelle in der Nähe.
17. Was sucht Frau Becker?	Frau Becker sucht den Photoapparat.
18. Wo ist der Photoapparat?	Er ist in der Aktenmappe.
19. Wie sieht der Himmel aus?	Es sind viele dunkle Wolken am Himmel.
20. Warum stellt Herr Becker das Radio an?	Er möchte die Nachrichten hören.
21. Was sagt der Wetterbericht?	Der Wetterbericht sagt: Mittags schweres Gewitter in den Voralpen, später wieder sonnig und wärmer.
22. Wo wollen Beckers und Wilsons zu Mittag essen?	Sie wollen in Garmisch zu Mittag essen.

23. Welches ist Ihre Heimatstadt?
24. Wie ist das Wetter dort im Sommer?
25. Wo ist es im Sommer in Amerika am kühlsten?
26. Wohin möchten Sie dieses Jahr am liebsten fahren?
27. Wo ist das Klima besser, - in Washington
    oder in New York?
28. Welche Jahreszeit finden Sie in Ihrer Heimat
    am schönsten?
29. Was sagt der Wetterbericht heute?
30. In welcher Jahreszeit regnet es in Washington viel?
31. Wann ist es hier am kältesten?
32. Welche Stadt ist grösser, München oder Bonn?
33. Welches ist das beste Hotel hier?
34. Wo wollen Sie heute zu Mittag essen?
35. Was machen Sie, wenn Sie eine Reifenpanne haben?

CONVERSATION PRACTICE (not recorded)

1

A: Welche Jahreszeit haben Sie am
   liebsten?
B: Hier in Deutschland habe ich den
   Frühling am liebsten. Der ist
   viel länger als bei uns in Amerika.
A: Ist es bei Ihnen zu Hause im Sommer
   sehr warm?
B: Jedenfalls viel wärmer als hier.
   Und die Luftfeuchtigkeit ist sehr
   hoch.
A: Und wie ist bei Ihnen der Winter?
B: Gewöhnlich haben wir nicht so viel
   Schnee wie hier. Der Winter in
   Deutschland ist auch viel kälter
   als bei uns.

3

A: Ich höre, Sie suchen eine neue
   Wohnung?
B: Ja, wir brauchen eine grössere.
   Unsere ist wirklich zu klein.
A: In der Schubertstrasse sind einige
   zu vermieten. Das ist nicht weit
   von hier.
B: Ich werde heute abend gleich hin-
   gehen. Hoffentlich ist die Miete
   nicht zu hoch.
A: Ich glaube, sie ist nicht viel
   höher als hier.

2

A: Wo kaufen Sie Ihre Anzüge, im
   Konfektionsgeschäft oder im Waren-
   haus?
B: Ich kaufe sie gewöhnlich im Kon-
   fektionsgeschäft. Man hat dort eine
   grössere Auswahl als im Warenhaus.
A: Ist es dort nicht viel teurer?
B: Nicht viel und die Qualität der
   Anzüge ist besser.

4

B: Was darf ich Ihnen zeigen?
A: Ich möchte gern einen Pullover
   haben.
B: Gern, - in welcher Grösse?
A: Grösse 42 und in grau, bitte.
B: Gefällt Ihnen dieser hier?
A: Ja, ganz gut, - aber ich hätte
   eigentlich lieber einen billigeren.
   Dieser ist mir etwas zu teuer.
B: Ich zeige Ihnen gern noch andere.
   Der hellgraue hier ist zum Beispiel
   auch sehr gut und preiswerter als
   der andere. Möchten Sie ihn mal
   anprobieren?
A: Nein, die Ärmel sind zu kurz.
   Ich brauche einen mit längeren
   Ärmeln.
B: Hier ist ein ähnlicher Pullover
   mit langen Ärmeln.
A: Ja, der gefällt mir.

SITUATIONS

Ein Wochenende in den Bergen

Herr Wilson sagt Herrn Becker, er
will am Wochenende in die Berge fahren.
Er sagt, er läuft gern Ski und er
hofft, es gibt viel Schnee in den
Bergen. Er möchte Herrn Becker gern
mitnehmen. Herr Becker hat am Wochenende nichts vor. Er kann leider nicht
Ski laufen, aber er möchte gern mitkommen. Er fragt, mit welchem Auto
sie fahren wollen. Er hat einen
grösseren Wagen als Herr Wilson.
Herr Wilson möchte aber lieber mit
seinem neuen Volkswagen fahren; der
fährt in den Bergen besser
als ein grosser Wagen.

Herr Becker kauft einen Pullover

Herr Becker fragt, was sie mitnehmen
wollen. Herr Wilson will sich noch
warme Unterwäsche kaufen und Herr
Becker braucht lange, warme Socken
und einen Pullover. Sie gehen zusammen in ein Konfektionsgeschäft und
der Verkäufer fragt sie, was er ihnen
zeigen darf. Erst suchen sie einen
Pullover. Aber der eine ist zu klein,
der andere ist zu auffällig und bei
einem anderen sind die Ärmel zu kurz.
Endlich findet Herr Becker einen
guten, einfarbigen Pullover. Er ist
leider ziemlich teuer, aber der Verkäufer hat nichts Preiswerteres.
Herr Becker nimmt den Pullover und
bezahlt an der Kasse.

Am Telephon

Herr Müller und Herr Becker sprechen
telephonisch zusammen. Herr Müller
fragt, wie es Herrn Becker geht und
wie es ihm in Frankfurt gefällt. Herr
Becker sagt, es gefällt ihm gut, leider
ist das Wetter schlecht.
Es regnet jetzt sehr viel. Herr Becker
möchte wissen, wie das Wetter in Süddeutschland ist. Herr Müller sagt,
es ist wärmer als in den letzten Tagen
und hoffentlich bleibt es so. Herr
Becker sagt, er muss in drei Tagen nach
München zum Generalkonsulat fahren.
Herr Müller möchte ihn gern sehen,
Herr Becker soll ihn dann besuchen.

In München

Herr Schulze trifft Herrn Becker vor
dem Rathaus. Herr Becker sagt, er
muss viele Geschäftsreisen machen und
er kommt nicht oft nach München. Herr
Schulze fragt ihn, wo er jetzt in
München wohnt. Herr Becker sagt, er
wohnt in einem Hotel in der Beethoven-
strasse. Herr Schulze fragt Herrn
Becker, was er jetzt vorhat. Herr
Becker muss noch einige Besorgungen
machen und dann möchte er gern essen
gehen. Er will Herrn Schulze in
einer Stunde wieder auf dem Parkplatz
vor dem Rathaus treffen. Dort steht
das Auto von Herrn Schulze und sie
wollen zusammen nach Schwabing fahren
und dort zu Mittag essen.

NARRATIVES

I

    Frau Meyer macht auf der <u>Autofahrt</u> am Wochenende im Juli viele Aufnahmen.
Sie photographiert die dunklen Wolken am Himmel, die Berge der Voralpen und die
Männer <u>beim Reifenwechsel</u>. Sie macht auch eine Aufnahme von der wunderbaren
Aussicht; die ist viel schöner als auf dem <u>Prospekt</u> vom <u>Reisebüro</u>. Leider wird
man später auf den Bildern nichts von den Wolken, den Bergen, dem Schnee und
dem Sonnenschein und dem Reifenwechsel sehen. Die Kamera ist nämlich kaputt.
Man wird auf den Bildern nichts als "<u>Nebel</u>" sehen.

die Autofahrt	the automobile trip
beim Reifenwechsel	changing tires
der Prospekt	the prospectus, leaflet
das Reisebüro	the travel agency
der Nebel	the fog

II

Konsul Thompson wird in einer Woche <u>Urlaub</u> haben. Er möchte gern eine Reise machen, weiss aber noch nicht, wohin. Er hat schon soviel von Bayern gehört, eine Rheinreise soll auch sehr schön sein, und gerade hat er eine Postkarte aus einem <u>Kurort</u> an der Ostsee von seinem Freund, Vizekonsul Wilson bekommen. Herr Wilson schreibt ganz <u>begeistert</u> von der Gegend in der Nähe von Lübeck. Konsul Thompson möchte über <u>verschiedene</u> Reisemöglichkeiten Auskunft haben, geht also in ein Reisebüro und spricht mit einem der Herren dort. Dieser gibt ihm viele Prospekte und fragt ihn, <u>ob</u> er eine <u>Gesellschaftsfahrt</u> <u>mitmachen</u> möchte oder ob er mit seinem Wagen fahren will. Gesellschaftsreisen sind am preiswertesten. Man bezahlt nichts extra für <u>Übernachtung</u> und Essen, und man kann viele <u>Sehenswürdigkeiten</u> sehen. Mit dem <u>eigenen</u> Auto ist man <u>unabhängiger</u>, aber man gibt natürlich viel mehr Geld aus. Herr Thompson <u>entscheidet</u> <u>sich</u> für eine Autofahrt nach Süddeutschland. Von Frankfurt bis Heidelberg wird er auf der Autobahn fahren. In den meisten <u>Rasthäusern</u> an der Autobahn kann man Tag und <u>Nacht</u> etwas zu essen bekommen, und in einigen kann man auch übernachten. Der Verkehr auf der Autobahn wird sehr <u>stark</u> sein. Also wird er hinter Heidelberg auf der <u>Bundesstrasse</u> langsamer weiterfahren und sich in Ruhe die schöne <u>Umgebung</u> ansehen. In Rothenburg möchte er alle Sehenswürdigkeiten sehen. Dann wird er <u>über</u> Augsburg nach München und <u>schliesslich</u> in die Berge fahren.

der Urlaub	the vacation, leave
der Kurort	the resort
begeistert	enthusiastic(ally)
verschieden	various, different
ob	if, whether
die Gesellschaftsfahrt	the tour
mitmachen	to take part in
die Übernachtung	the night's lodging
die Sehenswürdigkeiten (pl)	the sights
eigen	own.
unabhängig	independent
sich entscheiden für	to decide on
das Rasthaus	the "rest house"
die Nacht	the night
stark	strong, heavy
die Bundesstrasse	the federal highway
die Umgebung	the surroundings
über	via
schliesslich	finally

FINDER LIST

die	Aktenmappe, -n	briefcase
die	Alpen	Alps
	anhaben	have on
	er hat es an	he has it on
	anstellen	turn on
	er stellt es an	he turns it on
	anziehen	put on
	ich ziehe etwas an	I put something on
der	April	April
die	Aufnahme, -n	photograph
der	August	August
	ausgerechnet	it would have to be ... !
die	Aussicht	view
die	Autobahn, -en	parkway
sich	beeilen	hurry
	ich beeile mich	I hurry
	bei uns zu Hause	where we live
der	Berg, -e	mountain

	der	Dezember	December
		dick	thick, heavy
		dicker	thicker, heavier
		eben	just, simply
	das	Ehepaar,-e	(married) couple
		fast	almost
	der	Februar	February
es		fehlt mir	I need it
		es hat uns gefehlt	we needed it
		feucht	moist, humid
		feuchter	more humid
sich		freuen auf (plus acc)	look forward to
	der	Freund,-e	friend
		frieren	freeze
	der	Frühling,-e	spring
	das	Gebirge,-	(range of) mountains
	das	Gewitter,-	thunder storm
	das	Glück	luck
		Glück haben	be lucky
		heiss	hot
		heisser	hotter
	der	Herbst,-e	fall
	der	Himmel	sky
		höchste	highest
ich		hörte	I have heard
	die	Jahreszeit,-en	season
	der	Januar	January
		jeder	every, each
		jeden Sommer	every summer
	der	Juni	June
	der	Juli	July
		im Juli	in July
		kalt	cold
		mir ist kalt	I'm cold, chilly
		kühl	cool
		kühler	cooler
		länger	longer
		letzt-	last
		letzten Sommer	last summer
	die	Luftfeuchtigkeit	humidity (of the air)
	der	Mai	May
	der	Mantel,¨	overcoat
	der	März	March
		Meter	meters
zu		Mittag essen	eat lunch
		mittags	at noon
	die	Nachrichten	news
		nah	near, close
		näher	closer
		na ja	all right then
	der	November	November
		oben	up
		öfters	often
	der	Oktober	October
	der	Ort,-e	place
	die	Ostsee	Baltic Sea
	der	Photoapparat,-e	camera
	der	Pullover,-	sweater, pullover
	das	Radio,-s	radio
	der	Regen	rain
		regnen	rain
		es regnet	it's raining
	der	Reifen,-	tire
	die	Reifenpanne,-n	flat tire
	der	Schnee	snow
		schnell	fast

	schneller	faster
am	schönsten	nicest, most beautiful
der	Schwarzwald	Black Forest
	schwer	heavy, severe
	selbst	myself, himself, ourselves etc.
der	September	September
	Ski laufen	ski
	er läuft Ski	he skis
das	Skilaufen	skiing
	zum Skilaufen	for skiing
	so	that way, like that
	sonnig	sunny, fair
	später	later
	Süddeutschland	Southern Germany
das	Tal,-̈er	valley
die	Tankstelle,-n	filling station
	unten	down
der	Verkehr	traffic
	viel Regen	much rain
der	Volkswagen,-	Volkswagen
die	Voralpen	Lower Alps
	vorigen	last, previous
	warm	warm
	wärmer	warmer
	wenig	little, not much
	weniger	less
	weniger Verkehr	less traffic
	wenn	when
	werden	(future auxiliary)
	er wird	he will, he's going to
der	Wetterbericht,-e	weather report
der	Winter,-	winter
das	Wochenende,-n	week-end
die	Wolke,-n	cloud
wir	wollten	we were planning
	wunderbar	wonderful
die	Zeit,-en	time

ZUM WEISSEN HIRSCH

SPEISEKARTE

KALTE KÜCHE   DM

Nordseekrabben in Currymayonnaise	2.--
Hausmacher Wurstplatte, Kartoffelsalat	2.--
Kaltes Pökelrippchen, Mayonnaisesalat	2.40
Kalter Schweinebraten, mit verschiedenen Salaten umlegt	3.--
Geflügelsalat nach Art des Hauses, Butter, Toast	4.--

SUPPEN

Tagessuppe	-.40
Ochsenschwanzsuppe	1.--
Hühnerbrühe mit Nudeln	-.50

VOM KALB

Kalbskopf en tortue	3.--
Wiener Schnitzel mit Röstkartoffeln, gemischter Salat	3.50
Paprikarahmschnitzel mit Butterspaghetti, Bohnensalat	4.--
Kalbssteak mit Champignons, pommes frites, Buttererbsen	5.50
Kalbshaxen für 2-3 Personen	Preis nach Grösse

VOM RIND

Gehacktes Rindsteak mit Zwiebeln, Röstkartoffeln, Salat	2.75
Ungarisches Saftgoulasch mit Spaghetti, Salat	2.75
Rumpsteak mit Meerrettich, pommes frites, gemischter Salat	4.--
Lendensteak mit Kräuterbutter, pommes frites, junges Gemüse	5.--

VOM SCHWEIN

Hausmacher Bratwurst mit Sauerkraut, Kartoffelpüree	1.50
Leberkäse, abgebräunt, Kartoffelsalat	1.60
1 Paar Frankfurter Würstchen mit Meerrettich, Kartoffelsalat	1.82
Frankfurter Pökelrippchen auf Weinkraut, Kartoffelpüree	2.40
Schweineschnitzel paniert, Röstkartoffeln, Salat	2.50
Eisbein mit Sauerkraut, Kartoffelpüree	Preis nach Grösse

GEFLÜGEL

1/2 Masthähnchen in Butter, pommes frites, gemischter Salat	3.50
Fricassé vom Huhn im Reisrand	4.--

KOMPOTTE

Apfelmus	-.50
Ananas mit Sahne	1.--

IM GASTHOF "ZUM WEISSEN HIRSCH"

Basic Sentences

<table>
<tr><td>

I

the resort

Place: A resort in the mountains.

fourth
the fourth of July
during

Time: The fourth of July, at noon
during a thunder shower.

Cast: The Wilsons, the Beckers, a
waiter.

the inn
the stag
at the (sign of) the
White Stag

MR. BECKER

There's the White Stag Inn.

the impression
to make a good impression

It looks pretty good.

Shall we have lunch there?

if, whenever

MR. WILSON

All right, and later, if it's not
raining any longer perhaps we could
take a walk.

the dining room (of an inn)

MRS. WILSON

This is really a charming dining room!

Shall we sit here by the window?

MRS. BECKER

Yes, why don't we?

what a pity

MRS. WILSON

What a pity the weather's so bad.

</td><td>

I

der Kurort,-e

Ort: Ein Kurort in den Bergen.

vierten
am vierten Juli
während

Zeit: Am vierten Juli, mittags
während eines Gewitters.

Personen: Wilsons, Beckers, ein
Ober.

der Gasthof, -̈e
der Hirsch,-e
"Zum Weissen Hirsch"

HERR BECKER

Dort ist der Gasthof "Zum Weissen
Hirsch".

der Eindruck, -̈e
einen guten Eindruck machen

Der macht einen ganz guten Eindruck.

Wollen wir da zu Mittag essen?

wenn

HERR WILSON

Gut, und später, wenn es nicht mehr
regnet, könnten wir vielleicht noch
einen Spaziergang machen.

das Gastzimmer,-

FRAU WILSON

Das ist aber ein gemütliches Gast-
zimmer!

Wollen wir uns hier ans Fenster
setzen?

FRAU BECKER

Ja, warum nicht?

wie schade

FRAU WILSON

Wie schade, dass das Wetter so schlecht
ist.

</td></tr>
</table>

from this table	von diesem Tisch aus

Otherwise I'm sure there's a beautiful view from this table.

Von diesem Tisch aus hat man sonst sicher eine schöne Aussicht.

the menu	die Speisekarte,-n
to order	bestellen

The Beckers and the Wilsons look over the menu and make their orders.

Beckers und Wilsons sehen sich die Speisekarte an und bestellen.

II

calf's liver	die Kalbsleber
mashed potatoes	das Kartoffelpüree
apple sauce	das Apfelmus

MRS. BECKER

FRAU BECKER

Waiter, please bring me calf's liver with mashed potatoes and apple sauce.

Herr Ober, bringen Sie mir bitte Kalbsleber mit Kartoffelpüree und Apfelmus.

the special for today	das Tagesgericht,-e
without	ohne (prep with acc)
the soup	die Suppe,-n

MRS. WILSON

FRAU WILSON

The special for today for me please, but without the soup.

Für mich bitte das Tagesgericht, aber ohne Suppe.

the steak	das Rumpsteak,-s
fried potatoes	die Röstkartoffeln

MR. WILSON

HERR WILSON

I'd like steak with fried potatoes.

Ich hätte gern Rumpsteak mit Röstkartoffeln.

the trout	die Forelle,-n
the butter	die Butter
melted butter	zerlassene Butter

MR. BECKER

HERR BECKER

And I'll take the blue trout with melted butter.

Und ich nehme Forelle blau mit zerlassener Butter.

the ladies and gentlemen	die Herrschaften

WAITER

OBER

Would you care for something to drink? (' Would the ladies and gentlemen care for something to drink?')

Möchten die Herrschaften etwas zu trinken haben?

apple juice	der Apfelsaft

MRS. WILSON

FRAU WILSON

I'd like a glass of apple juice.

Ich hätte gern ein Glas Apfelsaft.

MRS. BECKER	FRAU BECKER
Bring me one too, please.	Bitte bringen Sie mir auch eins.
light	hell
MR. WILSON	HERR WILSON
A light beer, please.	Ein helles Bier, bitte.
Moselle wine	der Moselwein
MR. BECKER	HERR BECKER
I'd like a glass of Moselle wine.	Ich möchte gern ein Glas Moselwein haben.

III	III
what time	wieviel Uhr
MR. WILSON	HERR WILSON
What time is it anyway?	Wieviel Uhr ist es eigentlich?
quarter	viertel
MR. BECKER	HERR BECKER
It's exactly quarter past one.	Es ist genau viertel nach eins.
always	immer
MR. WILSON	HERR WILSON
Do you always eat at this time?	Essen Sie immer um diese Zeit?
usually, mostly since	meistens da
MR. BECKER	HERR BECKER
Usually not later than one o'clock, since I generally go home at noon.	Meistens schon um ein Uhr, da ich mittags gewöhnlich nach Hause gehe.
most (pl) the main meal	die meisten die Hauptmahlzeit
MR. WILSON	HERR WILSON
Don't most people anyway in Germany eat their main meal at noon?	Essen nicht überhaupt die meisten Leute in Deutschland mittags ihre Hauptmahlzeit?
necessarily, definitely	unbedingt
MR. BECKER	HERR BECKER
Not necessarily.	Nicht unbedingt.
to depend on the job, profession working hours	abhängen von der Beruf,-e die Arbeitszeit,-en
It depends on ⎾the⏋ job and working hours.	Es hängt von Beruf und Arbeitszeit ab.

in the evening	abends

MR. WILSON

HERR WILSON

If you yourselves eat your main meal at noon do you then have a warm meal again in the evening?	Wenn Sie selbst mittags Ihre Hauptmahlzeit essen, essen Sie dann abends nochmal warm?

sometimes, occasionally
    the rye bread
    the cold cuts
    the cheese
	manchmal
	    das Roggenbrot,-e
	    der Aufschnitt
	    der Käse

MR. BECKER

HERR BECKER

Only occasionally. Usually we have rye bread, butter, cold cuts and cheese.	Nur manchmal. Meistens gibt es bei uns Roggenbrot, Butter, Aufschnitt und Käse.

And we have tea with it.	Und dazu trinken wir Tee.

IV

IV

appetite
    I'm hungry for,
    have room for (something)
    the piece
    the cake
	der Appetit
	    ich habe Appetit auf (etwas)
	
	    das Stück,-e
	    der Kuchen,-

MRS. WILSON

FRAU WILSON

Now I still have room for a piece of cake and a cup of coffee.	Jetzt habe ich noch Appetit auf ein Stück Kuchen und eine Tasse Kaffee.

MR. WILSON

HERR WILSON

Yes, I would too.	Ja, ich auch.

MR. BECKER

HERR BECKER

Shall we order something more too?	Wollen wir uns auch noch etwas bestellen?

MRS. BECKER

FRAU BECKER

No, thank you, nothing more for me.	Danke, für mich nichts mehr.

I prefer to have my coffee later.	Ich trinke meinen Kaffee lieber später.

to think
    the concert
    the opportunity (for something)
	denken
	    das Konzert,-e
	    die Gelegenheit (zu etwas)

MR. BECKER

HERR BECKER

I think, we'll have the best opportunity for that afterward during the concert.	Ich denke, dazu haben wir nachher während des Konzerts die beste Gelegenheit.

V   V

well, that's a surprise!   na also
the sun   die Sonne
to shine   scheinen

MR. WILSON   HERR WILSON

Well, that's a surprise!   Na also, die Sonne scheint ja schon
The sun's shining again!   wieder!

MR. BECKER   HERR BECKER

Then we can go.   Dann können wir ja gehen.

to pay   zahlen

Waiter, the check please!   Herr Ober, bitte zahlen!

daily   täglich
concert in the resort   das Kurkonzert,-e

MR. WILSON   HERR WILSON

Is there a concert in the resort here   Ist hier eigentlich täglich
every day, can you tell me?   Kurkonzert?

if, whether   ob
to take place   stattfinden

WAITER   OBER

Yes, I just don't know whether it's   Ja, ich weiss nur nicht, ob es heute
going to be in the park or in the   im Park oder im Kurhaus stattfindet.
Kurhaus today.

MR. WILSON   HERR WILSON

Do you happen to know at what time   Wissen Sie zufällig, um wieviel Uhr
it begins?   es anfängt?

WAITER   OBER

I think it's at four.   Ich glaube, um vier.

MR. WILSON   HERR WILSON

What time is it now?   Wie spät ist es denn jetzt?

three-quarters   dreiviertel

MR. BECKER   HERR BECKER

Quarter to three.   Dreiviertel drei.

enough   genug
in order to   um ... zu

MR. WILSON   HERR WILSON

Then we still have enough time to take   Da haben wir noch genug Zeit, um uns
a look around the place.   den Ort etwas anzusehen.

the picture postcard   die Ansichtskarte,-n

MRS. WILSON	FRAU WILSON

MRS. WILSON

And I can buy a couple of picture postcards too at the same time.

FRAU WILSON

Dann kann ich mir auch gleich noch ein paar Ansichtskarten kaufen.

half past five
at the latest
to leave

halb sechs
spätestens
abfahren

MR. BECKER

We have to leave at five-thirty at the latest, though.

HERR BECKER

Um halb sechs müssen wir aber spätestens abfahren.

Notes on Grammar

(For Home Study)

A.   WORD ORDER IN LARGER SENTENCES

   I. Sentence Connectors

   1. It was noted in Unit 3 that the finite verb is the second element of statements. In Unit 8 we noted that an introductory phrase such as <u>ich glaube</u> may be considered to be a separate item and not the first element of a statement. We have also encountered three little words which in a similar way may precede a sentence but are not counted as its first element.

> Und ich nehme Forelle blau mit zerlassener Butter.
> Und dazu trinken wir Tee.
> Aber es ist auch kühler hier oben.
> Aber im Winter fahren wir öfters in die Berge zum Skilaufen.
> Oder wir fahren in den Schwarzwald.

<u>Und</u>, <u>aber</u> and <u>oder</u> actually connect these sentences to preceding utterances. We will call them SENTENCE CONNECTORS. In traditional terminology they are referred to as COORDINATING CONJUNCTIONS.

   2 Simple sentences may thus be joined together by Sentence Connectors into larger, compound sentences:

> Ich wohne in München, aber ich fahre sehr oft nach Frankfurt.
> Beckers haben ein neues Auto, und im Sommer fahren wir öfters mit ihnen in die Berge.
> Essen Sie immer um diese Zeit, oder essen Sie manchmal auch später?

Notice that the word order of both parts of these compound sentences is similar: the verb is the second element of statements, or the first element of yes-no questions, regardless of whether or not a sentence connector precedes. Grammatically speaking, sentence connectors occur <u>between</u> sentences, not <u>in</u> them.

  II. Clauses and Clause Introducers

   1. Two or more sentences joined together by sentence connectors are not the only type of larger sentences we have encountered, however. Sometimes one sentence is built into another as a subordinate part of it. Note the following examples:

> Können Sie mir sagen, <u>wo ich ein Visum beantragen kann</u>?
> <u>Wie ich sehe</u>, haben Sie eine schöne Bibliothek, Herr Wilson.
> Ich wusste garnicht, <u>dass Ihre Frau hier Verwandte hat</u>.
> Ich weiss nicht, <u>ob es heute im Park oder im Kurhaus stattfindet</u>.

The underlined parts of the above sentences are Clauses. They are sentences which are incorporated into the larger sentences as subordinate parts of them. Notice that they introduced in every case by special little words (<u>wo</u>, <u>wie</u>, <u>dass</u>, <u>ob</u>) which we will call CLAUSE INTRODUCERS. In traditional terminology they are referred to as SUBORDINATING CONJUNCTIONS.

2. Notice the order of words following the clause introducers above. The
clause may be very short, consisting only of the clause introducer,
subject pronoun and verb, or it may be quite long. The finite verb may
be by itself (sehe, hat), or it may be part of a verb phrase with an
infinitive (beantragen kann) or accented adverb (stattfindet). In every
case however THE FINITE VERB IS LAST WITHIN THE CLAUSE.

3. Now compare NORMAL WORD ORDER with CLAUSE WORD ORDER. Note especially
the position of the FINITE VERB:

Wo kann ich ein Visum beantragen?	... wo ich ein Visum beantragen kann?
Ihre Frau hat Verwandte hier.	... dass Ihre Frau hier Verwandte hat.
Findet es heute im Park oder im Kurhaus statt?	... ob es heute im Park oder im Kurhaus stattfindet.

Notice now too that a verb phrase with an accented adverb is written
as one word when it occurs at the end of a clause.

4. The list of Clause Introducers includes a number of words you are
already familiar with (all the question words, for instance) plus
several others. We give here only the ones which have been encountered
up to this point.

da	"since"
dass	"that"
ob	"whether"
wann	"when"
warum	"why"
was	"what"
welcher (welches, welche, etc.)	"what, which"
wenn	"if, when, whenever"
wer (wen, etc.)	"who, whom"
wie	"as; how"
wieviel (wieviele, etc.)	"how much, how many"
wo	"where"

Notice that some of these words sound just like other words which are
not clause introducers. Remember that CLAUSE INTRODUCERS AND CLAUSE
WORD ORDER GO TOGETHER.

Da wollen wir unseren Freund Meyer besuchen.	There we're planning to visit our friend Meyer.
Da wir unseren Freund Meyer besuchen wollen, fahren wir auch nach Frankfurt.	Since we're planning to visit our friend Meyer, we're also going to go to Frankfurt.
Das müssen wir morgen machen.	We have to do that tomorrow.
Ich weiss, dass wir das morgen machen müssen.	I know that we have to do that tomorrow.
Wie können Sie das verstehen?	How can you understand that?
Wie ich sehr gut verstehen kann, will er einfach nicht mehr dort arbeiten.	As I can very well understand, he simply doesn't want to work there any more.

III. Difficulties with Larger Sentences

Most of the difficulties students have with larger sentences result from
a) failure to remember the cardinal observations that Germans place the
verb second in statements last in clauses, and b) failure to recognize
what constitutes an element, i.e., what the first element of the sentence is.

Let us examine some more of the sentences we have encountered, plus a few additional examples, and observe the arrangement of their elements.

   a. Im Sommer fahren wir an die Ostsee, aber im Winter bleiben wir hier in München.
   b. Herr Müller weiss schon, dass wir jetzt in der Ludwigstrasse wohnen.
   c. Meistens essen wir schon um ein Uhr, da ich mittags gewöhnlich nach Hause gehe.
   d. Wir werden in einer halben Stunde, wenn meine Frau zurückkommt, die Kisten auspacken.
   e. Später, wenn es nicht mehr regnet, könnten wir vielleicht noch einen Spaziergang machen.
   f. Wenn Sie selbst mittags Ihre Hauptmahlzeit essen, essen Sie dann abends nochmal warm?

1. In each of the above sentences the finite verb is the second element. Everything that precedes the finite verb then is the first element.

2. The first element may thus be: a subject pronoun (d), a noun phrase (b) a preposition and its object (a), an adverb (c), an adverb plus a clause (e), or a clause by itself (f).

3. A clause may come at the beginning (e,f), middle (d), or end (b,c) or a larger sentence. It may be an element by itself (f) or part of another element (e).

4. Within the clause itself the verb is last.

5. When a clause comes at the beginning of a sentence, two finite verbs will occur next to each other (e,f).

B. ORDINAL NUMERALS

I. We have already noted that German numbers, except for <u>eins</u>, normally have no endings. They are not adjectives, although they may occur within the specifier-adjective-noun sequence. There are however number-like adjectives in German which do have endings. We have had one such example in this unit:

   Am <u>vierten</u> Juli, mittags   The fourth of July, at noon during
   während eines Gewitters.   a thunder shower.

These number-like adjectives, the words for "first, fourth, twentieth, etc." are called ORDINAL NUMERALS. Note how the numeral above is formed:

   am vier-t-en Juli   (on) the fourth of July.

The number is followed by a stem-lengthener -<u>t</u>- and then the regular adjective ending.

II. Look at some more examples of NUMBERS and ORDINAL NUMERALS:

   Wir fahren in <u>zehn</u> Tagen   Wir werden am <u>zehnten</u> Tag unserer
   nach Amerika.   Reise ankommen.
   Hier sind täglich <u>zwei</u>   Das <u>zweite</u> Konzert fängt um acht
   Konzerte.   Uhr an.
   <u>Ein</u> Sommer im Gebirge ist   Das ist mein <u>erster</u> Sommer im Gebirge.
   sehr schön.
   Ich lese jeden Tag <u>drei</u>   Die <u>dritte</u> Zeitung lese ich abends.
   Zeitungen.
   Im Sommer finden hier   Das <u>zwanzigste</u> Konzert war am
   <u>zwanzig</u> Konzerte statt.   schönsten.
   Kennen Sie seine <u>fünf</u> Söhne?   Kennen Sie seinen <u>fünften</u> Sohn?
   Wir fahren in <u>acht</u> Wochen   In der <u>achten</u> Woche unserer Reise
   nach Berlin.   fahren wir nach Berlin.
   Das sind ihre <u>sieben</u> Kinder.   Das ist ihr <u>siebtes</u> (<u>siebentes</u>) Kind.

1. Most Ordinal Numerals through "nineteenth" have the NUMBER plus STEM-LENGTHENER -t- plus ADJECTIVE ENDINGS:

am zehn-t-en Tag	on the tenth day
das zwei-t-e Konzert	the second concert
seinen fünf-t-en Sohn	his fifth son

2. Three Ordinal Numerals are irregular and one has an alternate, irregular form:

meir erst-er Sommer	my first summer
die dritt-e Zeitung	the third newspaper
der acht-en Woche	the eighth week
ihr siebt-es Kind	her seventh child
(ihr sieben-t-es Kind)	

3. The Ordinal Numerals from "twentieth" on up have the NUMBER plus STEM-LENGTHENER -st- plus ADJECTIVE ENDINGS:

das zwanzig-st-e Konzert	the twentieth concert

III. Ordinal Numerals are used for dates in both German and English. There are some differences in the way they are used, however:

Am vierten Juli besuchen wir meine Tante.	On the fourth of July On July the fourth we're going to visit my aunt. On July fourth
Heute ist der sechste Mai.	the sixth of May. Today is May the sixth. May sixth.

In English we have three choices; in German there is only one. Note that the date is always a der-sequence, although the noun (der Tag) is not expressed, and that the ordinal always immediately precedes the name of the month when it occurs. Here are some more examples:

Am 16. September komme ich wieder zurück.	On September 16th I'm coming back again.
Der 21. Juni ist der längste Tag des Jahres.	The 21st of June is the longest day of the year.
Ich freue mich auf den einunddreissigsten!	I'm looking forward to the thirty-first!
Wir fahren am Nachmittag des 18. ab.	We're leaving on the afternoon of the 18th.

When they occur in sentences, dates have whatever form (Nominative, Accusative, Dative, Genitive) the structure of the sentence may require. Notice that in the German writing system the ordinal may also be identified by a period placed after the Arabic numeral. When a date stands alone, as for example at the head of a letter, it has the Accusative form.

Bremen, den 31. Mai 1951

C.   PREPOSITIONS WITH THE GENITIVE

Numerous examples of prepositions with dative and/or accusative objects have occurred and have been discussed. In this unit we encounter the first example of a preposition followed by a genitive form:

Dazu haben wir nachher während des Konzerts die beste Gelegenheit.

The preposition während is one of a very small group of prepositons which are customarily followed by a genitive object. We will note the others as they occur.

D.   TELLING TIME

I. We have had several references to time by the clock. Let us examine a few
   of them.

Wie spät ist es denn jetzt?	What time is it now?
Wieviel Uhr ist es eigent- lich?	What time is it anyway?
Es ist genau viertel nach eins.	It's exactly quarter past one.
Wir essen meistens um ein Uhr.	We usually eat at one o'clock.
Das Kurkonzert fängt um vier Uhr an.	The concert begins at four o'clock.

There are two ways of asking the time in German; both are equally common.
In German as in English time expressions the word for "o'clock" may or may
not occur. Notice, however, that the word for "one" is <u>ein</u> when followed
by <u>Uhr</u> but is <u>eins</u> when the word <u>Uhr</u> does not occur.

II. There are different ways of telling time in German. Here are some more
    examples:

Ich werde um zehn Uhr dreissig bei Ihnen sein.	I'll be at your office at ten-thirty.
Um halb sechs müssen wir spätestens abfahren.	We have to leave at half past five at the latest.
Es ist viertel vor drei.	It's a quarter to three.
Es ist dreiviertel drei.	It's a quarter to three.
Viertel nach eins.	Quarter past one.
Viertel zwei.	Quarter past one.

Time between the hours may be designated with reference to the number of
minutes involved (<u>zehn Uhr dreissig</u>, <u>zwanzig Minuten nach fünf</u>). This
presents no problem. The use of fractions is a little more complicated,
however.

1. The word <u>viertel</u> may be used with the prepositions <u>nach</u> and <u>vor</u> (<u>viertel
   nach eins</u>, <u>viertel vor drei</u>). This is just like the English use of
   "quarter past" or "quarter to".

2. The words <u>viertel</u>, <u>halb</u> and <u>dreiviertel</u> also occur WITHOUT PREPOSITIONS.
   They then mean "a quarter", "a half" or "three-quarters" of the way
   through the hour, and the reference point is the hour which has not yet
   struck. You may, for instance, think of the hour from one o'clock to
   two o'clock as the second hour and the hour from two o'clock to three
   o'clock as the third hour. At 1:15 you are one-fourth of the way through
   hour number two (<u>viertel zwei</u>); at 1:30 you are halfway through the
   hour (<u>halb zwei</u>); at 1:45 you are three-quarters of the way through the
   hour (<u>dreiviertel zwei</u>).

III. Here is a tabular presentation of the different ways of telling time in
     German:

1:00	ein Uhr		eins
1:15	ein Uhr fünfzehn	viertel nach eins	viertel zwei
1:30	ein Uhr dreissig		halb zwei
1:45	ein Uhr fünfundvierzig	viertel vor zwei	dreiviertel zwei

IV. We have had three words referring to the general time of day: <u>abends</u>,
    <u>mittags</u>, <u>nachmittags</u>. These are adverbs and often occur together with a
    reference to clock time. There is one more which is of frequent occurrence:
    the word <u>morgens</u>. Here are further examples of their use:

Ich gehe <u>mittags</u> gewöhnlich nach Hause.	I usually go home at noon.
Essen Sie <u>abends</u> nochmal warm?	Do you eat a warm meal again in the evening?
Wir kommen um acht Uhr <u>morgens</u>.	We'll come at eight o'clock in the morning.
<u>Nachmittags</u> bin ich immer im Büro.	In the afternoons I'm always in the office.
<u>Abends</u> um sieben hören wir immer den Wetterbericht.	We always hear the weather report at seven in the evening.
Was haben Sie <u>mittags</u> um zwölf Uhr vor?	What do you have planned for twelve noon?

Note that these expressions for the time of day may be used BOTH to refer to something which takes place regularly or habitually AND to refer to a specific point of time on a particular day.

E. THE SUPERLATIVE STEM <u>MEIST</u>-

<u>Meist</u>- was noted as an irregular superlative stem in Unit 9. We have encountered some of the forms in which it occurs and will now add a few more examples in order to present a summary of its forms and their uses.

1. As attributive adjectives, forms of the stem <u>meist</u>- occur in the specifier-adjective-noun sequence:

Essen nicht <u>die meisten Leute</u> mittags ihre Hauptmahlzeit?	Don't <u>most people</u> eat their main meal at noon?
<u>Die meiste Zeit</u> arbeitet er überhaupt nicht.	<u>Most of the time</u> he doesn't work at all.
<u>Das meiste Geschirr</u> will ich in Deutschland kaufen.	<u>Most of the china</u> I intend to buy in Germany.
Von uns allen hat er <u>das meiste Geld</u>.	Of all of us he has <u>the most money</u>.
<u>Die meisten</u> sagen gar nichts.	<u>Most /</u>people_7 don't say anything at all.

Notice that in English we say "most", "the most", or "most of the ...". The forms of <u>meist</u>- in an attributive phrase in German are <u>always</u> preceded by a specifier. The noun can be omitted however.

2. The special predicate phrase <u>am meisten</u>:

Herr Köhler raucht <u>am meisten</u>.	Mr. Köhler smokes <u>the most</u>.
Abends lese ich <u>am meisten</u>.	I read <u>most</u> in the evenings.
Von allen Verwandten besucht uns meine Tante <u>am meisten</u>.	Of all / our_7 relatives my aunt visits us <u>the most</u>.

3. The adverb <u>meistens</u>:

Wir essen <u>meistens</u> um ein Uhr.	We <u>usually</u> eat at one o'clock.
Er schreibt <u>meistens</u> Romane.	He writes <u>mostly</u> novels.
Im Sommer fahren wir <u>meistens</u> ins Gebirge.	In the summer we <u>usually</u> go to the mountains.

Compare the sentences above and note the different meanings given by the forms of <u>meist</u>-. Note especially, however, the difference in the

way the two forms <u>meisten</u> and <u>meistens</u> are used: <u>Meisten</u> ALWAYS OCCURS
IN A PHRASE. <u>Meistens</u> NEVER IS PART OF A PHRASE.

<u>Die meisten</u> sagen nichts.	Most say nothing.
<u>Meistens</u> sagen sie nichts.	Mostly they say nothing.
<u>Am meisten</u> lese ich abends.	I read most in the evenings.
<u>Meistens</u> lese ich abends.	Usually I read in the evenings.

SUBSTITUTION DRILL - Part I

1. Ich weiss nicht, <u>wann</u> Herr Meyer
   kommt.

   ob – warum – mit wem – um wieviel Uhr

2. Wissen Sie, <u>dass</u> er nach England
   fährt?

   wann – ob – mit wem – warum

3. Das Konzert findet in <u>einer Woche</u>
   statt.

   sechs Monaten – drei Tagen – einem
   halben Jahr – einer Stunde – zwei
   Wochen – einer halben Stunde

4. Ich besuche <u>abends</u> manchmal Beckers.

   nachmittags – morgens – mittags

5. Ich möchte mir <u>eine Tasse Kaffee</u>
   bestellen.

   ein Stück Kuchen – ein Glas Apfelsaft –
   eine Tasse Tee – ein Glas Moselwein –
   ein Glas Bier – eine Tasse Milch

6. Das hängt von <u>seinem Beruf</u> ab.

   Ihrer Arbeit – dem Wetter – der Grösse
   des Wagens – meiner Frau – der Reise
   meines Kollegen – dem Besuch seiner
   Eltern

7. Ich glaube, dass er <u>in München
   wohnt.</u>

   zwei Kinder hat – gut deutsch spricht –
   im Konsulat arbeitet – nach Deutschland fährt – mit dem Omnibus kommt

8. Wissen Sie, wann er gewöhnlich
   <u>nach Hause kommt?</u>

   nach Berlin fährt – zu Mittag isst –
   seine Briefe schreibt – ins Kino geht –
   einen Spaziergang macht

9. Glauben Sie wirklich, dass Herr
   Jones <u>deutsch sprechen kann?</u>

   Briefe schreiben will – den Anzug
   kaufen möchte – soviel arbeiten muss –
   schon um eins kommen wird – bald nach
   Deutschland fahren kann

10. Wir wissen nicht, ob <u>sie heute
    oder morgen ankommt.</u>

    er um sechs oder um vier Uhr abfährt –
    es im Park oder im Kurhaus stattfindet –
    sie bald oder später anruft – wir am
    ersten oder am dritten einziehen – er
    ihn gleich oder nachher abholt

(End of Tape 10A)

Tape 10B   Part II

1. Heute ist der <u>achtzehnte Mai</u>.

   22. Juni – 3. April – 1. Januar –
   2. September – 5. August – 19. Dezember

   zweiundzwanzigste Juni – dritte April –
   erste Januar – zweite September –
   fünfte August – neunzehnte Dezember

2. Er kommt am <u>zwanzigsten April</u>.

   16. Mai – 4. Juli – 12. September –
   23. Oktober – 6. Juni – 31. Dezember

   sechzehnten Mai – vierten Juli –
   zwölften September – dreiundzwanzigsten
   Oktober – sechsten Juni – einund-
   dreissigsten Dezember

3. Ich freue mich auf den <u>zweiten Mai</u>.

    22. Februar - 10. März - 6. April -   zweiundzwanzigsten Februar - zehnten
    13. Mai - 26. Juni - 7. Juli -   März - sechsten April - dreizehnten
    19. August - 11. September -   Mai - sechsundzwanzigsten Juni - sieb-
    10. November   ten (siebenten) Juli - neunzehnten Au-
                                       gust - elften September - zehnten
                                       November

4. Der <u>dreiundzwanzigste Mai</u> ist ein Mittwoch.

    1. Dezember - 14. September -   erste Dezember - vierzehnte September -
    2. Januar - 8. August - 15. Juni -   zweite Januar - achte August - fünf-
    28. Mai - 10. Januar   zehnte Juni - achtundzwanzigste Mai -
                                        zehnte Januar

5. Am <u>sechsten Juni</u> wollen wir nach Bonn fahren.

    17. April - 3. Februar - 9. Dezem-   siebzehnten April - dritten Februar -
    ber - 30. August - 27. März -   neunten Dezember - dreissigsten August -
    3. November   siebenundzwanzigsten März - dritten
                                        November

6. Das Theater fängt um <u>acht Uhr fünf-
   zehn</u> an.

    8:45 - 7:30 - 6:20 - 5:15 - 9:00 -   acht Uhr fünfundvierzig - sieben Uhr
    4:10   dreissig - sechs Uhr zwanzig - fünf
                                        Uhr fünfzehn - neun Uhr - vier Uhr zehn

7. Wir essen meistens um <u>halb eins</u>.

    12:00 - 6:30 - 12:15 - 7:45 -   zwölf - halb sieben - viertel eins -
    6:00 - 1:30   dreiviertel acht - sechs - halb zwei

8. Es ist genau <u>viertel vor sieben</u>.

    6:10 - 2:45 - 11:05 - 3:40 - 5:15 - zehn nach sechs - viertel vor drei -
    9:55   fünf nach elf - zwanzig vor vier -
                                        viertel nach fünf - fünf vor zehn

CONVERSION DRILL - Part I

    Change the order of elements in the following sentences by beginning each sentence with the underlined word or words.

1. Wir fahren <u>nächsten Monat</u> in die   Nächsten Monat fahren wir in die Berge.
   Berge.
2. Die Sonne scheint <u>heute</u> sehr schön. Heute scheint die Sonne sehr schön.
3. Ich weiss nicht, <u>was wir machen</u>   Was wir machen sollen, weiss ich nicht.
   <u>sollen</u>.
4. Wir gehen zusammen einkaufen, <u>wenn</u> Wenn mein Mann nach Hause kommt, gehen
   <u>mein Mann nach Hause kommt</u>.   wir zusammen einkaufen.
5. Wir kommen <u>am Sonntag</u> zu Ihnen,   Am Sonntag kommen wir zu Ihnen, wenn
   wenn wir Zeit haben.   wir Zeit haben.
6. Wir werden <u>seine Frau</u> leider nicht Seine Frau werden wir leider nicht
   mehr sehen können.   mehr sehen können.
7. Wir essen gewöhnlich um eins, <u>da</u>   Da ich mittags nach Hause gehe, essen
   <u>ich mittags nach Hause gehe</u>.   wir gewöhnlich um eins.
8. Ich bestelle <u>meistens</u> Rumpsteak   Meistens, wenn ich ins Restaurant gehe,
   mit Röstkartoffeln, <u>wenn ich ins</u> bestelle ich Rumpsteak mit Röstkar-
   <u>Restaurant gehe</u>.   toffeln.
9. Wir essen immer <u>um diese Zeit</u>.   Um diese Zeit essen wir immer.
10. Wir kennen <u>ihn</u> nicht, aber sie.   Ihn kennen wir nicht, aber sie.
11. Ich habe nicht <u>das Geld für eine</u> Das Geld für eine grosse Reise habe
   <u>grosse Reise</u>.   ich nicht.

Part II

Combine the following pairs of sentences into larger sentences by using one of the sentence connectors <u>und</u>, <u>aber</u> or <u>oder</u>.

1. Mein Kollege hat ein neues Auto.
   Wir fahren öfters zusammen in die
   Berge.

   Mein Kollege hat ein neues Auto und
   wir fahren öfters zusammen in die Berge.

2. Ich möchte ihn sehr gern besuchen.
   Er wohnt zu weit von hier.

   Ich möchte ihn sehr gern besuchen,
   aber er wohnt zu weit von hier.

3. Ich möchte die Lampe kaufen.
   Ich habe kein Geld.

   Ich möchte die Lampe kaufen, aber ich
   habe kein Geld.

4. Sie können eine Taxe nehmen.
   Sie können mit Ihrem Wagen fahren.

   Sie können eine Taxe nehmen, oder
   Sie können mit Ihrem Wagen fahren.

5. Nehmen Sie Rumpsteak?
   Essen Sie lieber Kalbsleber?

   Nehmen Sie Rumpsteak oder essen Sie
   lieber Kalbsleber?

6. Der Vizekonsul gibt ihr ein Formular. Sie füllt es aus.

   Der Vizekonsul gibt ihr ein Formular
   und sie füllt es aus.

7. Meine Frau hat Appetit auf Bratwurst mit Sauerkraut.
   Ich esse lieber Forelle blau.

   Meine Frau hat Appetit auf Bratwurst
   mit Sauerkraut, aber ich esse lieber
   Forelle blau.

8. Herr Becker nimmt den Hörer ab.
   Die Sekretärin meldet sich.

   Herr Becker nimmt den Hörer ab und die
   Sekretärin meldet sich.

Part III

Change the following questions into clauses in the sentence beginning:
<u>Ich kann Ihnen nicht sagen</u>, ... In every case give the complete sentence!

1. Wann zieht Herr Becker ein?

   Ich kann Ihnen nicht sagen, wann
   Herr Becker einzieht.

2. Wann kommt Herr Becker an?
   ... wann Herr Becker ankommt.
3. Wen ruft Herr Becker an?
   ... wen Herr Becker anruft.
4. Wieviel gibt Herr Becker aus?
   ... wieviel Herr Becker ausgibt.
5. Warum fährt Herr Becker ab?
   ... warum Herr Becker abfährt.
6. Was füllt Herr Becker gerade aus?
   ... was Herr Becker gerade ausfüllt.
7. Wen holt Herr Becker ab?
   ... wen Herr Becker abholt.
8. Was packt Herr Becker ein?
   ... was Herr Becker einpackt.
9. Mit wem macht Herr Becker die
   Herren bekannt?
   ... mit wem Herr Becker die Herren
   bekannt macht.

Part IV

Change the following questions into clauses in the sentence beginning:
<u>Ich weiss nicht</u>, ... In every case give the complete sentence!

1. Bei wem klingelt Herr Meyer?

   Ich weiss nicht, bei wem Herr Meyer
   klingelt.

2. Mit wem spricht Herr Meyer?
   ... mit wem Herr Meyer spricht.
3. Auf was freut sich Herr Meyer?
   ... auf was Herr Meyer sich freut.
4. An wen schreibt Herr Meyer?
   ... an wen Herr Meyer schreibt.
5. Zu wem geht Herr Meyer?
   ... zu wem Herr Meyer geht.
6. Mit wem spricht Herr Meyer?
   ... mit wem Herr Meyer spricht.
7. Neben wem wohnt Herr Meyer?
   ... neben wem Herr Meyer wohnt.

VARIATION DRILL

1. **Ich höre, dass Sie nach Deutschland**
   fahren wollen.

   a. I know that my mother can come.

   b. I believe that I have to go to
      the bank.
   c. We know that he's planning to
      buy a new car.
   d. I hope that you can come too.
   e. I think that our trip is going
      to depend on the weather.

   I hear that you're planning to go to
   Germany.

   Ich weiss, dass meine Mutter kommen
   kann.
   Ich glaube, dass ich zur Bank gehen
   muss.
   Wir wissen, dass er sich einen neuen
   Wagen kaufen will.
   Ich hoffe, dass Sie auch kommen können.
   Ich denke, dass unsere Reise vom Wetter
   abhängen wird.

2. **Von diesem Tisch aus hat man eine**
   schöne Aussicht.

   a. From this window you ('one')
      can see the cathedral.
   b. Can you ('one') see the
      mountains from here?
   c. Can you ('one') see the Zug-
      spitze from this restaurant?
   d. I can see the Alps from my
      apartment.
   e. Can you see the Autobahn from
      your room?

   From this table there's a beautiful
   view.

   Von diesem Fenster aus kann man den
   Dom sehen.
   Kann man von hier aus die Berge sehen?

   Kann man von diesem Restaurant aus die
   Zugspitze sehen?
   Ich kann von meiner Wohnung aus die
   Alpen sehen.
   Können Sie von Ihrem Zimmer aus die
   Autobahn sehen?

3 **Bringen Sie mir bitte ein Glas**
   Moselwein.

   a. She orders a glass of milk.
   b. Please bring me a piece of cake.
   c. Shall I bring you a glass of
      water?
   d. He orders rye bread, butter and
      a piece of cheese.
   e. Please bring me a cup of coffee.

   Please bring me a glass of Moselle
   wine.

   Sie bestellt ein Glas Milch.
   Bitte bringen Sie mir ein Stück Kuchen.
   Soll ich Ihnen ein Glas Wasser bringen?

   Er bestellt Roggenbrot, Butter und ein
   Stück Käse.
   Bringen Sie mir bitte eine Tasse Kaffee.

4. **Ich muss nach Hause gehen, da es**
   schon sehr spät ist.

   a. If it rains today let's not
      drive to the mountains.
   b. Let's walk rather, since the
      weather is so nice.
   c. I can't buy the car now, since
      I don't have any money.
   d. Since we still have enough time,
      we can now take a walk.
   e. You'll have to call him up at
      home, since he's not in the
      office today.
   f. We can still buy a few picture
      postcards if we hurry.

   I have to go home, since it's already
   very late.

   Wenn es heute regnet, wollen wir nicht
   ins Gebirge fahren.
   Wir wollen lieber zu Fuss gehen, da
   das Wetter so schön ist.
   Ich kann das Auto jetzt nicht kaufen,
   da ich kein Geld habe.
   Da wir noch genug Zeit haben, können
   wir jetzt einen Spaziergang machen.
   Sie müssen ihn zu Hause anrufen, da er
   heute nicht im Büro ist.

   Wir können noch ein paar Ansichtskarten
   kaufen, wenn wir uns beeilen.

5. **Wissen Sie, ob er heute kommt?**

   a. We don't know yet whether we'll
      go.
   b. Ask him, please, if he wants to
      come along.
   c. Please write me whether you're
      going to travel to the mountains.

   Do you know if he's coming today?

   Wir wissen noch nicht, ob wir fahren
   werden.
   Fragen Sie ihn bitte, ob er mitkommen
   will.
   Schreiben Sie mir bitte, ob Sie in die
   Berge fahren werden.

d. Can you tell me if the concert
   is going to take place today?
e. He doesn't know yet whether
   he's going to leave as early
   as tomorrow.

Können Sie mir sagen, ob das Konzert
heute stattfindet?
Er weiss noch nicht, ob er morgen
schon abfährt.

6. **Er sitzt dort am dritten Tisch
   links.**

   **He's sitting there at the third table
   to the left.**

   a. This is my second trip to
      Germany.
   b. She lives on the sixth floor.
   c. Is that still your first car?
   d. That's her fourth book already.
   e. That's the third flat tire!

   Das ist meine zweite Reise nach
   Deutschland.
   Sie wohnt im fünften Stock.
   Ist das noch Ihr erster Wagen?
   Das ist schon ihr viertes Buch.
   Das ist die dritte Reifenpanne!

7. **Um wieviel Uhr essen Sie gewöhnlich?**

   At what time do you usually eat?

   a. At what time do you go home?
   b. Last week I was in Hamburg at
      this time.
   c. What will you be doing tomorrow
      at this time?
   d. What time are we supposed to
      meet them?
   e. Tomorrow morning at this time
      we'll be in Berlin already.

   Um wieviel Uhr gehen Sie nach Hause?
   Vorige Woche war ich um diese Zeit
   in Hamburg.
   Was werden Sie morgen um diese Zeit
   tun?
   Um wieviel Uhr sollen wir sie treffen?

   Morgen früh um diese Zeit werden wir
   schon in Berlin sein.

8. **Findet die Konferenz morgens oder
   nachmittags statt?**

   **Is the conference going to be in the
   morning or in the afternoon?**

   a. He's leaving in the afternoon
      already.
   b. The conference will be at nine
      o'clock in the morning.
   c. He goes home at twelve noon.
   d. They're planning to come to
      our place at seven in the
      evening.
   e. Every morning at eight o'clock
      we listen to ('hear') the news.

   Er fährt schon nachmittags ab.

   Die Konferenz findet um neun Uhr
   morgens statt.
   Er geht mittags um zwölf nach Hause.
   Sie wollen um sieben Uhr abends zu
   uns kommen.

   Morgens um acht Uhr hören wir die
   Nachrichten.

9. **Wissen Sie, dass Herr Becker heute
   kommt?**

   **Do you know that Mr. Becker is coming
   today?**

   a. Please tell him that we have
      to hurry.
   b. Can you tell me when the concert
      is going to be?
   c. Please write me whether the
      Beckers are going to Germany.
   d. Do you really believe that the
      furnace is out of order?
   e. Ask him, please, if there's a
      concert in the resort here
      daily.

   Sagen Sie ihm bitte, dass wir uns
   beeilen müssen.
   Können Sie mir sagen, wann das Konzert
   stattfindet?
   Schreiben Sie mir bitte, ob Beckers
   nach Deutschland fahren.
   Glauben Sie wirklich, dass die Heizung
   kaputt ist?
   Fragen Sie ihn bitte, ob hier täglich
   Kurkonzert ist.

10. **Wissen Sie, warum Herr Becker heute
    nicht kommt?**

    **Do you know why Mr. Becker isn't
    coming today?**

    a. I think ('find') that your
       apartment looks very nice now.
    b. I don't know whether Mr. Becker
       is going to call again.
    c. She says that there are beauti-
       ful picture postcards there.

    Ich finde, dass Ihre Wohnung jetzt
    sehr schön aussieht.
    Ich weiss nicht, ob Herr Becker
    nochmal anruft.
    Sie sagt, dass es dort schöne
    Ansichtskarten gibt.

d. Please tell me when the bus
leaves.

Sagen Sie mir bitte, wann der Omnibus
abfährt.

e. I think ('find') that the inn
looks very good.

Ich finde, dass der Gasthof einen sehr
guten Eindruck macht.

11. Nachher, wenn die Sonne wieder
scheint, wollen wir in die Stadt
fahren.

In a little while, if the sun is
shining again, we plan to drive
down town.

a. Tomorrow morning, if the weather
is good, we plan to go for a
walk.

Morgen früh, wenn das Wetter gut ist,
wollen wir einen Spaziergang machen.

b. Later, if it's not raining any
more, we can take a look around
the place.

Später, wenn es nicht mehr regnet,
können wir uns den Ort ansehen.

c. Sometimes when we have a warm
meal at noon we only eat bread
and cold cuts in the evening.

Manchmal, wenn wir mittags warm essen,
essen wir abends nur Brot und Aufschnitt.

d. Before, if we have enough time,
we'll take a few pictures.

Vorher, wenn wir genug Zeit haben,
werden wir ein paar Aufnahmen machen.

e. In the evening, if we have an
('the') opportunity for it, we
can unpack our dishes.

Abends, wenn wir die Gelegenheit dazu
haben, können wir unser Geschirr
auspacken.

VOCABULARY DRILL

1. während - "during"

a. Während eines Gewitters fahre
ich nicht gern mit dem Auto.

I don't like to take the car during a
thunder shower.

b. Während ihres Besuches will sie
viele Aufnahmen machen.

During her visit she wants to take
a lot of pictures.

c. Während des Kurkonzerts können
wir eine Tasse Kaffee trinken.

During the concert (in the resort) we
can have a cup of coffee.

d. Er trifft Herrn Meyer während
eines Spaziergangs.

He meets Mr. Meyer while he's out
walking ('during a walk').

e. Während der Konferenz soll man
nicht rauchen.

You're ('one is') not supposed to
smoke during the conference.

2. meistens - "usually, mostly"

a. Im Sommer fahren wir meistens
an die Ostsee.

In the summer we usually go to the
Baltic Sea.

b. Meistens essen wir in diesem
Hotel.

We eat mostly at this hotel.

c. Wir essen meistens schon um
ein Uhr.

We usually eat as early as one o'clock.

d. Nachmittags um vier Uhr trinken
wir meistens eine Tasse Kaffee.

At four in the afternoon we usually
have a cup of coffee.

e. Von hier aus hat man meistens
eine gute Aussicht.

From here you usually have a good
view.

3. die meisten - "(the) most ..., most of the ..."

a. Die meisten Leute in Amerika
essen abends ihre Hauptmahlzeit.

Most people in America eat their main
meal in the evening.

b. Die meisten Kurkonzerte finden
im Park statt.

Most of the concerts in the resort
are held in the park.

c. In den meisten amerikanischen
Restaurants gibt es auch deutsches Bier.

In most American restaurants they have
German beer too.

d. Mit den meisten kleinen Autos
kann man sehr schnell fahren.

In most small cars you can go very
fast.

e. Das meiste Essen bekommt man in
dem Restaurant in der Schubertstrasse.

You get the most food at the restaurant
on 'Schubertstrasse'.

4. am meisten - "(the) most"

   a. In diesem Geschäft kaufen wir
      am meisten.
   b. Am meisten fahren wir mit
      unserem Volkswagen.
   c. Wir gehen oft ins Kino, aber
      am meisten gehen wir ins
      Theater.
   d. Wir rauchen alle viel, aber
      Herr Becker raucht am meisten.
   e. Meine Frau und ich lesen viel,
      am meisten liest aber mein Sohn.

   a. We buy the most at this
      store.
   b. We do most of our driving in the
      Volkswagen.
   c. We often go to the movies, but we go
      to the theater most.
   d. We all smoke a lot, but Mr. Becker
      smokes the most.
   e. My wife and I read a lot; my son
      reads the most, however.

5. hätte(n) gern - "would like (something)"

   a. Ich hätte gern ein Glas Apfel-
      saft.
                      I'd like a glass of apple juice.
   b. Hätten Sie gern ein Stück
      Kuchen?
                      Would you like a piece of cake?
   c. Wir hätten gern drei Tassen
      Kaffee.
                      We'd like three cups of coffee.
   d. Er hätte gern ein Rumpsteak
      mit Röstkartoffeln.
                      He'd like a steak with fried potatoes.
   e. Hätten Sie gern etwas Käse
      dazu?
                      Would you like some cheese with it?

6. bestellen - "to order"

   a. Was möchten Sie bestellen?
                      What would you like to order?
   b. Ich glaube, ich bestelle ein
      Glas Bier.
                      I think I'll order a glass of beer.
   c. Er bestellt das Tagesgericht,
      aber ohne Suppe.
                      He orders the special for the day
                      but without soup.
   d. Nein danke, ich möchte nichts
      mehr bestellen.
                      No thanks, I don't care to order
                      anything more.
 ·e. Bestellen Sie mir bitte ein
      Glas Moselwein.
                      Order me a glass of Moselle wine,
                      please.

7. Appetit auf etwas haben - "to have room for something (to eat), to feel
                    like eating"

   a. Ich habe Appetit auf ein Stück
      Kuchen.
                      I have room for a piece of cake.
   b. Er hat Appetit auf ein Rump-
      steak.
                      He feels like a steak.
   c. Ich habe noch Appetit auf etwas
      Apfelmus.
                      I still have room for some applesauce.
   d. Auf was haben Sie heute Appetit?
                      What do you feel like eating today?
   e. Sie hat Appetit auf Kalbsleber
      mit Kartoffelpüree.
                      She feels like calve's liver with
                      mashed potatoes.

8. abhängen von - "to depend on"

   a. Unsere Reise hängt vom Wetter
      ab.
                      Our trip depends on the weather.
   b. Das hängt von der Qualität des
      Stoffes ab.
                      That depends on the quality of the
                      material.
   c. Es hängt von seiner Arbeitszeit
      ab, ob er heute zu uns kommen
      kann.
                      It depends on his working hours,
                      whether he can come and see us today.
   d. Ich glaube, das wird von seinem
      Beruf abhängen.
                      I think that will depend on his job.
   e. Das hängt von unserem Besuch in
      Deutschland ab.
                      That depends on our visit to ('in')
                      Germany.

9. <u>schade</u> - "(it's) a pity; too bad"

a. Wie schade, dass Sie heute nicht kommen können!	What a pity that you can't come today!
b. Schade, dass es schon wieder regnet.	It's a pity that it's raining again.
c. Zu schade, dass wir keinen Spaziergang machen können!	Too bad that we can't go for a walk!
d. Ist es nicht schade, dass das Konzert nicht stattfindet?	Isn't it a pity that the concert is not being held?
e. Schade, dass es hier keinen guten Moselwein gibt.	It's a pity that they don't have any good Moselle wine here.

10. <u>stattfinden</u> - "to take place, to be held, to be"

a. Können Sie mir sagen, wann das Kurkonzert stattfindet?	Can you tell me when the concert in the resort is going to be?
b. Die Reise findet in drei Wochen statt.	The trip is going to be in three weeks.
c. In welchem Monat findet der Sommerschlussverkauf statt?	In what month is the summer clearance sale being held?
d. Die Konferenz soll in einer halben Stunde stattfinden.	The conference is supposed to be in half an hour.

11. <u>abfahren</u> - "to leave"

a. Können Sie mir sagen, wann der Omnibus abfährt?	Can you tell me when the bus leaves?
b. In zehn Minuten müssen wir ab-fahren.	In ten minutes we have to leave.
c. Wann fährt er ab, heute oder morgen früh?	When is he leaving, today or tomorrow morning?
d. Wir fahren ab, wenn das Wetter besser ist.	We're going to leave when the weather is better.
e. Sie fährt am dritten März hier ab.	She's leaving on the third of March.

(End of Tape 10B)

TRANSLATION DRILL (not recorded)

1. It's the fourth of July.	Es ist der vierte Juli.
2. The Wilsons and the Beckers are at a resort in the mountains.	Wilsons und Beckers sind in einem Kurort in den Bergen.
3. During the thunder shower they intend to go to a restaurant and eat lunch (there).	Während des Gewitters wollen sie in ein Restaurant gehen und dort zu Mittag essen.
4. The White Stag Inn looks pretty good.	Der Gasthof "Zum Weissen Hirsch" macht einen guten Eindruck.
5. They drive into the parking lot of the inn in their car and then they go into the dining room.	Sie fahren mit dem Auto auf den Park-platz des Gasthofs und dann gehen sie ins Gastzimmer.
6. In the charming dining room they find a table by the window.	In dem gemütlichen Gastzimmer finden sie einen Tisch am Fenster.
7. They hope that they'll have a good view from the table.	Sie hoffen, dass sie von dem Tisch aus eine gute Aussicht haben.
8. The waiter brings the menu and Mrs. Becker orders calve's liver with mashed potatoes and applesauce.	Der Ober bringt die Speisekarte und Frau Becker bestellt Kalbsleber mit Kartoffelpüree und Apfelmus.
9. Mrs. Wilson takes the special for the day, but she'd like not to have the soup with it.	Frau Wilson nimmt das Tagesgericht, aber sie möchte keine Suppe dazu haben.
10. The waiter is to bring Mr. Wilson steak with fried potatoes.	Der Ober soll Herrn Wilson Rumpsteak mit Röstkartoffeln bringen.
11. Mr. Becker orders blue trout with melted butter.	Herr Becker bestellt Forelle blau mit zerlassener Butter.
12. He's especially fond of trout.	Forelle isst er besonders gern.

13. The waiter asks if they want to have something to drink.	Der Ober fragt, ob sie etwas zu trinken haben wollen.
14. Mrs. Wilson and Mrs. Becker would like a glass of apple juice.	Frau Wilson und Frau Becker möchten gern ein Glas Apfelsaft trinken.
15. Mr. Wilson prefers beer to apple juice.	Herr Wilson trinkt lieber Bier als Apfelsaft.
16. Mr. Becker orders a glass of Moselle wine, since that goes better with trout.	Herr Becker bestellt ein Glas Moselwein, da der besser zu Forelle passt.
17. Mr. Wilson asks Mr. Becker what time it is.	Herr Wilson fragt Herrn Becker, wieviel Uhr es ist.
18. It's quarter past one.	Es ist viertel zwei.
19. The Beckers usually eat lunch not later than one o'clock.	Beckers essen gewöhnlich schon um ein Uhr zu Mittag.
20. Mr. Becker's office is in the vicinity of his apartment, and at noon he usually goes home for lunch.	Das Büro von Herrn Becker ist in der Nähe seiner Wohnung, und mittags geht er meistens zum Essen nach Hause.
21. Mr. Wilson would like to know if most Germans eat their main meal at noon.	Herr Wilson möchte wissen, ob die meisten Deutschen mittags ihre Hauptmahlzeit essen.
22. Mr. Becker says that that depends on ⎡the⎤ job and working hours.	Herr Becker sagt, dass das von Beruf und Arbeitszeit abhängt.
23. The Beckers eat their main meal at noon, but then they don't have a warm meal again in the evening.	Beckers essen mittags ihre Hauptmahlzeit, aber abends essen sie dann nicht mehr warm.
24. Usually they have ('there is at their house') rye bread, butter, cold cuts and cheese.	Meistens gibt es bei ihnen Roggenbrot, Butter, Aufschnitt und Käse.
25. They usually have a cup of tea with it.	Sie trinken gewöhnlich eine Tasse Tee dazu.
26. Mrs. Wilson still has room for ('is still hungry for') a piece of cake.	Frau Wilson hat noch Appetit auf ein Stück Kuchen.
27. The Beckers don't want anything more to eat.	Beckers wollen nichts mehr essen.
28. They'd rather have a cup of coffee later on.	Sie möchten lieber später noch eine Tasse Kaffee trinken.
29. At last the sun is shining again.	Endlich scheint die Sonne wieder.
30. Mr. Becker calls the waiter ⎡the bill⎤.	Herr Becker ruft den Ober und zahlt.
31. Since the weather is nice now, they want to take a walk through the resort.	Da das Wetter wieder schön ist, wollen sie noch einen Spaziergang durch den Kurort machen.
32. They hear that there's a concert in the resort daily. ('a concert takes place ... ')	Sie hören, dass täglich ein Kurkonzert stattfindet.
33. If the weather is good, it takes place in the park, otherwise in the 'Kurhaus'.	Wenn das Wetter gut ist, findet es im Park statt, sonst im Kurhaus.
34. Mr. Wilson would like to know when the concert begins.	Herr Wilson möchte wissen, wann das Konzert anfängt.
35. The waiter thinks it begins at four o'clock.	Der Ober glaubt, es fängt um vier Uhr an.
36. They still have enough time to look around the city.	Sie haben noch genug Zeit, um sich die Stadt anzusehen.
37. Mrs. Wilson would like to buy a few picture postcards.	Frau Wilson möchte einige Ansichtskarten kaufen.
38. At four o'clock they want to have a cup of coffee in the 'Kurhaus'.	Um vier Uhr wollen sie im Kurhaus eine Tasse Kaffee trinken.
39. They plan to leave at half past five.	Sie haben vor, um halb sechs abzufahren. (Sie wollen um halb sechs abfahren.)

RESPONSE DRILL (not recorded)

1. Wo sind Wilsons und Beckers?
Sie sind in einem Kurort in den Bergen.

2. Welcher Tag ist es?
Es ist der vierte Juli.

3. Wie ist das Wetter?
Das Wetter ist schlecht, es regnet und es soll ein Gewitter geben.

4. Was wollen sie während des Gewitters machen?
Während eines Gewitters wollen sie in einem Gasthof zu Mittag essen.

5. Wie spät ist es?
Es ist viertel nach eins.

6. In welchen Gasthof gehen sie?
Sie gehen in den Gasthof "Zum Weissen Hirsch".

7. Was für einen Eindruck macht dieser Gasthof?
Er macht einen sehr guten Eindruck.

8. Was wollen sie nach dem Essen machen?
Wenn es nicht mehr regnet, wollen sie nach dem Essen einen Spaziergang machen.

9. Wie gefällt ihnen das Gastzimmer?
Das Gastzimmer gefällt ihnen sehr gut, es ist sehr gemütlich.

10. An welchen Tisch setzen sie sich?
Sie setzen sich an einen Tisch am Fenster.

11. Warum wollen sie am Fenster sitzen?
Sie denken, dass sie eine schöne Aussicht haben, wenn das Wetter wieder besser ist.

12. Was bringt ihnen der Ober?
Der Ober bringt ihnen die Speisekarte.

13. Was bestellen die Damen?
Frau Wilson bestellt das Tagesgericht, ohne Suppe. Frau Becker möchte Kalbsleber mit Kartoffelpüree und Apfelmus haben.

14. Und was bestellen die Herren?
Herr Becker hätte gern Forelle blau mit zerlassener Butter. Herr Wilson nimmt Rumpsteak mit Röstkartoffeln.

15. Was trinken Wilsons und Beckers dazu?
Die Damen trinken Apfelsaft, Herr Wilson trinkt ein Glas Bier und Herr Becker ein Glas Moselwein.

16. Um wieviel Uhr essen Beckers meistens zu Mittag?
Sie essen meistens schon um ein Uhr.

17. Warum essen sie schon um ein Uhr?
Herr Becker geht mittags gewöhnlich nach Hause.

18. Wann essen die meisten Leute in Deutschland ihre Hauptmahlzeit, mittags oder abends?
Das hängt von Beruf und Arbeitszeit ab.

19. Was essen Beckers abends, wenn sie schon mittags ihre Hauptmahlzeit essen?
Dann essen Beckers meistens Roggenbrot, Butter, Aufschnitt und Käse.

20. Was trinken sie dazu?
Sie trinken meistens Tee dazu.

21. Auf was haben Herr und Frau Wilson noch Appetit?
Sie haben noch auf ein Stück Kuchen und eine Tasse Kaffee Appetit.

22. Wann trinken Beckers ihren Kaffee lieber?
Beckers trinken ihren Kaffee lieber etwas später.

23. Wann werden sie dazu Gelegenheit haben?
Sie werden nachher während des Konzerts vielleicht Gelegenheit dazu haben.

24. Wie ist das Wetter nach dem Essen?
Das Wetter ist gut, die Sonne scheint wieder.

25. Warum ruft Herr Becker den Ober?
Er möchte zahlen.

26. An welchen Tagen finden in dem Kurort Kurkonzerte statt?
Die Kurkonzerte finden täglich statt.

27. Wo finden die Konzerte statt, wenn das Wetter gut ist?
Wenn das Wetter gut ist, finden die Konzerte im Park statt.

28. Und wo finden sie statt, wenn das Wetter schlecht ist?
Dann finden sie im Kurhaus statt.

29. Wann soll das Kurkonzert anfangen?
Der Ober glaubt, dass es um vier Uhr anfängt.

30. Was wollen Beckers und Wilsons vorher machen?
Sie wollen sich den Kurort ansehen.

31. Was möchte Frau Wilson kaufen?

Sie möchte einige Ansichtskarten kaufen.

32. Wann wollen sie spätestens abfahren?

Sie wollen spätestens um halb sechs abfahren.

33. Wieviel Uhr ist es?
34. Wann fahren Sie nach Deutschland?
35. Ist heute der dritte oder der vierte Mai?
36. Wann essen Sie meistens zu Mittag?
37. Wann essen Sie Ihre Hauptmahlzeit?
38. Was essen Sie gewöhnlich abends?
39. Wie ist das Essen in dem Restaurant auf der anderen Seite der Strasse?
40. Was essen Sie am liebsten?
41. Wann fahren Sie wieder auf Besuch nach Hause?
42. Wann fängt das Theater an?

CONVERSATION PRACTICE (not recorded)

1

A: Wollen Sie mit uns in die Alpen fahren?
B: Wann fahren Sie denn?
A: Am dritten Juli, - wenn es nicht regnet!
B: Ich möchte sehr gern mitkommen, aber leider muss ich schon am 25. Juni in München sein.
A: Schade!

2

A: Regnet es eigentlich noch?
B: Nein, die Sonne scheint schon wieder.
A: Ich möchte gern einen Spaziergang machen und mir den Ort ansehen. Kommen Sie mit?
B: Ja, gern. Gibt es hier in der Nähe ein Geschäft, wo ich Ansichtskarten kaufen kann?
A: Ich glaube, dass Sie die sogar hier im Restaurant bekommen.

3

A: Wann essen Sie eigentlich immer Ihre Hauptmahlzeit, Herr Meyer?
M: Gewöhnlich um sieben Uhr abends, wenn ich aus dem Büro komme.
A: Essen Sie mittags auch warm?
M: Nein, dann esse ich meistens etwas Roggenbrot mit Aufschnitt und Käse und trinke ein Glas Bier dazu.
A: Ich kann mittags zum Essen nach Hause gehen und wir essen meistens warm.

4

A: Was bestellen Sie?
B: Ich will mal den Ober fragen, ob sie hier Forellen haben.
A: Ich glaube, ich nehme Rumpsteak mit Röstkartoffeln.
B: Wollen Sie ein Glas Wein dazu trinken?
A: Nein, ich trinke lieber Bier.

SITUATIONS

Im Restaurant

1

Herr Becker und Herr Jones sitzen im Restaurant. Der Ober bringt ihnen die Speisekarte und sie bestellen.

2

Die beiden Herren sprechen zusammen. Herr Becker sagt, dass seine Frau und er am zehnten August nach Bonn fahren werden. Herr Jones möchte wissen, ob sie mit dem Auto fahren und wie lange sie in Bonn bleiben wollen.

3

Herr Becker und Herr Jones sprechen über das Essen in einigen Restaurants, was sie gern essen und was sie nicht gern essen. Dann bestellt Herr Becker das zweite Glas Bier. Der Ober fragt Herrn Jones, ob er ihm auch noch ein Glas Bier bringen darf. Aber Herr Jones hätte lieber eine Tasse Kaffee und dazu will er ein Stück Kuchen essen.

4

Herr Jones fragt Herrn Becker, wann er
meistens zu Mittag isst und ob er
abends kalt oder warm isst. Herr
Becker sagt es ihm und später fragt er
Herrn Jones, wann er seine Hauptmahlzeit gewöhnlich isst. Er weiss nicht,
dass man in Amerika oft mittags und
abends warm isst.

5

Herr Jones ruft den Ober, er möchte
gern zahlen. Sein Essen kostet fünf
Mark fünfunddreissig. Er gibt dem
Ober zehn Mark und der Ober wechselt
das Geld und gibt ihm vier Mark fünf-
undsechzig zurück. Dann bezahlt Herr
Becker für sein Essen.

NARRATIVE

Herr und Frau Burke kommen am 10. Juli auf dem Flughafen in Frankfurt an.
Sie sind zum ersten Mal in Deutschland. Ihre Freunde holen sie ab und da es
gerade Mittagszeit ist, gehen sie erst einmal in ein Restaurant. Der Ober bringt
die Speisekarte und Burkes sind froh, dass ihnen ihre Freunde helfen können.
Frau Burke hat zwar ein kleines Wörterbuch, aber das Lesen einer Speisekarte ist
ziemlich schwierig.
Das Essen schmeckt ihnen sehr gut. Sie wundern sich aber, dass der Ober ihnen
kein Eiswasser bringt. Salz, Pfeffer und Senf stehen auf dem Tisch.
Als Nachtisch bestellen sie sich später noch ein Stück Kuchen.
Frau Wilson erzählt Burkes, dass sehr viele Deutsche nachmittags in ein Café
gehen und dort Torte essen und Kaffee trinken, sofern sie es sich geldlich und
zeitlich leisten können.
Frau Burke fällt es auf, dass die Leute am Nebentisch nie beim Essen das Messer
aus der Hand legen. Sie haben die Gabel in der linken Hand und mit dem Messer
schieben sie das Gemüse, Fleisch und dieKartoffeln auf die Gabel. Sie haben
immer beide Hände auf dem Tisch. Ja, andere Länder, andere Sitten!

zum ersten Mal - for the first time
das Wörterbuch, ̈er - dictionary
schwierig - difficult
es schmeckt ihnen (gut) - it tastes
                        good to them
sich wundern - to be surprised
das Eis - ice
das Salz - salt
der Pfeffer - pepper
der Senf - (German) mustard
der Nachtisch - dessert

die. Torte,-n - cake
sofern - insofar as
geldlich - financially
zeitlich - with respect to time
nie - never
die Gabel,-n - fork
das Messer,- - knife
schieben - shove
das Gemüse,- - vegetable
das Fleisch - meat
die Sitten (pl) - customs

FINDER LIST

	abends	in the evening
	abfahren	leave
	abhängen von	depend on
die	Ansichtskarte,-n	picture postcard
das	Apfelmus	apple sauce
der	Apfelsaft	apple juice
der	Appetit	appetite
	ich habe Appetit auf (etwas)	I'm hungry (for something)
die	Arbeitszeit,-en	working hours
der	Aufschnitt	cold cuts
der	Beruf,-e	job, profession
	bestellen	order
die	Butter	butter
	da	since
	denken	think
	dreiviertel	three quarters
der	Eindruck, ̈e	impression
	einen guten Eindruck machen	make a good impression
die	Forelle,-n	trout
der	Gasthof, ̈e	inn

das	Gastzimmer,-	dining room (of an inn)
die	Gelegenheit (zu etwas)	opportunity (for something)
	genug	enough
	halb	half
die	Hauptmahlzeit,-en	main meal
	hell	light
der	Hirsch,-e	stag
	Zum Weissen Hirsch	at the (sign of) the White Stag
die	Kalbsleber	calves' liver
das	Kartoffelpüree	mashed potatoes
der	Käse	cheese
das	Konzert,-e	concert
der	Kuchen,-	cake
das	Kurkonzert,-e	concert in the resort
	manchmal	sometimes, occasionally
die	meisten	most (pl)
	meistens	usually, mostly
der	Moselwein	Moselle wine
	na also	well, that's a surprise
	ob	if, whether
	ohne	without (prep with acc)
das	Roggenbrot,-e	rye bread
die	Röstkartoffeln	fried potatoes
das	Rumpsteak,-s	steak
wie	schade	what a pity
	scheinen	shine
die	Sonne	sun
	spätestens	at the latest
die	Speisekarte,-n	menu
	stattfinden	take place
das	Stück,-e	piece
die	Suppe,-n	soup
das	Tagesgericht,-e	special for today
	täglich	daily
	um ... zu	in order to
	unbedingt	necessarily, definitely
	viertel	quarter
	vierten	fourth
	am vierten Juli	the fourth of July
	von diesem Tisch aus	from this table
	während	during
	wenn	if, whenever
	zahlen	pay
	zerlassene Butter	melted butter

Tape 11A   EIN WOCHENTAG

Basic Sentences

I   I

At the breakfast-table.   Am Frühstückstisch.

MR. NEUMANN   ### HERR NEUMANN

Where's Klaus?   Wo ist denn Klaus?

> to oversleep   sich verschlafen
> he overslept   er hat sich verschlafen

Did he oversleep again?   Hat er sich wieder verschlafen?

> to comb one's hair   sich kämmen
> hurry up   beeil' dich
> to miss   verpassen
> you miss   du verpasst

MRS. NEUMANN   ### FRAU NEUMANN

No, he's just combing his hair.   Nein, er kämmt sich gerade.

Hurry up, Klaus, or you'll miss the Beeil' dich, Klaus, sonst verpasst
bus.   du den Autobus.

> to wash   waschen
> I wash my hands   ich wasche mir die Hände

KLAUS   ### KLAUS

I'm coming; I'm just washing my hands. Ich komme gleich; ich wasche mir nur
                                     noch die Hände.

> the shoe   der Schuh,-e

Where are my brown shoes anyway?   Wo sind eigentlich meine braunen
                                     Schuhe?

> the shoemaker   der Schuster,-
> at the shoemaker's   beim Schuster
> to sole   besohlen
> to have something soled   etwas besohlen lassen
> he has something soled   er lässt etwas besohlen

MRS. NEUMANN   ### FRAU NEUMANN

At the shoemaker's; I had them   Beim Schuster; ich habe sie besohlen
soled.   lassen.

> you can   du kannst
> this afternoon   heute nachmittag[1]

You can pick them up this afternoon. Du kannst sie heute nachmittag abholen.

> the school outing   der Schulausflug,-̈e

KLAUS

We have a school outing today.

Can I have some money?

    you have

MR. NEUMANN

Here's six marks.

    get, have
    to you, for you
    the hair
    to cut
    to have something cut
    before
    you come

Get your hair cut (from it) too
before you come home.

    to forget
    forget
    your
    the snack, lunch
    to run
    run
    so that
    to be late

MRS. NEUMANN

Don't forget your lunch, and now run
so you won't be late.

II

MR. NEUMANN

Do you have to go down town Helga?

    to go (with someone)

MRS. NEUMANN

Yes, I'd really like to go along
with you now.

    a great deal
    to attend to,
    to take care of

I have a good deal to attend to.

MR. NEUMANN

What all are you planning to do?

    first
    the cleaners

KLAUS

Wir machen heute einen Schulausflug.

Kann ich etwas Geld haben?

    du hast

HERR NEUMANN

Hier hast du sechs Mark.

    lass
    dir (dative)
    das Haar,-e
    schneiden
    etwas schneiden lassen
    bevor
    du kommst

Lass dir davon auch noch die Haare[2]
schneiden, bevor du nach Hause kommst.

    vergessen
    vergiss
    dein
    das Frühstücksbrot,-e
    laufen
    lauf'
    damit
    zu spät kommen

FRAU NEUMANN

Vergiss dein Frühstücksbrot nicht
und nun lauf', damit du nicht zu
spät kommst.

II

HERR NEUMANN

Musst du in die Stadt, Helga?[3]

    mitfahren (mit jemandem)

FRAU NEUMANN

Ja, ich möchte am liebsten gleich mit
dir mitfahren.

    eine ganze Menge
    besorgen

Ich habe eine ganze Menge zu besorgen.

HERR NEUMANN

Was hast du denn alles vor?

    zuerst
    die Reinigung,-en

MRS. NEUMANN	FRAU NEUMANN
I have to go to the cleaners first.	Ich muss zuerst zur Reinigung gehen.

to clean	reinigen
to have something cleaned	etwas reinigen lassen

I want to have your grey suit cleaned.	Ich will deinen grauen Anzug reinigen lassen.

take	nimm

MR. NEUMANN	HERR NEUMANN
Take the blue one along too, please.	Nimm doch bitte auch den blauen mit.

at the same time	auch gleich
the shirt	das Oberhemd,-en
the laundry	die Wäscherei,-en

MRS. NEUMANN	FRAU NEUMANN
All right, and then I can take your shirts to the laundry at the same time.	Ja, und dann kann ich auch gleich deine Oberhemden in die Wäscherei bringen.

the dentist	der Zahnarzt,-̈e
the hairdresser	der Frisör,-e
at the hairdresser's	beim Frisör

At ten o'clock I have to be at the dentist's and at the hairdresser's at twelve.	Um zehn Uhr muss ich beim Zahnarzt, sein und um zwölf beim Frisör.

you will	du wirst
hardly, scarcely	kaum

MR. NEUMANN	HERR NEUMANN
Then you can hardly be home before half past one.	Da wirst du ja kaum vor halb zwei zu Hause sein.
Shall I come and pick you up at the hairdresser's?	Soll ich dich beim Frisör abholen?

it's possible	es geht
pick ... up	hol' ... ab

MRS. NEUMANN	FRAU NEUMANN
Yes, if you can pick me up at one.	Ach ja, wenn es geht, hol' mich dort um eins ab.

the way home	der Nachhauseweg
on the way home	auf dem Nachhauseweg
in addition , too	noch
the pharmacy	die Apotheke,-n
the watchmaker	der Uhrmacher,-

On the way home I'd like to go to the pharmacy and the watchmaker's too.	Auf dem Nachhauseweg möchte ich gern noch zur Apotheke und zum Uhrmacher.[3]

III

At the office in the afternoon:	Nachmittags im Büro:

Doctor	Herr Doktor[4]
he called	er hat ... angerufen

MISS KELLER | ### FRÄULEIN KELLER

Dr. Bergmann just called, Mr. Neumann.

Eben hat Herr Dr. Bergmann angerufen, Herr Neumann.

leave a message	bestellen lassen

MR. NEUMANN | ### HERR NEUMANN

Did he leave a message?

Hat er etwas bestellen lassen?

to expect	erwarten
the conference	die Besprechung,-

MISS KELLER | ### FRÄULEIN KELLER

Yes, he's expecting you at five o'clock for a conference.

Ja, er erwartet Sie um fünf Uhr zu einer Besprechung.

he said	er hat gesagt

MR. NEUMANN | ### HERR NEUMANN

Did he say what it was about?

Hat er gesagt, um was es sich handelt?

the customs regulations	die Zollbestimmungen

MISS KELLER | ### FRÄULEIN KELLER

Yes, it's about the new customs regulations.

Ja, um die neuen Zollbestimmungen.

the papers, documents	die Unterlagen
all the papers	alle Unterlagen

Here are all the papers.

Hier sind schon alle Unterlagen.

he wanted	er wollte
he wants to speak to him	er will ihn sprechen[5]

By the way a gentleman from the British Embassy wanted to talk to you.

Übrigens wollte Sie ein Herr von der englischen Botschaft sprechen.

MR. NEUMANN | ### HERR NEUMANN

What about?

In welcher Angelegenheit?

MISS KELLER | ### FRÄULEIN KELLER

I don't know. He's going to call back.

Das weiss ich nicht. Er will nochmal anrufen.

MR. NEUMANN | ### HERR NEUMANN

All right.

Na schön.

to dictate	diktieren

I'd like to dictate a few letters to you now, Miss Keller.	Ich möchte Ihnen jetzt einige Briefe diktieren, Fräulein Keller.

the Employment Office the Chamber of Commerce	das Arbeitsamt,-̈er die Handelskammer,-n

First, one to the Employment Office and then one to the Chamber of Commerce.	Zuerst einen an das Arbeitsamt und dann einen an die Handelskammer.

the article to translate to have something translated	der Artikel,- übersetzen etwas übersetzen lassen

And have this article translated please.	Und lassen Sie diesen Artikel doch bitte übersetzen.

IV

MISS KELLER

FRÄULEIN KELLER

Mr. Neumann, Mr. Meyer is on the wire.	Herr Neumann, Herr Meyer ist am Apparat.

to switch (from one line to another)	umschalten

MR. NEUMANN

HERR NEUMANN

Thank you, put him on please.	Danke, schalten Sie bitte um.
Neumann speaking.	Hier Neumann.

MR. MEYER

HERR MEYER

Hello, Gerhard, how are you?	Tag Gerhard, wie geht's?

except for too much	abgesehen von zu viel

MR. NEUMANN

HERR NEUMANN

All right, except for too much work of course.	Ganz gut, abgesehen von zuviel Arbeit natürlich.

the song loaded down, overburdened	das Lied,-er überlastet

MR. MEYER

HERR MEYER

Yes, the same old story; I'm pretty well loaded down too right now.	Ja, das alte Lied; ich bin zur Zeit auch ziemlich überlastet.

you know this evening, tonight the lecture to give a lecture	ihr wisst heute abend[6] der Vortrag,-̈e einen Vortrag halten

What I wanted to say was - you know that Professor Albers is giving a lecture tonight.	Was ich sagen wollte - ihr wisst doch, dass Professor Albers heute abend einen Vortrag hält.

you go	ihr geht
Are you going?	Geht ihr hin?

MR. NEUMANN HERR NEUMANN

Yes, you're going too, I hope.	Ja, ihr doch hoffentlich auch!
the repair shop	die Reparaturwerkstatt, ̈-en

MR. MEYER HERR MEYER

Unfortunately our car is still in the shop.	Unser Auto ist leider immer noch in der Reparaturwerkstatt.
your	eurem
Could we go with you in your car?	Könnten wir in eurem Wagen mitfahren?

MR. NEUMANN HERR NEUMANN

Of course, we'd be glad to have you.	Aber natürlich, gern.
shortly	kurz
before	vor (plus dative)
at your house	bei euch
to come by	vorbeikommen
We'll come by your house shortly before eight. Is that all right with you?	Wir kommen kurz vor acht bei euch vorbei. Passt euch das?

MR. MEYER HERR MEYER

Fine. Well then, we'll see you later.	Sehr gut. Also dann bis nachher.

Notes to the Basic Sentences

[1] Germans do not say: "this afternoon, this evening" but, literally, "today afternoon, today evening". Heute occurs in phrases with any of the words for the general time of day: heute morgen, heute mittag, etc.

[2] Both das Haar and the plural die Haare are used in German, whereas we use only the singular form "hair" in English.

[3] The infinitives gehen and fahren are often omitted with the auxiliary verbs müssen, können, möchte(n), dürfen, sollen and wollen when the idea of motion is clearly indicated by the rest of the sentence.

[4] As a sign of respect, both in direct address and in referring to a third person Germans use Herr plus the person's title: Herr Doktor, Herr Konsul, Herr Kollege, Herr Wachtmeister, Herr Ober, Herr Professor, etc.

[5] In an office situation Germans usually say: Er will ihn sprechen or Ich möchte Sie sprechen, with an accusative form. In a social situation they more often say: Er will mit ihm sprechen or Ich möchte mit Ihnen sprechen, with the preposition mit and a dative form.

[6] In English the choice of "this evening" or "tonight" depends on the formality of the situation in which the speaker finds himself. Both expressions indicate the period roughly from dinnertime to bed-time. Germans always say heute abend, however, in referring to this period of time.

Notes on Grammar

(For Home Study)

A.   VERB FORMS IN FAMILIAR SPEECH

I. German has three different words for <u>you</u>.

Wollen <u>Sie</u> nicht Platz nehmen, Herr Allen?	Won't <u>you</u> sit down, Mr. Allen?
Maria, <u>du</u> kennst doch Herrn Becker, nicht wahr?	Maria, <u>you</u> know Mr. Becker, don't you?
Geht <u>ihr</u> hin?	Are <u>you</u> going?

The different words for <u>you</u> in German indicate different situations and different social relationships. <u>Sie</u> indicates a formal relationship between the speaker and the person or persons addressed. There is no distinction between singular and plural. <u>Du</u> indicates a familiar or intimate relation- ship, but where only one person is addressed. <u>Ihr</u> indicates that two or more people are being addressed with whom the speaker is on familiar or intimate terms.

Outside of the family circle itself the familiar forms are used only with very close friends. Most Germans regard this relationship in a very special light and do not enter into it lightly after childhood years. The use of the familiar <u>du</u> and <u>ihr</u> forms is very much more restricted among Germans than the use of first names among Americans, for instance. The familiar forms are used by all adults in talking to children below the age of puberty, however. They are also used with animals and in addressing the deity.

II. New verb forms are also used with the familiar words for <u>you</u>.

1. The form of the verb with <u>du</u> is found from the er-form in the following ways:

a. In verbs whose er-form ends in -t, the final -t is replaced by -st.

er komm-t	er fähr-t	er ha-t	er arbeit-e-t	er find-e-t
du komm-st	du fähr-st	du ha-st	du arbeit-e-st	du find-e-st

Notice that the connecting vowel -e- is generally retained in the <u>du</u>-form when it occurs in the <u>er</u>-form (after -d- or -t-), although it is sometimes lost in rapid speech.

<u>Remember</u> that final -b or -g in <u>er</u>-form stems have the <u>sounds</u> of final $/\,p\,/$ or $/\,k\,/$!

er gib-t	"gip-t"	er leg-t	"lek-t"
du gib-st	"gip-st"	du leg-st	"lek-st"

b. In verbs whose er-form ending -t is preceded by -s- or -z-, the -s- of the <u>du</u>-form ending is lost, so that in these cases the <u>du</u>-form turns out to be identical with the <u>er</u>-form.

er lies-t	er läss-t	er sitz-t	er heiss-t	er vergiss-t
du lies-t	du läss-t	du sitz-t	du heiss-t	du vergiss-t

c. In verbs whose <u>er</u>-form does not end in -t, -st is added.

er will	er kann	er soll	er darf	er möchte
du will-st	du kann-st	du soll-st	du darf-st	du möchte-st

Note however that the -s- of the <u>du</u>-form ending is lost after a preceding -s-.

er muss	er weiss
du muss-t	du weiss-t

d. The following <u>du</u>- and <u>er</u>-forms show irregularities.

er ist   er wird   er hält
du bist   du wirst   du hältst

2. The form of the verb with <u>ihr</u> is arrived at as follows:

a. The -en ending of the <u>wir</u>-form is replaced by -t in most verbs.

| wir komm-en | wir les-en | wir müss-en | wir besuch-en | wir arbeit-en |
| ihr komm-t | ihr les-t | ihr müss-t | ihr besuch-t | ihr arbeit-e-t |

Notice that a connecting vowel appears here also after -d- or -t-.
<u>Remember</u> that stems ending in -b or -g will have the <u>sounds</u> $\underline{/}$ b $\underline{/}$ and $\underline{/}$ g $\underline{/}$
in the <u>wir</u>-form before the ending -en, but will have the <u>sounds</u> $\underline{/}$ p $\underline{/}$ and
$\underline{/}$ k $\underline{/}$ in the <u>ihr</u>-form before the ending -t!

wir geb-en   "geb-en"   wir trag-en   "trag-en"
ihr geb-t   "gep-t"   ihr trag-t   "trak-t"

b. There is one irregular form.

wir sind
ihr seid

III. There are three COMMAND or IMPERATIVE forms in German corresponding to
the three words for <u>you</u>.

1. In situations where the word for <u>you</u> is <u>Sie</u> the COMMAND form consists
of the verb form ending in -en followed by the pronoun <u>Sie</u>.

Grüssen Sie bitte Ihre   Please give my regards to Mrs. Allen.
Frau Gemahlin.
Herr Ober, bringen Sie   Waiter, please bring me calves' liver
mir bitte Kalbsleber mit   with mashed potatoes and apple sauce.
Kartoffelpüree und Apfel-
mus.

Note that the <u>Sie</u>-COMMAND form of the verb <u>sein</u> is irregular:

Seien Sie ruhig!   Be quiet!

2. In situations where the word for <u>you</u> is <u>ihr</u> the COMMAND form consists
of the <u>ihr</u>-form of the verb alone, with <u>no</u> pronoun following.

Kommt doch heute abend   Do come over and see us tonight!
zu uns!
Vergesst eure Bücher   Don't forget your books!
nicht!
Seid bitte um vier Uhr   Be at our house at four o'clock, now!
bei uns!

3. In situations where the word for <u>you</u> is <u>du</u> a special COMMAND form is
used with no pronoun following.

a. For the majority of German verbs this special COMMAND form is the
same as the infinitive or <u>wir</u>-for STEM, that is, the infinitive
or <u>wir</u>-form minus the ending -en.

Beeil' dich, Klaus!   Hurry up, Klaus!
Lass dir die Haare   Get your hair cut.
schneiden.
Lauf', damit du nicht   Run, so you won't be late.
zu spät kommst.
Hol' mich dort um eins   Pick me up there at one.
ab.

This COMMAND form alternatively has an ending -e which is often <u>written</u> or is indicated in the writing system by an apostrophe as above but is <u>not spoken</u> by most Germans.

Beeile dich.	Hole mich in einer Stunde ab.

b. For a few verbs the COMMAND form regularly has the ending -e added to the infinitive or <u>wir</u>-form stem. These are verbs whose stems end in -t or -d or in an <u>unstressed</u> syllable.

Entschuldige, dass ich störe.	Excuse me for disturbing you.
Arbeite nicht so viel!	Don't work so much!

c. In verbs like <u>sprechen</u> and <u>lesen</u> whose STEM sometimes has the vowel -e- and sometimes -i- (or -ie-) the COMMAND form is the same as the <u>du</u>-form STEM, that is, the <u>du</u>-form minus the ending -st (or -t).

Vergiss dein Frühstücksbrot nicht.	Don't forget your lunch.
Nimm doch bitte auch den blauen mit.	Take the blue one along too, please.
Lies den ganzen Artikel.	Read the whole article.

d. The verb <u>sein</u> has an irregular COMMAND form.

Sei bitte um vier Uhr bei uns.	Be at our house at four o'clock, now.

B.   PRONOUNS AND POSSESSIVE WORDS IN FAMILIAR SPEECH

I. The three forms of the pronouns used in familiar, or intimate speech are as follows:

Nominative	du	ihr
Accusative	dich	euch
Dative	dir	euch

We have seen how they are used in some of the basic sentences; here are a few additional examples:

Wie geht es Ihnen, Herr Becker?	How are you, Mr. Becker?
Wie geht es dir, Klaus?	How are you, Klaus?
Na, Klaus und Gerhard, wie geht es euch?	Well, Klaus and Gerhard, how are you?
Beeilen Sie sich!	
Beeil' dich!	Hurry up!
Beeilt euch!	
Lassen Sie sich die Haare schneiden.	
Lass dir die Haare schneiden.	Get your hair cut.
Lasst euch die Haare schneiden.	
Ich hole Sie dort um eins ab.	
Ich hole dich dort um eins ab.	I'll pick you up there at one.
Ich hole euch dort um eins ab.	
Darf ich mit Ihnen mitfahren?	
Darf ich mit dir mitfahren?	May I go along with you?
Darf ich mit euch mitfahren?	

II. The possessive words that go with <u>du</u> and <u>ihr</u> are <u>dein</u> and <u>euer</u>. Like the other possessive words (see Unit 4) they are <u>ein</u>-type specifiers and have the following forms:

	with <u>der</u>-nouns	with <u>das</u>-nouns	with <u>die</u>-nouns	with plural nouns
Nominative	dein	dein	deine	deine
Accusative	deinen	dein	deine	deine
Dative	deinem	deinem	deiner	deinen
Genitive	deines	deines	deiner	deiner
Nominative	euer	euer	eure	eure
Accusative	euren	euer	eure	eure
Dative	eurem	eurem	eurer	euren
Genitive	eures	eures	eurer	eurer

Note that the forms of <u>dein</u> correspond exactly to the forms of <u>mein</u>, <u>sein</u>, etc., as given in Unit 4. Note also that <u>euer</u> has a shorter form <u>eur-</u> before endings.

III. The familiar possessive words may occur in any of the <u>ein</u>-type specifier sequences and also, in the special forms noted in Unit 4, standing alone when the noun is understood.

> Hast du <u>dein</u> Frühstücksbrot?
> Ich will <u>deinen</u> grauen Anzug reinigen lassen.
> Kannst du auch meine Oberhemden mitnhemn, wenn du <u>deine</u> in die Wäscherei bringst?
> Das ist mein Pullover. Wo ist <u>deiner</u>?
> Könnten wir in <u>eurem</u> Wagen mitfahren?
> Wollt ihr <u>eure</u> Sommeranzüge auch reinigen lassen?
> Das ist aber ein schöner Wagen! Ist das <u>eurer</u>?

C.   THE AUXILIARY VERB <u>LASSEN</u>

The auxiliary verb <u>lassen</u> occurs in verb phrases with an infinitive, just as <u>können</u>, <u>müssen</u>, <u>werden</u>, etc. (see Units 2, 3 & 9). English has a similar verb phrase with a form of the verbs <u>have</u> or <u>get</u> and a participle.

> Lass dir auch die Haare schneiden.   Get your hair cut, too.
> Lassen Sie diesen Artikel doch bitte übersetzen.   Have this article translated, please.
> Ich lasse heute nachmittag meine Schuhe besohlen.   I'm getting my shoes soled this afternoon.
> Weisst du, wo Klaus seine Anzüge reinigen lässt?   Do you know where Klaus has his suits cleaned?

D.   COMPLEX VERB PHRASES

Most of the verb phrases encountered hitherto have consisted of two parts: an auxiliary verb and an infinitive (like the examples with <u>lassen</u> above) or a verb and an accented adverb (<u>Hol</u>' mich um eins <u>ab</u>). Some examples of verb phrases containing both an accented adverb and an infinitive have also occurred (Ich <u>werde</u> meinen Mantel <u>anziehen</u>). In this unit we now have an example of a verb phrase consisting of three parts:

> Ich <u>will</u> deinen grauen Anzug   I want to have your grey suit cleaned.
> <u>reinigen</u> <u>lassen</u>.

Here the auxiliary verb (<u>will</u>) has occurred together with a second auxiliary verb in the infinitive form (<u>lassen</u>) plus the infinitive (<u>reinigen</u>).

Let us examine some additional examples of COMPLEX VERB PHRASES:

Ich <u>werde</u> leider nicht vor acht Uhr <u>kommen</u> <u>können</u>.	Unfortunately I won't be able to come before eight o'clock.
Herr Schneider <u>soll</u> ausgezeichnet Ski <u>laufen</u> <u>können</u>.	Mr. Schneider is supposed to be an excellent skier.
Ich <u>werde</u> spätestens um halb vier <u>abfahren</u> <u>müssen</u>.	I'll have to leave at half past three at the latest.
<u>Wollen</u> Sie sich die Haare <u>schneiden</u> <u>lassen</u>?	Do you want to have your hair cut?

Note that when two infinitives stand together in this way the auxiliary infinitive is always last.

E.   DERIVATIVE NOUNS

In German as in English a number of nouns can be formed from other words (verbs, adjectives, other nouns), usually by the addition of a noun-forming suffix. Examples are such words as <u>print-ing</u>, <u>good-ness</u>, <u>friend-ship</u>, <u>practical-ity</u>. The process is not indiscriminate or automatic, however, and only certain words lend themselves to it.

1. The simplest formation consists in the use of the infinitive as a noun. Note that it is always a <u>das</u>-noun. The English equivalent may be either the <u>-ing</u> form of the verb (used as a noun) or a related noun or in some cases a completely different word.

essen	to eat	das Essen,-	food, meal
einrichten	to arrange	das Einrichten	the act of arranging
aussehen	to look, appear	das Aussehen	appearance
schreiben	to write	das Schreiben,-	writing (as a skill), official letter
wissen	to know	das Wissen	knowing (about something), knowledge

Form nouns 'from the following infinitives and give their English equivalents:

gehen   rauchen   können   reinigen   sprechen   treffen   leben   denken

2. There are a number of examples of a <u>die</u>-word formed from a <u>der</u>-word by the addition of the suffix <u>-in</u>. These words all designate the feminine counterpart of the masculine word. Compare the English suffixes <u>-ess</u> and <u>-ix</u>: <u>actr-ess</u>, <u>aviatr-ix</u>:

der Gemahl	husband (very formal)	die Gemahlin,-nen	wife (very formal)
der Sekretär	secretary (man)	die Sekretärin,-nen	secretary (woman)
der Freund	friend (man)	die Freundin,-nen	friend (woman)
der Amerikaner	American	die Amerikanerin,-nen	American (woman)

3. **Die**-words are formed from many infinitives by substitution of the suffix **-ung** for the ending **-en**.

besorgen	to attend to	die Besorgung,-en	errand
wohnen	to live, dwell	die Wohnung,-en	apartment
bestellen	to order	die Bestellung,-en	the order
ordnen	to put in order	die Ordnung	order, neatness
stellen	to put, place	die Stellung,-en	position

Form nouns of this type from the following infinitives and give their English equivalents:

> stören   verbinden   verzeihen   vorstellen   zahlen   bezahlen

4. **Der**-words are formed from many infinitives by substituting the suffix **-er** for the ending **-en**. Notice that these nouns all designate persons. A very few words have <u>umlaut</u> of the stem vowel with this suffix.

arbeiten	to work	der Arbeiter,-	worker
mieten	to rent	der Mieter,-	tenant, lessee
schreiben	to write	der Schreiber,-	clerk, scribe
verkaufen (¨)	to sell	der Verkäufer,-	sales clerk

Form nouns from the following infinitives and give their English equivalents:

> besuchen   denken   fahren   finden   hören   kaufen (¨)
> laufen (¨)   lesen   rauchen   trinken   übersetzen   vermieten

5. **Die**-words are formed from many adjectives by the addition of suffixes **-heit** or **-keit**. These suffixes thus work like English -ness, -ity, etc.

a. With suffix **-heit**:

schön	beautiful	die Schönheit,-en	beauty
rein	pure	die Reinheit,-en	purity
mehr	more	die Mehrheit,-en	majority

Form nouns from the following adjectives and give their English equivalents:

> berühmt   bestimmt   einfach   unbestimmt

b. With suffix **-keit**:

ähnlich	similar	die Ähnlichkeit,-en	similarity
möglich	possible	die Möglichkeit,-en	possibility
richtig	correct	die Richtigkeit	correctness

Form nouns from the following adjectives and give their English equivalents:

> gemütlich   langsam   natürlich   sauber
> wahrscheinlich   wichtig   wirklich   zufällig

6 **Die**-words are formed from certain other nouns by the addition of the suffix **-schaft**. This suffix works like English **-hood** and **-ship**. Some words have <u>umlaut</u> of the stem vowel with this suffix, and some nouns lose a final -e.

der Bruder (¨)	brother	die Brüderschaft,-en	brotherhood
der Bote	messenger	die Botschaft,-en	message; embassy
der Herr	gentleman	die Herrschaften (pl)	ladies and gentlemen
der Ort	place	die Ortschaft,-en	locality

Form nouns from the following nouns and give their English equivalents:

Bekannte   Freund   Nachbar   Vater   Verwandte

SUBSTITUTION DRILL

1. Ich muss <u>heute morgen</u> in die Stadt fahren.

heute abend - heute nachmittag - heute mittag

2. Hoffentlich verpassen wir <u>den Autobus</u> nicht.

die Strassenbahn - den englischen Konsul - Herrn Schneider - den Beamten - die französischen Diplomaten - Frau Kunze - den Polizisten - Ihren Bruder - seinen Freund - Ihre Tante

3. Er lässt <u>die Schuhe besohlen.</u>

den Wagen waschen - den Anzug reinigen - die Formulare ausfüllen - die Kisten heraufbringen - die Oberhemden waschen - die Briefe schreiben - den Artikel übersetzen

4. Ich will <u>deinen grauen Anzug</u> reinigen lassen.

meine braune Jacke - seinen hellgrauen Pullover - unsere weissen Wolldecken - deine gemusterte Krawatte

5. Nimm doch bitte auch <u>den blauen Anzug</u> mit.

deine schwarzen Schuhe - dein weisses Oberhemd - den langen Artikel - die neue Zeitung - die saubere Wäsche - deinen warmen Pullover - den alten Mantel - deine kurze Jacke

6. Beeil' dich, damit du <u>nicht zu spät kommst.</u>

nicht den Omnibus verpasst - noch zum Zahnarzt kommst - noch mitfahren kannst - nicht das Konzert verpasst

7. Ich gebe dir noch Geld, damit du <u>die Schuhe abholen</u> kannst.

zum Frisör gehen - die Wäsche abholen - die Reinigung bezahlen - zur Apotheke fahren - die Bücher kaufen

8. Es handelt sich um <u>den Vortrag von Professor Albers.</u>

die Besprechung in der Handelskammer - den Artikel in dieser Zeitung - den Schulausflug der Kinder - die Unterlagen für die Konferenz die neuen Zollbestimmungen - unsere Fahrt nach Deutschland

9. Passt es <u>dir</u>, wenn wir um acht vorbeikommen?

euch - ihnen - ihm - ihr - Ihnen

10. Ich hoffe, du <u>hebst das Geld nicht ab.</u>

probierst die Jacke zuerst an - rufst Herrn Jones bald an - füllst das Formular jetzt aus - packst die Kisten nicht aus - richtest ihm das aus - fährst nach München mit - kommst heute abend vorbei - kommst bald zurück - kümmerst dich um das Gepäck - nimmst den Koffer mit

11. Herr Becker holt <u>mich</u> um fünf Uhr ab.

dich - ihn - Sie - euch - uns - deine Eltern - eure Freunde - Ihre Tante - den Konsul - die Damen - Herrn Becker

12. Ich möchte <u>Herrn Dr. Bergmann</u> sprechen.

Herrn Professor Albers - Herrn Wachtmeister König - Konsul Jones - Herrn Dr. Müller

13. Ich will jetzt <u>die Briefe schreiben</u> lassen.

den Artikel übersetzen - den Mantel reinigen - die Schuhe besohlen - diese Formulare ausfüllen - die Kisten heraufbringen - die Unterlagen bringen

14. Ein Herr <u>von der Botschaft</u> möchte Sie sprechen.

Generalkonsulat - Arbeitsamt - Handelskammer - Apotheke - Rathaus - Post - Zoll

vom Generalkonsulat - vom Arbeitsamt - von der Handelskammer - von der Apotheke - vom Rathaus - von der Post - vom Zoll

15. Wäscht <u>er sich</u> die Hände?

du - Sie - ihr - sie

wäschst du dir - waschen Sie sich - wascht ihr euch - wäscht sie sich

16. Ich hole dich um zwei <u>beim Frisör</u> ab.

Wäscherei - Schuster - Reinigung - Uhrmacher - Zahnarzt - Bank - Apotheke

bei der Wäscherei - beim Schuster - bei der Reinigung - beim Uhrmacher - beim Zahnarzt - bei der Bank - bei der Apotheke

17. <u>Du</u> musst <u>dir</u> die Haare schneiden lassen.

wir - sie - ihr - er - unsere Kinder - sie

wir müssen uns - sie müssen sich - ihr müsst euch - er muss sich - unsere Kinder müssen sich - sie muss sich

(End of Tape 11A)

Tape 11B   CONVERSION DRILL

I. Convert the following questions in the <u>er</u>-form to the <u>du</u>-form and the <u>ihr</u>-form as indicated.

1. Kommt er um fünf nach Hause?

Kommst du um fünf nach Hause?
Kommt ihr um fünf nach Hause?

2. Geht er heute nachmittag zum Schuster?

Gehst du heute nachmittag zum Schuster?
Geht ihr heute nachmittag zum Schuster?

3. Bestellt er die Bücher bald?

Bestellst du die Bücher bald?
Bestellt ihr die Bücher bald?

4. Verschläft er sich oft?

Verschläfst du dich oft?
Verschlaft ihr euch oft?

5. Kämmt er sich öfters die Haare?

Kämmst du dir öfters die Haare?
Kämmt ihr euch öfters die Haare?

6. Diktiert er gewöhnlich so schnell?

Diktierst du gewöhnlich so schnell?
Diktiert ihr gewöhnlich so schnell?

7. Fährt er mittags meistens nach   Fährst du mittags meistens nach Hause?
   Hause?   Fahrt ihr mittags meistens nach Hause?

8. Läuft er immer so langsam?   Läufst du immer so langsam?
                                      Lauft ihr immer so langsam?

9. Vergisst er die Briefe auch   Vergisst du die Briefe auch nicht?
   nicht?   Vergesst ihr die Briefe auch nicht?

10. Will er den Vortrag halten?   Willst du den Vortrag halten?
                                      Wollt ihr den Vortrag halten?

11. Wohnt er in der Stadt oder   Wohnst du in der Stadt oder im Vorort?
    im Vorort?   Wohnt ihr in der Stadt oder im Vorort?

12. Wäscht er seine Wäsche selbst   Wäschst du deine Wäsche selbst oder
    oder bringt er sie in die   bringst du sie in die Wäscherei?
    Wäscherei?   Wascht ihr eure Wäsche selbst oder
                                      bringt ihr sie in die Wäscherei?

13. Zieht er in die Stadt?   Ziehst du in die Stadt?
                                      Zieht ihr in die Stadt?

14. Wechselt er das Geld in der   Wechselst du das Geld in der Bank?
    Bank?   Wechselt ihr das Geld in der Bank?

15. Vermietet er eins seiner   Vermietest du eins deiner Zimmer?
    Zimmer?   Vermietet ihr eins eurer Zimmer?

16. Tut er das gern?   Tust du das gern?
                                      Tut ihr das gern?

17. Trifft er sie immer auf dem   Triffst du sie immer auf dem
    Nachhauseweg?   Nachhauseweg?
                                      Trefft ihr sie immer auf dem
                                      Nachhauseweg?

18. Trägt er heute seinen neuen   Trägst du heute deinen neuen Anzug?
    Anzug?   Tragt ihr heute eure neuen Anzüge?

19. Steht er schon lange da?   Stehst du schon lange da?
                                      Steht ihr schon lange da?

20. Sitzt er gern in diesem Sessel?   Sitzt du gern in diesem Sessel?
                                      Sitzt ihr gern in diesem Sessel?

21. Setzt er sich wieder an diesen   Setzt du dich wieder an diesen Tisch?
    Tisch?   Setzt ihr euch wieder an diesen Tisch?

22. Schreibt er einen anderen   Schreibst du einen anderen Artikel?
    Artikel?   Schreibt ihr einen anderen Artikel?

23. Nimmt er wieder Kalbsleber mit   Nimmst du wieder Kalbsleber mit
    Kartoffelpüree?   Kartoffelpüree?
                                      Nehmt ihr wieder Kalbsleber mit
                                      Kartoffelpüree?

24. Mietet er die Wohnung in der   Mietest du die Wohnung in der Schubert-
    Schubertstrasse?   strasse?
                                      Mietet ihr die Wohnung in der Schubert-
                                      strasse?

25. Legt er die Briefe immer auf den Legst du die Briefe immer auf den
    Schreibtisch?   Schreibtisch?
                                      Legt ihr die Briefe immer auf den
                                      Schreibtisch?

26. Leiht er uns die Schreib-
    maschine?

Leihst du uns die Schreibmaschine?
Leiht ihr uns die Schreibmaschine?

27. Lebt er schon lange in
    Deutschland?

Lebst du schon lange in Deutschland?
Lebt ihr schon lange in Deutschland?

28. Kennt er den Uhrmacher gut?

Kennst du den Uhrmacher gut?
Kennt ihr den Uhrmacher gut?

29. Kauft er seine Anzüge im
    Herrenkonfektionsgeschäft?

Kaufst du deine Anzüge im
Herrenkonfektionsgeschäft?
Kauft ihr eure Anzüge im
Herrenkonfektionsgeschäft?

30. Hört er die Nachrichten um
    sieben oder um acht?

Hörst du die Nachrichten um sieben
oder um acht?
Hört ihr die Nachrichten um sieben
oder um acht?

31. Holt er heute seine Eltern ab?

Holst du heute deine Eltern ab?
Holt ihr heute eure Eltern ab?

32. Hilft er beim Einrichten?

Hilfst du beim Einrichten?
Helft ihr beim Einrichten?

33. Heisst er Bauer oder Brauer?

Heisst du Bauer oder Brauer?
Heisst ihr Bauer oder Brauer?

34. Hält er vor dem Hotel?

Hältst du vor dem Hotel?
Haltet ihr vor dem Hotel?

35. Hat er die Unterlagen bei
    sich?

Hast du die Unterlagen bei dir?
Habt ihr die Unterlagen bei euch?

36. Gibt er ihm ein Frühstücks-
    brot?

Gibst du ihm ein Frühstücksbrot?
Gebt ihr ihm ein Frühstücksbrot?

37. Findet er den Artikel?

Findest du den Artikel?
Findet ihr den Artikel?

38. Isst er abends gewöhnlich
    warm?

Isst du abends gewöhnlich warm?
Esst ihr abends gewöhnlich warm?

39. Denkt er, dass es in Deutsch-
    land kälter ist als hier?

Denkst du, dass es in Deutschland
kälter ist als hier?
Denkt ihr, dass es in Deutschland
kälter ist als hier?

40. Braucht er ein neues Auto?

Brauchst du ein neues Auto?
Braucht ihr ein neues Auto?

II. Convert the following commands in the Sie-form to commands in the du-form
    and in the ihr-form.

1. Zeigen Sie mir bitte Ihr Gepäck.

Zeig' mir bitte dein Gepäck.
Zeigt mir bitte euer Gepäck.

2. Gehen Sie hier durch den Park.

Geh' hier durch den Park.
Geht hier durch den Park.

3. Kommen Sie doch mal am nächsten
   Sonntag zu uns.

Komm' doch mal am nächsten Sonntag
zu uns.
Kommt doch mal am nächsten Sonntag
zu uns.

4. Entschuldigen Sie, dass ich   Entschuldige, dass ich störe.
   störe.   Entschuldigt, dass ich störe.

5. Sehen Sie mal diese dunklen   Sieh mal diese dunklen Wolken am
   Wolken am Himmel.   Himmel.
                                         Seht mal diese dunklen Wolken am
                                         Himmel.

6. Sagen Sie ihm doch bitte, er   Sag' ihm doch bitte, er möchte mich
   möchte mich anrufen.   anrufen.
                                         Sagt ihm doch bitte, er möchte mich
                                         anrufen.

7. Bringen Sie bitte die Wäsche   Bring' doch bitte die Wäsche in die
   in die Wäscherei.   Wäscherei.
                                         Bringt doch bitte die Wäsche in die
                                         Wäscherei.

8. Kommen Sie doch bitte nicht   Komm' doch bitte nicht zu spät.
   zu spät.   Kommt doch bitte nicht zu spät.

9. Bleiben Sie bitte noch eine   Bleib' bitte noch eine Stunde hier.
   Stunde hier.   Bleibt bitte noch eine Stunde hier.

10. Lesen Sie doch mal diesen   Lies doch mal diesen Artikel.
    Artikel.   Lest doch mal diesen Artikel.

III. Change the following sentences into clauses in the sentence beginning
     Ihr wisst doch, dass ...

   1. Professor Albers hält heute   Ihr wisst doch, dass Professor Albers
      den Vortrag.   heute den Vortrag hält.

   2. Sie ist beim Frisör.   Ihr wisst doch, dass sie beim Frisör
                                        ist.

   3. Die Schuhe sind beim Schuster.   Ihr wisst doch, dass die Schuhe beim
                                        Schuster sind.

   4. Er sitzt am Frühstückstisch.   Ihr wisst doch, dass er am Frühstücks-
                                        tisch sitzt.

   5. Die Hemden sind noch in der   Ihr wisst doch, dass die Hemden noch
      Wäscherei.   in der Wäscherei sind.

   6. Beckers vermieten ihr Haus.   Ihr wisst doch, dass Beckers ihr Haus
                                        vermieten.

   7. Die Besprechung findet heute   Ihr wisst doch, dass die Besprechung
      nicht statt.   heute nicht stattfindet.

   8. Unser Auto ist noch in der   Ihr wisst doch, dass unser Auto noch
      Reparaturwerkstatt.   in der Reparaturwerkstatt ist.

IV. Change the following questions into clauses in the question beginning
    Weisst du, ...

   1. Wann will er sich die Haare   Weisst du, wann er sich die Haare
      schneiden lassen?   schneiden lassen will?

   2. Wo kann ich mir die Schuhe   Weisst du, wo ich mir die Schuhe
      besohlen lassen?   besohlen lassen kann?

3. Wo soll ich den Anzug   Weisst du, wo ich den Anzug reinigen
   reinigen lassen?   lassen soll?

4. Warum möchte er den Artikel   Weisst du, warum er den Artikel
   übersetzen lassen?   übersetzen lassen möchte?

5. Wo können wir uns die Sachen   Weisst du, wo wir uns die Sachen
   einpacken lassen?   einpacken lassen können?

6. Wo willst du die Hemden   Weisst du, wo du die Hemden waschen
   waschen lassen?   lassen willst?

7. Muss ich mich vorstellen   Weisst du, ob ich mich vorstellen
   lassen?   lassen muss?

8. Wann darf ich deine Eltern   Weisst du, wann ich deine Eltern ab-
   abholen lassen?   holen lassen darf?

9. Wen muss ich nach Hause   Weisst du, wen ich nach Hause bringen
   bringen lassen?   lassen muss?

10. Was soll ich Herrn Becker   Weisst du, was ich Herrn Becker aus-
    ausrichten lassen?   richten lassen soll?

VARIATION DRILL

1. <u>Du schreibst doch den Brief, nicht</u>   <u>You're going to write the letter,</u>
   <u>wahr?</u>   <u>aren't you?</u>

   a. You're going to the post office,   Du gehst doch zur Post, nicht wahr?
      aren't you?
   b. You're going to pick up the   Du holst doch die Schuhe ab, nicht
      shoes, aren't you?   wahr?
   c. You're going to give him the   Du gibst ihm das Geld doch, nicht
      money, aren't you?   wahr?
   d. You're driving down town, aren't   Du fährst doch in die Stadt, nicht
      you?   wahr?

2. (the same sentences in the familiar plural)

3. <u>Ihr kommt zu spät.</u>   <u>You're late.</u>

   a. You read too much.   Ihr lest zu viel.
   b. You won't reach him today.   Ihr erreicht ihn heute nicht.
   c. You ask too many questions ('too   Ihr fragt zuviel.
      much').
   d. You don't work enough.   Ihr arbeitet nicht genug.
   e. You are somewhat loaded down.   Ihr seid etwas überlastet.

4. (the same sentences in the familiar singular)

5. <u>Ich treffe dich morgen hier.</u>   <u>I'll meet you (sg) here tomorrow.</u>

   a. We'll take you (pl) with us   Wir nehmen euch heute abend mit.
      tonight.
   b. I'll pick you (sg) up shortly   Ich hole dich kurz vor acht Uhr ab.
      before eight o'clock.
   c. She's expecting you (pl) at six.   Sie erwartet euch um sechs.
   d. He'll call you (sg) this after-   Er ruft dich heute nachmittag an.
      noon.
   e. We don't need you tomorrow,   Wir brauchen Sie morgen nicht,
      Miss Becker.   Fräulein Becker.

6. <u>Sie wäscht sich gerade die Hände.</u>   <u>She's just washing her hands.</u>

   a. I'm combing my hair.   Ich kämme mir die Haare.
   b. Are you buying yourselves a   Kauft ihr euch einen neuen Wagen?
      new car?
   c. Do you cut your hair yourself?   Schneidest du dir die Haare selbst?
   d. Do you want to borrow my little   Willst du dir mein kleines Radio
      radio?   leihen?
   e. Do you (all) want to wash your   Wollt ihr euch die Hände waschen?
      hands?

7. <u>Geht ihr auch zum Vortrag?</u>   <u>Are you going to the lecture too?</u>

   a. Are you coming to the concert   Kommt ihr auch zum Konzert?
      too?
   b. Are you staying down town too?   Bleibt ihr auch in der Stadt?
   c. Are you eating at the restaurant   Esst ihr auch im Restaurant?
      too?
   d. Do you buy at this store too?   Kauft ihr auch in diesem Geschäft?
   e. Do you live in the suburbs too?   Wohnt ihr auch im Vorort?

8. <u>Ist das eure Zeitung?</u>   <u>Is that your newspaper?</u>

   a. Do you have a telephone in your   Habt ihr ein Telephon in eurem Zimmer?
      room?
   b. Do you visit your parents often?   Besucht ihr eure Eltern oft?
   c. Is that the address of your   Ist das die Adresse eures Hotels?
      hotel?
   d. I really like your new car.   Euer neues Auto gefällt mir wirklich
                                            gut.
   e. Does Mr. Schneider live in your   Wohnt Herr Schneider auch in eurem
      apartment house too?   Etagenhaus?

9. (the same sentences in the familiar singular)

10. <u>Das ist wirklich ein schöner Mantel.</u>   <u>That really is a beautiful coat.</u>
   <u>Ist das deiner?</u>   <u>Is it yours?</u>

   a. My, but that's a small car. Is   Das ist aber ein kleines Auto. Ist
      it yours (pl)?   das eures?
   b. My, but those are nice-looking   Das sind aber schöne Schuhe. Sind das
      shoes. Are they yours (sg)?   deine?
   c. That really is a warm coat. Is   Das ist wirklich ein warmer Mantel.
      it yours (sg)?   Ist das deiner?
   d. My, but those are short jackets.   Das sind aber kurze Jacken. Sind das
      Are they yours (pl)?   eure?
   e. My, but that's an old book. Is   Das ist aber ein altes Buch. Ist das
      it yours(sg)?   deins?
   f. That really is a nice tie. Is   Das ist wirklich eine schöne Krawatte.
      it yours (sg)?   Ist das deine?

11. <u>Komm' schnell nach Hause!</u>   <u>Come home quickly!</u>

   a. Don't forget the shoes!   Vergiss die Schuhe nicht!
   b. Go to the shoemaker's first!   Geh' erst zum Schuster!
   c. Take the blue suit with you.   Nimm den blauen Anzug mit.
   d. Comb your hair!   Kämm' dir die Haare!
   e. Wash your hands!   Wasch' dir die Hände!

12. <u>Wisst ihr, dass wir bald nach</u>   <u>Do you know that we're going to Germany</u>
   <u>Deutschland fahren?</u>   <u>soon?</u>

   a. Do you know, whether the school   Wisst ihr, ob der Schulausflug morgen
      outing is tomorrow?   stattfindet?
   b. Are you hoping too that the   Hofft ihr auch, dass Meyers bald
      Meyers leave soon?   abfahren?

c. Do you believe that the conference is going to begin tomorrow?

Glaubt ihr, dass die Konferenz morgen anfängt?

d. Do you think that the secretary can translate that?

Denkt ihr, dass die Sekretärin das übersetzen kann?

e. Do you expect that they will visit you?

Erwartet ihr, dass sie euch besuchen?

13. Findest du nicht auch, dass die Wohnung sehr teuer ist?

Don't you think too that the apartment is very expensive?

a. Do you think ('believe') that we're late?

Glaubst du, dass wir zu spät kommen?

b. Are you going to tell him that you want him to come to the conference?

Sagst du ihm, dass er zur Besprechung kommen möchte?

c. Do you know whether he's going to the Chamber of Commerce?

Weisst du, ob er zur Handelskammer geht?

d. Do you think that the car is still out of order?

Denkst du, dass das Auto noch kaputt ist?

e. Do you expect that he's going to call up soon?

Erwartest du, dass er bald anruft?

14. Lassen Sie diesen Artikel doch übersetzen, Herr Meyer.

Have this article translated, Mr. Meyer.

a. Have these shirts washed, please (fam sg).

Lass diese Oberhemden bitte waschen.

b. Have the shoes soled too (fam pl).

Lasst die Schuhe auch besohlen.

c. Have your hair cut, please (fam sg).

Lass dir die Haare bitte schneiden.

d. Have the apartment cleaned too, please, Mrs. Köhler.

Lassen Sie die Wohnung bitte auch saubermachen, Frau Köhler.

15. Du musst den Artikel übersetzen lassen.

You (fam sg) will have to have the article translated.

a. You (fam pl) can have the laundry picked up.

Ihr könnt die Wäsche abholen lassen.

b. They're supposed to have the forms filled out.

Sie sollen die Formulare ausfüllen lassen.

c. I have to have my shoes soled.

Ich muss mir die Schuhe besohlen lassen.

d. She wants to have the tire changed.

Sie will den Reifen wechseln lassen.

16. Hol' doch bitte die Schuhe beim Schuster ab.

Pick up the shoes at the shoemaker's please.

a. Go to the post office and get ten stamps, please.

Geh' doch bitte zur Post und hol' zehn Briefmarken.

b. Don't expect us too early.

Erwarte uns nicht zu früh.

c. Take these letters along with you to the post office.

Nimm doch diese Briefe mit zur Post.

d. Turn the radio on, please.

Stell' bitte das Radio an.

e. Please give me Gerhard's telephone number.

Gib mir doch bitte mal Gerhards Telephonnummer.

17. (the same sentences in the familiar plural)

18. Seid nicht so langsam, sonst verpasst ihr noch die Strassenbahn.

Don't be so slow, or else you miss the streetcar.

a. Please be at our house at quarter past five (fam pl).

Seid bitte um viertel sechs bei uns.

b. Please be at my house tonight
   at seven o'clock (fam sg).

Bitte sei heute abend um sieben Uhr
bei mir.

c. Be quiet; father's working
   (fam sg).

Sei ruhig, Vater arbeitet.

d. Please be at my place at nine-
   thirty, Mr. König.

Seien Sie bitte um neun Uhr dreissig
bei mir, Herr König.

e. Be nice to your friend, Klaus!

Sei nett zu deinem Freund, Klaus.

f. Please be quiet, gentlemen;
   there's an important conference
   next door.

Seien Sie bitte ruhig, meine Herren --
nebenan ist eine wichtige Besprechung.

19. Er muss heute nachmittag zur Bank.

He has to /‾go‾/ to the bank this
afternoon.

a. I'd like to /‾go‾/ down town
   tomorrow.

Ich möchte morgen gern in die Stadt.

b. I have to /‾go‾/ to the post
   office, too.

Ich muss noch zur Post.

c. I want to /‾go‾/ to the dentist
   today.

Ich will heute zum Zahnarzt.

d. Do you have to /‾go‾/ to the
   watchmaker's too?

Musst du noch zum Uhrmacher?

e. She wants to /‾go‾/ to the hairdresser's this afternoon.

Sie will heute nachmittag zum Frisör.

20. Ein Herr von der englischen
    Botschaft will Sie sprechen.

A gentleman from the British Embassy
wants to talk to you.

a. May I please talk to Dr. Bergmann?

Darf ich bitte Herrn Dr. Bergmann
sprechen?

b. I'd like to talk to Professor
   Albers.

Ich möchte gern Herrn Professor
Albers sprechen.

c. Do you wish to speak to Consul
   Wilson?

Wollen Sie Herrn Konsul Wilson
sprechen?

d. I must speak to Officer König.

Ich muss Herrn Wachtmeister König
sprechen.

e. Can I talk to your colleague?

Kann ich Ihren Herrn Kollegen
sprechen?

VOCABULARY DRILL

1. zu spät kommen - "to be late"

a. Hoffenltich kommt er nicht
   wieder zu spät!

I hope he's not late again!

b. Ich möchte wirklich nicht zu
   spät kommen.

I really shouldn't like to be late.

c. Beckers kommen meistens zu spät.

The Beckers are usually late.

d. Wahrscheinlich kommen wir zu
   spät.

We'll probably be late.

e Er wird sicher wieder zu spät
  kommen.

He'll surely be late again.

2. besorgen - "to attend to, take care of"

a. Hast du heute viel zu besorgen?

Do you have a lot to attend to today?

b. Wir haben heute nichts (nicht
   viel) zu besorgen.

We don't have anything to attend to
today.

c. Ich will morgen einige Sachen
   besorgen.

I want to attend to a few things
tomorrow.

d. Habt ihr heute etwas zu besorgen?

Do you have something to attend to
today?

e Könnt ihr das nicht nächste
  Woche besorgen?

Can't you take care of that next
week?

3. <u>erwarten</u> - "to expect"

a. Wann erwarten Sie uns?	When do you expect us?
b. Herr Becker erwartet Sie heute um drei Uhr.	Mr. Becker expects you at three o'clock today.
c. Erwartet der Konsul, dass ich ihn anrufe?	Does the consul expect me to call him up ('that I call him up') ?
d. Der Zahnarzt erwartet dich morgen um eins.	The dentist expects you tomorrow at one.
e. Herr Dr. Bergmann erwartet uns zu einer Besprechung.	Dr. Bergmann is expecting us for a conference.

4. <u>abgesehen von</u> - "except for, apart from"

a. Abgesehen von zuviel Arbeit geht es mir ganz gut.	Except for too much work I'm quite all right.
b. Abgesehen von der Reifenpanne war die Reise sehr schön.	Apart from the flat tire the trip was very nice.
c. Abgesehen von dem Klima gefällt es mir hier sehr gut.	Apart from the climate I like it here very much.
d. Abgesehen vom Gewitter war der Spaziergang sehr schön.	Except for the thunder shower the walk was very nice.

5. <u>einen Vortrag halten</u> - "to give a lecture"

a. Herr Professor Albers hält heute in der Handelskammer einen Vortrag.	Professor Albers is giving a lecture at the Chamber of Commerce today.
b. Wann werden Sie Ihren Vortrag halten?	When will you be giving your lecture?
c. Nächsten Monat soll Dr. Bergmann einen Vortrag halten.	Next month Dr. Bergmann is supposed to be giving a lecture.
d. Ich weiss nicht, wann er seinen Vortrag hält.	I don't know when he's giving his lecture.

6. <u>bevor</u> - "before"

a. Bevor ich zur Konferenz gehe, möchte ich Ihnen noch einen Brief diktieren, Fräulein Neumann.	Before I go to the conference I'd like to dictate a letter to you, Miss Neumann.
b. Wasch' dir die Hände, bevor du dich an den Frühstückstisch setzt.	Wash your hands before you sit down at the breakfast table.
c. Bevor ich dich abhole, will ich noch zum Uhrmacher.	Before I pick you up I just want to /_go_/ to the watchmaker's.
d. Ich muss die englische Botschaft anrufen, bevor ich zur Besprechung gehe.	I have to call up the British Embassy before I go to the conference.
e. Bring' bitte erst den Brief zur Post, bevor du ins Kino gehst.	Take the letter to the post office, please, before you go to the movies.

7. <u>noch</u> - "too"

a. Dann möchte ich noch zur Apotheke gehen.	Then I'd like to go to the pharmacy too.
b. Dann kann ich noch zur Bank gehen.	Then I can go to the bank too.
c. Ich will mir noch ein paar Ansichtskarten kaufen.	I want to buy (myself) a few picture postcards too.
d. Wir möchten noch zum Arbeitsamt fahren.	We'd like to go to the employment office too.
e. Ihr müsst noch die Kisten wegschaffen.	You'll have to clear away the crates too.

(End of Tape 11B)

TRANSLATION DRILL (not recorded)

1. Mr. and Mrs. Neumann are seated at the breakfast-table.
   Herr und Frau Neumann sitzen am Frühstückstisch.
2. Mr. Neumann would like to know where Klaus is.
   Herr Neumann möchte wissen, wo Klaus ist.
3. He has to hurry so that he doesn't miss the bus.
   Er muss sich beeilen, damit er den Autobus nicht verpasst.
4. He just has to comb his hair still and wash his hands.
   Er muss sich nur noch kämmen und seine Hände waschen.
5. Then he looks for his brown shoes.
   Dann sucht er seine braunen Schuhe.
6. Mrs. Neumann tells him that they're at the shoemaker's.
   Frau Neumann sagt ihm, dass sie beim Schuster sind.
7. Klaus can pick them up in the afternoon.
   Klaus kann sie nachmittags abholen.
8. Klaus would like to have some money, since he has a school outing today.
   Klaus möchte gern etwas Geld haben, da er heute einen Schulausflug hat.
9. Mr. Neumann gives him six marks.
   Herr Neumann gibt ihm sechs Mark.
10. He's supposed to get his hair cut (from it) too before he comes home.
    Er soll sich davon auch die Haare schneiden lassen, bevor er nach Hause kommt.
11. Mrs. Neumann gives him his lunch.
    Frau Neumann gibt ihm sein Frühstücksbrot.
12. Now Klaus has to run quickly however, or else he'll be late.
    Jetzt muss Klaus aber schnell laufen, sonst kommt er zu spät.
13. A little later the Neumanns drive down town together.
    Etwas später fahren Neumann zusammen in die Stadt.
14. Mrs. Neumann has a good deal to attend to.
    Frau Neumann hat eine ganze Menge zu besorgen.
15. First she has to go to the cleaners.
    Zuerst muss sie zur Reinigung gehen.
16. She wants to have her husband's grey suit cleaned.
    Sie will den grauen Anzug ihres Mannes reinigen lassen.
17. She's supposed to take the blue one along with her to the cleaners too.
    Den blauen soll sie auch zur Reinigung mitnehmen.
18. She'd like to take the shirts to the laundry.
    Die Oberhemden möchte sie zur Wäscherei bringen.
19. At ten o'clock she has to go to the dentist and be at the hairdresser's at twelve.
    Um zehn Uhr muss sie zum Zahnarzt gehen und um zwölf beim Frisör sein.
20. Mr. Neumann asks if he is (supposed) to pick up his wife there.
    Herr Neumann fragt, ob er seine Frau dort abholen soll.
21. Otherwise she can hardly be home before half past one.
    Sonst kann sie kaum vor halb zwei zu Hause sein.
22. She says she'd like him to be there at one.
    Sie sagt, er möchte um eins dort sein.
23. On the way home they have to /go/ to the watchmaker's and the pharmacy.
    Auf dem Nachhauseweg müssen sie zum Uhrmacher und zur Apotheke.
24. After lunch Mr. Neumann goes /back/ to the office again.
    Nach dem Essen fährt Herr Neumann wieder ins Büro.
25. The secretary says that Dr. Bergmann expects Mr. Neumann at five o'clock for a conference.
    Die Sekretärin sagt, dass Dr. Bergmann Herrn Neumann um fünf Uhr zu einer Besprechung erwartet.
26. It's about the new customs regulations, and Miss Keller gives him all the papers.
    Es handelt sich um die neuen Zollbestimmungen und Fräulein Keller gibt ihm alle Unterlagen.
27. A gentleman from the British Embassy wanted to talk to Mr. Neumann too, but the secretary doesn't know what about.
    Ein Herr von der englischen Botschaft wollte Herrn Neumann auch sprechen, aber die Sekretärin weiss nicht, in welcher Angelegenheit.
28. He's going to call back later.
    Er wird später nochmal anrufen.
29. Then Mr. Neumann dictates two letters to his secretary, one to the Chamber of Commerce and one to the employment office.
    Dann diktiert Herr Neumann seiner Sekretärin zwei Briefe, einen an die Handelskammer und einen an das Arbeitsamt.

30. He gives her an article also, and she is (supposed) to have it translated.	Er gibt ihr auch einen Artikel, und sie soll ihn übersetzen lassen.
31. A little later the telephone rings, and the secretary answers.	Etwas später klingelt das Telephon und die Sekretärin meldet sich.
32. Miss Keller tells Mr. Neumann that Mr. Meyer is on the wire.	Fräulein Keller sagt Herrn Neumann, dass Herr Meyer am Apparat ist.
33. Mr. Neumann tells her (he'd like her) to put him on please and then speaks with his friend.	Herr Neumann sagt ihr, sie möchte bitte umschalten und spricht dann mit seinem Freund.
34. He says that he's well, except for too much work.	Er sagt, dass es ihm gut geht, - abgesehen von zuviel Arbeit.
35. Mr. Meyer is pretty well loaded down too right now.	Herr Meyer ist zur Zeit auch ziemlich überlastet.
36. Then he would like to know if the Neumanns are going to Professor Albers' lecture.	Dann möchte er wissen, ob Neumanns zu dem Vortrag von Professor Albers gehen.
37. Mr. Neumann says that they are planning it.	Herr Neumann sagt, dass sie es vorhaben.
38. Unfortunately the Meyers' car is in the shop.	Leider ist das Auto von Meyers in der Reparaturwerkstatt.
39. They would like to ride in the Neumann's car with them.	Sie möchten gern in Neumanns Wagen mitfahren.
40. They plan to drive to the lecture together shortly before eight.	Kurz vor acht wollen sie zusammen zum Vortrag fahren.

RESPONSE DRILL (not recorded)

1. Warum sitzt Klaus nicht mit seinen Eltern am Frühstückstisch?.	Er kämmt sich gerade und muss sich noch die Hände waschen.
2. Warum muss er sich beeilen?	Er muss sich beeilen, da er sonst den Autobus verpasst.
3. Was sucht Klaus?	Er sucht seine Schuhe.
4. Wo sind die Schuhe?	Sie sind beim Schuster.
5. Warum sind sie beim Schuster?	Frau Neumann lässt sie besohlen.
6. Wann kann er die Schuhe abholen?	Er kann sie heute nachmittag abholen.
7. Warum will Klaus etwas Geld haben?	Er macht einen Schulausflug.
8. Wieviel Geld gibt ihm sein Vater?	Sein Vater gibt ihm sechs Mark.
9. Warum gibt er ihm soviel Geld?	Er soll sich die Haare schneiden lassen, bevor er nach Hause kommt.
10. Was soll er nicht vergessen, bevor er geht?	Er soll sein Frühstücksbrot nicht vergessen.
11. Warum soll er schnell laufen?	Er soll schnell laufen, damit er nicht zu spät kommt.
12. Wohin fahren Neumanns?	Sie fahren in die Stadt.
13. Warum fährt Frau Neumann mit?	Sie hat eine ganze Menge zu besorgen.
14. Warum nimmt sie zwei Anzüge von ihrem Mann mit?	Sie will sie zur Reinigung bringen und sie reinigen lassen.
15. Wohin bringt sie die Oberhemden?	Die Oberhemden bringt sie in die Wäscherei.
16. Was hat sie auch noch vor?	Sie muss noch zum Zahnarzt und zum Frisör gehen.
17. Wann soll sie dort sein?	Beim Zahnarzt soll sie um zehn Uhr sein und beim Frisör um 12.
18. Wann wird sie wieder zu Hause sein?	Sie kann kaum vor halb zwei zu Hause sein.
19. Wann will Herr Neumann seine Frau abholen?	Er will sie um eins beim Frisör abholen.
20. Wo müssen sie auf dem Nachhauseweg noch halten?	Auf dem Nachhauseweg müssen sie beim Uhrmacher und bei der Apotheke halten.
21. Wohin geht Herr Neumann nachmittags?	Nachmittags geht er ins Büro.
22. Was sagt ihm die Sekretärin?	Sie sagt, dass Herr Dr. Bergmann angerufen hat.

23. Was hat er bestellen lassen?

Er erwartet Herrn Neumann um fünf zu einer Besprechung.

24. Um was handelt es sich?

Es handelt sich um die neuen Zollbestimmungen.

25. Was gibt Fräulein Keller Herrn Neumann?

Sie gibt ihm alle Unterlagen.

26. In welcher Angelegenheit wollte ein Herr von der englischen Botschaft Herrn Neumann sprechen?

Fräulein Keller weiss das nicht. Der Herr will nochmal anrufen.

27. An wen diktiert Herr Neumann später zwei Briefe?

Er diktiert einen Brief an die Handelskammer und einen an das Arbeitsamt.

28. Was soll Fräulein Keller übersetzen lassen?

Sie soll einen Artikel übersetzen lassen.

29. Wer ruft Herrn Neumann an? - Wie heisst er?

Herr Meyer ruft Herrn Neumann an. Er heisst Gerhard.

30. Warum ruft er ihn an?

Er möchte wissen, ob Neumanns zu dem Vortrag von Professor Albers gehen.

31. Warum möchte Herr Meyer das wissen?

Sein Auto ist noch in der Reparaturwerkstatt, und er und seine Frau möchten in Neumanns Wagen mitfahren.

32. Um wieviel Uhr wollen Neumanns bei ihnen vorbeikommen?

Sie wollen um acht Uhr bei ihnen vorbeikommen.

CONVERSATION PRACTICE (not recorded)

1

A: Gehst du heute abend ins Theater?
B: Ich weiss nicht, ob ich ins Theater gehen soll oder zum Vortrag von Professor Albers.
A: Ach, hält Albers heute einen Vortrag? Den möchte ich eigentlich auch gern hören! Um wieviel Uhr und wo?
B: Um acht Uhr in der Handelskammer.
A: Wenn du hingehst, komme ich mit dir mit.
Wir können ja auch morgen ins Theater gehen.

2

B: Um wieviel Uhr ist heute die Besprechung bei Dr. König, Fräulein Keller?
K: Um fünf Uhr fünfzehn, Herr Doktor.
B: Haben Sie alle Unterlagen da?
K: Ja, sie liegen in Ihrer Aktenmappe auf dem Schreibtisch.
B: Gut. - Bitte rufen Sie doch gleich mal Herrn Becker an und sagen Sie ihm, dass ich gern heute mit ihm zu Mittag essen möchte.
K: Um wieviel Uhr, Herr Doktor?
B: Um ein Uhr, und wenn es Herrn Becker recht ist, im Ratskeller.
K: Soll ich diesen Artikel aus der französischen Zeitung übersetzen lassen?
B: Ja, er ist sehr wichtig. - Bevor ich zum Essen gehe, möchte ich Ihnen noch einige Briefe diktieren. Bringen Sie sie bitte noch vor eins zur Post.

3

Lee: Ich möchte diesen Anzug und die hellgraue Jacke reinigen lassen.
Frl: Bitte sehr; - am Freitag nachmittag können Sie die Sachen wieder abholen.
Lee: Wieviel kostet das Reinigen des Anzugs?
Frl: Der Anzug kostet zwei Mark fünfzig, die Jacke eine Mark fünfundneunzig.
Lee: Kann ich bei Ihnen auch meine Wäsche waschen lassen?
Frl: Unsere Wäscherei ist hier nebenan. Darf ich um Ihren Namen und die Adresse bitten?
Lee: Frank Lee, Schubertstrasse 12, erster Stock.
Frl: Vielen Dank.

SITUATIONS

Am Telephon

Gerhard Becker ruft seinen Freund,
Klaus König an. Er fragt ihn, ob er
mit ihm am Wochenende nach München
fahren will. Klaus hat leider keine
Zeit, er muss am Sonnabend zum Zahnarzt
und Sonntag früh erwartet er seine
Eltern. Gerhard fragt, wie lange seine
Eltern bleiben wollen und was sie vorhaben. Klaus sagt, dass seine Eltern
nur zwei bis drei Tage bleiben werden
und dass er ihnen die Stadt zeigen
will. Am Sonntag abend will er mit
ihnen ins Theater gehen. Dann fragt
Gerhard seinen Freund, ob er jetzt mit
ihm zu Mittag essen will. Klaus hat
Zeit und beide wollen um 12:30 Uhr im
Restaurant am Markt sein.

Im Büro

Sagen Sie Ihrer Sekretärin, dass Sie
zu einer wichtigen Konferenz gehen
müssen. Es handelt sich um die neuen
Einfuhrbestimmungen, und Sie brauchen
dafür die Unterlagen. Bevor Sie gehen, sagen Sie ihr, was sie noch machen soll. Zum Beispiel soll sie noch
zur Post gehen, einen Artikel übersetzen, Herrn Dr. Bergmann anrufen,
einige Formulare ausfüllen und Ihrer
Frau ausrichten, dass sie Sie heute
abend um sechs Uhr abholen möchte

Besorgungen

Fragen Sie den Portier Ihres Hotels,
wo in der Nähe eine Reinigung und
eine Wäscherei ist. Dann bringen Sie
Ihre Wäsche und zwei Anzüge dorthin.
Das Fräulein in der Wäscherei zählt
Ihre Wäsche, - vier Oberhemden, zwei
Sporthemden, Socken, Unterwäsche -
und Sie fragen, wann Sie wieder alles
abholen können. Dann gehen Sie zum
Schuster und holen Ihre Schuhe ab.
Sie fragen ihn, wieviel das Besohlen
kostet. Auf dem Nachhauseweg fragen
Sie ein Kind, wo eine Apotheke ist.
Das Kind sagt es Ihnen und dann
sprechen Sie noch etwas mit ihm,
fragen es, wo es wohnt, wie es heisst
usw.

NARRATIVE

Die beiden Fuhrleute (Nach J.P. Hebel)

Zwei Fuhrleute treffen sich mit ihrem Wagen auf einer engen Strasse und
können sich nicht gut ausweichen. "Fahre mir aus dem Wege!" ruft der eine.
"Ei, so fahre du mir aus dem Wege!" ruft der andere. "Ich will nicht!" sagt der
eine. "Ich brauche es nicht!" sagt der andere. Keiner gibt nach und sie werden
beide sehr ärgerlich. "Höre", sagt endlich der erste, "jetzt frage ich dich
zum letzten Mal: willst du mir aus dem Wege fahren oder nicht? Wenn du es nicht
tust, mache ich es mit dir, wie ich es heute schon mit einem anderen gemacht
habe." Der andere Fuhrmann wird vorsichtig und sagt:"Nun, dann hilf mir doch
wenigstens deinen Wagen etwas auf die Seite zu schieben, ich habe ja sonst nicht
Platz, um mit meinem auszuweichen." Das ist dem ersten Fuhrmann recht und nach
einigen Minuten ist alles in Ordnung. Bevor sie weiterfahren, fragt der zweite
Fuhrmann den ersten:"Hör' mal, vorhin sagtest du doch, du willst es mit mir machen
wie du es heute schon mit einem gemacht hast. Sag' mir doch, wie hast du es mit
ihm gemacht?" "Ja, denke dir", sagt der andere, "der Grobian wollte mir nicht
aus dem Wege fahren, da - fuhr ich ihm aus dem Wege."

der Fuhrmann, Fuhrleute	teamster	zum letzten Mal	for the last time
eng	narrow	vorsichtig	cautious
(sich) ausweichen	get out of	wenigstens	at least
	(each other's) way	schieben	push
ei	ho!	weiterfahren	drive on
nachgeben	give in	vorhin	a little while ago
werden	become	der Grobian	lout
ärgerlich	angry	fuhr	drove

FINDERLIST

heute	abend	this evening
	abgesehen von	except for, apart from
die	Apotheke, -n	pharmacy
das	Arbeitsamt, ¨er	employment office
der	Artikel, -	article
	beeil' dich	hurry up
	besohlen	sole
etwas	besohlen lassen	have something soled
	er lässt etwas besohlen	he has something soled
	besorgen	attend to, take care of
die	Besprechung, -en	conference
	bestellen lassen	leave a message
	bevor	before
	damit	so that
	dein	your
	dir (dat)	to you, for you
Herr	Doktor	Doctor
	erwarten	expect
bei	euch	at your home
	eurem	your
der	Frisör, -e	hairdresser
beim	Frisör	at the hairdresser's
das	Frühstücksbrot, -e	snack, lunch
es	geht	it's possible
ihr	geht	you go
er hat	gesagt	he said
das	Haar, -e	hair
die	Handelskammer, -n	Chamber of Commerce
du	hast	you have
	hol' ... ab	pick ... up
sich	kämmen	comb one's hair
du	kannst	you can
	kaum	hardly, scarcely
du	kommst	you come
	kurz	shortly
	lass'	get, have
	laufen	run
	lauf'	run
das	Lied, -er	song
eine ganze	Menge	a great deal
	mitfahren	go (with someone)
der	Nachhauseweg	the way home
	auf dem Nachhauseweg	on the way home
heute	nachmittag	this afternoon
	nimm	take
	noch	in addition, too
das	Oberhemd, -en	shirt
	reinigen	clean
etwas	reinigen lassen	have something cleaned
die	Reinigung, -en	cleaners
die	Reparaturwerkstatt, ¨en	repair shop
	schneiden	cut
etwas	schneiden lassen	have something cut
der	Schuh, -e	shoe
der	Schulausflug, ¨e	school outing
der	Schuster, -	shoemaker
beim	Schuster	at the shoemaker's
zu	spät kommen	to be late
er will ihn	sprechen	he wants to speak to him
	überlastet	loaded down, overburdened
	übersetzen	translate
etwas	übersetzen lassen	have something translated

der	Uhrmacher,-	watchmaker
	umschalten	switch (from one line to another)
die	Unterlagen	papers, documents
alle	Unterlagen	all the papers
	vergessen	forget
	vergiss	forget
	verpassen	miss
du	verpasst	you miss
sich	verschlafen	oversleep
	er hat sich verschlafen	he overslept
	vorbeikommen	come by
der	Vortrag,⸚e	lecture
	einen Vortrag halten	give a lecture
	waschen	wash
	ich wasche mir die Hände	I wash my hands
die	Wäscherei,-en	laundry
du	wirst	you will
ihr	wisst	you know
er	wollte	he wanted
der	Zahnarzt,⸚e	dentist
die	Zollbestimmungen	customs regulations
	zuerst	first
	zuviel	too much

Tape 12A   AUF EINER GESELLSCHAFT

Basic Sentences

I   I

MR. BERGMANN

How long have you been here,
Mrs. Jones?

> only

MRS. JONES

Only two months.

> he arrived

We arrived in Bremerhaven on the
second of March.

> pleasant, agreeable
> the crossing
> he had

MR. BERGMANN

Did you have a pleasant crossing?

> in general, on the whole

MRS. JONES

On the whole, yes.

> seasick
> she was

Only our daughter was seasick almost
all the time.

> I'm sorry

MR. BERGMANN

I'm sorry /¯to hear that_7.

> the voyage
> the recovery, recuperation

MRS. JONES

Aside from that the voyage was a real
vacation for us.

HERR BERGMANN

Wie lange sind Sie denn schon hier,
gnädige Frau?

> erst

FRAU JONES

Erst zwei Monate.

> er ist ... angekommen

Wir sind am zweiten März in Bremerhaven angekommen.

> angenehm
> die Überfahrt,-en
> er hat ... gehabt

HERR BERGMANN

Haben Sie eine angenehme Überfahrt
gehabt?

> im Grossen und Ganzen

FRAU JONES

Im Grossen und Ganzen, ja.

> seekrank
> sie ist ... gewesen

Nur unsere Tochter ist fast die ganze
Zeit seekrank gewesen.

> es tut mir leid

HERR BERGMANN

Das tut mir aber leid.

> die Seereise,-n
> die Erholung

FRAU JONES

Abgesehen davon war die Seereise eine
richtige Erholung für uns.

II

to get settled	sich einleben
he has gotten settled	er hat sich eingelebt

MR. KELLER

HERR KELLER

Have you gotten well settled, Mr. Allen?

Haben Sie sich gut eingelebt, Herr Konsul[1]?

to feel well	sich wohl fühlen

MR. ALLEN

HERR ALLEN

Yes, we feel very much at home here already.

Ja, wir fühlen uns hier schon recht wohl.

fortunately	glücklicherweise
he has found	er hat ... gefunden

We've found a nice apartment fortunately.

Wir haben glücklicherweise eine nette Wohnung gefunden.

the colony, settlement	die Siedlung,-en

MR. KELLER

HERR KELLER

In the American Colony?

In der amerikanischen Siedlung?

for two weeks	seit vierzehn Tagen
the two-family house	das Zweifamilienhaus,-̈er
the south	der Süden

MR. ALLEN

HERR ALLEN

No, we've been living in a two-family house in the southern part of town for two weeks.

Nein, wir wohnen seit vierzehn Tagen in einem Zweifamilienhaus im Süden der Stadt.

the problem	das Problem,-e
the school question	das Schulproblem,-e
the family	die Familie,-n
to solve, settle	lösen
he solved, settled	er hat ... gelöst

MR. KELLER

HERR KELLER

How did you settle the school question in your family?

Wie haben Sie das Schulproblem in Ihrer Familie gelöst?

the boy	der Junge,-n
to attend	besuchen
(a secondary school in the German educational system)	das Realgymnasium[2],-en

MR. ALLEN

HERR ALLEN

The two boys are attending a German 'Realgymnasium'.

Die beiden Jungen besuchen ein deutsches Realgymnasium.

the little girl	die Kleine,-n
the kindergarten	der Kindergarten,-̈

Our little girl goes to an American kindergarten.

Unsere Kleine geht in einen amerikanischen Kindergarten.

III

the opera

MR. BRUCE

You were at the opera yesterday too, weren't you?

  the performance
  you liked it

How did you like the performance?

MR. JONES

Very much.

  glad, happy
  the subscription
  the season ticket for the theater
  he took

I'm glad I got a season ticket for the theater.

  stupid
  to bad
  he did

MR. BRUCE

That's what I should have done, too. ('Too bad I didn't do that too.')

  one and a half
  the ticket
  to stand in line
  he had to stand in line

I had to stand in line an hour and a half for my ticket.

  to be worthwhile
  it was worthwhile

MR. JONES

But it was worth it, wasn't it?

MR. BRUCE

Definitely!

  in a week
  the Berlin Philharmonic

III

die Oper,-n

HERR BRUCE

Sie sind doch gestern auch in der Oper gewesen, nicht wahr?

  die Aufführung,-en
  es hat Ihnen gefallen

Wie hat Ihnen die Aufführung denn gefallen?

HERR JONES

Sehr gut.

  froh
  das Abonnement,-s
  das Theater-Abonnement,-s

  er hat ... genommen

Ich bin froh, dass ich ein Theater-Abonnement genommen habe.

  dumm
  zu dumm
  er hat ... getan

HERR BRUCE

Zu dumm, dass ich das nicht auch getan habe.

  anderthalb
  die Karte,-n
  anstehen
  er hat anstehen müssen

Ich habe anderthalb Stunden[3] für meine Karte anstehen müssen.

  sich lohnen
  es hat sich gelohnt

HERR JONES

Aber es hat sich doch gelohnt, nicht wahr?

HERR BRUCE

Unbedingt!

  in acht Tagen
  die Berliner Philharmoniker (pl)

Do you know by the way, that the Berlin Philharmonic is giving a concert here in a week?	Wissen Sie übrigens, dass die Berliner Philharmoniker in acht Tagen hier ein Konzert geben?
he has read	er hat ... gelesen
MR. BRUCE	HERR BRUCE
Yes, I've read about it. Are you going to go?	Ja, das habe ich gelesen. Werden Sie hingehen?
MR. JONES	HERR JONES
I'd like to if there are still tickets.	Ich möchte schon, wenn es noch Karten gibt.
to inquire, ask	sich erkundigen
MR. BRUCE	HERR BRUCE
I intend to inquire tomorrow. May I get you a ticket too?	Ich will mich morgen mal erkundigen. Darf ich für Sie auch eine Karte besorgen?
would be	wäre
MR. JONES	HERR JONES
Yes, that would be nice.	Ja, das wäre nett.
IV	IV
MR. MEYER	HERR MEYER
How is your son getting along?	Was macht Ihr Sohn?
MR. KÖNIG	HERR KÖNIG
Thank you, he's fine.	Danke, es geht ihm gut.
to study (at a university)	studieren
He's studying at (the university of) Göttingen now.	Er studiert jetzt in Göttingen.
in the capacity of the (university) student the exchange student	als der Student,-en der Austauschstudent,-en
MR. MEYER	HERR MEYER
Wasn't he in America as an exchange student?	Ist er nicht als Austauschstudent in Amerika gewesen?
MR. KÖNIG	HERR KÖNIG
Yes, he was able to study there for two years in fact.	Ja, er hat sogar zwei Jahre dort studieren können.
foreign contries	das Ausland
Wasn't your daughter also abroad?	War Ihre Tochter nicht auch im Ausland?

the (woman) teacher	die Lehrerin,-nen
the physical education teacher	die Sportlehrerin,-nen
Norway	Norwegen

MR. MEYER

Yes, in Norway as a physical education teacher.

HERR MEYER

Ja, als Sportlehrerin in Norwegen.

married	verheiratet

Now she's married and has been living in Munich since last summer.

Jetzt ist sie verheiratet und wohnt seit letztem Sommer in München.

to see each other	sich sehen[4]

MR. KÖNIG

Then you undoubtedly see each other frequently.

HERR KÖNIG

Dann sehen Sie sich sicher öfters.

every few months	alle paar Monate

MR. MEYER

No, unfortunately only every few months.

HERR MEYER

Nein, leider nur alle paar Monate.

V

V

(head of the administration of a district corresponding roughly to a county)	der Landrat,⸚e

MR. ALLEN

Isn't that the Landrat over there?

HERR ALLEN

Ist das da drüben nicht der Landrat?

the editor	der Redakteur,-e

MR. JONES

No, that's an editor.

HERR JONES

Nein, das ist ein Redakteur.

the hostess	die Gastgeberin,-nen

The Landrat is sitting beside our hostess.

Der Landrat sitzt neben unserer Gastgeberin.

MR. ALLEN

The lady on his left is Frau von Rothenburg, isn't she?

HERR ALLEN

Die Dame links von ihm ist doch Frau von Rothenburg, nicht wahr?

MR. JONES

Yes, that's right.

HERR JONES

Ja, ganz recht.

the Red Cross	das Rote Kreuz

She works for the Red Cross.

Sie arbeitet für's Rote Kreuz.

recently	neulich
the reception	der Empfang, ̈-e
the consul general	der Generalkonsul, -n
he met	er hat ... kennengelernt

MR. ALLEN

HERR ALLEN

I met her recently at a reception at the consul general's.

Ich habe sie neulich auf einem Empfang beim Generalkonsul kennengelernt.

to converse	sich unterhalten

Do you know the gentleman she's talking to?

Kennen Sie den Herrn, mit dem sie sich unterhält?

the director	der Leiter, -
the Board of Health	das Gesundheitsamt, ̈-er

Yes, that's Dr. Maler, the director of the Board of Health.

Ja, das ist Dr. Maler, der Leiter des Gesundheitsamtes.

VI

VI

the player	der Spieler, -
the tennis player	der Tennisspieler, -

MR. MÜLLER

HERR MÜLLER

I've heard that you're a good tennis player.

Ich habe gehört, dass Sie ein guter Tennisspieler sind.

MR. BRUCE

HERR BRUCE

Oh, just fair.

Na, es geht.

to engage in athletic activities	Sport treiben

Anyway I do like athletics.

Ich treibe jedenfalls gern Sport.

since a short time ago	seit kurzem
modern	modern
the bath, bathing place	das Bad, ̈-er
the swimming pool	das Schwimmbad, ̈-er

MR. MÜLLER

HERR MÜLLER

Then you undoubtedly know that we've had a very modern swimming pool here since a short time ago.

Wissen Sie eigentlich, dass wir hier seit kurzem ein ganz modernes Schwimmbad haben?

to be present, to be there	da sein

MR. BRUCE

HERR BRUCE

Yes, but I've never been there.

Ja, aber ich bin noch nie dagewesen.

(No English equivalent, implies that agreement with the statement made is assumed.)	ja

MR. MÜLLER	HERR MÜLLER

If it's all right with you, we can
go together sometime.

Wenn es Ihnen recht ist, können wir
ja mal zusammen hingehen.

MR. BRUCE	HERR BRUCE

Yes, I'd be glad to.   Gerne.

Notes to the Basic Sentences

¹ In a social situation such as this it would be natural for the German to use
Mr. Allen's titel in speaking to him, just as he would say "gnädige Frau"
in speaking to a lady. An American of course would just say "Mr. Allen" or
"Mrs. Jones".

² In the German educational system after Elementary School (die Volksschule)
there are two principal secondary schools for students planning to go on
to the university. One is the <u>Oberrealschule</u>, or the <u>Realgymnasium</u> where
modern languages and natural sciences are given prominence. The other is the
<u>Humanistisches Gymnasium</u>, often referred to just as <u>Gymnasium</u>, where the
humanities, classical languages and literature are given more prominence.

³ <u>anderthalb Stunden</u> is plural in German (it is <u>more</u> than one), although in
English we say "an hour and a half" and the noun remains singular.

⁴ <u>sich sehen</u>. The pronoun here indicates a reciprocal relationship: "see each
other, see one another". The pronouns <u>sich</u>, <u>uns</u>, <u>euch</u> may occur with a
number of German verbs to indicate this relationship: <u>besuchen</u>, <u>kennen</u>,
<u>schreiben</u>, <u>treffen</u>, <u>verstehen</u>, etc.

Notes on Grammar
(For Home Study)

A.   VERBS.   PAST TIME.

I. In English we use several devices in order to talk about <u>past time</u>, some
   of which are illustrated in the following examples:

   1) We <u>had</u> a very pleasant crossing.
   2) <u>Was</u> he <u>living</u> in Berlin then?
   3) They <u>did</u> not <u>buy</u> the house.
   4) I <u>have</u> <u>written</u> a long letter to Bill.
   5) We <u>have been living</u> in this house for two months already.

   Notice that one of these devices (sentence 1) consists solely of a PAST TENSE
   form of the verb (<u>had</u>). All the other sentences contain VERB PHRASES
   consisting of an AUXILIARY VERB (<u>was</u>, <u>did</u>, <u>have</u>) plus a PRESENT PARTICIPLE
   (<u>living</u>), or an INFINITIVE (<u>buy</u>), or a PAST PARTICIPLE (<u>written</u>), or a
   PAST and a PRESENT PARTICIPLE together (<u>been living</u>).

II. In German there are three devices which are used to talk about past time.

   1) Die Seereise <u>war</u> eine   The voyage was a real vacation
      richtige Erholung für uns.   for us.
   2) Wie <u>haben</u> Sie das Schul-   How did you settle the school
      problem <u>gelöst</u>?   question?
   3) Sie <u>wohnt</u> seit letztem   She's been living in Munich since
      Sommer in München.   last summer.

   Sentence 1) contains a PAST TENSE form of the verb; sentence 2) contains
   a VERB PHRASE with an AUXILIARY VERB plus a PAST PARTICIPLE;

sentence 3) contains a PRESENT TENSE form of the verb. Notice that some
of the devices used in English do not occur in German and one of the
devices used in German does not occur in English.

III. In <u>some</u> cases (particularly where the verbs <u>sein</u> and <u>haben</u> are concerned)
two German devices for talking about past time are interchangeable.

1) <u>Haben</u> Sie eine angenehme Überfahrt <u>gehabt</u>?
2) <u>Hatten</u> Sie eine angenehme Überfahrt?

<u>Did</u> you <u>have</u> a pleasant crossing?

3) Die Seereise <u>war</u> eine richtige Erholung für uns.
4) Die Seereise <u>ist</u> eine richtige Erholung für uns <u>gewesen</u>.

The voyage <u>was</u> a real vacation for us.

Sentences 1) and 3) occurred in the basic sentences of this unit.
Sentences 2) and 4) could just as well have occurred in their stead.
See if you could substitute any other English sentence for the one given
in each case. Does the situation seem different to you, the time and
place and circumstances under which the comments are made? GERMAN AND
ENGLISH DEVICES FOR TALKING ABOUT PAST TIME DO NOT COINCIDE EXACTLY.
The SIMPLE PAST TENSE of the one language is not necessarily equivalent
to the SIMPLE PAST TENSE of the other, and a VERB PHRASE in the one
language is not necessarily equivalent to a VERB PHRASE in the other.

B   VERBS. THE PERFECT PHRASE.

I. The most frequent device used in <u>conversation</u> in German is the VERB PHRASE
consisting of an AUXILIARY VERB plus a PAST PARTICIPLE. This is called
the PERFECT PHRASE.   The form is like our English PERFECT PHRASE <u>have sent</u>,
<u>have gone</u>, etc., but note that an English PERFECT PHRASE does not always
occur where a German PERFECT PHRASE is used.

1. Notice the following examples, most of which have occurred in our units:

Wir <u>haben</u> Sie lange nicht <u>gesehen</u>, Herr Becker.
We <u>haven't seen</u> you for a long time, Mr. Becker.

Sie <u>haben</u> vorhin bei mir <u>angerufen</u>, Herr Bauer.
You <u>called</u> my office a little while ago, Mr. Bauer.

<u>Hat</u> er <u>gesagt</u>, um was es sich handelt?
<u>Did</u> he <u>say</u> what it was about?

Sie <u>hat</u> lange vor dem Geschäft <u>gestanden</u>.
She <u>stood</u> in front of the store for a long time.

Wissen Sie, wo seine Eltern in Deutschland <u>gewohnt haben</u>?
Do you know where his parents <u>lived</u> in Germany?

<u>Most</u> German verbs make the PERFECT PHRASE with the AUXILIARY VERB <u>haben</u>.

2. Notice further:

Wir <u>sind</u> am zweiten März in Bremerhaven <u>angekommen</u>.
We <u>arrived</u> in Bremerhaven on the second of March.

Meine Zeitung <u>ist</u> heute nicht <u>gekommen</u>.
My paper <u>didn't come</u> today.

Die Handwerker <u>sind</u> jedenfalls gestern <u>dagewesen</u>.
At any rate the workmen <u>were</u> here yesterday.

Wie lange <u>bist</u> du denn dort <u>geblieben</u>?
How long <u>did</u> you <u>stay</u> there?

Ich glaube nicht, dass sie heute <u>mitgefahren ist</u>.
I don't think she <u>went</u> along today.

Certain German verbs make the PERFECT PHRASE with the AUXILIARY VERB sein.
The following is a list of the verbs in the first twelve units which
do this:

auswandern	fahren	kommen	laufen
	abfahren	ankommen	
bleiben	mitfahren	hereinkommen	sein
		hinkommen	
	gehen	mitkommen	ziehen
	ausgehen	vorbeikommen	einziehen
	hingehen	zurückkommen	

You will remember that these verbs do not occur with accusative objects.
Notice that all except bleiben and sein are also verbs which indicate
motion or change of position.

II. The verbs dürfen, können, möchte (n), müssen, sollen, wollen and lassen
have a SPECIAL PERFECT PHRASE.

   Ich habe die Schuhe besohlen lassen.
   Er hat sogar zwei Jahre dort studieren können.
   Ich habe anderthalb Stunden für meine Karte anstehen müssen.

Instead of a PAST PARTICIPLE the INFINITIVE form of these verbs occurs
in the PERFECT PHRASE. Since they all function as auxiliary verbs with
another infinitive, two infinitives stand together at the end of the
sentence, the auxiliary infinitive last. This construction is sometimes
referred to as the DOUBLE INFINITIVE construction. Notice that this is
exactly the same construction as we noted in Unit 11 under COMPLEX VERB
PHRASES. THE AUXILIARY VERB in the SPECIAL PERFECT PHRASE is always
haben, however. Compare:

   Ich habe die Schuhe besohlen lassen.
   Ich muss die Schuhe besohlen lassen.
   Ich werde die Schuhe besohlen lassen.

C.   VERBS. PAST PARTICIPLE FORMS

There are two form classes of PAST PARTICIPLES in German. Most verbs have
PAST PARTICIPLES which end in a -t like gekauft, gelöst, gewohnt and are
called WEAK VERBS. A relatively small group of very common verbs have
PAST PARTICIPLES which end in -n like gefahren, gesehen, gestanden and are
called STRONG VERBS.

I. Weak Verbs.

   1. Most WEAK VERBS have a PAST PARTICIPLE CONSISTING of a form which is
      identical with the er-form of the PRESENT TENSE preceded by the
      prefix ge-:

         ge-kauft   ge-wohnt   ge-hört   ge-arbeitet   ge-regnet

   2. When the verb has an accented adverb this precedes the prefix ge-
      and the whole thing is written as one word:

         ein-ge-lebt   auf-ge-macht   ein-ge-richtet   vor-ge-stellt

   3. When the verb is not stressed on the first syllable, the PAST PARTICIPLE
      consists only of a form identical with the er-form of the PRESENT TENSE
      and has no additional prefix ge-.

         besucht   vermietet   gehört   erwartet   studiert   übersetzt

4. A few WEAK VERBS have irregular PAST PARTICIPLES:

ge-habt   ge-kannt   ge-bracht   ge-wusst   ge-dacht

Notice that most of these verbs also have other forms which are irregular.

II. Strong Verbs.

1. The PAST PARTICIPLES of many STRONG VERBS incorporate arbitrary changes in the STEM which cannot be predicted from the infinitive or present tense forms. The following is a complete list of all STRONG VERBS which have occurred in the first twelve units, together with their PAST PARTICIPLES:

abheben	abgehoben	laufen	*gelaufen
anbieten	angeboten	leihen	geliehen
anfangen	angefangen	lesen	gelesen
anrufen	angerufen	liegen	gelegen
behalten	behalten	nehmen	genommen
bekommen	bekommen	abnehmen	abgenommen
bitten	gebeten	mitnehmen	mitgenommen
bleiben	*geblieben	scheinen	geschienen
empfehlen	empfohlen	schneiden	geschnitten
essen	gegessen	schreiben	geschrieben
fahren	*gefahren	sehen	gesehen
abfahren	*abgefahren	ansehen	angesehen
mitfahren	*mitgefahren	aussehen	ausgesehen
finden	gefunden	sitzen	gesessen
stattfinden	stattgefunden	sprechen	gesprochen
geben	gegeben	stehen	gestanden
ausgeben	ausgegeben	anstehen	angestanden
gefallen	gefallen	tragen	getragen
gehen	*gegangen	treffen	getroffen
ausgehen	*ausgegangen	treiben	getrieben
hingehen	*hingegangen	trinken	getrunken
halten	gehalten	tun	getan
heissen	geheissen	unterhalten	unterhalten
helfen	geholfen	verbinden	verbunden
kommen	*gekommen	vergessen	vergessen
ankommen	*angekommen	verschlafen	verschlafen
hereinkommen	*hereingekommen	verstehen	verstanden
hinkommen	*hingekommen	waschen	gewaschen
mitkommen	*mitgekommen	ziehen	*gezogen
vorbeikommen	*vorbeigekommen	anziehen	angezogen
zurückkommen	*zurückgekommen	einziehen	*eingezogen

*Note that these PAST PARTICIPLES occur in a PERFECT PHRASE with the AUXILIARY sein.

2. The verb sein, which is irregular, has the PAST PARTICIPLE gewesen.

D. VERBS. PAST TIME CONTINUING IN THE PRESENT.

I. To indicate that an action or state begun in the past is still continuing in the present German uses a PRESENT TENSE of the verb with an expression indicating continuation or duration of time.

1. The most common of these expressions are:

a. The question phrase wie lange accompanied by schon (or jetzt).

Wie lange sind Sie denn schon hier?	How long have you been here?
Wissen Sie, wie lange sie schon in dieser Strasse wohnt?	Do you know, how long she has been living on this street?

b. An adverb or an <u>accusative</u> phrase, usually accompanied by <u>schon</u>, <u>jetzt</u> or <u>erst</u>.

Wohnen Sie schon <u>lange</u> in Berlin?	Have you been living in Berlin long?
Ich bin jetzt ein <u>halbes Jahr</u> in Deutschland.	I've been in Germany for six months now.
Meine Frau ist erst <u>zwei Monate</u> hier.	My wife has only been here for two months.
Ich habe diesen Anzug schon <u>drei Jahre</u>.	I have had this suit for three years.
Ich glaube, sie sitzt schon eine <u>ganze Stunde</u> da drüben im Café.	I think she has been sitting over there in the café for a whole hour.

c. The preposition <u>seit</u> followed by an adverb, a question word or a <u>dative</u> phrase.

Der Brief liegt <u>seit gestern</u> auf seinem Schreibtisch.	The letter has been on his desk since yesterday.
<u>Seit wann</u> arbeiten Sie in diesem Büro?	How long have you been working in this office?
Sie wohnt <u>seit letztem Sommer</u> in München.	She has been living in Munich since last summer.
Wir sind erst <u>seit einer Stunde</u> hier in Frankfurt.	We've only been here in Frankfurt for an hour.

Note that <u>schon</u> and <u>erst</u> are ADVERBS and occur EITHER with an <u>accusative</u> phrase OR with <u>seit</u> and a <u>dative</u> phrase.

Ich bin schon eine Woche hier.	Ich bin schon einen Monat hier.
Ich bin erst eine Woche hier.	Ich bin erst einen Monat hier.

Ich bin seit einer Woche hier.	Ich bin seit einem Monat hier.
Ich bin schon seit einer Woche hier.	Ich bin schon seit einem Monat hier.
Ich bin erst seit einer Woche hier.	Ich bin erst seit einem Monat hier.

2. You will have noticed that past time which continues into the present is indicated in English by a VERB PHRASE. Notice the implication of the following sentences:

Wie lange <u>haben</u> Sie in München <u>gewohnt</u>?	How long <u>did</u> you <u>live</u> in Munich?
Ich <u>bin</u> ein halbes Jahr in Deutschland <u>gewesen</u>.	I <u>was</u> in Germany for six months.
Sie <u>hat</u> eine ganze Stunde da drüben im Café <u>gesessen</u>.	She <u>sat</u> over there in the café for the whole hour.

The use of the VERB PHRASE in German with expressions indicating continuation or duration of time indicates that the state or action lies <u>entirely in the past</u>.

E.   TIME EXPRESSIONS

It is possible to measure time alternatively in large or small units. We speak of "thirty minutes" or of "half an hour", for instance; we may say "four weeks" or "a month". Most of the basic units of time have now been presented in our units, and it will be interesting to note some of the alternatives which Germans use in speaking about a period of time.

Wir wohnen seit <u>vierzehn Tagen</u> hier.	Wir wohnen seit <u>zwei Wochen</u> hier.
Die Philharmoniker geben in <u>acht Tagen</u> hier ein Konzert.	Die Philharmoniker geben in <u>einer Woche</u> hier ein Konzert.
Die Aufführung war sehr lang, <u>neunzig Minuten</u>.	Die Aufführung war sehr lang, <u>anderthalb Stunden</u>.
Wir kommen in <u>vier Wochen</u> wieder zurück.	Wir kommen in <u>einem Monat</u> wieder zurück.
Ich bin nur <u>acht Tage</u> in Frankfurt geblieben.	Ich bin nur <u>eine Woche</u> in Frankfurt geblieben.
Das Konzert fängt in <u>dreissig Minuten</u> an.	Das Konzert fängt in <u>einer halben Stunde</u> an.
Wir waren <u>sechs Monate</u> in Amerika.	Wir waren <u>ein halbes Jahr</u> in Amerika.
Sie sehen sich alle <u>vierzehn Tage</u>.	Sie sehen sich alle <u>zwei Wochen</u>.
Er arbeitet schon <u>achtzehn Monate</u> bei uns.	Er arbeitet schon <u>anderthalb Jahre</u> bei uns.
<u>Zwölf Monate</u> sind eine lange Zeit.	<u>Ein Jahr</u> ist eine lange Zeit.

SUBSTITUTION DRILL

1. Das habe ich <u>gehört</u>.

gelesen - gesehen - bestellt - bekommen - ausgerichtet - beantragt - gefunden - bezahlt - geholt - getan - vorgehabt - vergessen

2. Meyers sind vorige Woche <u>abgefahren</u>.

zurückgekommen - eingezogen - hinge- gangen - angekommen - ausgewandert - vorbeigekommen

3. Wie hat Ihnen <u>die Aufführung</u> gefallen?

das Konzert - die Oper - die Ansichts- karte - das Theater - die Briefmarken - die Aussicht - die Berliner Philhar- moniker - die Seereise

4. <u>Unsere Tochter</u> ist seekrank gewesen.

meine Frau - wir - mein Vater - ich - unsere Kinder - die Eltern meiner Frau

5. Ich habe Sie gestern <u>in der Oper</u> gesehen.

in der Stadt - Im Theater - auf dem Empfang im Schwimmbad - beim General- konsul - in der Botschaft - bei Schwarz & Co.

6. Wir sind erst <u>am zweiten März</u> an- gekommen.

am Freitag - gestern - vorige Woche - heute - vorhin - in dieser Woche

7. Wir wohnen schon <u>vier Wochen</u> in einem Zweifamilienhaus im Süden der Stadt.

lange - einen Monat - sechs Jahre - anderthalb Monate - sechs Wochen

8. Sie wohnen seit <u>letztem Sommer</u> in München.

vorigem Herbst - dem ersten April - letztem Winter - dem 22. Juni - einem halben Jahr

9. Die Berliner Philharmoniker geben in <u>acht Tagen</u> ein Konzert.

drei Wochen - vierzehn Tagen - einer Woche - zwei Tagen

10. Ich bin <u>sehr lange</u> dort geblieben.

eine Stunde - drei Tage - zwei Wochen - ein halbes Jahr - zwei Monate - nicht lange - vier Stunden

11. Er arbeitet schon seit <u>drei</u> <u>Monaten</u> in Frankfurt.

einem Jahr - kurzem - sechs Wochen - einem halben Jahr - vierzehn Tagen - einer Woche - anderthalb Jahren

12. Wir wohnen schon <u>sechs Monate</u> hier.

zwei Wochen - vierzehn Tage - anderthalb Jahre - lange - ein halbes Jahr - drei Monate - einen ganzen Monat

13. Ich bin erst <u>zwei Jahre</u> in Hamburg.

drei Monate - vier Tage - einen Monat eine Woche - einen Tag

14. Ich habe sie neulich <u>kennengelernt</u>.

gefragt - abgeholt - getroffen - verpasst - besucht - angerufen - mitgenommen - gesprochen

15. Ich habe <u>gehört,</u> dass Sie ein guter Tennisspieler sind.

gesehen - gewusst - gelesen - gedacht - erwartet

16. Ich bin erst seit <u>zwei Monaten</u> hier.

zwei Wochen - drei Tagen - einer halben Stunde - zwanzig Minuten - kurzem - anderthalb Stunden

17. Ist das da drüben nicht <u>der</u> <u>Landrat</u>?

Konsul - Professor - französische Schriftsteller - Leiter des Gesundheitsamtes - Redakteur - englische Diplomat - Generalkonsul

(End of Tape 12A)

Tape 12B   CONVERSION DRILL

1. Wann heben Sie das Geld ab?
2. Er bietet ihr ein Glas Moselwein an.
3. Wann fangen Sie an?
4. Die Sekretärin meldet das Gespräch an.
5. Sie probiert die braune Jacke an.
6. Das können wir uns nicht leisten.
7. Er zieht sich ein sauberes Oberhemd an.
8. Wo arbeitet sie?
9. Ich esse oft in diesem Restaurant.

10. Was richten Sie ihm aus?
11. Sie wandert nach Amerika aus.
12. Stellst du dich heute für die Karten an?
13. Ich beantrage ein Visum.
14. Hoffentlich beeilt er sich.
15. Er erkundigt sich beim Arbeitsamt.
16. Sie macht ihn mit Dr. Becker bekannt.
17. Bekommt ihr heute die Pässe?
18. Wann besuchen Sie ihre Tochter?
19. Bezahlst du heute die Miete?
20. Wie lange bleibt ihr in München?
21. Die Männer tragen die Kisten in den Keller.
22. Sie bringt ihm die Ansichtskarten.

23. Er buchstabiert seinen Namen.
24. In dieser Tankstelle lasse ich die Reifen wechseln.
25. Wo geht ihr heute hin?
26. Musst du noch zur Apotheke gehen?
27. Wann richtest du dein Zimmer ein?

Wann haben Sie das Geld abgehoben?
Er hat ihr ein Glas Moselwein angeboten.
Wann haben Sie angefangen?
Die Sekretärin hat das Gespräch angemeldet.
Sie hat die braune Jacke anprobiert.
Das haben wir uns nicht leisten können.
Er hat sich ein sauberes Oberhemd angezogen.
Wo hat sie gearbeitet?
Ich habe oft in diesem Restaurant gegessen.

Was haben Sie ihm ausgerichtet?
Sie ist nach Amerika ausgewandert.
Hast du dich heute für die Karten angestellt?
Ich habe ein Visum beantragt.
Hoffentlich hat er sich beeilt.
Er hat sich beim Arbeitsamt erkundigt.
Sie hat ihn mit Dr. Becker bekannt gemacht.
Habt ihr heute die Pässe bekommen?
Wann haben Sie ihre Tochter besucht?
Hast du heute die Miete bezahlt?
Wie lange seid ihr in München geblieben?
Die Männer haben die Kisten in den Keller getragen.
Sie hat ihm die Ansichtskarten gebracht.
Er hat seinen Namen buchstabiert.
In dieser Tankstelle habe ich die Reifen wechseln lassen.
Wo seid ihr heute hingegangen?
Hast du noch zur Apotheke gehen müssen?
Wann hast du dein Zimmer eingerichtet?

28. Die Sonne scheint den ganzen Tag.   Die Sonne hat den ganzen Tag geschienen.
29. Wann fährt er nach Deutschland?   Wann ist er nach Deutschland gefahren?
30. Hoffentlich finden Sie die Zoll-   Hoffentlich haben Sie die Zollbe-
    bestimmungen.   stimmungen gefunden.
31. Der Frisör schneidet ihm die   Der Frisör hat ihm die Haare ge-
    Haare.   schnitten.
32. Sie freut sich auf seinen Besuch.   Sie hat sich auf seinen Besuch
        gefreut.
33. Gehen Sie heute in die Stadt?   Sind Sie heute in die Stadt gegangen?
34. Das Buch gefällt ihr nicht.   Das Buch hat ihr nicht gefallen.
35. Sie geben ihm den Artikel, nicht   Sie haben ihm den Artikel gegeben,
    wahr?   nicht wahr?
36. Können Sie sich an unser Klima   Haben Sie sich an unser Klima ge-
    gewöhnen?   wöhnen können?
37. Hat er das Buch?   Hat er das Buch gehabt?
38. Hilft Ihnen Frau Meyer beim   Hat Ihnen Frau Meyer beim Einrichten
    Einrichten?   geholfen?
39. Sie holt gerade die Schuhe ab.   Sie hat gerade die Schuhe abgeholt.
40. Ich bearbeite seinen Antrag.   Ich habe seinen Antrag bearbeitet.
41. Kennen Sie Herrn Becker?   Haben Sie Herrn Becker gekannt?
42. Der Generalkonsul kommt heute.   Der Generalkonsul ist heute gekommen.
43. Er wechselt das Geld in der Bank.   Er hat das Geld in der Bank gewechselt.
44. Ich leihe dir das Buch.   Ich habe dir das Buch geliehen.
45. Er liest gerade den Artikel in   Er hat gerade den Artikel in der
    der Zeitung.   Zeitung gelesen.
46. Der Ausweis liegt auf seinem   Der Ausweis hat auf seinem Schreib-
    Schreibtisch.   tisch gelegen.
47. Nehmen Sie die Formulare mit?   Haben Sie die Formulare mitgenommen?
48. Schreibst du heute den Brief?   Hast du heute den Brief geschrieben?
49. Wir sitzen meistens an diesem   Wir haben meistens an diesem Tisch
    Tisch.   gesessen.
50. Er spricht sehr langsam.   Er hat sehr langsam gesprochen.
51. Er gibt sich immer grosse Mühe.   Er hat sich immer grosse Mühe gegeben.
52. Das tue ich gern für Sie.   Das habe ich gern für Sie getan.
53. Versteht ihr ihn gut?   Habt ihr ihn gut verstanden?
54. Wo studierst du?   Wo hast du studiert?
55. Ihr kommt wieder zu spät!   Ihr seid wieder zu spät gekommen.
56. Er kümmert sich nicht um sie.   Er hat sich nicht um sie gekümmert.
57. Wäscht er sich die Hände?   Hat er sich die Hände gewaschen?
58. Du übersetzt doch diesen Artikel,   Du hast doch diesen Artikel übersetzt,
    nicht wahr?   nicht wahr?
59. Ihr verschlaft euch fast jeden   Ihr habt euch fast jeden Tag verschla-
    Tag.   fen.
60. Der Redakteur unterhält sich   Der Redakteur hat sich gerade mit dem
    gerade mit dem Landrat.   Landrat unterhalten.

VARIATION DRILL

1. Haben Sie eine angenehme Überfahrt   Did you have a pleasant crossing?
   gehabt?

   a. Have you (fam pl) found a nice   Habt ihr eine nette Wohnung gefunden?
      apartment?
   b. Where did you (fam sg) do your   Wo hast du eigentlich studiert, Klaus?
      university work anyway, Klaus?
      ('Where did you study ... ?')
   c. Who were you just talking to?   Mit wem haben Sie gerade gesprochen?
   d. How much did the season ticket   Wieviel hat das Theater-Abonnement
      to the theater cost?   gekostet?
   e. When did you meet Mrs. Meyer?   Wann haben Sie Frau Meyer kennenge-
          lernt?

2. __Ich bin um zehn Uhr nach Hause__
   __gekommen.__

   a. The Consul General went to
      London for a conference.
   b. Where were you (fam pl) yester-
      day evening?
   c. Dr. Maler has gone to Bonn.
   d. Were you at the theater
      yesterday, too?
   e. I stayed home all Sunday.

__I came home at ten o'clock.__

   Der Generalkonsul ist zu einer
   Konferenz nach London gefahren.
   Wo seid ihr gestern abend gewesen?

   Dr. Maler ist nach Bonn gefahren.
   Sind Sie gestern auch im Theater
   gewesen?
   Ich bin den ganzen Sonntag zu Hause
   geblieben.

3. __Haben Sie sich an das Klima__
   __gewöhnt?__

   a. Have you (fam pl) inquired yet?
   b. Did you (fam sg) oversleep
      again already?
   c. Did he feel at home there?
   d. Was it worth it?
   e. Have you (fam pl) been looking
      forward to the visit?

__Have you gotten accustomed to the__
__climate?__

   Habt ihr euch schon erkundigt?
   Hast du dich schon wieder verschlafen?

   Hat er sich dort wohlgefühlt?
   Hat es sich gelohnt?
   Habt ihr euch auf den Besuch gefreut?

4. __Ich habe heute drei Briefe__
   __geschrieben.__

   a. Professor Albers gave a very
      good lecture last night.
   b. Mr. Kunze didn't drink any wine.
   c. I ran into Dr. Becker yesterday
      evening.
   d. He took the book with him.
   e. You (fam sg) went to the museum
      this afternoon, didn't you?

__I've written three letters today.__

   Professor Albers hat gestern abend
   einen sehr guten Vortrag gehalten.
   Herr Kunze hat keinen Wein getrunken.
   Ich habe gestern abend Dr. Becker
   getroffen.
   Er hat das Buch mitgenommen.
   Du bist heute nachmittag ins Museum
   gegangen, nicht wahr?

5. __Ich habe anderthalb Stunden für__
   __meine Karte anstehen müssen.__

   a. Have you had the article
      translated, Miss Keller?
   b. I wasn't able to (go and) get
      the tickets unfortunately.
   c. I wasn't permitted to smoke for
      two years.
   d. Did you (fam sg) have to work
      yesterday?
   e. She didn't want to give me her
      telephone number.

__I had to stand in line an hour and a__
__half for my ticket.__

   Haben Sie den Artikel übersetzen
   lassen, Fräulein Keller?
   Ich habe die Karten leider nicht
   besorgen können.
   Ich habe zwei Jahre nicht rauchen
   dürfen.
   Hast du gestern arbeiten müssen?

   Sie hat mir ihre Telephonnummer nicht
   geben wollen.

6. __Wir haben zwei Jahre in Berlin__
   __gewohnt.__

   a. I read for two hours last night.

   b. How long did you live in Frank-
      furt?
   c. He worked at the embassy for
      four years.
   d. My brother studied in Bonn for
      six months ('half a year').
   e. We stayed in Munich for a month.

__We lived in Berlin for two years.__

   Ich habe gestern abend zwei Stunden
   gelesen.
   Wie lange haben Sie in Frankfurt
   gewohnt?
   Er hat vier Jahre bei der Botschaft
   gearbeitet.
   Mein Bruder hat ein halbes Jahr in
   Bonn studiert.
   Wir sind einen Monat in München
   geblieben.

7. <u>Ich habe sie seit letztem Sommer</u>   <u>I haven't seen her since last summer.</u>
   <u>nicht gesehen.</u>

   a. My sister hasn't written for   Meine Schwester hat seit drei Monaten
      three months.   nicht geschrieben.
   b. You (fam pl) haven't called us   Ihr habt uns seit einer Woche nicht
      for a week.   angerufen.
   c. They haven't visited us since   Sie haben uns seit Februar nicht
      February.   besucht.
   d. We haven't heard anything from   Wir haben seit einem Jahr nichts von
      him for a year.   ihm gehört.
   e. I haven't received a letter from   Ich habe seit sechs Monaten keinen
      her for six months.   Brief von ihr bekommen.

8. <u>Haben Sie sich gut eingelebt,</u>   <u>Have you gotten well settled,</u>
   <u>Herr Konsul?</u>   <u>Mr. Allen?</u>

   a. I've spoken to Professor   Ich habe Herrn Professor Neumann
      Neumann, Dr. Allen.   gesprochen, Herr Doktor.
   b. An editor from the 'Frankfurter   Ein Redakteur von der Frankfurter
      Allgemeine' called, Sir ('Consul   Allgemeinen hat angerufen, Herr
      General').   Generalkonsul.
   c. Miss Keller, did you place the   Fräulein Keller, haben Sie das Fern-
      long-distance call for Dr. Klein?   gespräch für Herrn Dr. Klein ange-
                                             meldet?
   d. Do you know the Consul General,   Kennen Sie den Herrn Generalkonsul,
      Mrs. Allen?   gnädige Frau?
   e. May I please introduce Vice   Darf ich bitte Herrn Vizekonsul
      Consul Wilson?   Wilson vorstellen?

9. <u>Ist das da drüben nicht der Land-</u>   <u>Isn't that the 'Landrat' over there?</u>
   <u>rat?</u>

   a. Have you met the Director of   Haben Sie den Leiter vom Gesundheits-
      the Board of Health?   amt kennengelernt?
   b. He was talking to a ⌐newspaper⌐   Er hat vorhin mit einem Redakteur
      editor a little while ago.   gesprochen.
   c. The French consul is sitting   Der französische Konsul sitzt neben
      beside the hostess.   der Gastgeberin.
   d. My secretary just called the   Meine Sekretärin hat gerade den Leiter
      Director of the Employment   des Arbeitsamtes angerufen.
      Office.
   e. Mrs. von Rothenburg was at the   Frau von Rothenburg ist auch auf dem
      reception too.   Empfang gewesen.

10. <u>Wir wohnen erst zwei Monate hier.</u>   <u>We've only been living here for two</u>
                                             <u>months.</u>

   a. I've only been here three days.   Ich bin erst drei Tage hier.
   b. He has only known her for a   Er kennt sie erst einen Monat.
      month.
   c. We've been living in America   Wir wohnen jetzt einige Jahre in
      for several years now.   Amerika.
   d. He has been working in the   Er arbeitet schon zwei Monate in der
      embassy for two months already.   Botschaft.
   e. I've been studying German for   Ich studiere schon ein halbes Jahr
      half a year now.   deutsch.

11. <u>Wir wohnen seit vier Wochen in Bonn.</u>   <u>We have been living in Bonn for</u>
                                             <u>four weeks.</u>

   a. They have been living in a new   Sie wohnen seit acht Tagen in einem
      house on the outskirts of town   Neubau am Rande der Stadt.
      for a week.
   b. Do you know that we have had a   Wissen Sie, dass wir seit kurzem hier
      new theater here since a short   ein neues Theater haben?
      time ago?

c. You've had a new car since a few   Du hast seit einigen Tagen ein neues
days ago, haven't you?   Auto, nicht wahr?

d. He has been working here in the   Er arbeitet seit dem 15. April hier im
consulate since the 15th of April.   Konsulat.

12. **Wissen Sie übrigens, dass die**   **Do you know by the way that the Berlin**
    Berliner Philharmoniker hier ein   **Philharmonic is giving a concert here?**
    Konzert geben?

   a. Do you (fam pl) know by the way   Wisst ihr übrigens, dass Meyers bald
      that the Meyers are going to   nach Deutschland fahren?
      Germany soon?

   b. Do you know by the way whether   Wissen Sie übrigens, ob der General-
      the Consul General drove to the   konsul zur Konferenz gefahren ist?
      conference?

   c. Do you (fam sg) know by the way   Weisst du übrigens, wie lange er dort
      how long he attended the   studiert hat?
      university there?

   d. Do you know by the way that the   Wissen Sie übrigens, dass der Landrat
      'Landrat' gave a lecture?   einen Vortrag gehalten hat?

   e. Do you know by the way who   Wissen Sie übrigens, wer den Artikel
      translated the article?   übersetzt hat?

VOCABULARY DRILL

1. <u>erst</u> - "only, not until"

   a. Sie hat erst nach der Überfahrt   Only after the voyage was she able to
      wieder richtig essen können.   eat again properly.

   b. Wohnt ihr erst eine Woche in dem   Have you only been living a week in
      Zweifamilienhaus?   the two-family house?

   c. Sie geht erst morgen in die Oper.   She's not going to the opera until
                              tomorrow.

   d. Er wird sich erst in zwei Jahren   He's not going to buy a new car until
      ein neues Auto kaufen.   two years /̲ from now̲_/.

   e. Wir haben erst nach einem Monat   We found a nice apartment only after
      eine nette Wohnung gefunden.   a month /̲ of looking̲_/.

2. <u>alle</u> - "every"

   a. Die Omnibusse fahren hier alle   The busses go every ten minutes here.
      zehn Minuten.

   b. Alle drei Jahre besuchen wir   Every three years we visit our relatives
      unsere Verwandten in Deutschland. in Germany.

   c. Wir bekommen alle paar Wochen   We get a picture postcard from him
      eine Ansichtskarte von ihm.   every few weeks.

   d. Alle drei Minuten hat das Tele-   Every three minutes the telephone rang.
      phon geklingelt.

   e. Wir machen alle zwei Jahre eine   We take a long trip every two years.
      lange Reise.

3. <u>verheiratet</u> - "married"

   a. Wie lange sind Sie schon verhei-   How long have you been married?
      ratet?

   b. Ich habe gehört, dass ihr seit   I heard that you have been married
      Oktober verheiratet seid.   since October.

   c. Sie ist jetzt verheiratet und   She's married and has two children
      hat zwei Kinder.   now.

   d. Du bist seit letztem Sommer   You've been married since last summer,
      verheiratet, nicht wahr?   haven't you?

4. <u>der Junge</u> - "the boy"

a. Der Junge ist seekrank gewesen.	The boy was seasick.
b. Wie geht's Ihrem Jungen?	How is your boy?
c. Haben Sie meinen Jungen dort gesehen?	Did you see my boy there?
d. Unser ältester Junge studiert jetzt in Bonn.	Our oldest boy is attending the university in Bonn.
e. Wird Ihr Junge eine deutsche Schule besuchen?	Will your oldest boy be going to a German school?

5. <u>ganz</u> - "all, whole"

a. Sie haben den ganzen Tag gearbeitet.	They worked all day.
b. Habt ihr den ganzen Monat keinen Brief von ihm bekommen?	Haven't you received a letter from him all month?
c. Hier hat es die ganze Woche geregnet.	It rained here the whole week.
d. Ich habe eine ganze Stunde anstehen müssen.	I had to stand in line a whole hour.
e. Sie haben den ganzen Monat keine Miete bezahlt.	They haven't paid any rent for a whole month.
f. Er ist den ganzen Nachmittag geblieben.	He stayed all afternoon.

6. <u>zu dumm</u>! - "I wish, ... should have ..."

a. Zu dumm, dass du soviel arbeiten musst!	I wish you didn't have to work so much!
b. Zu dumm, dass ihr nicht mitkommen könnt!	I wish you could come along!
c. Zu dumm, dass wir die Aufführung nicht gesehen haben!	I wish we had seen the performance!
d. Zu dumm, dass ihr zu spät gekommen seid!	You shouldn't have been late!
e. Zu dumm, dass ich Ihnen nicht vorher geschrieben habe!	I wish I'd written you earlier!
f. Zu dumm, dass Sie ihn verpasst haben!	Too bad you missed him!
g. Zu dumm, dass er uns nicht erreicht hat!	I wish he'd gotten ahold of us!

7. <u>es tut ... leid</u> - " ... is (are) sorry"

a. Es tut mir leid, dass Ihre Tochter seekrank gewesen ist.	I'm sorry that your daughter was seasick.
b. Es tut uns leid, dass wir Herrn Neumann nicht besucht haben.	I'm sorry that we didn't visit Mr. Neumann.
c. Es tut mir leid, dass du noch keine Wohnung gefunden hast.	I'm sorry that you haven't found an apartment yet.
d. Es tut ihm leid, dass du keine Theaterkarten bekommen hast.	He's sorry that you didn't get any theater tickets.
e. Es tut mir leid, dass ihr das Schulproblem noch nicht gelöst habt.	I'm sorry that you haven't settled the school question yet.
f. Es tut uns leid, dass wir die Nachrichten nicht gehört haben.	We're sorry that we didn't listen to the news.

8. <u>sich erkundigen</u> - "inquire, find out, ask"

a. Wir haben uns erkundigt, wie es seiner Tochter geht.	We inquired how his daughter is.
b. Erkundigt euch bitte, wann der Omnibus abfährt.	Find out when the bus leaves (fam pl).

c. Erkundige dich bitte, wo das   Find out where the new swimming pool
   neue Schwimmbad ist.   is (fam sg)
d. Hast du dich erkundigt, wo die   Did you (fam sg) ask where the
   Aufführung stattfinden wird?   performance will be?
e. Habt ihr euch erkundigt, ob die   Did you (fam pl) inquire whether the
   Philharmoniker nächste Woche   Philharmonic is playing here next
   hier spielen?   week?

9. besorgen - "get, go and get"

a. Hast du für mich auch eine Karte   Did you get a ticket for me, too?
   besorgt?
b. Ich muss unbedingt den franzö-   I definitely have to get that French
   sischen Roman für ihn besorgen.   novel for him.
c. Hast du für deine Schwester eine   Did you get a newspaper for your
   Zeitung besorgt?   sister?
d. Er hat für seinen Vater gute   He got some good cigars for his
   Zigarren besorgt.   father.
e. Ich muss noch einen Papierkorb   I have to go and get a waste-basket
   für mein Zimmer besorgen.   for my room too.

(End of Tape 12B)

TRANSLATION DRILL (not recorded)

1. Mr. and Mrs. Jones have gone to   Herr und Frau Jones sind mit ihren
   Germany with their children.   Kindern nach Deutschland gefahren.
2. On the second of March they arrived   Am zweiten März sind sie in Bremer-
   in Bremerhaven.   haven angekommen.
3. On the whole they have had a pleasant Im Grossen und Ganzen haben sie eine
   crossing.   angenehme Überfahrt gehabt.
4. Unfortunately their little daughter   Leider ist ihre kleine Tochter fast
   was seasick almost all the time.   die ganze Zeit seekrank gewesen.
5. Aside from that the voyage was a   Abgesehen davon ist die Seereise für
   real vacation for the others.   die anderen eine richtige Erholung
                                         gewesen.
6. Now they have been living in Munich   Nun wohnen sie schon seit zwei Monaten
   for two months.   in München.
7. Mr. Keller and Mr. Allen are   Herr Keller und Herr Allen unterhalten
   conversing.   sich.
8. Mr. Allen is a consul in the   Herr Allen ist Konsul im Generalkon-
   Consulate General in Frankfurt.   sulat in Frankfurt.
9. He's gotten very well settled there   Er hat sich dort schon sehr gut
   now.   eingelebt.
10. Mr. Keller asks him if he still   Herr Keller fragt ihn, ob er noch in
    lives in the American Colony.   der amerikanischen Siedlung wohnt.

11. Consul Allen says, that he has   Konsul Allen sagt, dass er ein Zwei-
    rented a two-family house.   familienhaus gemietet hat.
12. His wife, his children and he feel   Seine Frau, seine Kinder und er fühlen
    very much at home there.   sich dort sehr wohl.
13. They are glad that they're now   Sie sind froh, dass sie jetzt im Süden
    living in the southern part of   der Stadt wohnen.
    town.
14. Fortunately they have been able to   Glücklicherweise haben sie auch das
    settle the school question, too.   Schulproblem lösen können.
15. Their two boys have been attending   Ihre beiden Jungen besuchen seit
    a German Realgymnasium for two   vierzehn Tagen ein deutsches Real-
    weeks.   gymnasium.
16. The little girl has been going to   Die Kleine geht schon vier Wochen in
    an American kindergarten for four   einen amerikanischen Kindergarten.
    weeks already.
17. Mr. Jones and Mr. Bruce were at the Herr Jones und Herr Bruce sind gestern
    opera yesterday.   in der Oper gewesen.
18. They liked the performance very much, Die Aufführung hat ihnen sehr gut ge-
    and Mr. Jones is glad that he got a fallen und Herr Jones ist froh, dass er
    season ticket for the theater.   sich ein Theater-Abonnement genommen hat.

19. Mr. Bruce unfortunatley had to stand in line for an hour and a half for his ticket.

Herr Bruce hat leider für seine Karte anderthalb Stunden anstehen müssen.

20. He has read in the paper that the Berlin Philharmonic is giving a concert in a week.

Er hat in der Zeitung gelesen, dass die Berliner Philharmoniker in acht Tagen ein Konzert geben.

21. Mr. Jones has heard about it too and would like to know if there are still tickets.

Herr Jones hat auch davon gehört und möchte wissen, ob es noch Karten gibt.

22. Mr. Bruce doesn't know that, but he intends to inquire the next day.

Das weiss Herr Bruce nicht, aber er will sich am nächsten Tag mal erkundigen.

23. If there still are tickets, he'll get one for Mr. Jones too.

Wenn es noch Karten gibt, besorgt er auch eine für Herrn Jones.

24. Mr. Meyer and Mr. König are talking together.

Herr Meyer und Herr König sprechen zusammen.

25. Mr. König's son is studying at ⎣the university of⎦ Göttingen.

Der Sohn von Herrn König studiert in Göttingen.

26. Last year he returned from America.

Voriges Jahr ist er aus Amerika zurückgekommen.

27. He was able to study there for two years as an exchange student.

Er hat als Austauschstudent zwei Jahre dort studieren können.

28. The Meyers' daughter is now living in Munich.

Die Tochter von Meyers lebt jetzt in München.

29. She was in Norway last year, but since last August she has been married.

Sie war letztes Jahr in Norwegen, aber seit letztem August ist sie verheiratet.

30. Unfortunately the Meyers only see their daughter every few months.

Leider sehen Meyers ihre Tochter nur alle paar Monate.

31. Mr. Allen would like to know, whether the 'Landrat' is sitting over there.

Herr Allen möchte wissen, ob der Landrat dort drüben sitzt.

32. Mr. Jones tells him, that that is an editor and that the 'Landrat' is sitting beside the hostess.

Herr Jones sagt ihm, dass das ein Redakteur ist und dass der Landrat neben der Gastgeberin sitzt.

33. To the left of the 'Landrat' sits Frau von Rothenburg.

Links vom Landrat sitzt Frau von Rothenburg.

34. She's just conversing with Dr. Maler, the director of the board of health.

Sie unterhält sich gerade mit Herrn Dr. Maler, dem Leiter des Gesundheitsamtes.

35. Mr. Jones met Frau von Rothenburg recently at a reception at the consul general's.

Herr Jones hat Frau von Rothenburg neulich auf einem Empfang beim Generalkonsul kennengelernt.

36. Mr. Bruce likes athletics, and Mr. Müller has heard that he is a good tennis player.

Herr Bruce treibt gern Sport und Herr Müller hat gehört, dass er ein guter Tennisspieler ist.

37. Mr. Müller asks him if he knows that there's a very modern, new swimming pool in the vicinity.

Herr Müller fragt ihn, ob er weiss, dass in der Nähe ein ganz modernes neues Schwimmbad ist.

38. Mr. Bruce has heard of it and would like to go there with him sometime.

Herr Bruce hat davon gehört und möchte gern mal mit ihm hingehen.

RESPONSE DRILL (not recorded)

1. Wie lange ist Familie Jones schon in Deutschland?

Familie Jones ist erst zwei Monate in Deutschland.

2. Wann sind Jones' in Bremerhaven angekommen?

Sie sind am zweiten März in Bremerhaven angekommen.

3. Wie ist die Überfahrt gewesen?

Die Überfahrt ist im Grossen und Ganzen sehr angenehm gewesen.

4. Ist keiner seekrank gewesen?

Doch, leider ist ihre Tochter fast die ganze Zeit seekrank gewesen.

5. Seit wann wohnt Konsul Allen mit seiner Familie in einem Zweifamilienhaus?

Er und seine Familie wohnen seit zwei Wochen in einem Zweifamilienhaus.

6. In welcher Gegend der Stadt wohnen sie?

Sie wohnen im Süden der Stadt.

7. Wo haben sie vorher gewohnt?

Sie haben vorher in der amerikanischen Siedlung gewohnt.

8. Wie haben er und seine Frau das Schulproblem ihrer Kinder gelöst?

Ihre beiden Söhne besuchen ein deutsches Realgymnasium und ihre kleine Tochter geht in einen amerikanischen Kindergarten.

9. Wo sind Herr Bruce und Herr Jones gestern gewesen?

Sie sind in der Oper gewesen.

10. Wie hat ihnen die Aufführung gefallen?

Die Aufführung hat ihnen sehr gut gefallen.

11. Warum hat Herr Bruce anderthalb Stunden für seine Karte anstehen müssen?

Er hat leider kein Theater-Abonnement genommen.

12. Wann werden die Berliner Philharmoniker hier ein Konzert geben?

Sie werden in acht Tagen hier ein Konzert geben.

13. Werden Herr Bruce und Herr Jones in das Konzert gehen?

Ja, wenn sie noch Karten bekommen können.

14. Was macht der Sohn von Herrn Meyer?

Er studiert in Göttingen.

15. Wo hat er voriges Jahr studiert?

Voriges Jahr hat er als Austauschstudent in Amerika studiert.

16. Wie lange war er in Amerika?

Er ist zwei Jahre dort gewesen.

17. Wo ist die Tochter von Herrn Meyer gewesen?

Sie war in Norwegen.

18. Was hat sie in Norwegen getan?

Sie ist dort als Sportlehrerin gewesen.

19. Wo wohnt sie jetzt?

Sie wohnt jetzt in München.

20. Seit wann wohnt sie dort?

Sie wohnt seit letztem Sommer dort.

21. Wie oft sehen Meyers ihre Tochter?

Sie sehen sie leider nur alle paar Monate.

22. Wer sitzt neben dem Landrat?

Neben dem Landrat sitzt die Gastgeberin.

23. Wie heisst die Dame links vom Landrat?

Sie heisst Frau von Rothenburg.

24. Wo arbeitet sie?

Sie arbeitet für's Rote Kreuz.

25. Wo hat Herr Allen Frau von Rothenburg kennengelernt?

Er hat sie neulich auf einem Empfang kennengelernt.

26. Mit wem unterhält sich Frau von Rothenburg gerade?

Sie unterhält sich gerade mit Herrn Dr. Maler.

27. Wer ist Herr Dr. Maler?

Er ist der Leiter des Gesundheitsamtes.

28. Treibt Herr Bruce gern Sport?

Ja, er ist ein guter Tennisspieler.

29. Was möchte Herr Müller Herrn Bruce gern zeigen?

Er möchte ihm gern das neue, moderne Schwimmbad zeigen.

30. Seit wann gibt es dort ein Schwimmbad?

Erst seit kurzem.

31. Wie lange wohnen Sie schon in Washington?
32. Um wieviel Uhr sind Sie gestern nach Hause gekommen?
33. Wie lange haben Sie in New York gewohnt?
34. Wo haben Sie studiert?

(This drill is continued on the next page.)

35. Wie lange arbeiten Sie schon hier?
36. Wo sind Sie letztes Jahr hingefahren?
37. Wann haben Sie dieses Buch gelesen?
38. Wann haben Sie Herrn Keller angerufen?
39. Wo haben Sie eigentlich Herrn und Frau
    Müller kennengelernt?
40. Wo sind Sie gestern abend gewesen?
41. Seit wann wohnen Sie in der Mozartstrasse?
42. Wie lange sind Sie schon verheiratet?
43. Seit wann rauchen Sie?
44. Wie lange sprechen Sie schon deutsch?
45. Wie lange regnet es schon?

CONVERSATION PRACTICE

1

A: Gehen Sie heute abend auch ins
   Konzert?
B: Nein; ich habe leider keine Karten
   bekommen können.
A: Haben Sie denn kein Abonnement?
B: Voriges Jahr habe ich eins gehabt.
   Dieses Jahr habe ich mir keins
   genommen, da ich viele Geschäfts-
   reisen machen muss.
A: Ach ja, Herr Dr. Bergmann hat mir
   gesagt, dass Sie nächste Woche nach
   Norwegen fahren.
   Sind Sie schon einmal dort gewesen?
B: Nein, noch nicht.
   Ich freue mich schon auf diese
   Reise.

2

A: Seit wann sind Sie hier in München?
B: Seit dem ersten Oktober.
A: Haben Sie eine nette Wohnung ge-
   funden?
B: Leider nein. Wir wohnen noch im
   Hotel.
A: Sind Ihre Möbel schon angekommen?
B: Noch nicht; aber wenn die da sind,
   müssen wir unbedingt eine Wohnung
   haben.

3

A: Wohnen Sie noch immer im Hotel,
   Herr Generalkonsul?
B: Nein, gnädige Frau, seit gestern
   wohnen wir in der amerikanischen
   Siedlung.
   Meine Frau ist jetzt auch hier.
A: Hat Ihre Frau Gemahlin eine an-
   genehme Überfahrt gehabt?
B: Leider nein; sie ist fast die
   ganze Zeit seekrank gewesen.

4

A: Sind Sie gestern in der Oper
   gewesen, Herr Doktor?
B: Ja.
A: War die Aufführung gut?
B: Die Aufführung ja, aber nicht die
   Musik!
   Es war eine ganz moderne Oper.
A: Gefällt Ihnen die moderne Musik
   nicht?
B: Nein.
A: Warum sind Sie denn dann in die
   Oper gegangen?
B: Weil ich ein Theater-Abonnement
   habe.

SITUATIONS

Auf einer Gesellschaft

Auf einer Gesellschaft macht Herr König
Sie mit Herrn Jones bekannt. Sie fragen
ihn, wie lange er schon in Bonn ist, wie
ihm die Stadt gefällt, ob er eine schöne
Wohnung gefunden hat und ob er vorher
schon einmal in Deutschland gewesen ist.
Später fragt Herr Jones Sie, wer die
Dame neben dem Landrat ist; er glaubt,
dass er sie vorige Woche auf einem Empfang beim Generalkonsul kennengelernt
hat.

Zwei unterhalten sich

Unterhalten Sie sich mit Ihrem Freund
über Ihre Universitäten, wo Sie studiert haben, ob Sie Sport getrieben
haben, ob Sie oft ins Theater oder
Kino gehen und sagen Sie ihm, dass die
berühmten Berliner Philharmoniker bald
kommen werden. Ihr Freund möchte wissen,
ob man für das Konzert noch Karten bekommen kann. Sie sagen, dass Sie das
nicht genau wissen. Sie selbst haben
ein Abonnement, aber Sie werden sich
gern mal erkundigen, ob es noch Karten
gibt.

Unterhaltung im Büro

Sie unterhalten sich im Büro mit Herrn
Becker. Sie waren beide gestern in der
Oper. Herr Becker sagt, die Oper hat
ihm nicht gut gefallen. Er hört moderne
Musik nicht gern. Sie sagen, dass Ihnen
die Oper ganz gut gefallen hat, aber
dass Sie auch lieber andere Musik hören.
Dann fragen Sie Herrn Becker, ob er gestern auch den amerikanischen Generalkonsul gesehen hat. Sie sprechen noch
über einige andere Bekannte und dann
gehen Sie zusammen essen.

Ankunft in Deutschland

Sie sind gerade in Bonn angekommen,
nehmen sich eine Taxe und fahren zum
Hotel. Dort nehmen Sie sich ein Zimmer
und rufen dann Ihren Kollegen, Vizekonsul Jones an. Herr Jones fragt Sie,
ob Sie eine angenehme Reise gehabt
haben und wie es Ihrer Familie geht.
Sie sagen, dass Ihre Familie etwas
später kommt. Sie wollen erst ein
Haus mieten. Herr Jones sagt, dass
es sehr schwer ist, ein Haus zu bekommen, aber Sie können doch erst mal in
eine Wohnung in der amerikanischen
Siedlung ziehen. Dann fragt Herr Jones,
ob Sie mit ihm ins Restaurant zum Essen
gehen wollen. Sie sagen ja, aber Sie
wollen sich erst noch waschen und einen
anderen Anzug anziehen. Sie werden in
anderthalb Stunden im Restaurant sein.

NARRATIVE

Bonn, den 15. Mai 1961

Lieber Fritz!

Seit acht Tagen sind wir in Bonn und fühlen uns hier eigentlich recht wohl.
Wir sind erst mit dem Auto nach Heidelberg gefahren und haben dort Freunde besucht
und von dort habe ich Dir auch eine Ansichtskarte geschrieben. Glücklicherweise
ist das Wetter jetzt sehr schön. Es hat <u>furchtbar</u> geregnet, als wir in Bremerhaven
<u>ankamen</u>. Unsere Kisten, Bilder und Teppiche sind endlich <u>eingetroffen</u> und wir
haben uns jetzt sehr gemütlich eingerichtet. Leider müssen wir in der amerikanischen Siedlung wohnen. Die Wohnungen sind sehr schön und gross, – aber es ist
eben "Klein-Amerika" und nicht Deutschland. <u>Allerdings</u> muss ich im Büro fast nur
deutsch sprechen. Ich arbeite in der Visa-Abteilung und <u>stelle</u> Visen <u>aus</u>. Für
meine Frau ist es etwas <u>schwieriger</u>. Sie kauft natürlich in der "Commisary" ein
und spricht fast den ganzen Tag nur englisch. Die Kinder wollen wir in eine deutsche Schule <u>schicken</u>, damit sie gut deutsch lernen und deutsche Freunde finden. –
Wir wollen uns ein Theater-Abonnement nehmen und viel ins Theater und in die Oper
gehen. Im Sommer wollen wir oft mit dem Auto in die <u>Umgebung</u> fahren. Vieles ist
neu für uns; wenn wir uns etwas besser hier eingelebt haben, schreibe ich Dir
<u>ausführlicher</u>. Ich hoffe, dass es Dir und Deiner ganzen Familie gut geht und dass
Ihr uns auch bald einmal schreibt. Grüss' bitte Alle <u>herzlich</u> von uns.

Viele Grüsse

Dein Bill

furchtbar	awfully (hard)	schwierig	difficult
ankamen	arrived	schicken	send
eingetroffen	come	die Umgebung	surrounding country
allerdings	to be sure	ausführlich	in detail
ausstellen	issue	herzlich	cordially

FINDER LIST

das	Abonnement,-s	subscription
	alle paar Monate	every few months
	als	in the capacity of
	anderthalb	one and a half
er ist	angekommen	he arrived
	angenehm	pleasant, agreeable
	anstehen	stand in line
er hat	anstehen müssen	he had to stand in line
die	Aufführung,-en	performance
das	Ausland	foreign countries
der	Austauschstudent,-en	exchange student
das	Bad,¨er	bath, bathing place
die	Berliner Philharmoniker (pl)	Berlin Philharmonic
	besuchen	attend
	da sein	be present, be there
	dumm	stupid
zu	dumm	too bad
sich	einleben	get settled
er hat sich	eingelebt	he has gotten settled
der	Empfang,¨e	reception
die	Erholung	recovery, recuperation
sich	erkundigen	inquire, ask
	erst	only
die	Familie,-n	family
	froh	glad, happy
die	Gastgeberin,-nen	hostess
es hat Ihnen	gefallen	you liked it
er hat	gefunden	he has found
er hat	gehabt	he had
er hat	gelesen	he has read
der	Generalkonsul,-n	Consul General
er hat	genommen	he took
das	Gesundheitsamt,¨er	board of health
er hat	getan	he did
sie ist	gewesen	she was
	glücklicherweise	fortunately
im	Grossen und Ganzen	in general, on the whole
	ja	(no English equivalent, implies that agreement with the statement made is assumed)
der	Junge,-n	boy
die	Karte,-n	ticket
er hat	kennengelernt	he met
der	Kindergarten,¨	kindergarten
die	Kleine,-n	little girl
der	Landrat,¨e	(head of the administration of a district corresponding roughly to a county)
die	Lehrerin,-nen	(woman) teacher
der	Leiter,-	director
sich	lohnen	be worthwhile
	lösen	solve, settle
	er hat gelöst	he solved, settled
	modern	modern
	neulich	recently
	Norwegen	Norway
die	Oper,-n	opera
das	Problem,-e	problem
das	Realgymnasium,-en	(a secondary school in the German educational system)
der	Redakteur,-e	editor
das	Rote Kreuz	Red Cross
das	Schulproblem,-e	school question

das	Schwimmbad, ̈er	swimming pool
	seekrank	seasick
die	Seereise, -n	voyage
sich	sehen	see each other
	seit kurzem	since a short time ago
	seit vierzehn Tagen	for two weeks
die	Siedlung, -en	colony, settlement
der	Spieler, -	player
die	Sportlehrerin, -nen	physical education teacher
	Sport treiben	engage in athletic activities
der	Student, -en	(university) student
	studieren	study (at a university)
der	Süden	south
in acht	Tagen	in a week
der	Tennisspieler, -	tennis player
das	Theater-Abonnement, -s	season ticket for the theater
es	tut mir leid	I'm sorry
die	Überfahrt, -en	crossing
sich	unterhalten	converse
	verheiratet	married
	wäre	would be
sich	wohl fühlen	feel well
das	Zweifamilienhaus, ̈er	two-family house

☆ U.S. GOVERNMENT PRINTING OFFICE : 1976 O−202−323

More selected BARRON'S titles:

DICTIONARY OF ACCOUNTING TERMS
Siegel and Shim
Nearly 2500 terms related to accounting are defined.
Paperback, $9.95, Can. $13.95 (3766-9)

DICTIONARY OF ADVERTISING AND DIRECT MAIL TERMS
Imber and Toffler
Nearly 3000 terms used in the ad industry are defined.
Paperback, $9.95, Can. $13.95 (3765-0)

DICTIONARY OF BANKING TERMS
Fitch
Nearly 3000 terms related to banking, finance and money
management.
Paperback, $10.95, Can. $14.95 (3946-7)

DICTIONARY OF BUSINESS TERMS
Friedman, general editor
Over 6000 entries define business terms.
Paperback, $9.95, Can. $13.95 (3775-8)

BARRON'S BUSINESS REVIEW SERIES
These guides explain topics covered in a college-level business
course.
Each book: paperback
ACCOUNTING, 2nd EDITION. *Eisen*. $11.95, Can. $15.95 (4375-8)
BUSINESS LAW, *Hardwicke and Emerson*. $11.95, Can. $15.95 (3495-3)
BUSINESS STATISTICS, *Downing and Clark*. $11.95, Can. $15.95 (3576-3)
ECONOMICS, *Wessels*. $11.95, Can. $15.50 (3560-7)
FINANCE, 2nd EDITION. *Groppelli and Nikbakht*. $11.95,
Can. $15.95 (4373-1)
MANAGEMENT, *Montana and Charnov*. $11.95, Can. $15.50 (3559-3)
MARKETING, *Sandhusen*. $11.95, Can. $15.95 (3494-5)
QUANTITATIVE METHODS, *Downing and Clark*. $10.95,
Can. $14.95 (3947-5)

TALKING BUSINESS SERIES: BILINGUAL DICTIONARIES
Five bilingual dictionaries translate about 3000 terms not found in
most foreign phrasebooks.
Each book: paperback
TALKING BUSINESS IN FRENCH, *Le Gal*. $9.95, Can. $13.95
(3745-6)
TALKING BUSINESS IN GERMAN, *Strutz*. $9.95, Can. $12.95
(3747-2)
TALKING BUSINESS IN ITALIAN, *Rakus*. $8.95, Can. $11.95
(3754-5)
TALKING BUSINESS IN JAPANESE, C. *Akiyama and* N. *Akiyama*.
$9.95, Can. $12.95 (3848-7)
TALKING BUSINESS IN KOREAN, *Cheong*. $8.95, Can. $11.95
(3992-0)
TALKING BUSINESS IN SPANISH, *Fryer and Faria*. $9.95,
Can. $13.95 (3769-3)

Barron's Educational Series, Inc.
250 Wireless Boulevard, Hauppauge, NY 11788
Call toll-free: 1-800-645-3476, in NY 1-800-257-5729
In Canada: Georgetown Book Warehouse
34 Armstrong Ave., Georgetown, Ontario L7G 4R9
Call toll-free: 1-800-247-7160